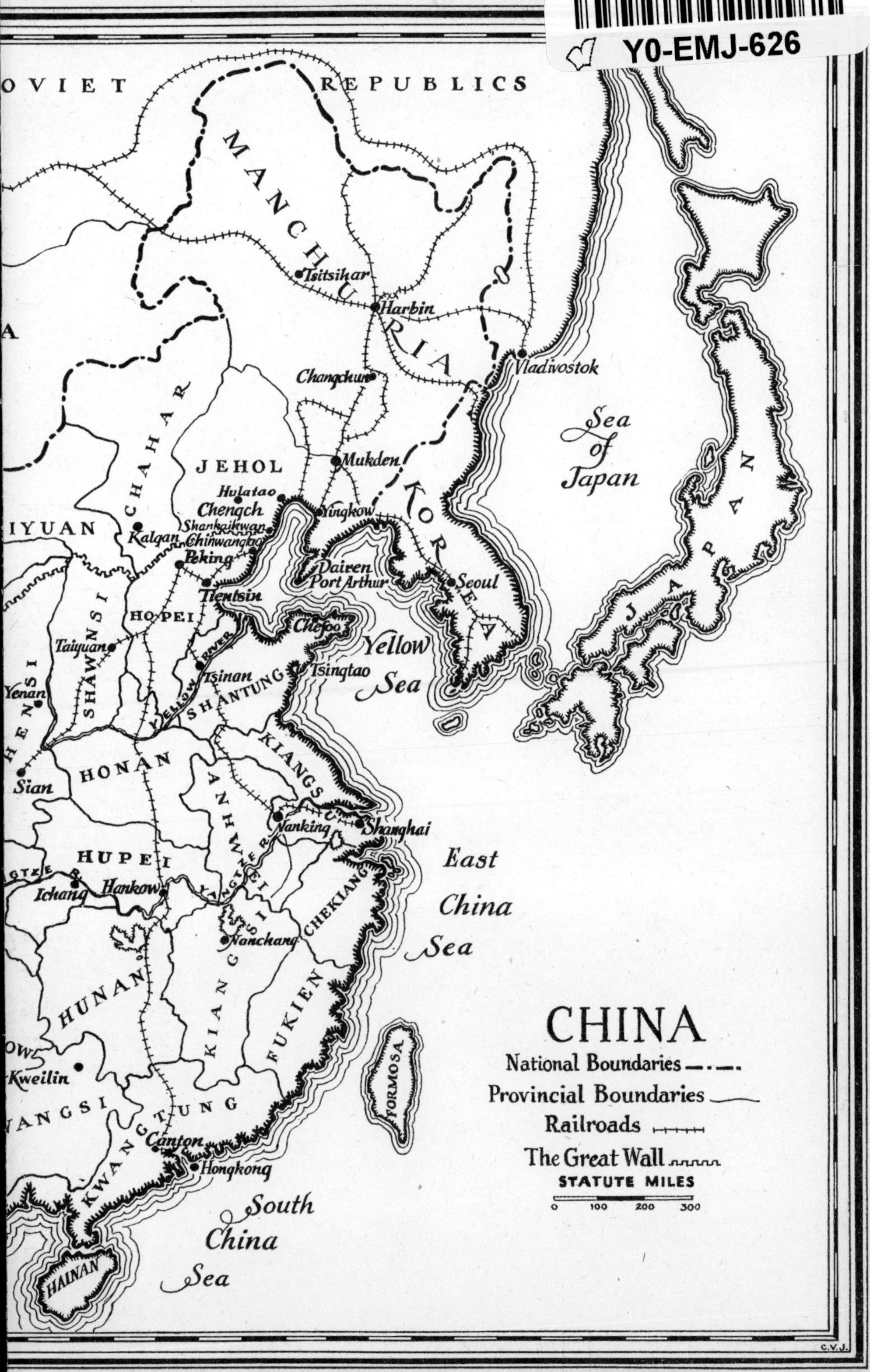

OVIET REPUBLICS
MANCHURIA
Tsitsihar
Harbin
Vladivostok
Changchun
Mukden
JEHOL
Hulatao
Chengch
Yingkow
KOREA
Sea of Japan
JAPAN
IYUAN
CHAHAR
Kalgan
Shankaikwan
Chinwangtao
Peking
Tientsin
Dairen
Port Arthur
Seoul
HOPEI
SHANSI
Taiyuan
Chefoo
Yellow Sea
Tsinan
YELLOW RIVER
SHANTUNG
Tsingtao
Yenan
SHENSI
Sian
HONAN
KIANGSU
ANHWEI
Nanking
Shanghai
HUPEI
YANGTZE R.
Ichang
Hankow
East China Sea
KIANGSI
Nanchang
CHEKIANG
HUNAN
FUKIEN
FORMOSA
Kweilin
KWANGSI
KWANGTUNG
Canton
Hongkong
South China Sea
HAINAN
CHINA
National Boundaries
Provincial Boundaries
Railroads
The Great Wall
STATUTE MILES
0 100 200 300
C.V.J.

LAST CHANCE IN CHINA

By FREDA UTLEY

LANCASHIRE AND THE FAR EAST
JAPAN'S FEET OF CLAY
JAPAN'S GAMBLE IN CHINA
CHINA AT WAR
THE DREAM WE LOST: SOVIET RUSSIA THEN AND NOW

Last Chance in CHINA

by

Freda Utley

THE BOBBS-MERRILL COMPANY

INDIANAPOLIS *Publishers* NEW YORK

First Edition

To P. M. A. L.

Foreword

It would be impossible for me to list the names of all the Chinese and Americans to whom I am indebted in writing this book. Some of them are mentioned in its pages; others to whom I owe as much are not referred to since one cannot always quote those from whom one has learned most.

For interviews and hospitality and other kindnesses I wish to thank Generalissimo and Madame Chiang Kai-shek, Dr. H. H. Kung and Dr. Wang Ch'ung-hui. Foreign Minister Wang Shih-chieh and Vice-Foreign Ministers Kan and Liu Chieh, Chen Li-fu, K. C. Wu, Wu Te-chen and my old friend Francis Yao who was working with him at Kuomintang Headquarters, Chang Kuo-san of the Chinese Central News Service, Cheng Ming-shu and Ma Yin-Ch'u, S. Y. Wu, Secretary of the Executive Yuan, Generals Tang En-po and Li Tsung-jen, Dr. Wong Wen-hao, Premier Chang Chun, Yu Ta-wei, Wang Yun-wu, Chu Chia-hua, Fu Ssu-nien, Y. C. Koo, T. F. Tsiang, K. C. Wu, Carson Chang, Hsu Tao-liu, Shu Shen-yu (Lao-shu), Lo Lung-chi, Wei Tao-ming, Dr. Robert K. S. Lim, Mary Chen and Loo Chi-teh; "Sinmay" and other Shanghai friends too numerous to mention.

I am particularly indebted to Counselor Chen Chih-mai of the Chinese embassy in Washington (a former collaborator of Dr. Hu Shih's on the *Independent Review* in prewar days), who combines a profound understanding of China's political and economic problems and culture with a Western liberal outlook. My thanks are also due to Dr. Hu Shih himself, the former Chinese Ambassador to the United States who has been my friend for many years and first helped me to understand the Chinese attitude toward life. I am also particularly indebted to Dr. Fu Ssu-nien, the distinguished historian who combines the learning of China with that of the West and who, while fearlessly criticizing the government of his country, has a deep understanding of its difficulties.

I wish also to express my gratitude to my Communist hosts in

Yenan who received me with every courtesy in spite of my pronounced anti-Communist views. Although we are on opposite sides of the barricades, so to speak, General Chu Teh, Ching Ling my interpreter, the editor of the *Emancipation Daily,* Chiang Lung-chi, the doctors at the International Peace Hospital, and many another Chinese Communist made me welcome in Yenan, showed me everything I asked to see and spent hours talking to me. I am especially grateful to Chou En-lai, the Communist representative in Chungking, who made it possible for me to visit the Communist Northwest.

Among the Americans to whom I am indebted for information and assistance are General Albert C. Wedemeyer, Colonel "Bill" Mayer and Captain Gates of the Public Relations office, Generals George E. Stratemeyer and Paul Caraway and George Olmsted, Colonel Pendleton Hogan, Brigadier Middleton, Colonel Don Scott, Colonel Ivan Yeaton, Admiral Daniel E. Barbey, General Worton of the U.S.M.C., his aide Captain Tom Watson who died in China, and other Marine officers, Colonel Kellis of the O.S.S., Dr. Logan Roots of UNRRA, Walter Robertson, the United States Charge d'Affaires, Bland Calder of the United States Embassy, and John L. Kullgren of the War Department, Tillman Durdin of the *New York Times* and Arch Steele of the *New York Herald Tribune.*

My special thanks are due to Dr. J. Lossing Buck, the foremost American expert on China's agrarian problem who gave me invaluable assistance in writing the chapter on "Poverty and the Land."

I have also to thank General Victor Odlum, the Canadian Ambassador and perhaps the best informed and wisest of all the diplomats I met in China; also Sir George Sansom, British Representative on the Far Eastern Commission. Finally I must express my gratitude to Dr. Paul Linebarger of the School for Advanced International Studies in Washington for his help in the preparation of this book; his personal encouragement has been as valuable as his readiness to answer my inquiries.

My thanks are due to the authors or publishers who have given me permission to quote from the following books and articles: Random House: *Battle for Asia,* by Edgar Snow; William Sloane Associates: *Thunder Out of China,* by Theodore White and Annalee Jacoby; Doubleday & Company, Inc.: *Wrath in Burma* by Fred Eldridge; The Macmillan Company: *China's Destiny,* by Chiang

Kai-shek; Harold Isaacs: *The Tragedy of the Chinese Revolution;* Lin Yu-tang: *The Vigil of a Nation;* Paul Linebarger, for permission to quote from his books and his article in the *Yale Review;* Emily Hahn, for permission to quote from one of her articles; the Associated Press, for allowing me to reproduce extracts from the dispatches sent by Richard Cushing and Spenser Davis about Manchuria.

I have not attempted to follow Sinological academic style in the rendering of Chinese names into English; I have used the spelling employed by the persons referred to or by the American Press.

While I acknowledge my indebtedness to others the opinions expressed in this book are my own, unless otherwise clearly indicated by quotations. My acknowledgments are a record of thanks and in no way attribute responsibility for the views I have expressed.

FREDA UTLEY
Martha's Vineyard, Mass.
July 25, 1947

Table of Contents

CHAPTER		PAGE
I	"We Want to Go Home"	15
II	Gray Dawn in China	31
III	Coué Diplomacy	61
IV	Shanghai	84
V	Last Days of Chungking	113
VI	The Fascination of Yenan	139
VII	Are They Real Communists?	170
VIII	Success of the Democratic Masquerade	185
IX	The Struggle for Manchuria	219
X	Why Marshall Failed	242
XI	General Wedemeyer in China	265
XII	The Dilemma of the Chinese Liberals	282
XIII	Poverty and the Land	310
XIV	Can China Remain Chinese?	327
XV	China: Focus of Conflict	353
XVI	Conclusion: America's Stake in China	382

LAST CHANCE IN CHINA

CHAPTER I

"We Want to Go Home"

THE flight traffic clerk asked me in mid-Atlantic why on earth I was flying *from* America. It was October 1945 and I was on my way to China via India. The giant Air Transport Command plane carried only three passengers from the United States to Calcutta.

Why, indeed, was I flying to the Orient now that the war was over?

If I had replied that I wanted to learn who had won the war, this GI would surely have thought me mad. Like most Americans he no doubt considered that the war was won once the fighting stopped, and that after victory one simply went home.

Nor could I have truthfully told him that I wanted to write an impartial book on China. The test of a tale is the teller thereof. Everyone's views are the result of prejudice and experience, and behind cool, so-called neutral books there often lurks a deceitful author whose real aim is to show that the world ought to be run according to his own pet ideas or illusions. I am fully aware that my own views are the result of the life I have led, and that I am not at all impartial in the world-wide struggle between Communism and democracy.

I simply replied that I was a writer and earned my living that way.

To have explained further why the fate of China seemed to me so important, I would have needed to tell him the story of my life. That would certainly have taken too long. Moreover my past experiences in Russia, Japan and China would have been as incomprehensible to this young American as a life lived on another planet. So I did not mention that I had left behind, in a boarding school in Connecticut, a son born in Moscow, who was all I had left from the days when I lived under the Communist dictatorship with my Soviet husband. Nor did I tell him that my husband had been carried off one night by the secret police to disappear without trial into one of Russia's concentration camps.

It is also difficult to explain in a few words why my feeling about China has remained constant through all my experiences and disillusionments. In my childhood and youth the Chinese appeared as a people victimized by Western imperialism in general, and in particular by England, the country of my birth. Nearly twenty years ago I had come overland from Russia to China believing that only Communist leadership could free the oppressed people of Asia and the rest of the colonial world from exploitation, oppression and grinding poverty. The year I had spent in Japan with my husband in 1928-1929 had given me an inside view of Japanese tyranny and conditioned me to champion China. In Russia where I lived from 1930 to 1936 I had learned to know a despotism more cruel even than Japan's. This new "progressive" Soviet imperialism was now menacing China as Japan had formerly done.

The Chinese seemed fated to be forever the victims of injustice and aggression. For them the Allied victory in World War II had only opened the door to a new menace. Had the long war of resistance against Japan been fought in vain?

In 1938 I had come to America for the first time to speak for the American Committee for Non-Participation in Japanese Aggression. In those days I had spent my energies trying to get America and England to stop war supplies to the Japanese aggressors. Now America, my adopted country, was blindly helping Russia by giving encouragement to the Chinese Communists. It seemed to me that history was repeating itself. First Japan had been helped to conquer China. Now Soviet Russia, through her agents the Chinese Communists, was being assisted by America to get into position to acquire dominion over China. One had to start all over again the struggle to awaken American public opinion to the issues at stake in the Far East, lest a worse Pearl Harbor befall us in the future.

At Casablanca, where we stopped four hours during the night for the plane to be checked over, the Red Cross hall was filled with soldiers waiting their turn to go home. Most of the other rooms and buildings were empty. It was like wandering round the stage of an empty theater after the actors had all gone.

Next morning in bright sunlight we breakfasted at Tripoli. Late that afternoon, after hours of flying over blue seas and brown deserts, the green ribbon of the Nile Valley appeared in the distance. On the desert's edge we saw the Pyramids below, and the Sphinx seemingly no larger than a cat.

Impossible to stop in Egypt even for one day of sight-seeing. The plane traveled day and night, never stopping for more than the scheduled forty minutes or four hours.

Everywhere we were asked why we were flying to the Orient and not away from it. The men one talked to eating a quick meal in the Army mess halls had only one desire, to get the hell out of Africa or Asia and be home.

American demobilization and its results were apparent in the spring of 1946 when I left China to return to the United States by the Pacific route. I traveled then by Marine plane to Hawaii. Neither the Marines nor the Navy nor the Air Transport Command could any longer send their giant transports by day and night over the oceans. The shortage of personnel made it impossible to service the planes after dark.

From Newfoundland to the Azores, from Casablanca across North Africa and the Holy Land, over the burning sands of Arabia, across Persia, on to Karachi and Calcutta, across Burma to Kunming and Chungking, across Central China to Shanghai, up to Marine territory in North China, on the islands and atolls of the vast Pacific Ocean—everywhere were the unmistakable signs of American power, American efficiency and American prestige. But everywhere too the visible power of the United States was fading away as its soldiers and sailors returned to their homes.

Passing over the Dead Sea in the moonlight, with the lights of Bethlehem far away to the west, I thought: The devil can take you to the top of a high mountain and tempt you with dominion over all the kingdoms of the earth only if you come from a desert or from an overpopulated, backward and poor or misgoverned land. Not if you come from a prosperous and free country with an abundance of resources and little poverty. Americans, sailing in their great ships high up over the earth, are not even aware of any temptation to dominate the world. They just want to go home. . . .

Empires have been built by merchants and adventurers leading paupers, or by tyrants seeking to keep their own people enslaved by diverting their thoughts away from dreams of liberty to the "glories" and rewards of foreign conquest.

Ancient Rome conquered the Mediterranean World after her peasants had lost their lands to the rich while fighting for "security." Britain began her empire-building in the days when freebooters like Drake plundered the galleons of Spain in the Atlantic. Next came the colonization of America by men and women escaping religious persecution, or seeking freedom from feudal restraints, longing for liberty, opportunity and enough to eat.

But the greatest expansion of Britain's power came in the late eighteenth and nineteenth centuries when her dispossessed peasants were impressed into the navy, or enlisted in the army to avoid starvation, while trade followed the flag in Africa and Asia.

Today the British Empire is contracting and the British people are too weakened to maintain the world order they established in the nineteenth century. Germany lies in ruins but a new imperialist power has arisen. Soviet Russia is driven to expand by incentives which are both new and very old. The Communist ideology is new and the world order which Moscow seeks to impose is radically different from the old British concept. But the economic and political motivation for Russian expansion is similar to that which drove the Czars or ancient Persia and Assyria to conquest: the need of tribute from abroad in order to maintain tyranny at home.

Russia has abundant raw material resources and a starved internal market. But the Soviet economic and political system, which they call Socialist, is too oppressive and cumbersome, and therefore inefficient, to give the Russian people tolerable material conditions of existence. The loss of freedom under the Communist dictatorship has therefore not been compensated for by the gain of security.

The Kremlin is driven to a policy of conquest by the permanent crisis in the Soviet economy. A complete breakdown can be avoided only if Russia can obtain goods from abroad without the necessity of paying for them.

Before the war the younger generation of Russians knew nothing better than their own subsistence scale of living. Today many Red Army men have had a glimpse of the far higher standard of living in the "capitalist world." Stalin and the Communist bureaucracy can never sleep easy if outside the confines of the Soviet Union there are prosperity and freedom. Imperialist expansion offers the only hope of stilling the longing of the Russian people for liberty and better material conditions. If the capitalist world can be first weakened and then destroyed, the Communist dictatorship can be made secure. If other nations can be forced to work for Russia her people may obtain the necessities of life which the Soviet system fails to produce. If there is no freedom anywhere the Russian people can be expected to accept their lot. As Stalin himself has written:

> It is inconceivable that the Soviet Republic should continue to exist interminably side by side with imperialist states. Ultimately one or the other must conquer.*

To the Communists all capitalist states are by their very nature "imperialist," and they regard the United States as the leading "Imperialist Power." Yet in the United States, which combines the natural resources of Russia with the freedom and efficiency which can make full use of them, there is no social basis for imperialism nor much economic need for it—as yet. America's resources are still great and her land not overpopulated. Above all, the American people participate in and control their government.

Foreign trade, which is a question of life and death for Britain as for Germany, still seems unimportant to the majority of Americans. American exports for three decades have represented, in the main, gifts to foreigners in the form of unrepayable loans, Lend-Lease or UNRRA contributions. The fact that the United States tariff has prevented repayment except in gold is a proof of America's near self-sufficiency.

Why should the American people accept the responsibilities of empire since they neither need nor desire its profits and glory? This was the basic truth which gave American isolationism its strength. Today, however, the terrible march of science has created such long-range and devastating weapons of destruction that the United States has lost the security which geography once afforded her. Today also there exists a great power determined to extinguish America's attraction for Europeans and Asiatics, and confident that American policy can be rendered nugatory by domestic pressures manipulated from abroad while her potential allies are dragged one by one into Russia's sphere in anticipation of the battle of the giants to come. Each country unable to resist Russia or weakened from within by the Communist

---

* *Problems of Leninism.* International Publishers, New York City. This book is circulated in thirty languages to millions of people.

disease is not only a lost ally, it is also a potential ally of the enemies of democracy.

America is the only country strong enough with her allies to impose universal peace, and possessing both the resources and the political freedom not to be tempted to enslave other peoples. But whoever heard of, or imagined, a country giving peace and security to others without oppressing and exploiting them? How is it to be expected that any nation will give the world the benefits of imperialism without its curses? This is the dilemma of our age. Those who want power want it for bad ends. Those who reject power are the only ones who could use it for the good of mankind.

In China I saw America's power and prestige being whittled away and her hands tied by misunderstanding of the international situation and the strident demand to "bring the boys home." America's strength was also her weakness. However privileged their position abroad, Americans long for home. In the nineteenth century the British Tommy, born in the slums of London or some other city of the Empire over which the sun never sets, lived better in India or elsewhere in the Colonial Empire than in England, and he could enjoy feeling superior to the "natives." But the attitude of most Americans was summed up for me in the words of GI's I talked to in Kunming. Parked waiting in the warm sun of lovely Yunnan they said: "China! Let the Chinese have it; we want to go home."

It may be different if mass unemployment comes following the postwar boom, and foreign trade seems a solution for economic crisis and a substitute for the vanished frontier. America's lavish use of her raw material resources has already created some shortages. We are no longer free of the necessity to import vital strategic materials. There may soon be an economic basis for American interest in free trade and a free world obtainable only through the exertion of American power.

Already many demobilized men look back on their life in the Army, Navy or Marine Corps with some faint regret. Or so at least I was told by some of their buddies in China. Some few re-enlist without going home, saying they "never had it so good." Certainly it is better than a civilian job at $25 a week. The soldier, sailor and marine has no housing difficulties to contend with. And there is always the type of man who cannot settle down again to work on the farm, or in a factory or office, after a war. But so long as the American people control their own destiny, so long as neither demagogues nor dictators deprive them of freedom, world power is not likely to attract them. This is the tragic paradox of the world situation. By rejecting their historical opportunity to establish an American world order the American people may leave a free field for those whose every effort is bent toward the attainment of world hegemony.

You have here a strange situation, a situation without historical precedent. While other nations strive, or have striven, for empire or world domination, the United States refuses the prize which her arms and her industrial might have won. No one could challenge the United States if her people desired empire over the earth. Their power is predominant. If the eagle felt like screaming the other nations would listen and obey. Without America there would have been no German or Japanese defeat. But, having fallen into the war, the American people hastened only to scramble out of the lands which would gladly have seen them stay.

It is understandable that every American soldier wants to go home. It is less comprehensible that the American people, having proclaimed themselves overwhelmingly opposed to an isolationist policy, should have demanded that we "bring the boys home" and refrain from using our power to make secure the aims for which we fought.

Wars are not football matches fought only to be won. They would be senseless unless an effort were made to achieve an objective and insure a lasting peace. As Congressman Walter Judd said shortly after V-J Day, "It is most unfortunate that so many Americans concluded that the war was over and we had won it when as a matter of fact all we had done was to defeat the Germans and the Japanese. Who wins the war depends largely on what we do from here on. It will be won by whatever forces and ideas dominate in the reconstruction of Europe and the development of Asia."

The issue of world hegemony is most clearly presented in China. Here is the arena where a clash could occur which would lead to a third world conflagration as surely as Japan's rape of Manchuria in 1931. The Far Eastern policy which the United States has pursued more or less consistently for decades, here comes into conflict with a Russian policy as inimical to it as was Japan's.

Russia today, even more positively than Japan yesterday, threatens the complete extinction of American rights and interests in China. Not only this. A Russia dominant in Asia with bases in the Kuriles and in Siberia facing Alaska constitutes a far greater threat to American security than Japan ever did.

Since the end of the nineteenth century the United States has opposed the domination of China by any one power, has sought to preserve the integrity of China and insisted upon the open door for the commerce of all nations. This policy has, however, been negatively rather than positively applied. Principle has time and again been sacrificed to expediency.

Up to Pearl Harbor neither national interest nor security was ever thought to be sufficiently involved for the United States to take a positive and strong line of action in defense of either China's integrity or American interests in China. Japan's territorial conquests were not "recognized" but Americans continued to do business with her at China's expense. The United States, like the British Empire, supplied the Japanese with oil, scrap iron, machinery and anything else needed for war, confining her protests to the infringement of American rights, not China's.

For four decades the United States strove to avoid war over China by giving only lip service to the principle of maintaining China's integrity. War came nevertheless in December 1941. This was not only because Japan had allied herself to Germany. It was also because there came a moment when principle and self-interest required the same action, when it was no longer possible to maintain the second without the first. Thus American insistence on the preservation of China's integrity and national independence was the immediate, although not the basic cause for her involvement in World War II. If the United States had not refused to sanction the territorial gains of Japan's long series of aggressions against China, Japan would never have joined with Germany and Italy in a military alliance, nor have challenged the United States in December 1941. On the other hand, if the United States and Britain had firmly and actively supported China, there would have been no Pearl Harbor.

The essential weakness in United States Far Eastern policy has not been inconsistency but vacillation as regards the means to be adopted to achieve its aims. Over and over again we have failed to take strong diplomatic action in time to save the necessity for future military action. It is obvious now that the war with Japan which cost so many American lives in the bloody battles on the islands and atolls of the Pacific could have been avoided had we applied economic sanctions against Japan when she first attacked China. We know that Japan was ready to surrender before the atom bomb was launched on Hiroshima. Once cut off from imports of oil and other war materials she had no chance at all to survive.

Today we are faced with a very similar situation to the one we failed to cope with in the thirties. Russia has stepped into Japan's shoes. She has inherited the "divine mission" of keeping China disunited and powerless. Russia today, like Japan in the early thirties, exploits the centrifugal forces in China in order to convert her into a satellite.

President Roosevelt at Yalta promised Stalin to bring pressure upon the Chinese Government to force it to give up to Russia the imperialist privileges in Manchuria which China had struggled fifteen years to deny to Japan. In so doing he not only disregarded China's legitimate interests, but he forgot that Japan had originally been raised up and supported by his relative Theodore Roosevelt as a counterweight to Russia whose Czars, at the end of the nineteenth century, threatened to acquire hegemony over the whole of China.

The elimination of Japan and the unnecessary concessions made at Yalta to Stalin's imperialist ambitions have put Russia back into the position she occupied at the beginning of the century. The great game begins anew. The conflict between the West and Russia for predominant power over the body and soul of China has been resumed, following the episode of Japan's rise and fall. But today it has become part of the world struggle between the opposing forces of Communist Russia and democratic America.

In the nineteenth century Britain and Russia met face to face in China, but Britain supported by the United States managed to push Russia back by building up Japan. Today it is America, not the weakened British Empire, which faces Russia across the huge body of China. Today the conflict between the West and Muscovy in the Far East is primarily an American-Russian conflict. The Russians understand this only too well and act accordingly. But Americans are loath to see in yesterday's ally the enemy of today and tomorrow.

Japan never really had a chance to establish control over China.

Her armies could advance and do untold damage, but too few Chinese were ready to co-operate with her to establish effective rule over the occupied areas. Russia enjoys great advantages over Japan in this respect. Her resources are much greater, she has a land approach to China and she has something more than a Fifth Column in the shape of the Chinese Communists with their own army controlling large territories in the North. Moreover, Soviet Russia, never having gone to war against China, can hope to succeed where Japan failed. She may be able to revive and exploit the latent anti-imperialist and anti-Western sentiments of the Chinese people so skillfully used by Russia from 1924 to 1927 when she almost succeeded in shutting out the Western Powers from China. Her failure then was due to Chiang Kai-shek and the moderate elements in the revolutionary Kuomintang which he represented. Stalin has never forgotten or forgiven the Generalissimo for orientating China toward the West. Now, twenty years after, it is a primary object of his policy to destroy China's national leader and National Revolutionary Party.

How few Americans today remember that only two decades ago Russia, not Japan, constituted the greatest menace to American, as well as British, interests in China! The struggle with the USSR from 1922 to 1927 was the bitterest that American influence had ever faced in the Far East. If the alliance between the Chinese Nationalists and Russia which existed in the twenties had been continued, it would have proved irresistible. The threat of a Russian hegemony over China led America, from 1927 onward, to join with Britain in strengthening the non-Communist majority in the Kuomintang, led by Chiang Kai-shek. Only eighteen years later General Marshall came to China to try to revive in the name of unity and democracy the Kuomintang Communist coalition which America had been intent on destroying in 1927.

My three visits to China have coincided with three distinct phases of her history and her relations with the West.

In 1928, when I visited China for the first time, I had come from Moscow to Shanghai across Siberia bearing secret messages from the Comintern. It was shortly after the split between the Kuomintang and the Communists and the establishment of the Nanking Government headed by Chiang Kai-shek. The Communists who had survived the massacre in the spring of 1927 were either in hiding or with the Red Army in Kiangsi.

The documents, which I carried "in my bosom" in the style of old-fashioned melodrama, had to be delivered in Shanghai with elaborate precautions. My instructions were to register at the Palace Hotel and telephone to a certain "Herr Doktor Haber" saying I had arrived with "the samples of silk stockings." When he came I handed over with relief the sealed and silk-encased package which contained I know not what secret instructions for the furtherance of Comintern aims in China. I had been chosen to bring them because I was English and the holders of British and American passports were least likely to be searched at the border. Nevertheless I was glad my mission was accomplished, for I am not the stuff of which conspirators are made.

Before sailing for Japan with more secret messages I was allowed to spend an evening with the leaders of the Shanghai underground.

We met after midnight in a whitewashed cellar somewhere off Nanking Road. The Comintern agents plied me with questions about happenings in Moscow, which in my innocence I was unable to answer. The men I met, Americans and Germans or German-speaking Europeans, must have been, if not Trotskyists, at least extremely unhappy revolutionaries. They had witnessed Stalin's sacrifice of the Chinese Communists and were watching with dismay the beginnings of his transformation of the Comintern into a suboffice of the Russian state.

Exactly ten years later I was to meet two of them again. In October 1938 when about to leave Shanghai for America, I was awakened early in the morning by the telephone ringing. A man's voice asked me if he could come up but would give no name. I was still half-asleep when a white-faced, emaciated and shabbily dressed man entered the room. I did not remember him but he gave me such full details of my visit to Shanghai in 1928 that I was convinced. He was pitifully nervous and begged me to come and visit him and his wife that evening.

They were the once famous couple called Noulens who had been arrested as Comintern agents around 1933 and made the headlines when they went on a hunger strike.

I agreed to visit them but I was nervous because Noulens had insisted on my telling no one. For all I knew he might still be Moscow's agent or he might even be working for the Japanese, and both might want to have me quietly disappear.

I took Randall Gould, editor of the *Shanghai Evening Post,* into my confidence. He offered to wait for me in his car at the end of the street and to come and rescue me if I did not rejoin him in an hour's time.

The Noulens told me they had been released from prison in 1937 and Madame Sun Yat-sen was supplying them with enough money to exist. But they had been warned to see no one—or so they said and I believed them. They said they had so longed to speak to someone they had once known and trusted that they had risked asking me to their home. They were obviously terrified. They were Austrians without passports and with nowhere to go, for it was clear that they feared to be liquidated if they returned to Russia. They knew too much. I urged them to meet Randall Gould, who was a liberal and a kindly man and who I knew would try to help them. But they dared not.

Poor devils. I left full of pity for these two white-faced derelicts of an age in Comintern history long past. They had left one prison only to fear incarceration in another. Rejected by everyone, they were too broken in spirit to save themselves and start a new life. I had known men and women like them in Moscow, old revolutionaries whose hopes were dead but who could not break with their past and waited only for death.

"Dr. Haber" seems to have had better luck and more sense. He had organized a real import business as a façade for his Comintern activities and developed it into a flourishing enterprise. Some of his employees acted in the double capacity of traveling salesmen and agents of the Comintern with their salaries halved between Moscow and Haber's business account. According to the account given of him in *Pattern for World Revolution* by the former Communist "Ypsilon," Haber, whom he calls Comrade L, decided in the early thirties that the Revolution was dead and he would henceforth become simply a businessman. His business was by then netting him a hundred thousand dollars a year profit. He calmly returned the amount of the original capital advanced to him by Moscow, arguing that this was all the Comintern had a right to expect since he had all along paid ten percent interest besides performing his duties as a Comintern agent.

I had not seen much of the Chinese on my first brief visit in 1928. Hatred of the "Western Imperialists" was then still so great that my Communist friends warned me against walking in the streets of the city. I spent most of my time investigating the cotton industry as a bona fide research student of the London School of Economics. I also tasted Shanghai's gay and opulent social life with Britishers who were shocked to hear that I was writing articles for "that Red rag," the *Manchester Guardian.* All values are indeed relative. Five years later in Moscow in one of the periodic "cleansings of the apparatus" it was brought up against me as a sign of bad bourgeois connections that I had once worked for the *Manchester Guardian*!

The attitude of most white people in Shanghai toward the Chinese twenty years ago made me understand and sympathize with the burning desire of the Chinese people to throw them out of China. Now as I write, in 1947, Communist-inspired anti-American demonstrations prove how easy it is to revive latent hatred of the West among the ill-fed, ragged masses of the Chinese cities.

On my second visit to China, in 1938, I had come by sea from England. By that time I was anti-Communist, having lived for six years in Soviet Russia. The change in China was as great as the change in me. I had learned that, compared with the tyranny and oppression, misgovernment and poverty under Russia's Communist Government, British imperialism is enlightened. The Chinese, far from wanting to oust the British and Americans, were hoping against hope that the West would come to her aid to rout the Japanese.

The attitude of the British and Americans in China had undergone a similar transformation. The old China hands who had once seen Japan as a useful junior partner in the business of holding China down and preserving foreign rights and privileges, were now cheering on the Chinese. Of course, they still did business with Japan, but they recognized and admired the stubborn courage of the Chinese and hoped that China would continue to resist Japan in spite of the material help the latter was getting from the United States and the British Empire.

Then as now the Western democracies were backing both sides. From 1937 to 1941 America and England had tried to avoid antagonizing Japan while giving China just sufficient aid and encouragement to keep her fighting. Following V-J Day, they tried to conciliate Russia and the Chinese Communists while giving strictly limited aid to the Chinese Nationalists.

In spite of all the changes in international alignments, China on my third visit seemed as far as ever from her goal of national liberation. As so often in the past hundred years she had exchanged one aggressor for another. Russia instead of Japan held Manchuria and was seeking to keep China disunited and powerless until she should submit and "co-operate."

Because the odds against her had been too great, victory had found China too weak to profit by it. Her people had borne too-heavy burdens for too long. The "diseases of defeat" had taken too heavy a toll for her to have strength to resist either Russia or the Communist infection unless aided by Western science, Western supplies and the heartening medicine of American sympathy and support. But America was vacillating once again. She refused wholly to repudiate the Communists as she had formerly refused to cease all aid to Japan.

At the time of my arrival in China it seemed that the policy of the United States might be taking a logical course. The clamor of the Left coupled with the overriding desire to "get along with Russia" had not succeeded in stopping aid to the National Government of China in its postwar efforts to re-establish its control over the provinces formerly occupied by Japan.

One of the best-informed diplomats in Chungking, General Victor Odlum, the Canadian ambassador, told me he was inclined to believe that the United States had decided upon a courageous and far-sighted Far Eastern policy.

"There are," he said, "Russian clouds on the international horizon. The only sound American policy would be to strengthen China, dominate the internal armed strife, improve Chinese communications and help train her army.

"If the United States does not vacillate in its support of the National Government, economic recovery will be rapid and the Communists will no longer be in a position to disrupt Chinese unity in Russia's interests. Time is flowing against the Communists. It will increase their difficulties and their problems, provided only that American policy does not switch back to the Stilwell line of favoring and encouraging Communism."

General Wedemeyer, whom I interviewed two months later in Shanghai, was convinced that the security of the United States required a strong China freed from the Communist menace.

In private conversation he said to me:

"Were the United States to abandon China now, all our costly sacrifices in the war against Japan would have been in vain. Both the honor and the interests of the United States require that we continue to support our most faithful ally and greatest potential friend, the Republic of China.

"China is the sincerest friend of the United States, for the simple reason that, whereas American interests and those of her other great allies are often in conflict, the interests of the United States and China coincide. It is only natural that other nations should try to get as much as they can out of America, while at the same time competing with her. China is the least involved in such an approach.

"Russia's goal is the establishment of puppet or satellite regimes along her Asiatic borders as well as in Europe. Stalin wants to have the psychological as well as the political and military initiative in Sakhalin, Korea, Manchuria, Jehol, Chahar, Hupeh, Inner Mongolia and Sinkiang, as well as in Persia. If the Chinese Communists are not forced to give up their private army and autonomous administration, Russia will get what she wants."

Both during and since my last visit to China there has been a continual seesaw in the relations between the National Government of China on the one side, and Russia and the Chinese Communists on the other side, depending on the amount of backing China received from the United States.

The Chinese Government never knew whether, in a showdown, America would use her power to prevent Russia from encroaching on China or whether China would be abandoned to her fate.

When America appeared to be taking a line of strong and uncompromising support of China, Russian pressure on China was relaxed and the Communists became less intransigent. In the summer of 1945 when General Hurley and General Wedemeyer represented the United States Government and armed forces in China; when America's hands were about to be freed by the collapse of Japan and there was a prospect that President Truman would not continue the Roosevelt policy of giving Stalin everything he asked for, Moscow ceased denouncing the Government of China and negotiated the Soong-Molotov Treaty of August 18. Thereafter, however, General Hurley's recall again gave Russia and the Communists hope that America was vacillating in its support of China. The Chinese Communists broke off negotiations in Chungking and started to tear up railroad lines and grab as much territory as they could.

From the Communist point of view, the greater the economic chaos and misery in China, the better their chance to dominate. Moreover the worse communications became and the greater the difficulties of the government in reviving trade and industry, the greater the disillusionment of the Americans with their ally China and the greater their desire to "leave China to the Chinese."

The Japanese had comforted themselves all through the war with the belief that even if they lost, China could not win. In August 1937 *The Oriental Economist* had written:

> In any event before Japan could fall in the struggle, China's movement to mould herself into a modern state and her programme of economic reconstruction would both go crashing down, leaving little of such Central Government as there is at present.

The Japanese were a little too optimistic. This dire prophecy has not been quite fulfilled. But since V-J Day China has moved perilously close to the abyss of disintegration. Economically and politically she is far worse off than in 1937, and the Communist menace which Japan pretended to see in the thirties is now a grim reality.

Can the United States, and will the United States, give China the necessary backing and assistance to prevent her crashing down? When I first arrived in China it seemed that we should.

When I left China in the spring of 1946, it appeared far more doubtful that America would pursue a policy to her own and China's advantage.

CHAPTER II

Gray Dawn in China

THE large and luxurious C-54 which had carried me so quickly from Washington to India terminated its flight at Calcutta. I was not, however, able to stay in India, even for a few days. The British authorities after keeping me waiting two months for a visa had given it to me only on condition that I fly straight through to China. No doubt the fact that I had been a Communist two decades ago was recorded and I was still a suspicious character.

After a day's sight-seeing and a much needed night in bed, I left Calcutta in the early dawn, sitting now on a bucket seat in a smaller plane filled to capacity with UNRRA personnel and other civilians.

We had expected to fly over the Hump and were disappointed that with the war's end the Army Transport Command had abandoned the beautiful if perilous route over the Himalayas. We flew instead over the vast green jungles of "liberated" Burma to Yunnan province.

The C-47's did not travel by night and the traffic in as well as out of China was still heavy, so we were delayed twenty-four hours in Kunming among bored GI's waiting their turn to go home.

In the evening Dr. Logan Roots, who had been my fellow passenger from Washington and who was a friend from Hankow days, took me to visit missionary friends who had lived in China through the whole war. We talked far into the night and then drove back through the old city to the army post at the airfield. Here I found the English doctor who shared my hut asleep with DDT powder liberally scattered on the blankets and floor. I reflected that she was going to find life insupportable in the interior of China if she feared vermin even in the spotlessly clean U. S. Army billets.

Next afternoon we reached Chungking, just seven days out of Washington, and seven years after I had left China in the second year of her war against Japan.

The road from the Chiulungpo airport to the city was inches deep in mud and rutted. At each hairpin bend up and down the steep hill-sides I clung to the jeep with both hands. The rain veiled the beautiful hills of Szechwan in mist. In my tired and melancholy mood I felt that the heavens themselves might weep for the tragedy of the Chinese people. Though they were patient, intelligent, industrious, tolerant and good-humored, history had not given them a break for over a hundred years.

First Britain and France, and on their heels Germany, Russia and Japan, had taken advantage of China's military weakness to despoil her; to wrest territories, concessions and privileges by force from a people who wished only to be left alone.

Now even in victory the Chinese were tasting only the fruits of defeat. Russia, instead of Japan, had control of Manchuria. The extraterritorial rights in China given up by the Western Powers had been revived in Russia's favor in the unequal Sino-Russian Treaty of August 1945.

The Chinese people seemed never able to acquire a breathing space. If they quenched the flames on one side of their house, they had immediately to turn to battle a conflagration on the other side.

I remembered how, when the Sino-Japanese War began, China's optimists and pessimists had alike believed that China could not hold on unaided against Japan's overwhelming military might unless she soon acquired allies. Both had been wrong. China had resisted alone longer than anyone had believed possible in that long-ago summer of 1937. Yet help when it came had been too little and too late. Japan, not Germany, had attacked the United States in December 1941, but America decided that Germany was the greater menace. Blockaded China was told to go on sticking it out while we defeated Hitler first. China's situation had become ever more desperate. The British loss of Malaya and Burma left her completely blockaded. The flow of Lend-Lease, denied to China, when it could easily have reached her, was turned over to Russia. Paeans of praise arose in America for the valiant armies of Stalin, armed by America. Adding insult to injury, scorn was heaped on the Chinese, the flower of whose armies had been cut down years before in the three-months' battle for Shanghai and the nine-months' struggle to save the Wuhan cities.

It was almost dark when we arrived in the suburbs of Chungking and I looked down for the first time on the calm clear waters of the Chialing River far below. We rushed through the narrow streets miraculously avoiding accidents. The danger from speeding American trucks and jeeps in the narrow crowded streets was an old story by now to the people of Chungking. To me the vehicles and the American soldiers offered a striking contrast to the China I had known. If only a little of this American aid had been given sooner! In 1937 and 1938 it could have saved China from the long series of defeats and retreats which had broken her people's morale.

I had never before been in Chungking. In 1938 when I had reported the war for the *London News Chronicle,* Hankow, or rather the three Wuhan cities on the Yangtze, had been China's temporary capital. I had left them on the eve of their capture by Japan. Canton had fallen ignominiously a few days later, adding the terrors of cowardice and treason to the burdens, already heavy, of the invasion.

The heroic days of China's long war of resistance had ended when I sailed to the United States in the fall of 1938. The coastal cities and provinces were all in Japanese hands. China was settling down to a weary, grim and seemingly hopeless struggle for survival.

The much-bombed city of Chungking came to symbolize the patience and courage of the Chinese people. But it was also a byword for corruption, misgovernment and misery.

I was returning to a China cleared of the "dwarf robbers from the East," but a strange nostalgia gripped my heart for the Hankow days when China had been battered but proud in her determination to go on fighting alone at whatever cost. Now although victorious she was regarded by her allies more as a victim saved than as the oldest fighter of them all against aggression.

Drained dry both by the Japanese and the demands of the long war on her primitive economy, the Chinese were still unable to undertake the gigantic tasks of reconstruction and reform. An undeclared civil war was raging in eleven provinces. The destruction begun by Japan was being completed by the Communists, who were busy destroying railroads, bridges, industrial equipment and mines.

Communist military strategy required that they thus prevent the Nationalist Armies from taking over the provinces liberated by Japan. But it also seemed that they were counting upon economic collapse to bring about the fall of the government and the establishment of their own dictatorship.

Nor was China threatened only by the breakaway of the North under a Communist administration. The Russian Army was still in occupation of Manchuria. Moscow was already violating the Sino-Soviet Treaty of August 1945, in which Russia had promised not only to evacuate China's Northeastern provinces within three months but also to give moral support and material aid only to the National Government of China.

China was once again threatened by a choice between partition and submission. Russia and the Communists, in place of Japan and her collaborators, menaced her integrity and independence. The Communists were playing a role which was compared by some Chinese to that of the war lords in the past, or to that of the Japan-sponsored "autonomous" regimes in North China in the thirties. China was even less united than before the Sino-Japanese War began. As for a century past, foreigners were taking advantage of her weakness. As one Chinese newspaper expressed it, China had seen the dawn but not yet the sun.

My first two weeks in Chungking I felt like a Rip Van Winkle in the Press Hostel. I had hoped to find a few old friends, for I knew that some of the "Hankow Last Ditchers," as we used to call ourselves in the fall of 1938, were back in China. But no veteran correspondents of China's war were then in Chungking. I got involved in fierce and futile arguments with young men who, in the days when China fought alone with little besides flesh and blood to oppose the modern armaments of the invaders, had probably hardly known there was a war going on in the Far East.

They had forgotten that, whereas the Poles, Danes, Norwegians, Belgians and even the French had gone down to speedy defeat, the ragged, ill-armed, badly led Chinese had continued year after year to deny victory to Japan's military machine.

These correspondents had arrived too late on the scene and they knew too little history to understand or sympathize with China. Like most Americans they had not been looking while the Chinese were fighting bravely in the early stages of the war, without adequate arms, without allies or any hope of outside aid. All they had seen, or knew about, was the exhausted and demoralized China of the last four years of the eight-year war.

It was, in any case, natural that these young Americans, fresh from the most prosperous, free and technologically advanced country in the world, should attribute all the ills of China to its government. They lacked even the smattering of knowledge of medieval history which Europeans acquire in school. Nor had they ever seen the poverty of Eastern Europe. Their experience and knowledge were in general as remote from the bitter realities of life for nine-tenths of mankind as those of an inhabitant of Mars. Seeing for the first time the age-old poverty of Asia and the corruption which is so much more obvious in a poor country than in a land flowing with milk and honey, they had concluded that the Chinese people were worthless. Or they belonged to the Teddy White-Edgar Snow school which believed that the Communists were the hope of China.

A few months later when I returned to Chungking from Shanghai, the whole atmosphere of the Press Hostel had changed and I felt as much at home as with the intelligent, well-informed, cynical, but sympathetic and realistic Americans I had known in Hankow. But in October of 1945 the American correspondents, with the exception of Spencer Moosa of the Associated Press, were the type to whom the following words of Colonel Linton, published in *Stars and Stripes,* might have been addressed:

> It is almost tragic that American soldiers have eyes and do not see, ears and do not hear, minds and do not understand. They see the poverty, the filth, and humanity serving as beasts of burden, but they do not see how all these things are inherent in the history of a great nation struggling to emerge from the days of handicraft to the day of modern technology. They hear a strange language, but they do not hear the voice of a people singing faith and hope for its future. Their minds tell them that China is different, very different from the life they know, but they do not understand that, like ourselves, and like all peoples, China must begin today from where she is.

In the old days before China became our ally by action of Japan, American correspondents had lived on about the same level as middle-class Chinese or foreign missionaries. Moreover their attitude had not been one of lordly superiority. They had been ashamed that these poor, inadequately armed pacific people were fighting to hold off Japan's tyranny while Americans aided the aggressors by letting them buy all they needed in the way of war materials and machines.

Now American correspondents had the privileges, as well as the uniforms, of United States Army officers. They received the same rations and PX privileges and had little contact with ordinary educated Chinese.

Sitting at our all-too-abundant meals at the Press Hostel, warmed by a roaring fire in a country where few Chinese even of high rank had fuel, the correspondents would comment on the venality of Chinese officials and the general rottenness of China. The idea never struck them that, possibly, on the salary of a Chinese official inadequate to provide the barest necessities of life for a family, they too might not have been so pure. As a Chinese official in the Executive Yuan said to me one day: "The Americans in China are Sons of Heaven; what can they know of our trials and our temptations?"

Yet I found American officers and men in Chungking, Kunming and Shanghai who, having served in the interior and being themselves inured to hardships, had a quite different attitude toward the Chinese. There were, for instance, the two happy and handsome young officers I had met at the Red Cross Club in Kunming. One, a Major Bohlen from Indiana, had walked two thousand miles along the Burma road in charge of a convoy of mules. The other, a Texan, had served as an artillery instructor with the Chinese Army in Hupeh. Both told me they had started by thinking the Chinese hopelessly backward and uncivilized but had soon changed their minds after living and working with them.

"My God," said the Texan, Captain Wilson, "I don't know how they do it! Their guts and good humor, the way they smile in pain and the dreadful conditions they endure so cheerfully—it makes one feel ashamed to complain."

He told me how the soldiers, half-starved themselves, often had to carry the guns because the animals were too weak through underfeeding to bear their burdens. Yet the Chinese soldiers had been apt pupils. Both these officers criticized those who thought that the American way of doing things was always the best. They had learned what the Chinese were up against and had marveled at their ingenuity in coping with difficulties which had seemed insurmountable to the Americans.

In Shanghai when dining with General Tang En-po, the commander of the area, I met a certain Colonel Don Scott who had been chief American supply officer in the South in the last year of the war. An elderly, hard-bitten regular officer and a former Olympic champion, Colonel Scott was certainly no sentimentalist. But he was anxious to impress on me that "there are some good Chinese."

"General Tang En-po," he said, "used our equipment right. He corrected many abuses. His soldiers were properly taken care of. General Tang, he's a man. He does things right."

Colonel Scott came to see me next day because he wanted to give me information to counteract some of the calumny against the Chinese Army in the American papers. He painted a vivid picture of the difficulties the Chinese had had to contend with. On his way to Kunming from Chungking he had seen the starved recruits prodded on with bayonets. In Kweichow he had been impressed by the contrast.

Colonel Scott and General Tang En-po had had "rice sessions" once a week. Tang did the procuring and the Americans supplied the transport. Kweichow was the poorest province in China and rice had to be brought clear from Chungking. Seventeen thousand U. S. Army trucks were used to haul the rice for hundreds of miles. Tang En-po saw to it that there was no "squeeze"; that all the rice went to feed the Chinese soldiers.

"I've seen what the Chinese have done; how they're coming along," said the colonel. "But how could any Chinese general feed his soldiers until we gave them transport?"

I had met General Tang En-po at the front in 1938 and liked him. But I also knew that he had got himself a bad name in Honan in the 1943 famine. He had roused the violent hostility of the peasants because he forced food out of them to feed his soldiers.

A country such as China, with poor communications or none at all, with a backward peasant economy and her few industrial cities and all her ports in the hands of the enemy, simply did not have the means to supply her huge armies and her refugee-swollen city population. It could be done at all only by squeezing the peasants. There were many Chinese generals who cared nothing either for their soldiers or the common people and used their power only to enrich themselves. But some of the best generals had sometimes been forced to oppress the people to secure food for their men.

The foreigners who cried loudly that the government should have instituted land reforms in the midst of the war, thereby ensuring the good will of the peasants and their willing support of the war effort, ignored economic realities. If the landowners had been expropriated and the land divided, it would have been impossible to supply China's armies and the population of the cities with even the meagerest rations. Since blockaded Free China could produce few manufactured goods, the peasants would not voluntarily have sold their grain to the government. China would have been in the same state as Russia from 1919 to 1922, the period of "War Communism" when the peasants, after acquiring possession of the land, refused to sell their produce for worthless paper and had to be forced to give up their grain at the point of the bayonet.

Land reform in China in the years 1938 to 1945 could have led only to a similar situation. Instead, China kept her old agrarian system and used the landowners as tax collectors. Grain was forced out of the peasants as rent and as taxes through the machinery provided by the old land system. It was not a pretty process, but no more was War Communism in Soviet Russia. Since the war in China was also financed by the government's printing presses, mounting inflation tended to improve the lot of the peasants in some places. Many were at least freed of their old cash debt burdens.

Of course there was and is a lot of cheating. The landowners pass as much as possible of the burden of taxation onto the peasants. But they themselves could not escape the government's exactions. China's financial system during the war was, and had to be, a so-called "feudal" one. The government used the landlords to squeeze the peasants and in turn squeezed them.

The Communists place all the emphasis of their propaganda on redistribution of the land. But an examination of Chinese resources shows that expropriation of the landowning class could not afford a lasting solution of the agrarian problem. China's situation is entirely different from Russia's. The Soviet Union has vast territories and a comparatively small population. There is no lack of land. China on the other hand has even less arable land than India and a larger population.

My first week in Chungking I looked up Dr. Robert Lim with whom I had visited the front in 1938 when he was head of the Chinese Red Cross Medical Commission. In those days he had been working without government funds and with precious little help from anyone in authority. Together with a group of Western-trained Chinese doctors and with funds supplied by overseas Chinese and a few foreign friends he had been trying to create in the midst of war a medical service to save some of the wounded soldiers.

The grim sights I had seen at the front in the days of Japan's offensive against the Wuhan cities were indelibly burned on my mind. The wounded limping back from the front. The men dying in the hovels called collecting stations. The complete absence of ambulances or even trucks to move them. The gallant efforts made by Bobby Lim and his helpers and by his friend, Dr. Loo Chi-teh, the surgeon general, to provide dressing stations, to train first-aid workers, to acquire a few trucks from abroad to move the wounded.

Bobby Lim had to contend not only against the callous indifference, incompetence and corruption of the old-style Chinese generals who did not consider it worth while to save the wounded but the International Red Cross had also refused him aid because it had to be "neutral" in the war, and would only help civilian victims of the air raids.

The New Life Movement under the direction of Colonel (now General) J. L. Huang and others in Madame Chiang's confidence had hindered rather than helped him. They constantly interfered with serious relief work by publicity stunts and had been jealous of Bobby Lim's success. Since he is not a Christian he had no contact with Madame Chiang through foreign missionaries and I had myself secured him his first interview with her in 1938, following which she had allocated funds to his organization from the foreign donations she received.

Since Bobby Lim, whenever able, had sent medical supplies and doctors to all the fronts, his enemies had accused him of Communist sympathies. He had been regarded as a hero by Agnes Smedley, the American whose heart and soul are with the common people of China and who believes that the Chinese Communists are China's hope.

I had always regarded Lim as one of the best Chinese I had ever met, a man with the highest medical qualification who had given up an easy living abroad or in Shanghai to give all his talents and energies to his country at the worst period of her fortunes. It was therefore to me a proof that everything is not now so wrong with the state of

China as her critics maintain, that such a man as Bobby Lim had become surgeon general of the National Armies while Dr. Loo Chi-teh was now in charge of the training of army medical personnel. The redoubtable Tai Li, the almost legendary figure who headed the Chinese secret police and co-operated with the American OSS in intelligence work during the war, had cleared Lim of any suspicion of Communist sympathies. And the Generalissimo himself had recognized Lim's worth, talents and devotion to his country, by putting him in charge of the army's medical services, backing him in his efforts at reform and making him a two-star general.

Bobby Lim came to fetch me at the Press Hostel as soon as he got my message that I was back in China. After my first two depressing days in Chungking it was wonderful to spend a week end at the army medical headquarters at New Bridge, fifteen miles outside Chungking. With Bobby I found another old friend, Mary Chen, whose husband had recently been reunited with her after nearly four years as a guerrilla fighter in the Philippines. There was also Dr. Wang, one of the few survivors of the original Changsha group, who now also was a general but just the same unassuming, honest doctor I had known in the old days.

Mary cooked us a Chinese dinner and Bobby opened a bottle of Scotch whisky which he had been saving for just such an occasion. Sitting on the terrace, with the flooded rice paddies in the valley below faintly illuminated by the moonlight, we talked far into the night. There was a lot of "do you remember?" but I also learned a good deal about what had happened in the years between. Next day we talked again, but Bobby was as busy as he had been in Changsha in 1938, when he had not even a secretary or a typist to help him with his administrative work and his appeals for medical supplies from abroad. Now he had a large staff and smart sentries guarded his headquarters. But he still gave his talents and his time and energies as unstintingly as before to the service of the Chinese soldiers.

An American Medical Service officer arrived in the morning and spent his day with us. It was, he said, his pleasure and his relaxation to come out to Lim's headquarters. Other days he came out on duty; on Sundays he came out to enjoy himself. This Major Puy was one of the many American officers I met who showed understanding, appreciation and sympathy for the Chinese, and felt completely at his ease with them. The Chinese doctors, for their part, were only too happy to be receiving expert advice and help from the United States Army.

Bobby told me that many reforms had been carried through in the army. He now had authority to reform the formerly hopelessly inefficient and corrupt Army Medical Service. Wounded soldiers in the later stages of the war had had a far better chance of surviving. Reforms in the methods of recruiting soldiers and in their treatment had been inaugurated. They were now somewhat better fed. Abuses whereby the commanding officers could profit by misappropriating the funds which should have bought food for the rank and file had been remedied by the direct issue of rations. American officers had helped a great deal. Above all Lend Lease, scanty as it was, had been of great help in improving the Chinese soldier's lot. For, after all, it was China's extreme poverty and the loss of resources to Japan which had been the root cause of the miserable plight of the Chinese soldier.

Bobby Lim was one among many old Chinese friends and acquaintances with whom I spent my time in Chungking. I was surprised and moved to find myself still remembered, after so many years, as the author of *Japan's Feet of Clay.* This book, which attempted to expose both Japan's basic weakness and the falsity of her democratic pretensions, and to awaken the Western world to the need to call her bluff and stop her aggression, had been translated into Chinese and widely sold. Even now, nearly ten years after its publication, I was remembered as a friend by both "reactionaries" and liberals because I had been one of the few foreigners who had tried to help China in the early days of her war of resistance when most Westerners were indifferent to her fate.

General Chen Ming-shu, who had commanded the Kuomintang forces which took Hankow in 1926, who had been a member of the Wuhan Government the following year, who had fought with the Nineteenth Route Army from Fukien against the Japanese in Shanghai in 1932 without Chiang Kai-shek's support or encouragement and who was now an unemployed general and one of the government's bitterest critics, often invited me to dine at Chungking's "Canton restaurant" of which he was part owner. Chen Ming-shu himself, no longer young but slim and handsome with the eyes of a dreamer, had been a friend of mine in 1938. He represented to a greater degree than any other Chinese I knew the hopes, the fire and enthusiasm and the sincerity which had inspired the Kuomintang in its early days.

I could not but agree with him that China's primary need was the separation of civil and military power, and that there can be no democracy until civil liberties are secured. It was obviously true that as long as the provinces were governed by military men with armies at their disposal there could be no civil liberty or popularly elected administrations. It was perhaps true that Chiang Kai-shek considered China's armies as "his" rather than the nation's. It was undoubtedly true that many able, experienced and honest men in China were not employed by the administration because they failed to give allegiance to Chiang Kai-shek personally while many "blockheads" belonged to the Central Executive Committee of the Kuomintang. I could also well believe that Chen Ming-shu was right in saying that the National Government had become a "clique which stands together," and that many Kuomintang members were dissatisfied and sympathized with the opposition. I hoped that he was right in believing that "the democratic elements in the Kuomintang" now out of office and impotent would soon become powerful and "show the world" a real implementation of the *San Min Chu I*.

But it seemed to me that Chen Ming-shu, like other sincere and honest liberals, ignored the terrible compulsions of the international situation. How could a civil government be established, the armed forces drastically reduced and democratic liberties be made a reality as long as China was threatened with destruction by the internal and external enemies of democracy?

Chen Ming-shu and others like him were not Communists but they practically ignored the Russian threat to Chinese independence. They were still living in the world of twenty years earlier.

For all his criticisms of Chiang Kai-shek's dictatorial nature and desire for personal power, Chen Ming-shu was still not his enemy.

"If only," he exclaimed, "his attitude were different! Chinese of all parties, in particular the able and sincere men of the Kuomintang, would sympathize and co-operate with him. But Chiang is like Louis XIV who said 'I am the state.' He considers himself to be the law, justice, everything. He kills men without trial. Even provincial magistrates may not be appointed without his consent.

"Chiang Kai-shek," he continued, "has two natures. The one is lawless since he himself transgresses the laws and destroys them. The other side of his nature is good. He sincerely loves his country and desires to lead China to independence and good government. He could be a great leader if only he would not insist on everyone in the government being a 'yes man.' I myself still love Chiang from the bottom of my heart. I wish I could help him to be China's George Washington."

Chen Ming-shu and his friends all lived in the simplest fashion with the exception of some of the wealthy members of the Democratic League. But so also did most of the government leaders except for a few millionaires like T. V. Soong and H. H. Kung and some others who had inherited or married money.

In few of the Chinese homes I visited did I find what would have been considered in America as tolerable conditions of living. Some of my old acquaintances, even those holding positions in the government or in the Kuomintang Party organization, were so poor that they had sold almost everything they possessed to buy food for their children.

I was often reminded of Moscow in Chungking because both the similarity and the differences were so striking. The Chinese capital was as dilapidated as the Russian, and the majority of the people lived in the same squalor and poverty. There were the same scarcity of manufactured goods and lack of housing except for the leading members of the bureaucracy. But, in Chungking, human ingenuity had free play. Every little bit of everything was used either to repair the bomb damage or to make something useful. Discarded American cans and other refuse were manufactured into all sorts of implements and utensils. Every bit of land outside the town was intensively cultivated. The hillsides were green with vegetables almost all the year round. Nothing was wasted.

In China you are not rated a capitalist or an enemy of the state if you try to help yourself by hard work and ingenuity. The bureaucracy might control large-scale enterprise, but at least the dew of freedom allowed small enterprises to burgeon and grow and hide the scars of war.

I dined often in restaurants and private homes with high officials. Never once did I find anything approaching the luxury and wealth of the Soviet bureaucracy. Of course, one must reckon with the difference in culture or lack of it. Display, luxury and barbaric ostentation are as alien to Chinese civilization as they are natural to the Russians. Nevertheless it was obvious that belonging to the top ranks of the ruling Kuomintang Party in China conferred nothing comparable in the way of privilege and material advantage to the perquisites of the leading members of the Communist Party in Russia.

Nor was the contrast between the living standards of rulers and ruled nearly so great. Many people are starving or living on the border line of starvation in both countries. But the difference in living standards between the majority of the people and those of the bureaucracy is far greater in Russia than in China.

No doubt the Chinese bureaucracy is as self-seeking as the Russian. But its income and its powers are far more limited. A Chinese government official can live in comfort only if he takes bribes; can get rich only through speculation and the manipulation of the country's finances. In a developed Communist society such as the Soviet Union the corruption of the ruling class is both of a subtler nature and more far-reaching. The Communist big shots simply allocate to themselves an inordinately large share of the national income. The high Soviet functionary is paid a huge salary and also has the right to the free use of all kinds of so-called state property: apartments, country houses, automobiles, hospitals, special schools for his children and other services. Like an aristocrat or a millionaire he is not subject to temptation.

In China, which like Russia does not produce enough of the bare necessities of life to go around, the bureaucracy has not been lifted up into such a high-income bracket that it is above temptation. The inflation which was the unavoidable result of the long war, the blockade and the civil war, has reduced the value of an official's salary so low that only the most high-principled and honest men, or those with private incomes, abstain from some method or another of supplementing their inadequate salaries.

At the time of writing (June 1947) the salary of a divisional chief in a Chinese Ministry is around 600,000 CN a month plus a rice allowance while a skilled worker earns about 800,000 without a rice allowance. In Soviet Russia when I lived there the average wage for the working class was less than 300 rubles a month as against ten or more times that sum for the director of a state enterprise, and up to 10,000 rubles for commissars and other big shots.

During the war years in China only payment of salaries and wages in kind, rationing and the severest regimentation could have prevented gross inequalities and have produced uniformity in poverty. Rationing is well-nigh impossible in a loosely organized and economically backward country, and price control without rationing has proved unworkable even in countries where the government exercises far greater power than in China.

It should be remembered that during the first eight months of the Sino-Japanese War the value of China's currency had been maintained in terms of foreign exchange. This was no mean achievement and bears testimony to the confidence of the Chinese people in the National Government. But, following Japan's occupation of the coastal provinces, the government was deprived of the customs dues, which had been its main source of revenue. There was no way of preventing the depreciation of the yuan with foreign trade drying up, military expenditures increasing and trade and industry stultified. Once the government could no longer afford to give foreign exchange for the great quantity of yuan offered, a flight from the currency began. The demand for goods as the only stable store of value continually decreased the value of the currency and pushed the price of the small available supply of goods to greater and greater heights. The spiral of inflation which no country avoids in wartime naturally proceeded at an accelerated tempo in blockaded China whose war lasted so much longer and was fought with so much less American help than that of other countries.

The Chinese Government should, no doubt, have made a greater effort to impose direct taxes on the rich. The political results of forcing the Soongs, Kungs and the other few rich families in China to disgorge a part of their American-invested fortunes would have been excellent. But it would not have ameliorated materially the basic causes of inflation, at least so long as China was blockaded. The basic problem of how to feed the army and the officials out of a diminishing revenue would have remained.

The National Government might perhaps have been able, if it had tried harder, to finance the war in part by internal loans. But since the Chinese middle classes had for the most part lost their sources of income through Japan's occupation of the coastal provinces, there was in fact little possibility of selling war bonds.

Inflation as a method of financing war expenditures has its compensations. At least China faces the future without a huge internal debt, while the blockade also precluded her burdening herself with future interest payments to foreign countries. If the rise in prices had been uniform and affected all classes equally, the depreciation of the currency would not have been harmful so long as the inflation was kept within bounds.

During the war years the inflation does not, in fact, appear to have had generally injurious effects. Some elements in the population suffered greatly but the workers and a substantial proportion of the peasants seem to have positively benefited by it.

Collection of the land tax in kind, instituted by Dr. Kung in 1941, enabled the government to collect a revenue which, if it did not keep pace with the advance in prices, followed closely behind. But the land tax could not produce sufficient revenue to finance war expenditures so that prices rose continually through the ever-increasing quantity of paper currency put into circulation, as well as on account of the scarcity of commodities. Naturally everyone who could "invested" in goods as the only stable store of value, and hoarding and speculation further intensified the inflation.

Nevertheless Dr. H. H. Kung's so-called feudal methods kept the inflation within what were to seem moderate limits a year or so after he was succeeded in the management of Chinese finances by Chiang Kai-shek's other brother-in-law, T. V. Soong. Moreover, by supplementing the salaries of government officials with rice payments, the much maligned Dr. Kung did something toward checking the graft which riddles the administration. Not all officials succumbed to temptation once they were no longer driven to be venal by the impossibility of feeding their families on their almost worthless money salaries.

The postwar attempt to adopt Western fiscal policies, at a time when civil war was wrecking the country and American financial support was lacking, resulted in far worse inflation and social injustice, less production and more misery. It was after V-J Day that the Chinese yuan plunged catastrophically.

Taking the period January to June 1937 as 100, the price of all commodities in Szechwan in terms of Chinese currency stood at 1,950 by June 1945. But by April 1947 the index of wholesale prices in Nanking had risen to 18,000.

When I arrived in China in October 1945 one could get only about 1,000 yuan for an American dollar. Six months later one could obtain 2,000 in Shanghai. At the time of writing (May 1947) the free or black-market rate has jumped to 23,000. The most spectacular fall in the exchange value of the yuan followed General Marshall's recall at the beginning of 1947 and the subsequent announcement of the withdrawal of U. S. armed forces from China. There is little doubt that the many indications of withdrawal of full American support from the Chinese National Government have diminished confidence in the currency equally with growing Chinese distrust of the administration.

Nor should it be forgotten that the cessation of dollar expenditures of American soldiers, marines and sailors in China constituted a severe blow to the exchange.

Some foreign experts, notably Dr. J. Lossing Buck, attribute the present inflation in large part to the government's mistaken exchange policy. According to his view the government's policy increased the intensity of the blockade during the war years and has created an artificial blockade since V-J Day. For, because the exchange rate of the yuan was set artificially high instead of being allowed to find its natural level, Chinese goods became too dear to export. Thus, he argues, the pegging of the exchange rate, far from curbing the inflation, probably intensified it by cutting off the source of foreign credits. Exports are naturally discouraged when the foreign buyer can obtain too few yuan for his dollars to buy Chinese products at a price at which they can be sold abroad. The artificially high exchange rate also cut off remittances from Chinese overseas who saw no sense in sending dollars to their relatives so long as the dollars could be exchanged for so few yuan as to make the gift almost worthless.

Although the government insisted on maintaining the exchange value of the currency in order to import and in order to maintain confidence, there is evidence that it actually defeated its own purpose.

In economics as in politics China fell between two stools. It was neither liberal enough nor sufficiently totalitarian. Either a policy of free trade and free exchange, or complete control of the national economy, could have prevented the present disastrous situation. The mixture of the two has stymied the whole economy. The government has neither the power nor the machinery nor the will to control and direct all economic activity in the interests of the state or the ruling party. But, at the same time, it interferes enough with private business, trade and exchange to hamper and destroy independent private economic activity. China hangs suspended between the capitalist democratic world and the Soviet so-called socialist world of state-administered production and trade.

Unless China receives American loans and American technical aid she cannot afford a laissez-faire economy. Nor is it possible to imagine that graft can be eliminated until there is a middle class independent of state patronage and free from the dreadful fear of sinking back into the abysmal poverty of the masses. Insecurity is so widespread and the fear of destitution so strong in China that even the comparatively well-to-do are obsessed by it.

Unless outside aid is forthcoming to help solve China's economic problem and set her on her feet, she faces disintegration or colonization by Russia or regimentation by her own rulers on Communist, National Socialist or state capitalist lines.

Nothing could be farther from the truth than to call China's National Government a "fascist tyranny." If Chiang Kai-shek had been a dictator and the Kuomintang a totalitarian party, China would have fought a better war. It would have been possible to force equality of sacrifice and equal poverty on all except the members of the ruling party. Everyone would have been compelled to fight or work for the nation.

China has, it is true, a secret police and men are sometimes imprisoned without trial. But speech is comparatively free and everyone is not terrorized by fear of condemnation to forced labor. Even its worst enemies have never accused the National Government of keeping millions of political prisoners in concentration camps. There is nothing comparable in China to the slave labor which has become an integral part of the Soviet economy.

I spent a morning at the university with Professor Ma Yin-ch'u, who is represented by Communist sympathizers as a martyr who spent two years in a concentration camp for his wartime diatribes against the government. He told me himself that he had never been ill-treated. He had simply been under house arrest in a remote district. He laughed as he related how he had made his guards climb mountains with him, and how he had lectured to them on economics and made them take notes. The young men of the secret police, he said, were decent fellows and he had proposed that they all be given university tuition at government expense. This large, robust and happy ex-Yale man bore no resemblance whatever to the tortured and starved inmates of a Russian or German concentration camp.

To everyone who has lived under a totalitarian tyranny as I did for six years in Soviet Russia, it is absurd to describe the National Government of China as such. Of course, China is not yet a democracy. But there is no sign of the all-pervading terror which bows down the Russian people. The Chinese criticize the government to their hearts' content, meet and talk to foreigners without fear of the secret police, go about their business without being haunted by dread of arrest and the concentration camp.

The main defect of the Chinese Government is not its dictatorial character but its failure to govern, the graft with which it is riddled and its inability to check abuses and carry out the reforms to which it is pledged. Its impotence is partly due to the wide variety of political and economic theories held by the leading members of the Kuomintang Party. In an administration where some want to go Right, some Left and some to stay where they are, there is practical immobility or utter confusion.

The principal complaint I heard from Chungking businessmen concerned the uncertainty caused by the government's vacillating economic policy and the contradictory orders given by various branches of the administration. T. V. Soong, who was Premier and also controlled the Central Bank of China, was issuing one set of instructions while the Legislative Yuan headed by Sun Fo passed laws which went directly against them.

Mr. T. A. Hu, managing director of the China Industry Company, told me that his most difficult problem was not knowing what degree of freedom of enterprise was to be allowed to private business in the future.

"Look," he said, pointing to his company's sprawling factories across the river from his downtown office. "During the war we produced pig iron, steel, cement and china. When Mr. Donald Nelson came to Chungking he congratulated us on our achievement in building up an efficient industry here in wartime. Our steel mill employed three thousand people and produced ten thousand tons of steel a year. Now we may have to stop production altogether."

"Your factories are still working, aren't they?"

"Yes, but only to about half their capacity and soon we may have to shut down."

"Why?" I asked. "Is it because you no longer receive orders from the government? Surely there must be a huge peacetime demand for your products?"

"That's the whole trouble," replied Mr. Hu. "We don't know where we stand. Not long ago the Executive Yuan passed a resolution that China should in general have a free economy. Subsequently strong opposition to this policy in certain government circles led to its modification in favor of more government control of industry. An Executive Yuan decision today may always be countermanded tomorrow. No Chinese industrialist can be certain that if he invests his capital in what has been declared a free field for private enterprise, he may not wake up one morning and find it has been declared a government monopoly."

Other Chungking businessmen told me the same story. They were all waiting anxiously to know what kind of private undertakings were to be allowed to survive and develop. There were rumors that the textile industry would be nationalized. The former Japanese or puppet-owned Shanghai mills were being organized by T. V. Soong into a state corporation. Fears were expressed that the native cotton growing and manufacturing developed in Szechwan during the war might be jettisoned in favor of the Eastern mills using imported cotton.

At a small meeting of Chungking industrialists arranged for me by the Democratic League I heard bitter complaints concerning T. V. Soong's policies. T. V., as the Generalissimo's Harvard-educated brother-in-law is called, although well known and liked in America where he is regarded as a liberal, seemed to be regarded as a Chinese J. P. Morgan by these Western businessmen. They all considered that the native industry they had built up in the Southwest during the war was being ruined by the "Eastern financiers." Everyone knew, they said, that T. V. had a tremendous fortune salted away in America and that his interests lay with the Shanghai bankers and merchants allied to foreign financial and merchant interests. An executive of the West China Development Company said:

"The government has spent three hundred and fifty million Chinese dollars to send workers home to the East, when only fifty million would have sufficed to start us up again here following the post-war depression in Szechwan. T. V. Soong knows how to make money so he is regarded as a specialist in economics. But it is production which is important, not financial speculation. Here the mines and mills are closing because there is no money to carry on; and the government is trying only to resurrect the industries in the liberated coastal provinces instead of also preserving those built up here during the war."

The attitude of the politically impotent Chinese industrialists toward the Soongs seemed not unlike that of a Midwestern American toward "New York financiers" or the big corporations operating from the Atlantic seaboard. Most of the Chungking industrialists, I was told, would welcome Kung back as the lesser of two evils. In their view, although unable to curb graft among his subordinates, Old Man Kung was at least not a monopolist who used his power as Minister of Finance to squeeze the independent businessman out of existence. He "broke no one's rice bowl" if he could help it.

The resignation of T. V. Soong in 1947 did not surprise me in view of what I had heard in Chungking. He was hated even by the Leftists inside and outside the Kuomintang. This was brought home to me forcibly one evening when I dined with my old friend S. Y. Wu, Secretary of the Legislative Yuan and Sun Fo's "brain truster," and some Chungking businessmen.

"We'd rather have the old man back" was their unanimous opinion. "Kung had his faults but Soong is far worse. Kung at least gave the small manufacturer and merchant a chance to live. But T. V. is trying to get into his own hands control over the whole Chinese economy. He is like an American trust magnate; he is trying to establish his own monopolies in textiles, shipping and anything else he can lay his hands on.

"Kung had some regard for China's interests even while promoting his own. But Soong is concerned primarily with his private interests. Even now while the Political Consultative Council is sitting in Chungking to decide the political future of China, T. V. Soong who is Premier is not participating. He is not even here. He is too busy founding his huge personal monopolies in Shanghai."

"Why then," I said, "does Chiang Kai-shek keep him in office, since it is generally thought that the Generalissimo does not like or trust T. V.?"

"Soong is America's favorite. The Americans like and trust him, so Chiang keeps him in office as the price of American support, hoping he will get China a big loan."

Perhaps it was the feeling that H. H. Kung at least adhered to more traditional and easily understood methods of acquiring wealth which made him less unpopular than T. V. Or perhaps it was just that in China's wretched situation whoever was responsible for the public finances was bound to be hated.

This was the picture of "Daddy Kung" given me by a Chinese newspaperman who had formerly worked under him.

"Kung," he said, "is the descendant of generations of Shansi bankers, which means the only bankers in existence among us before Western civilization opened our doors. The bankers of Shansi were the Jews of China. Shansi is a poor province and many of its sons went elsewhere to make a living. They stuck together and pooled their credit. Eventually they spread over the whole of China, their business depending upon mutual trust. But they were disinclined to trust anyone but men from Shansi. Kung likewise trusts men from his ancestral province first; it is easiest to get a job with him if you are from Shansi. But he also favors graduates of Oberlin College and of Yenching University because he was a student at the former and is President of the latter.

"Once you get a job with Kung he trusts you. So naturally people take advantage. If they make mistakes or are caught in wrong doing, they know it is their wisest course to confess to the old man. This impresses him with their honesty and he just says, 'Don't do it again, my boy.'

"He treats his own employees very generously; he overpaid his staff when in office. So he is naturally popular with those who work for him.

"On the other hand he is henpecked by his wife and is too indulgent to his children who are spenders. Thus despite his patriotism and his own personal honesty he was not keen enough or strong enough to stop corruption among those near to him or who worked under him. He was weak too in his dealings with the Generalissimo. He just couldn't say 'no' when the latter demanded money, and of course it had to be raised somehow."

In other words Dr. Kung seems to have both the virtues and vices of an old-style Chinese in his loyalty to his family, friends and associates and his inability to be as hard in his dealings with individuals he knows personally as China's situation demands. His methods of acquiring wealth may be suspect in Western eyes, but they are old and well-established in China, and he was always ready to "share the wealth" so to speak, by helping his subordinates and his friends.

T. V. Soong, on the other hand, is hated for his arrogant manner, and his methods of acquiring personal wealth being those of Western executives or trust magnates, not those of an old-style Chinese official, seem more reprehensible in Chinese eyes.

Even Leftist journalists liked Kung personally while inveighing against him. Like Emily Hahn I have a warm regard for him, but perhaps I am prejudiced by the fact that it was Kung who circulated my *Japan's Feet of Clay* among the delegates to the Brussels Conference of the signatories of the Nine Power Treaty, and tried to make Nevil Chamberlain read my book to awaken him to the necessity of stopping Japan.

Soong is hard and Kung is soft, and China needs hard men now. If Soong had been successful in his efforts to curb corruption among his subordinates, his unpopularity in China would have been proof of his virtue. But he was found to be no more capable than Kung of curing the disease which debilitates the Chinese Government. He was accused of showing favoritism to corporations with which he or his friends were connected and in general of ruining small business.

Nor can Soong be said to have done anything to promote democratic government in China. He showed disdain for the Legislative Yuan, refusing to account to them later for his actions while Premier of China. Impatient and arrogant, he has few friends and is disliked in particular for his un-Chinese rudeness of manner. Professor Fu Ssu-nien, the distinguished historian, wrote of him, "I would request the chemists to have his body analyzed and see if there is one molecule that gives a trace of Chinese culture."

In his speech to the Legislative Yuan on March 1, 1947, following his resignation as President of the Executive Yuan (Cabinet), T. V. made a spirited defense of his actions in a speech which graphically described the insurmountable difficulties faced by anyone in charge of the finances of a country in as desperate a situation as China. He justly claimed that the managed currency system which he had inaugurated in 1935 had enabled China to stand the eight-year war against Japan, but that the system also "contained the germs of the poison that the country is suffering from now." "When expenditure exceeded receipts," explained T. V., "the only resource was the printing presses. On the part of all agencies of the Government the argument became: Why should the Ministry of Finance limit expenditures when it has only to print a little more currency?"

Whatever T. V. Soong's personal faults, no one could deny the truth of his words when he said:

When the war ended, the course of inflation could have been stopped, that is, if there had been internal peace. Military expenditures could have been cut down, and revenues increased, and with the assistance of receipts like the Government sales of enemy property and gold, further issue of notes could have been avoided, and prices stabilized.

We know what did happen. Instead of peace and reconstruction the country was plunged into a state of war and destruction by the Communists that was even fiercer than during the Japanese occupation. With the Japanese, destruction of property was largely incidental to the war, with the Communists it was deliberate and conscious, and their aim was to destroy the economic system so that the Government would collapse, and they could then introduce their Communist system. Hence railways were destroyed, factories dynamited, mines flooded, and where they could hold they erected their own administration, set up their economic blockades and issued their own currency. Instead of the healing process of peace that the people looked forward to, they were plunged into civil war cumulatively more exhausting than the war with Japan. Revenues could not increase as rapidly as we hoped, more and more appropriations had to be given to the repair of railways, mines and industries, and military expenditures swelled to huge proportions.

This is the answer to the question raised in the beginning of my talk. Compared to the Communist war, the civil wars in the past were child's play. Those were the wars between rival armies, there was not the deliberate destruction of all means of communications and production, and the disruption of the social system which the Communists have as their conscious aims.

Even more important, as I have already pointed out, in the days of specie-backed bank notes, there were natural limits to inflation that were lost when we adopted the managed currency system. From the resulting unchecked increase in bank note issue came rising prices, speculation, and high interest rates; in fact, all the evils that the Legislative Yuan is contemplating today.

During my years as Minister of Finance, I was the watchdog of the treasury, I was the one who stood up against expenditures that could not be borne by the Treasury. When I became President of the Executive Yuan, events unfortunately made me the first and only line of resistance to demands for more and more money.

I have nothing but sympathy for our people who have suffered during eight years of war, and who ask for some surcease from pain now that the war with Japan is over. But facts are facts, and when the Ministry of Finance could not raise the necessary funds it had to be a struggle with me every time a larger appropriation was asked for. I had to help the Ministry of Finance to devise new sources of receipts such as the sale of enemy property and the organization of the China Textile Industries, Incorporated. I need only mention in passing that although there were charges of corruption in the disposal of enemy property practically every case related to the time before the Executive Yuan took over the assets and set up the Alien Property Custodian. Last summer an investigation body made up of the Control Yuan, the People's Political Council and representatives of public organizations organized many teams and went over the Alien Property Custodian operations throughout the country with a fine comb. Not a single case of corruption was discovered among the responsible heads of the organization. There were cases of petty larceny, and that was perhaps inevitable, but not a single one of the responsible men broke his faith with the country.

I shall also mention in passing the China Textile Industries, Incorporated. Had I listened to public clamors and sold the Japanese cotton mills, I would have enriched a few persons at the expense of the nation, I would have secured perhaps 200 or 300 billions sale price for the Treasury. Last year the net profit of the China Textile Industries, Incorporated, was 400 billions, this year it will reach 1,000 billions. If as the Government intends to do so now, the China Textile Industries, Incorporated, is offered for sale to the public, it will have an asset worth between 3,500 and 4,000 billions. No, I do not have to apologize for organizing the China Textile Industries, Incorporated.

I have often been accused of being arbitrary. I have only striven to conduct affairs of the state without fear or favor. From my own point of view, indeed I have looked upon myself as the most oppressed person in the whole country. The Ministry of Finance turns in very limited amounts of revenues and to meet Government expenditure it has to resort to the printing press. I know what that adds up to and night and day my colleagues and I worried over the situation. I have striven time and again to limit expenditures because I knew the danger that confronted us. Nearly all Government agencies, be it military or civilian, came to look upon me as the man responsible for frustrating their wishes for increased appropriations. When I asked for reconsideration on some item of expenditure forthwith there were inspired articles in the newspapers that while everyone had sanctioned the increase the President of the Executive Yuan was holding it up. I have borne this unpopularity because I considered it was in the line of duty.

The truth can be told in one sentence. The present economic crisis is the cumulative result of heavily unbalanced budgets carried through eight years of war and one year of illusory peace, accentuated to some degree by speculative activities.

T. V. Soong used to be well liked by the Communists and is always classed as a liberal by Western writers antagonistic to the National Government. Yet Dr. Lo Lung-chi, the voluble spokesman of the Democratic League, described him as a "comprador." The explanation undoubtedly lay in the League's tie-up with the small businessmen of Szechwan and Yunnan left out in the cold since the liberation of Shanghai and the coastal provinces. The Democratic League, for all its friendship with the Communists, was financed by such men as Miao Chia-min who owned some forty factories in Yunnan.

Although my first interviews with Chungking industrialists were arranged by members of the Democratic League, I found a wide divergence in the views expressed by the League's leaders and Chungking's businessmen. They had been brought together only by a certain community of interest in opposing the government. The heavy hand of the administration, coupled with the inflation and the transfer back to the East of China's capital, was ruining the industrialists who had flourished in wartime fulfilling government orders. It was natural that the Chungking businessmen and Szechwan bankers should now consider that government best which governed least, and support the opposition.

However, the Democratic League's alliance with the Communists was alienating its capitalist supporters. It was also alienating the best elements inside the League. Dr. Carson Chang, leader of the Social Democratic Party, when I interviewed him in Chungking, made it very clear that he had no sympathy with the Democratic League's policy of trying to ride to power by hanging onto the Communist Party's coattails. Carson Chang is an intelligent liberal, an economist and a patriot, not a politician mainly interested in securing a cushy job in the government. According to him China had other alternatives than the present administration or a coalition with the Communists.

There were, he said, plenty of good men in China and efficient administrators who could cleanse and rejuvenate the government. The Democratic League was making a great mistake in identifying liberalism with Communism which was antiliberal and totalitarian.

Nor did Carson Chang think that the choice for China in the administration of her finances was one between Kung and Soong. China, he said, had several able and honest bankers who could run the Finance Ministry and the Central Bank far better than Kung, who was incapable of eliminating corruption, or Soong, whose main interest was the accumulation of a fortune in U. S. dollars.

It seemed to me after talking to them that the leaders of the Democratic League had no more right to call themselves representatives of the people than the Kuomintang. According to its own claims the League's membership in Yunnan and Szechwan was only five thousand, and elsewhere it had even less support. They appeared to be a small group of "outs" hoping to force their way into office through an alliance with the Communists, and equally ready to ally themselves to old style war lords if this could help them to acquire power.

The Democratic League was linked up with some of the most "reactionary feudal" elements in China. It had been protected by "Tiger Lung," the war lord of Yunnan, who encouraged all dissident elements in his attempt to remain independent of the Central Government. In Chungking the League's meeting place was a large and beautiful mansion owned by a bearded old gentleman of the old school who had made a fortune in opium in his younger days as a petty war lord.

In my first meeting with the Democratic League leaders I had been surprised—almost shocked—to hear them describe Tiger Lung as a democrat whose deposition by Chiang Kai-shek had been an outrage.

For Lung's oppressive and corrupt governorship of Yunnan Province had been responsible for the bad impression of China received by the many American soldiers and airmen stationed at Kunming, the provincial capital, during the war.

One afternoon in Chungking at a Democratic League press conference after listening to a long dissertation against the government for its failure to make way for a "democratic" government, I asked a simple question: "How would you hold an election in China? There is not even a reliable estimate of China's population, let alone an electoral register. And how could the peasants possibly know who to vote for, given their ignorance of everything outside their village, the lack of communications and newspapers and informed public opinion?"

My question obviously stumped the leaders of the Democratic League. They had never considered the practical difficulties. To them, it is not unfair to say, democracy meant giving them jobs in the government.

During the Political Consultative Council negotiations in January and February 1946, which proposed to draw up an agreement for a coalition government, it was obvious that the Democratic League, like the Communist Party, was not interested in anything like a general election. The Communists frankly admitted that they wanted the coalition government then envisaged to continue, not majority rule by elected representatives. Hence their opposition to the summoning of a National Assembly.

A coalition government is not, in the nature of things, democratic. If all parties are represented in the government there is no opposition. Moreover, except in times of grave national emergency such as war, a coalition government can be counted upon to be impotent, since it must be pulled all ways by the contending parties within it. A coalition government in China, far from giving her better government, would probably be even worse than the present one.

We should understand China better if we recognized that Chinese parties and factions are little more than organizations of individuals, not popular movements. China is still too backward, economically, politically and in social organization, for the mass of the people to play a role in politics. It is not even generally correct to describe the parties, factions and cliques inside or outside the government as representing any particular class or interest. To a limited degree they stand for certain political ideas or economic and social policies but they are far more representative of powerful individuals or families. In China they don't usually say, "So and so has such and such political convictions." They say, "So and so is a Kung man" or a "Soong man," or one of "Sun Fo's group," or "So and so belongs to the Szechwan group."

Various cliques and groups inside and outside the government are connected with certain banking, merchant and industrial interests, or with a particular provincial faction and so forth. Other leaders are connected with the conservative or "feudal" elements in society, such as the reconditioned war lords or quasi-independent provincial governors or generals of provincial armies. Some leaders are more representative than others of the old-style literati, the scholar rural gentry. But one cannot truthfully say that any faction inside or outside the Kuomintang represents a particular class or a clearly defined vested interest. Too many government officials act in the interests of their relatives and friends but it is hard to point to any who act in the interests of a class.

Individual loyalties, family connections and personal striving for power play the predominant roles in Chinese politics.

Even before the long war ruined the young, independent middle class in China, industry and trade were largely dependent on the government which alone had large capital resources and the possibility of obtaining foreign credits. It depended even then very largely on government orders and subsidies or on credits from the banks whose directors were also government officials influential in its councils.

During the war the bureaucrats inevitably acquired both more power and greater opportunities for graft. It was perhaps always easier to acquire wealth through obtaining a high position in the government than by enterprise. Today with the government in control of almost the whole economy the independent capitalists find it harder than ever to exist. Hence the opposition to the government and the outwardly curious alliance at times between such reactionary elements as ex-war lords and "progressive" capitalists, and between both and the Communists.

Basically the trouble in China is that the war led to government control over the national economy, while not at the same time developing the democratic techniques for popular control over the administration.

During my first two weeks in Chungking, I heard enough and learned enough, to realize that the pattern of Chinese politics is too confused for anyone to be able to pronounce simple judgments concerning right and wrong as between the ins and the outs, and the good and the bad inside and outside the government. The views of Professor Chen Chih-mai, Counselor of the Chinese Embassy in Washington, seem sound. Speaking to the Harvard Law School he said:

It seems to me that many experts have treated the problem of China much as they would treat a mathematical problem, which is to be solved by arranging correctly the symbols involved. They would classify Chinese politicians into reactionaries, progressives, liberals, democrats, fascists, landlords, Communists, friends of America and foes of America . . . labels which are just as meaningless in China as they are in other lands. Having done so, they proceed to propose solutions by rearranging these individual groups, just as a mathematician would rearrange his symbols. . . .

I may go one step further in saying that I do not consider China as a problem, both in her internal and external relationships. China is, rather, a mass of problems, just like any other country, problems which assume ever-varying shapes and relationships in accordance with the subtle and complex laws of human character and the ever-changing colors of the general world scene. These problems are highly intricate, and must not under any circumstances be viewed in isolation from each other. . . .

We wish that you would pass judgment upon us not with your own yardstick but with one which fits in with the historical tradition and present conditions of China.

CHAPTER III

Coué Diplomacy

THE late Dr. Coué taught that when sick you could make yourself well by saying over and over, "Every day in every way I feel better and better." Although he failed to convince many people that will power and optimism are worth more than medical advice, his theory is constantly applied in international affairs. In the year following the defeat of Germany and Japan its adherents practically monopolized the press and radio, and the statesmen of the victorious nations seemed convinced that the world's ills could be cured by refusing to believe they existed.

The newspapers and statements of public men were full of optimism and we were continually reassured that international relations were getting better and better. When Russia began to roar like a lion we insisted that she was cooing like a dove. The more clearly Molotov and Stalin revealed in their speeches that Russia's conception of collaboration was that of a boa constrictor with the lamb it has eaten, the more ruthlessly the Soviet Union extinguished the liberties of its small neighbors in preparation for the war between the Communist and capitalist worlds, which the Kremlin proclaimed to be "inevitable," the more determinedly cheerful the American press became.

As the red danger signals multiplied the greater became the public rejoicing at Russia's "expressed desire" for international collaboration.

The United States being strong and healthy was able to survive the Coué treatment. It diminished her influence, lost her friends and allies, and made well-nigh impossible the fulfillment of her war aims without another war, but she remained the arbiter of the world's destiny.

China, weak and sick, hungry and poor, desperately required a scientific diagnosis of her illness and healing medicine or perhaps a major operation. But the United States insisted that all China had to do was to wish herself well. We told her she could become united and strong by persuading herself that she alone was responsible for the civil war which ravaged her.

In the winter of 1945-1946, not one word was released by the Chinese or American authorities about Russia's "preventive wrecking" of China's industrial base in Manchuria, or her refusal to get out of the Chinese Northeast. American diplomatic and intelligence officers had ample reports, but none of these was allowed to reach the public. A few columnists of the Right, such as Constantine Brown and George Sokolsky, hinted at the truth, but for the most part the American press was silent.

By ignoring Russian looting, America gave tacit acquiescence. The Soviet Government cannot be blamed if it regarded the United States State Department as both naïve and silly for failing to protest during the process of robbery, only to bleat a meek "Alas!" upon revelation of the crime.

It was made clear to me in my conversations with Chinese Government leaders in Chungking and Shanghai that they were hoping against hope that if China pretended that the Soviet Government was friendly, it would in fact become friendly; that if no word of protest was uttered against Russia's breaking of the Sino-Soviet Treaty, Russia would begin to live up to it; that if it were assumed that the Chinese Communist Party did not take orders from Moscow, it would in fact become a Chinese party and make possible a political settlement and an end to the civil war.

When it had been Japan who filched territory from China, set up autonomous regimes and said that all she wanted was a "friendly" Chinese Government which would "co-operate," no one had believed her. When Japan said she was not committing acts of aggression but merely extirpating Communism in China, everyone realized it was a lie. But now that Russia was doing the same sort of things as Japan had done and making the same kind of excuses, there was a conspiracy of silence.

Even the terminology used by the Russians was similar to that formerly employed by the Japanese. The Soviet Union also said she merely wanted "friendly" governments on her borders. The Communists did not, of course, claim to be endeavoring to prevent China going Communist. They said instead that they were trying to make China "democratic." But the underlying purpose was the same and the hypocrisy equally blatant.

When Japan was the aggressor, China received little help, but at least she got sympathy. Now she was deprived even of that. Those who should have been her allies took Communist professions seriously and belabored the Chinese authorities with abuse.

The Chinese Government did its best to make Couéism work. In November 1945, at the very time when Russia had refused the Chinese National armies the use of the Port of Dairen (which according to the Sino-Soviet Treaty was to remain Chinese, unlike Port Arthur which was to be "shared" with Russia), and when the Chinese were being prevented from landing at Yingkow by Russian-equipped Chinese Communist forces in whose favor the Red Army had vacated the port, Dr. Sun Fo and other members of the Chinese Government were speaking in the warmest terms of Sino-Soviet relations. And Shao Li-tze, former Chinese ambassador to Russia, declared categorically that China's internal imbroglio was "not influencing Sino-Soviet relations."

The make-believe was, of course, transparent. When I returned to Chungking in mid-January 1946, every correspondent knew more or less what was happening in Manchuria. Stories of the Red Army's looting of the Chinese provinces were rife, and it was no secret that the Soviet Government was demanding a codominion over all Manchuria as the price of peace in China. Yet even in off-the-record press conferences General Marshall, like the Chinese Government spokesmen, refused to answer questions or comment on what was going on in Manchuria.

The American correspondents in Chungking early in 1946, unlike those I had met the preceding October, were for the most part men of experience and knowledge who knew the score. But when they tried to get information at the press conferences the government spokesmen had nothing to say. Poor "Wordless Wu," as the then Minister of Information was nicknamed, together with his colleagues from the Foreign Office and Executive Yuan, had to parry all enquiries and profess complete ignorance of what everyone in Chungking was talking about privately.

In an interview with the press in Chungking I gave what it seems to me is still an accurate description of China's position. "China," I said, "is like a little boy being bullied by a big one. He fears that if he cries out no one will come to his assistance and the big boy will just beat him harder."

The Chinese Government issued no word of protest at the Soviet Government's breaches of the terms of the Sino-Soviet Treaty of August 1945. In that treaty the government of the USSR promised not only to respect the sovereignty of the National Government over the whole of China, including Manchuria; not only pledged itself to "noninterference in China's internal affairs," but also agreed:

To render to China moral support and aid in military supplies and other material resources, *such support and aid to be given entirely to the National Government as the Central Government of China.*

China had paid a high price for this promise. She had given up Port Arthur to Russia as a naval, army and air base; she had agreed to make Dairen a free port to and from which Russia could move goods without inspection or the payment of customs dues, and in which Russia would own half the harbor installations and equipment; and she had also been obliged to give Russia "joint ownership" of the railways of Manchuria. Since a Soviet citizen was also to be manager of the railways, China had in fact given Russia *de facto* control of her Northeastern provinces. In addition to all this China had agreed to recognize Outer Mongolia as an "independent state."*

The wheel had come full circle. In 1905 Lenin had welcomed the defeat of Russia by Japan and denounced the Czar's government for laying "its greedy paws upon China." In 1919 the Bolshevik government had voluntarily annulled all the treaties which "through force and corruption enslaved the Chinese nation." But in 1945, at Yalta, Stalin insisted on the restoration of the imperialist privileges on Chinese territory which Lenin had denounced. Following World War I the Western Powers had refused to relinquish their special rights and privileges in China, but in 1943 they released China from

* According to the terms of the treaty a plebiscite was to be held in Outer Mongolia. Since Soviet Russia had been ruling there for years no one, of course, had any illusions as to the result of the voting. Russia's MVD (secret police) would attend to any citizen of Outer Mongolia who would dare vote against "independence" under Soviet control.

the unequal treaties. Yet, while abandoning imperialist privileges for themselves, the British and Americans promised Stalin to wring such rights from the Chinese Government on Soviet Russia's behalf. History affords few examples of such complete reversals of policy in so short a period of time.

The reversed roles of the Western Powers and Russia was not immediately apparent to the Chinese public, since the government in its efforts to make Couéism work did its best to keep the Chinese people unmindful of the re-establishment of Russian imperialist rights on Chinese soil. This was brought home to me in somewhat amusing fashion when, together with Tillman Durdin of the *New York Times* and George Weller of the *Chicago Daily News,* I followed a students' demonstration in Chungking in February 1946.

The marching students had banners protesting against practically everything wrong in China and everywhere else in the world. They wanted peace, democracy and economic reconstruction at home and international collaboration. They wanted the British to give up Hong Kong, the Portuguese to give up Macao, and the French to abandon the extraterritorial rights in Shanghai, which they, alone among the Western Powers, were trying to retain. But the students carried no banners demanding the return of Port Arthur and Dairen.

George Weller, with the disarmingly innocent air which is his greatest asset, asked one of the student leaders to explain this omission. The youth was nonplused. There was a buzz of talk. Finally a young man from the head of the procession came over to us as we stood outside the British Embassy. In halting English he explained, "Russia's rights in Port Arthur and Dairen were given to her by treaty."

I remarked softly, "So also were Hong Kong and Kowloon given to Britain by treaty."

"Ah," said the boy, "but *that* was an unequal treaty."

A few weeks later Chinese students had become aware that the new imperialists had taken from China far more than the old retained, and there were huge demonstrations demanding that Russia "quit Manchuria." But the National Government was not responsible. It was still trying to make Couéism work and to restrain public protest at Russia's breaking of the Sino-Soviet Treaty for fear Stalin would deliver some new blow at China.

The Chinese Government had had no choice but to sign the Sino-

Soviet Treaty since President Roosevelt had promised Stalin that his claims against China would be "unquestionably fulfilled," and China had been in no position to refuse a United States demand. But by failing to protest at the Soviet Union's failure to honor its commitments in that treaty, the Chinese Government weakened its position at home as well as abroad.

This was amply demonstrated in 1947 when huge student demonstrations demanded an end to the civil war. Many of these students, had they realized that Russia menaced China and that the Communists were Moscow's agents, would not have come out against the National Government. But the pretense, so unwaveringly kept up by the government, that China's civil war was an "internal affair," had been all too successful. Naturally if the civil war was simply one between Chinese factions, the students were justified in believing that it would be stopped if the government would make concessions. How could they realize that the price of internal peace was subjection to Russian domination since the government and most of the press maintained the fiction that the Soviet Union was not interfering in Chinese internal affairs?

Although China had been forced to sign the Sino-Soviet Treaty of August 1945, the more optimistic members of the government had evidently persuaded themselves that the Soviet Government would honor its promise not to give arms or other support to the Chinese Communists. T. V. Soong, who negotiated the treaty, may have been primarily concerned with pleasing America, but he and others like him seem to have genuinely believed that it guaranteed internal peace in China.

The so-called Left Wing of the Kuomintang, led by Sun Yat-sen's son Sun Fo, had for years been in favor of a Russia-orientated foreign policy, and there were others who had argued that if China had to make concessions to Russia she had best make them herself in return for tangible benefits. "Why," it had been said in 1944 and 1945, "should the United States receive the *quid pro quo* for Chinese sacrifices; why should we let the American Government barter our rights and territories for what Roosevelt wants from Stalin; why not see if we can get a better deal by negotiating ourselves?"

The members of the National Government who put no trust in Stalin's word had to go along with T. V. Soong and Sun Fo and accept the Sino-Soviet Treaty at its face value. They had no choice on account of China's dependence on American support and America's insistence on amity with Russia at almost any price. But in private the "reactionaries" expressed to me their complete disbelief in Russia's promises and their conviction that China's ostrichlike diplomacy was senseless and self-defeating.

The treaty proved worthless to China. Moscow refused to vacate Manchuria until it was thoroughly wrecked, and started arming the Chinese Communists and fostering disunity in China immediately after V-J Day. The Red Army prevented the Chinese Government from getting its troops into Manchuria until the Communists had been so well ensconced there that Russia could expect them to be able to keep control and convert it into a Russian "Manchukuo."

If the United States had continued the realistic support of China pursued at the time of Japan's surrender, the National Government might have regained Manchuria in spite of Russia's cynical disregard of the terms of the Sino-Soviet Treaty. The Japanese had then been ordered to surrender themselves and their equipment only to the National forces, and the United States China Theater Commander had moved these forces rapidly by air to occupy the liberated areas ahead of the Communists. But in the fall and winter of 1945 General Wedemeyer, who was being attacked in the Communist press, found himself restricted in the use of American sea and air transport by certain officers in the Far Eastern Division of the State Department who placed their own interpretation on United States policy to the advantage of the Communists.

On November 2, 1945, Vice-Admiral Barbey, in command of American ships transporting Nationalist troops to Manchuria, withdrew from the port of Yingkow after a conference ashore with Soviet representatives, and after viewing several thousand Chinese Communists digging trenches under Russian protection. A few days earlier Barbey had retreated from another Manchurian port, Hulutao, after Communist riflemen had fired on a launch from his flagship.

Dairen and Port Arthur, Yingkow and Hulutao were the only ports in Manchuria; so the American Navy, retreating before the Russians and the Chinese Communists, finally landed its convoy of Nationalist troops at Chingwangtao in North China, whence they proceeded overland to capture Yingkow. A little later Yingkow was retaken by the Communists with the help of Russian tanks.

Ammunition and other necessary supplies were also denied to the

Chinese Government, this embargo continuing until June 1947, when it was at long last allowed to buy some ammunition and arms in America.

The United States, having forced China to sign away vital economic and strategic rights in Manchuria in the Sino-Soviet Treaty, did nothing to compel the Soviet Government to honor the treaty and left China almost defenseless in the face of Russian aggression.

The attitude of the United States was a severe blow to China, but the greatest disappointment of all to the Chinese people was the fact that all the concessions made to Russia had not brought internal peace.

There is little doubt that a word from Stalin would have caused the Chinese Communists to come to terms with the National Government, preserving the unity of China. This was apparent following the December 1945 Moscow conference of the Big Three which issued a communiqué pledging Russia as well as Britain and the United States to promote "a unified and democratic China *under the National Government.*"* At once the Communists, after months of refusal to negotiate, came to Chungking to talk peace.

China then as now was up against the problem which the United States and Britain also face: that of dealing with an aggressor nation which has two hands to use in international diplomacy. Stalin's right hand is the Russian Foreign Office and its diplomatic representatives abroad. His left hand, the Communist Parties and fellow travelers in all countries, can always take over the implementation of Moscow's policy when it seems advisable that the Soviet state should beat a retreat.

The Chinese Government was itself largely to blame for the predicament in which it found itself. During the war years it had refrained from answering the Communist accusations which had been given so much publicity in America. The Chinese Government and the Kuomintang Party rarely issue blanket orders to their press and information organs, but throughout the war they adhered with suicidal naïveté to the prohibition of anti-Communist propaganda. Occa-

* In the March 1947 Conference at Moscow, Molotov endeavored to falsify the record by saying that in December 1945 there had been agreement on the necessity for "the unification and democratization of China under *a* (instead of *the*) National Government."

sionally the realists at Kuomintang Party Headquarters would get out a schedule of Communist outrages, and the government would circulate a top-secret memorandum to its own officials, informing them of current Communist provocations. These were never released for publication. The Chinese public heard little of them; the world public, nothing. This was at the time when the Communists were ruthlessly sabotaging the National Government in the midst of its life-and-death struggle with Japan, and Communist irregulars were following Imperial Japanese divisions in occupying National Chinese territory. The Chinese Communists never actually allied themselves to Japan but they made Japanese positions secure in many places by preventing the Generalissimo's guerrillas from operating behind Japanese lines. All this occurred behind the silence of Chungking, either self-imposed or inspired by Washington's orders.

Either because he believed that it was futile to appeal to the American public over the head of the Roosevelt administration, or because he was under contrary orders from Chungking, the Chinese ambassador in Washington never tried to counteract the Communist propaganda which gave the American public an erroneous conception of the situation in the Far East.

One of the Vice-Ministers of Foreign Affairs in Chungking, from whom I asked an explanation of China's inept treatment of the Communist issues, explained it somewhat differently. "If," he said, "we were to admit that the Chinese Communists are Moscow's subordinates, we might land ourselves in even more trouble. Russia would have an excuse for interfering in our internal affairs. Since Russia says she has no interest in the Chinese Communists, she will not be in a position to protest or interfere when we set out to deal with them in earnest. Moreover, during the war years, we were always in deadly fear that the Russo-Japanese friendship pact might lead Moscow to take active measures against us. Our Communists were a sufficient problem as things were. It would have been even worse if they had actually joined hands with the Japanese against us."

Perhaps, however, the truest explanation I heard of Chungking's inept diplomacy was given me by General Wu Te-chen, former mayor of Shanghai and at that time in charge of the Kuomintang Party Headquarters in the capital.

"Our Chinese mentality was the cause of our mistake. We were ashamed that the world should know of our internal disagreements. The desire to save face was the primary reason why we never met Communist propaganda abroad. We thought that if we ignored it we would be able to cover up the split in China which was such a disgrace to the Chinese people."

If General Wu Te-chen was right, it means only that the Chinese share the rest of the world's inclination to deny realities if they are unpleasant and harmful and cause loss of face. The American and British people, who for so long went on pretending there was no fundamental disagreement between the democracies and "their gallant Russian allies," were behaving just like the Chinese. The falsity of wartime propaganda would have become too apparent to the voters if it had been recognized that victory meant merely the substitution of one totalitarian tyranny for another.

It was true that since the Chinese Communists were not openly recognized as Moscow's allies or subjects, Russia could have no valid objection to their being crushed in an all-out military campaign. The Soviet Government itself would not for a moment have tolerated the existence in Russia of a dissident party complete with its own army, challenging Stalin's authority. It could have had no shadow of an excuse for coming to the rescue of the Chinese Communists if Chiang Kai-shek decided to liquidate them by force. But Moscow had no need to intervene openly in China for the purpose of saving the Communists from destruction. Americans performed this service for her.

Prior to the appointment of General Marshall as special envoy to China in December 1945, it had seemed as if the United States might at long last face up to the realities of the situation in China and decide on a clear and unequivocal policy.

General Patrick Hurley while ambassador to China had learned by his experience in trying to bring unity to China that the Communists could not be trusted to keep their word, that every time he persuaded Chiang Kai-shek to agree to their demands they asked for more. He had returned to the United States convinced that the only way to unite China was to back the legitimate government recognized by Russia as by all the other United Nations.

Like most other Americans who have come into close contact with the Generalissimo, Hurley believed that Chiang Kai-shek was sincere in his reiterated statements that he was determined to solve the problem of Communism by political, not military, means; that he did not want to be a dictator and was ready to relinquish his powers as soon as a democratic government could function in China. On the other hand, it was clear to Hurley that the problem could never be solved if the United States continued its backhanded encouragement of the Communists. Naturally, as long as the Communists believed that they had the support of many State Department officials as well as of a large section of the American press, they would continue to be intransigent.

Chinese hopes that General Hurley would convince America that she must adopt a strong realistic policy in China were doomed to disappointment. The fiery general from Oklahoma did not have the historical perspective necessary to statesmanship of the long view. He accused his enemies in the State Department of "sabotaging" United States policy by privately advising the Communists that "his efforts to prevent the collapse of the Nationalist Government didn't represent the policy of the United States." But he seems to have taken Stalin at his word when assured by him in Moscow that the Soviet Government had no interest in the Chinese Communists. Or he considered himself bound to support the general American line of policy, that of seeing, hearing and speaking no evil of the Soviet Union. In any case, when he resigned he said that there was "no question" but that the Soviet as well as the British Government supported the United States' policy of unifying China.

In thus exonerating the Soviet Government from responsibility for the intransigence of the Chinese Communists General Hurley left himself without any strong argument against those who wanted the United States to favor neither of what they called "the two factions" in China, or against those who hoped to make a Mikhailovitch out of Chiang by the transfer of American support to the Communists. I myself in Shanghai had General Hurley's words quoted against me by the Russian press to prove I was wrong in blaming the Soviet Union for the actions of the Chinese Communists.

Clever propaganda in America had convinced a large part of the public that the Chinese Communists were liberal reformers and the best men in China, and that the Chinese National Government was a bunch of "fascists," "reactionaries" and what not. If the Chinese

Communists were not Moscow's puppets but sincere democrats, then General Hurley's opponents in the State Department had a good case for urging that the United States abandon Chiang Kai-shek and support the Communists instead.

"Love me, love my dog." General Hurley's mistake in thinking that he could be lacking in affection for the Chinese Communists without incurring the violent opposition of their masters was immediately apparent. The *Daily Worker* shrieked imprecations and consigned him to the "fascist" limbo to which critics of Russia are condemned.

Editorial opinion in the American press showed little or no awareness of the issues at stake in China. To judge from the extracts published by the United States Information Service in Shanghai, the newspapers which did not favor the Communists advocated a hands-off policy in order to avoid a clash with Russia. One of the very few informed comments was made by the *Philadelphia Record* which wrote:

> Withdrawal of our support would mean a full-scale civil war in China. Continued support of Chiang Kai-shek may help China on her difficult road toward democracy. We don't want an Asiatic Spain as the prelude to another world war.

The tide of appeasement was at this time running strong in the United States. Even those who had no sympathy for Communism wanted us to let Russia have her way in China. Distinguished "internationalists," such as Walter Lippmann, took a similar line in 1945 to the one they had advocated in pre-Pearl Harbor days. Mr. Lippmann had then urged noninterference with Japanese aggression and a settlement of American-Japanese differences at China's expense. He now advocated a "united political front" of Russia, Britain and the United States to force the reorganization of the Chinese Government on a "broader democratic basis" by inclusion of the Communists. Lest there should be any doubt that what he meant was forcing China to become a Russian satellite, he wrote that the "formula" for such a united front "is clearly indicated and is in principle like that made at Yalta for Poland." The *New York Herald Tribune*, among other newspapers, published editorials suggesting that the "same degree of sanity" should be shown by the United States in dealing with China as President Roosevelt had displayed at Yalta with regard to Poland.

Since the first country to take up arms against Nazi Germany had been sacrificed by Roosevelt and Churchill in their attempt to buy Stalin's good will, why should not China, the first country to resist Japanese aggression, suffer the same fate for the same good cause?

For China the policy favored by Mr. Lippmann and other less distinguished advocates of *Realpolitik* was all too familiar. For a hundred years the European Powers had settled their differences at her expense. Now with Poland's unhappy fate to warn them, the Chinese saw no course but submission to American-Russian demands. Whenever I argued with members of the Chinese Government in Chungking that their policy of silence was disastrous, they answered: "The Polish Government protested and look what happened to Poland. It is better to be patient and make sacrifices than risk extinction. We can't fight Russia, so our only hope is that the United States will restrain her if we follow American advice."

Viewed in historical perspective United States policy in 1945-1946 was a continuation of the line followed not merely for a decade, but for fifty, even a hundred years. To risk a little but not too much. To stand for the integrity of China but with reservations. To accept compromises at China's expense, if only the aggressors or imperialists or disruptors of Chinese unity could be induced to pay lip service to the principles which the United States supports, and to guarantee the preservation of American interests.

This was not due to hypocrisy or duplicity or a Machiavellian purpose. It was simply that Americans were not sufficiently interested in the Far East to commit themselves to a strong and definite policy and take the consequences. They would put one foot into the stormy Chinese sea, but they saw no valid reason why they should plunge right in and sink or swim with China. Moreover the real issues at stake in the Far East had been confused by the flood of writings in favor of the Communists and lack of understanding of Chinese problems, even on the part of anti-Communists.

The foreign policy of every country is largely determined by domestic politics. This is particularly true of the United States because it has the most democratic form of government of any people. Inevitably the administration responds to pressure groups at home and determines its course abroad according to its calculated effect at the next election. The ambiguity of American policy in China was the direct result of the confusion and misconceptions in the minds of the American public, and the administration's efforts to please everybody.

President Truman's statement of policy on December 15, 1945, told China that there must be a cessation of hostilities and a broadening of the government to accord "fair and effective representation" to *all* political elements. He promised that as China "moved toward peace and unity along these lines, the United States would assist the National Government in every reasonable way." China was told that she had a "clear responsibility to all the United Nations to eliminate armed conflicts within her territories."

The whole statement assumed that the Chinese civil war had nothing to do with Russia's policy of expansion by revolution. It also assumed that the promise of American loans and other aid in the reconstruction of China, once unity was achieved, would act as a powerful inducement to *both sides* to come to terms. In a word America's Far Eastern policy was based on the idea that the United States was in a position to mediate by putting pressure on both sides in the civil war.

In fact we had no means of exerting pressure on the Communists to come to an agreement or to honor their pledges if an agreement were worked out. Only Stalin was in a position to do this.

America's compulsions could be exerted only against the National Government. By ignoring the ties which link the Chinese Communists with Moscow and insisting on "unity" by agreement with the Communists, we immensely strengthened Stalin's hand. Since unity could not be achieved unless Moscow willed it, the Chinese Government was put in a position in which it seemed to have no choice but to make concessions to Russia if it were to retain American sympathy and obtain American economic assistance.

The Soviet Government was thus left free to impose unrestricted pressure on China. The Communists could keep the central authorities weak and deprived of full American support while Russia sequestered or destroyed all that China had sought to save in the eight-year war against Japan.

General Marshall's "veto power" over loans to China was accordingly worse than useless as a means to exert pressure on the Communists. Far from desiring that China receive credits for reconstruction, they were counting on economic decay to bring down the National Government and enable them to seize power.

By withholding economic aid from the National Government until it came to terms with those who profited from China's economic crisis, we put the Communists into a position in which they could blackmail the government.

One after another America's representatives in China, civil and military, had learned through experience that there is no middle way in China between support of the recognized government and support of the Communists. General Stilwell had looked with favor on the Communists; Generals Hurley and Wedemeyer had become convinced that effective support of the National Government was the only way to bring peace to China.

Instead of profiting from past experience General Marshall also had to learn the hard way. For months he tried with extraordinary patience and energy to mix oil and water into some new element. He confessed his failure long before he left China.

The Chinese people paid the price for the education of the United States representatives in China and of the American public.

As might have been expected the Communists welcomed General Marshall's assignment to China. A year later they admitted that he was not partial to Chiang Kai-shek "during the first two months of his stay in China."

Immediately following President Truman's December 1945 statement, the Communists suddenly, after months of refusal, announced their readiness to talk peace in Chungking.

This was not because of any change of heart or purpose in the Communist Chinese leader, but because it was necessary to convince America of their sincere desire for unity, and because a move toward reconciliation with the National Government synchronized with Stalin's policy.

The Red Army had already pretty well completed its dismantling of the factories in Mukden and Changchun and the removal of this machinery to Russia, and Moscow had promised to withdraw its forces by January 3 and to facilitate the entry of the Chinese Nationalist forces. It was not known what further concessions China had made to Russia but Stalin was demanding joint ownership of all Manchurian resources and industries. He evidently expected to get what he wanted, because General Chu Teh, the commander in chief of the Chinese Communist armies, had announced on December 5 that the Communist Party did not dispute the Central Government's sovereignty over Manchuria.

The Chinese Communists themselves were in need of a breathing space. In Southern Manchuria they had learned that even when equipped by the Russians with modern arms they were no match for Chiang Kai-shek's soldiers. They needed time to be trained by their Russian instructors. In Lenin's classic phrase, one step backward would enable them to take two steps forward later on.

The truce arranged by General Marshall, effective from January 13, gave the Communists exactly what they required to consolidate their gains, extend their power and get ready to play their part if and when Russia failed to extort what she wanted in Manchuria from the Government of China.

It "froze" the existing positions of the Communist and government forces in North and Central China. Mixed teams, composed of one American officer, one Chinese and one Communist representative, flew out from the Executive Headquarters established by General Marshall in Peiping to stop the civil war.

There was a last-minute hitch in the truce negotiations overcome by General Marshall's intervention. This episode is worth relating, because it demonstrates how the Chinese Government gave way to American representations, even when the Communists were clearly in the wrong.

According to the truce agreement Nationalist forces were to be allowed, without Communist interference, to take over from the Russians as the Red Army vacated the Northeastern provinces. On January 9, however, a dispute arose as concerns Jehol, the province adjoining Manchuria which had been administered by Japan as part of Manchukuo. The government insisted that since no Chinese and only Soviet troops were in Chihfeng, a railway junction city in Jehol, it should be occupied by the Nationalist armies under the agreement covering Manchuria. The Communists insisted on a standstill agreement there as in North China, and claimed that their forces had already taken over Chihfeng from the Russians.

General Chou En-lai that evening, according to Arch Steele of the *New York Herald Tribune*, was very depressed. He told the press that the government was insisting on its right to occupy both Chihfeng and Tolun—an important trading and communications center in Chahar just outside Jehol's western boundary. Occupation of these two strategic points by the Nationalist forces would throw a barrier across the middle of Jehol and effectively block Communist connections with the Red Army in Manchuria, threaten the Communist stronghold at Kalgan, and sandwich Communist-held Chengteh (capital of Jehol) between government armies north and south of the Great Wall. The Communists declared they would never agree.

At 10:30 that night General Marshall visited Chiang Kai-shek at his home and stayed there till midnight. At 12:30 Chou En-lai had a telephone call telling him to come to Marshall's house at 8:00 A.M. to meet Chiang Kai-shek. By 10:00 A.M. a truce draft had been worked out and given to the press. The Communists had won. Chihfeng, and with it control of Jehol, was theirs.

Soon afterward it was learned that the government's contention had been correct. The Red Army, not the Chinese Communists, had been in Chihfeng when the truce was signed. But the Chinese communists kept the town until driven out in the new phase of the civil war which began the following summer. As an official of the Chinese Foreign Office said to me, "General Marshall need not have forced us to give Jehol to the Communists. It was not necessary as part of the appeasement of Russia since it was covered by the Sino-Soviet agreement."

When I returned to Chungking a week or two after the truce had been signed, the Political Consultative Council meetings were in full swing. The government, Communists, Democratic League, Chinese Youth Party, and nonparty representatives were trying to hammer out an agreement for a coalition government. Marshall's truce had been signed as the preliminary for such an agreement, and everyone hoped that the civil war had ended.

Maybe it might have if Russia's policy had not changed, or if the Communists had not conceived themselves strong enough to try the military game again soon after the agreements were signed. The liberals or Westernizers were in the ascendant in the Kuomintang during the period of the Political Consultative Council negotiations. Chiang Kai-shek showed himself ready to make very great concessions for peace and a chance for reconstruction and reform. Even the most pessimistic Chinese had a little hope in January and February 1946.

Chou En-lai played an important role in this period. He must have convinced certain key personages that he represented a section of the Communist Party which sincerely wanted peace, unity and a democratic development for China. He almost convinced me in the hour and a half's conversation I had with him in Chungking. He avoided the subject of Russia and at the end he patted me on the shoulder, told me I might visit Yenan and, looking me straight in the eyes with an expression which made his last words significant, said: "The Chinese Communist Party is grown-up now and no longer needs assistance from anyone."

A day or two later I asked one of the Chinese Ministers who is very close to Chiang Kai-shek whether he and others believed that Chou En-lai was actually sincere in wanting collaboration. After a moment's thought he replied, "In strict confidence 'yes.' That accounts for the weakness and delicacy of his position in his own party."

It soon became evident that Marshall's policy was based on the assumption that it was possible to "detach" the Communists from their Russian affiliation; or at least "bring together the Right Wing of the Communists with the Left Wing of the Kuomintang," and thus create a real democratic party.

Walter Robertson, the United States chargé d'affaires in China, said to me in Peiping just before I left China: "Make no mistake about it, Marshall is a great man and he is doing a wonderful job in which I think he will succeed."

"Have you changed your mind about the Communists then?" I said. "When I talked to you a few months ago in Shanghai, you put no trust in them at all and believed they were Stalin's puppets?"

"No, I don't deny the Russian connection. But, after all, what are the Chinese Communist leaders but men with an army out for power? Why should they not get what they want on our side? Some of them would prefer it."

I remembered then how once at a press conference in Chungking, Chou En-lai had replied to a question whether Mao Tse-tung was about to visit Russia "for his health," by saying, "He would prefer to visit the United States."

There were rumors in the capital that Mao had in fact declined an invitation to come to Moscow. Soviet Russia's ex-puppet war lord of Sinkiang, who had gone over to the Kuomintang a few years before and never went outside his house without a bodyguard, told General Odlum that Mao had once said he would never go to Moscow because he was afraid he might be kept there. All this rumor and hearsay may have had some basis in fact. It could as likely have been deliberately encouraged by the Communists for their own ends.

Chou En-lai and others must have thrown out hints to make the Americans believe that there was a real possibility of Kuomintang-Communist collaboration. We may never know what was said between him and Chiang when they met alone. We shall probably not know for years what Chou said to Marshall and how much of what he said General Marshall believed.

Certainly Chou En-lai's attractive personality, his intelligence and wit and charm played a considerable part in convincing America's representatives in China that the Communists meant what they said.

It is impossible to say whether he was sincere or not. Historically it is of little importance. The Comintern record shows that it makes no difference when there is a section of a Communist Party which wants to follow the democratic path. It can never swing the whole party because of Moscow's control.

In the years preceeding Hitler's rise to power there was a considerable section of the German Communist Party which opposed the Comintern policy of regarding the Socialists and liberals as the main enemy and concentrating Communist efforts on the overthrow of German democracy to the benefit of the Nazis. All that resulted was their excommunication. Either you toe the Moscow line or you cease to be a Communist.

When I asked S. J. Wu, secretary of the Legislative Yuan and Sun Fo's close friend, whether it was actually believed that the Chinese Communists wanted to break with Russia and collaborate with the liberals and America in reconstructing China as a democracy, he replied without hesitation: "They would like to but they can't."

This was an acute observation. The Chinese Communists have no particular reason to love the Soviet Union. It disorganized and betrayed them in 1926 to the exigencies of Russia's domestic politics. Their success in later years in establishing a provincial government and army of their own was due to their own efforts, to the shortcomings of the National Government and to Moscow's inability to subject them to the same tight control as the Comintern exerted over Communist Parties in other countries. Their strength is undoubtedly largely due to their past geographical and political isolation. But today they are in close contact with their Russian masters through Manchuria.

Kungchantang representatives had, I was reliably informed in Chungking, been cold-shouldered by the Russian Red Army dignitaries in Manchuria following their poor showing against the Nationalist armies in the fall of 1945. The Russians, it was said, had been disgusted with them for their military failures against the Nationalists and had favored the ex-Japanese (Manchukuo) puppet forces. In a sense Russia had treated *her* Chinese as America treated hers. Both had been expected to accomplish the impossible task of winning battles without arms against well-armed adversaries: the Nationalists against the Japanese, and the Communists against the National armies. After my return to America, in the spring of 1946, Michael Lindsey, who is one of the warmest foreign friends of the Chinese Communists and who lived among them for years and married a Chinese, told me that his wife feared that the Chinese Communists were once again being sacrificed by Moscow.

One could almost sympathize with the Chinese Communists at times. Moscow was always ready to place them in the forefront of the battle, and retire and let them be killed if it suited her world strategy. Intelligent men like Chou En-lai, possibly Mao Tse-tung himself, probably understood very well that Russia would no more welcome a strong Communist China than a strong Kuomintang China. The function of the Chinese Communists, in Stalin's plans for world conquest, was to weaken China, prevent her unification and reconstruction and prepare her for absorption into a Russia-centered Soviet bloc. The last thing that Russia desired was their sincere co-operation with the liberal elements in the Kuomintang to convert China into a democracy and a strong united nation.

The Chinese Communists were only pawns and the more intelligent ones must have known it. In the tragic drama being played out in China, Chiang Kai-shek was not only the adversary of the Communists but was also the prop which sustained them. If Chiang could have been induced to play an anti-American role, there is little doubt that Stalin would have embraced him as readily as he had General Peron. The Soviet Government would not have scrupled to sacrifice the Chinese Communists if in so doing an advantage could be won over the United States.

Chiang's loyalty to the democracies, in the face of all the insults and injuries they had inflicted upon him, was the Chinese Communist guarantee of continued existence. Their usefulness to Russia depended on the National Government's loyalty to the United States.

On the other hand, there was no way out for the Chinese Communists even if they understood the situation. They might not love or trust Stalin but they dared not give up their army and submit themselves, defenseless, to the government of Chiang Kai-shek. Too much blood had flowed since 1927; too many promises had been broken and too much mistrust engendered. How could either side believe that the other would forgive and forget?

The Kuomintang could not believe in the sincerity of the Chinese Communist conversion to the principles of Sun Yat-sen until they broke with Moscow. The Communists could not prove their sincerity by breaking the tie with Moscow unless convinced that the National Government would not exterminate them if they did.

Chiang Kai-shek tried hard to break the deadlock, and maybe Chou En-lai did so too. It was Chou En-lai who had brought about a temporary reconciliation at Sian in December 1936, when war with Japan had become inevitable. Chou, who had lived in the national capital all through the war as the Communist representative, had a far better understanding of China's problems and the government's difficulties than the Communists far off in the mountain retreat of Yenan. He was an old companion in arms of the Generalissimo and the two men respected each other, perhaps liked each other.

I found it hard to believe that Chou En-lai, who charmed me as he did everyone else, is a liar and a cheat. He may have only been carrying out a clever stratagem in Moscow's interests, but it is barely possible that for a short period of time he saw a possibility, through American support, of cutting the umbilical cord which binds the Communists to Moscow without killing his party.

If, in fact, this was the case, any such outcome was prevented by America's vacillation and weakness in her dealings with Russia in both Europe and Asia, and the fading away of American military might.

Whether or not there was in fact ever any possibility of "detaching" the Chinese Communists from Russia, the only hope of success lay in America's strength and her readiness to use it. Our attraction would be powerful enough to pull the Chinese Communists into our sphere only if we appeared as stronger than Russia and as willing to protect our friends. Otherwise the Chinese Communists must of necessity remain attached to Russia. They must have known that should they ever join sincerely in a coalition government under American auspices, Russia would repudiate them and denounce them as fascists or Trotskyists or "running dogs of the imperialists." Russia is close to them while America is far away. And it was clearly demonstrated in Europe in 1945 and 1946 that, whereas Russia protects her own, the United States was willing to sacrifice millions of people on her side in order to avoid a clash with Russia.

There were all the elements of a Greek tragedy in China. Neither the Kuomintang nor the Communists could escape their fate. It was no simple conflict of right and wrong but one between two opposite principles. Chiang Kai-shek and Chou En-lai might both be noble men, but the stature of the protagonists on either side could not solve the irreconcilable conflict. No real compromise was possible. The past of both Kuomintang and Communists determined their future. Neither could escape from the impasse into which their different loyalties, aims and beliefs had brought them. Both sides were equally convinced that the path they desired China to follow was the only way to salvation, and neither dared trust the other.

The coalition government which America was so anxious they should form could not, in the nature of things, be more than an armed truce, or a "marriage of convenience in which both sides hoped to cheat the other."

General Marshall had been catapulted into the midst of a situation with which even Solomon could not have coped. Maybe the Gordian knot could be cut; it certainly could not be unraveled by an American general whose experience and knowledge were so far removed from the titanic struggle in China. He did his best to understand it, and he labored diligently, but he never had a chance to succeed. He not only had to try to solve in China alone the world-wide conflict between the United States and Russia for domination over the earth but he also had to pretend that the problems of China had no connection with the wider conflict. Coué diplomacy was still the order of the day in China, even after the United States had begun to face the facts of the international situation in Europe.

CHAPTER IV

Shanghai

THE Air Transport Command flights to Shanghai from Chungking were being canceled day after day on account of bad weather, so I decided to try the Chinese line. The pilots of the Chinese National Aviation Corporation, many of whom are Americans, must be among the best in the world. In the war years they could only fly when weather conditions precluded the danger of Japanese attack. So CNAC flights are rarely canceled.

On the other hand traveling by ATC is so simple that I had not anticipated the complications involved in traveling by the Chinese line. The Chinese have passport control and customs inspection and the airport is crowded with all the relatives of all the passengers.

I had undertaken to bring with me some baggage belonging to a correspondent who had left his possessions in Chungking when rushing to Shanghai for the Japanese surrender. His bags were locked and at first the customs would not pass them. This caused a long delay. The CNAC baggage allowance is much less than the ATC, and I had already wasted time among the crowd at the airport exchanging United States dollars for Chinese currency in order to pay the excess baggage fee. Now I found my passport missing—some official had demanded it from me earlier and not returned it. The plane was about to depart and I got into a panic. Trying to hurry through the crowds carrying my heavy bags, I tripped and fell over an iron weighing machine on the floor which I had not seen in the dim light.

I got up and found that I could not lift my right arm. I managed to explain to the customs people that I was in great pain, and got my stuff lifted into the plane. The passengers were all Chinese so I sat in dumb misery for hours, hoping against hope that my arm was only dislocated. To the left, to the right and in front of me were women and children sick most of the way. The smell was unpleasant, there was no food or water, and I had left the Press Hostel breakfastless at 5:30 A.M. Altogether it was an ordeal.

By the time we got to Shanghai after a stopover in Nanking it was late afternoon and I was dazed with pain and exhaustion. I could hardly get out of the plane much less climb up onto the truck to get to the town. One of the pilots, speaking English, came to my rescue and drove me in his car to the Cathay Hotel.

Here I hoped to find my friend, Cornelius V. Starr, publisher of the *Shanghai Evening Post*. Thanks to him I was soon in bed at the Shanghai Country Hospital with a shot of morphine. I had a double fracture where the arm joins the shoulder.

Next day my arm was set and strapped and for five weeks I was kept on my back with strict instructions not to move. I was disconsolate at having to waste so much time but Cornelius Starr, for whose insurance companies I had formerly worked in New York as Economic Adviser, produced a secretary for me and asked me to write a regular column for his newspaper. I had never before had the opportunity to write anything I liked and get it published, and this gave me a satisfaction which enabled me to forget the pain and the prospect of never again having completely normal use of my arm.

This was in November and December 1945 when the fiction that the Chinese Communists were just a liberal party unconnected with Moscow was being maintained in almost all the newspapers. It was then still fashionable to pretend that Russia was a democracy and a friend to China, who had no intention of trying either to take over Manchuria or establish a puppet government there and in North China.

I pulled no punches. I showed how Russia's actions paralleled Japan's in the thirties. I wrote of what was happening in Manchuria, from what I had learned in Chungking and from Chinese friends who visited me in the hospital. I demonstrated the connection between Chinese Communist acts and Moscow's policy. I insisted that in helping the Chinese Government to move its troops, guard communications and otherwise prevent anarchy or the partition of China, the United States was defending its own interests and seeking to ensure that the war should not have been fought in vain.

When I was at last able to get up and go out I found myself

warmly received in United States Army and Navy circles for having written what many officers thought, but about which there was a conspiracy of silence in the American and Chinese press. To my considerable satisfaction I found also that I had managed to annoy the Communists. My articles brought down on my head the wrath of the Russian press and radio in Shanghai and gave my views greater publicity than they would otherwise have had.

The Soviet Government had captured the formerly "White Russian" (*emigré*) newspapers in Shanghai; they published also an English-language propaganda sheet; and they had one of the main radio stations which they had run all through the Japanese occupation. The articles and radio talks in which they denounced me contained little substance and much verbiage and abuse. I was smeared as "illiterate," "reactionary," "childish," "fascist," an "enemy of the toiling masses," "an agent of reactionary capitalism," and "working in the interests of the war provocators." I have preserved one typical example, by Lev Grosse in *Novosty Dnya* of December 12, which as translated from the Russian under the heading ILLITERATE, INTRANSIGENT MISS UTLEY read as follows:

Many local newspapers pay much attention to a certain Miss Utley, arrived here to carry on anti-Soviet propaganda. This "emancipated" creature obviously has no understanding concerning the Soviet Union. But this—to the foreign reactionary point of view—doesn't matter.

The doubly impervious ignorance of this woman can be judged by the fact that she puts the Soviet Union in the same class with Germany and Japan. Russia, it seems, also is imperialistic and aggressive as was formerly Japan and Nazi Germany. The USSR wishes to exploit China, prevent China from becoming a powerful nation, and wishes to get from China all possible concessions and privileges for the purpose of weakening her (China) and provoking civil war.

It appears that this stranger imagines that the whole world consists of idiots who do not know that the USSR is, first of all, a country of toilers, the country which protects the interest of the working class. It seems that Miss Utley has overlooked the October revolution, all of Stalin's 5-year plans, and the meaning of Soviet Socialism. It seems that she has not emerged from the kindergarten of elementary political education. Even elementary school children would laugh at the articles she writes about the Soviet Union because they know more about it than she does. For instance, they know that the Soviet Union sacrificed 20,000,000 of her sons and daughters to save the world from the infection Nazi-ism and Samurai-ism, that Russia returned Manchuria to China at a cost of 10,000 lives, and that Russia wants to create a stable peace for the whole world and for the workers of the whole world, of which, it seems, Miss Utley does not consider herself a part. It appears that Miss Utley belongs to the enemies of these toilers and answers to some other interest, but not to the interest of humanity. She serves world reaction, provocators of war and the fascist beast. . . .

It is useless work, Miss Utley! Every honest Chinese as well as every honest American will say that the Soviet Union cannot be an aggressive country because of its internal structure, because of its Soviet ideology—the ideology of the toilers, who do not wish to shed the blood of their children for the interest of egoistic and extravagant reactionary capitalists. I have no doubt that Miss Utley will receive deserving gratitude for her activity from her masters—in the form of a proposal (recommendation) to leave China as soon as possible. . . .

Really isn't it clear to you, Miss Utley, that it is not Russia which is a menace to China . . . but you and your brother reactionaries? In fact it is you, but not Soviet Russia, who wants China to be a backward country and wholly dependent on the capitalists of all nationalities, on the industrial magnates who are afraid of losing their market in China! China will stand on her own feet and will create her great industry. In that the Soviet Union will lend her strong support.

No, Miss Utley, you are not worth the blood of our people, you do not merit the respect of humanity!

Having no citizenship and being fearful that the Soviet Government might soon be in a position to force them to return to Russia or have them thrown out of China, the majority of Shanghai's huge Russian colony were most anxious to do nothing to offend the Soviets. Some became Moscow's abject tools prepared to say anything and do anything to please their masters. The more actively anti-Communist they had been in the past the farther they now felt it necessary to go in adulation and subservience to Stalin in order to redeem themselves.

Lev Grosse is a son of the former Czarist consul general in Shanghai, and had once been bitterly anti-Bolshevik. Yet it must have been easier for a former loyal servant of the Czar to believe that Stalin can do no wrong, than for a liberal or Socialist "White Russian."

Many former reactionaries, conservatives, even aristocrats, had been enticed or driven to embrace the Soviet Union and act as its propagandists, spies and informers. The Social Democrats and Social Revolutionaries for the most part remained unreconciled and had the courage to defy the Soviet Government which was trying to force or persuade all Russians to become Soviet citizens.

There were some young people among the Russians in China who sincerely believed that Soviet Russia was all the propagandists said, and who having had their patriotic fervor aroused by the war longed to return to the fatherland. They had been born in China or having left Russia as young children had no memories of the Revolution. The background of their lives was one of hardship, humiliation and distress. "White Russians" were looked down on by the English, French and Americans as inferiors, and they had had to struggle in the labor market and in small business enterprises against their Chinese hosts. It was little wonder that they longed to believe in the New Russia and to live in their own country instead of as exiles or refugees in a world in which they belonged nowhere. Others again found it pleasant to be able to bully the Chinese who were in such mortal fear of the Soviet Government that the Shanghai police dared not arrest Soviet citizens when they got drunk and disorderly or committed other misdemeanors.

For the most part the former "White Russians" who had fled to China during or shortly after the Revolution were proving as useful to the Soviet Government as they had formerly been to Japan. Most of them had collaborated wholeheartedly with the Japanese and for that very reason were now ready to save themselves by jumping on the Soviet band wagon. Today they constitute valuable Communist auxiliaries. Most of them speak Chinese and few have any affection for China. In any case they are all terrorized by fear of being dragged back to Russia.

I was told in Tientsin that some of them were being used as dummies for the acquisition of Chinese properties by the Soviet Government. According to Vincent Torossian, a United States Marine Intelligence officer, there was evidence that Tientsin Russians both pumped the marines for military information to pass on to the Communists, and offered them fantastic prices to steal American arms, ammunition, trucks and jeeps.

Farther north, in Harbin and other Manchurian cities, the large, formerly "White" Russian colony was forced to act as Soviet citizens.

The Chinese who have a facility for apt description called the *emigré* Russians radishes—red outside and white inside.

As Sergeant Dick Wilson, of the *Stars and Stripes,* reported in February, 1946, from Mukden, "Once again the threat of railroading to the Siberian salt mines is haunting Russians in Manchuria who years ago fled the Soviet Union." "Hounded residents" of Mukden and Dairen revealed to this young United States correspondent that their lives were "shadowed by NKVD (Soviet secret police), their every move noted, recorded, and interpreted by skilled agents who keep them in line with a program of terror, espionage and intrigue."

Both the longings and fears of the Russians in China were brought home to me when Alla, my secretary, told me she did not dare to continue working for me, now that I was being attacked in the Russian press. I was sorry to lose her as we had become very friendly, and she was efficient, intelligent and amiable. It was hard to make out whether she was moved more by fear or by the wish to return to her native land. She did not want to believe the terrible things she had read and heard about the Soviet Union. Her mind told her they were true; her heart longed to disbelieve. She kept on saying that she must go and see for herself even if they killed or imprisoned her when she got there.

In any case she was fearful of the consequences of incurring the anger of the Soviet authorities by working for me, their enemy. She spoke and thought and felt like a character out of Dostoevski, ready for martyrdom, deliberately letting her heart instead of her head guide her actions; longing for love and happiness but believing she was doomed to sorrow, and feeling an inner compulsion to help the fates destroy her. She was clever and well qualified and quite nice-looking, but so sensitive and proud and self-sacrificing that her whole life had been spent in letting herself be victimized. She had for years supported her mother and her brother and her husband, but the last was now happily dead after having lived on her earnings without even being faithful to her.

It was a satisfaction to me before I left China to find she had become engaged to an American officer, and had finally decided against offering herself as a sacrifice to Mother Russia, and for emigration to the United States.

There could be no greater contrast than that between the mystical and unpractical old-style Russians, exemplified by Alla, and my Chinese nurses. The nurses had little to make them happy from a Western point of view. They worked very hard, they had little free time and very little money; several of them had been cut off from their families for years by the war and did not know if their parents were dead or alive. But they thought they were lucky and they were always smiling, cheerful and ready to go to any amount of trouble to make one comfortable. They were extremely fond of the matron, an exceptional English woman who spoke Chinese fluently and had devoted her life for twenty years to training nurses in China. Miss Bowerman astonished and pleased them by promoting her nurses according to their qualifications and their capacities instead of according to whether they were English, Russians, Eurasians or Chinese, as had been the custom in Western hospitals in China. I am sure that one could not have been better nursed anywhere, and in addition the whole atmosphere of the place was kind and friendly instead of stiff with discipline.

My favorite nurses were a charming and very pretty girl called Gloria, who had nursed in an American Army hospital during the war, and Miss Wu, an older, sadder woman who had worked in Shanghai all through the Japanese occupation. Neither of them wished to marry. Why, said the vivacious Gloria, should she exchange her pleasant useful independent life for that of a Chinese wife? And she would tell me what a dreadful life her mother had had with her father who spent his time and money on concubines while his wife slaved at home.

Without conscious cynicism Gloria told me how her father "being a patriot" had gone off to Chungking with all the money, and left her mother to manage anyway she could to support the family in Shanghai.

The hospital I was in was being run by a British Red Cross unit for the sick who had been in Japanese concentration camps, but there was one floor for paying patients. On the whole, the ex-prisoners told me, they had not been brutally treated. But they had always been hungry and had suffered terribly from cold. It was chilly enough in the hospital, but we were among the lucky few in Shanghai whose radiators had not been carted off by the Japanese and we had enough coal to have heat for three hours every day.

Miss Bowerman had been in the retreat with the Chinese Army in Kweichow the previous winter. She had slept on the ground in the snow and shared all the hardships of the Chinese soldiers. She had organized a hospital for the children among the starving frozen refugees and saved many lives with food obtained from Australia by the Red Cross. She was one of those rare people whose motivating force in life is healing and helping. She wasted no time condemning the Chinese for all the misery around her, but at once set out to do something about it. She loved the country and the people, understood their philosophy and recognized their qualities as well as their defects. Her sane and merciful attitude, her cool competence, sense of humor and kindness made her a most satisfactory person to talk to. When the time finally came for me to leave the hospital I departed with regret.

"The Chinese now are in a very suspicious mood after their long ordeal. Everybody is suspicious of everybody else. There is suspicion of the capitalists, of the foreigners, of the landowners, of the government; the people who lived through the occupation hate those who come from Free China; the Chungking people accuse the people of the liberated areas of having been collaborators. Hate and jealousy are today the driving force of politics."

This was the melancholy verdict of an old Chinese friend I talked to in Shanghai. In formerly Japanese-occupied territory as in the countries which Germany had occupied, liberation had brought neither bread nor warmth nor justice and freedom. It was a bitterly cold winter and coal was almost as precious as gold. The Communists had destroyed the railways and stopped the mines from working. Finally the Americans and the British brought fuel to Shanghai by boat but most of it had to be used for light and power. Broadway Mansions, where the United States Army Air Forces and the press lived, and where I secured a room when I left the hospital, was about the only building in Shanghai with regular hot water and heating.

The majority of the Chinese had neither heat nor warm clothing nor enough to eat. Since organization and distribution of supplies was worse than under the Japanese the people were suffering even more now than before the liberation. The most bitter disappointment was the behavior of the liberators. There was not, it is true, anything in the nature of the wholesale killings and executions which marked the return of the *emigré* government to France. It was not in the Chinese character to condemn as traitors all who had in any way "collaborated" with the Japanese in order to earn a living. But much property was confiscated and there was some outright robbery of the people of Shanghai by the "patriots" or carpetbaggers from Chungking.

As always in China, there was more corruption than persecution.

In Europe, lust for vengeance rather than desire for money motivated the atrocities and injustices perpetrated by the "liberators.". In China many were dispossessed of their property or ruined by exactions but few were murdered "legally" or by mob violence. What was most shocking was the fact that the representatives of the Chungking Government used the opportunity to enrich themselves either by taking possession of or selling to others the property of the "collaborators," or letting real collaborators or ex-puppets continue to enjoy their ill-gotten gains in return for fat bribes.

The Chinese, left to themselves, would probably never have had the idea of confiscating private property. They might also have been expected to have the common sense to encourage every factory in Shanghai to continue working instead of confiscating the Japanese and puppet-owned ones, thus closing them down. If they had followed their natural rational behavior pattern, they would not have treated as collaborators, whose property had to be confiscated, those who had merely bowed to necessity and kept themselves and their workers alive through the long hard years of the Japanese occupation. But their allies were continually criticizing the lack of democracy in China, and vengeance was now held to be a primary democratic virtue. If they had not sealed up enemy and puppet property, if reconstruction had been recognized as more immediately important than retribution, the factories would have been kept working and there would not have been such wide unemployment and such a steep rise in commodity prices. But there would have been a storm of criticism from the Left. Thus the debased standards of Western democracy gave the worst elements in China a good excuse to feather their own nests to the hurt of the nation.

The best as well as the worst aspects of the Chinese character as of their government were to be seen in Shanghai. The Chinese are venal, but they lack the revengeful and self-righteous spirit of the West. They showed themselves more humane and rational in their national and individual behavior toward the vanquished enemy than we, the Americans, British and French. The Chinese were capable of saying, "There but for the grace of God, go I," even when they had had at their mercy the people whose soldiers and government had ravaged and oppressed China for eight years. To the Chinese, the Japanese and Germans remained individual *people*. The conception of collective guilt which we have taken over from the Nazis and the Communists is foreign to their ethics and their reason.

China's essentially civilized attitude toward the defeated was often misconstrued. There were not wanting American correspondents in Shanghai who interpreted it as "sympathy with the fascists" and continually urged the Chinese to adopt the maxim, "Do as you have been done by," instead of adhering to the Confucian and Christian saying, "Do unto others as you would that they should do unto you."

One of the most unpleasant manifestations of the so-called Christian Western world's attempt to teach the Chinese how to be civilized and modern was the reiterated demand that they lock up every Japanese and German in Shanghai. Several of the American correspondents seemed to think that the main purpose of a victorious "democratic" nation was to extract an eye for an eye. They were indignant when they visited the camp for interned Germans and found that the prisoners had plenty to eat and were not otherwise ill-treated. They thought the Chinese very remiss because the Japanese civilian population of Shanghai was allowed freedom of movement in Hongkew, the former Japanese concession. When Chiang Kai-shek came to Shanghai in February 1946, the only question the Scripps-Howard correspondent had was one concerning the freedom of some Germans in China. The Generalissimo in his answer showed both courage and a truly democratic outlook. He said, "The Nazis who were our enemies are imprisoned. We do not consider every German national an enemy."

Thus in spite of their failure as yet to establish a democratic government, in some respects the Chinese have shown a greater regard than the Western powers for the moral and legal precepts which are the foundation of democratic government. We have abandoned the concept of equality before the law in favor of racial discrimination in our treatment of the conquered. As Anne O'Hara McCormick reported in the *New York Times,* there is an "interallied convention that the word of a German shall never be taken against that of an ally."

The Chinese, having themselves suffered so long by being treated as racial inferiors, might be expected to abhor such race distinctions. But it is not always that a people has the fairness and wisdom to recognize that the precepts it wishes applied to itself must also be adhered to in the treatment of others.

The Chinese are also loyal people. They remembered that in the early stages of Japan's war against them Germany had been a main source of China's armament imports, and that even when the Nazi Government withdrew the German military mission in the summer of 1938, some German officers had braved Hitler's wrath by remaining in Chiang Kai-shek's service.

It was more than a little ironical that the same Americans who had continued for years to help Japan by letting her buy scrap iron, oil and machinery, now insisted that even Germans who had helped China should be interned or sent to a ruined Germany. It was one of the best traits of the Chinese that, at a time when America held over them the power to save them from Russia or abandon them, their government refused to treat all Germans as "war criminals," and to hand over the individual officers who in 1938 had refused to return to Germany, sacrificed their careers in the German Army and risked the loss of their citizenship in order to continue serving China.

One evening in Shanghai I was invited by General Tang En-po, the commander of the Chinese forces in the area, to a dinner given by the Japanese interned in Hongkew. There were five American officers present and a few Chinese. Our Japanese "hosts" served a Japanese dinner in a Japanese room and afterward gave us an excellent concert.

When I arrived and seated myself on the floor with the others, I felt ill at ease. For years I had inveighed against the Japanese for their bullying of China, their aggression, the atrocities they had committed and their hypocrisy. But now they were defeated, broken and defenseless. The last thing I wanted to do was to crow over them now that they were the oppressed instead of the oppressors.

In a very short time I ceased to feel uncomfortable because the Chinese were so courteous and unconstrained. As the sake flowed and the geishas sang, the American officers also came to feel at ease. Brigadier General Middleton who was so huge and genial that I thought he must be a Texan, but who actually came from Connecticut, sang an American ballad following the Japanese songs. Tang En-po congratulated the Japanese performers, asked about conditions in the camp and in general behaved as Europeans once did, or are supposed to have done, in the Age of Chivalry. Altogether it was a heart-warming occasion which showed up the best qualities of victors and vanquished alike.

Left alone, the Chinese would probably have had the common sense to make use of the technical capacities of the defeated enemy. One reason why Chinese industry is today in such a parlous condition is the lack of engineers, mechanics and other qualified personnel. The factories taken over from the Japanese, or liberated after having been confiscated by Japan, are of little use without competent people to run them. And China's claim to reparations from Japan proper are often met with the argument that the Chinese could not make much use of machinery taken from Japan. Having defeated her, the Chinese would have done well for themselves to utilize Japanese talent and training in Chinese interests. I am not advocating that China should have copied the Russians, French and even the English, who are keeping millions of German ex-prisoners of war as slave laborers in farms and factories. It would have been easy for the Chinese to hire, on a voluntary basis, thousands of Japanese technicians now jobless and homeless. The Chinese cannot afford to employ Americans or British on a wide scale, but they could afford to employ Japanese and even Germans. A wonderful opportunity was indeed open to China to reverse the prewar relations with Japan by using the Japanese and exploiting their talents and training instead of being used and exploited by them.

It seemed to me that what prevented the adoption of such an intelligent and rational policy was mainly the attitude of China's allies in the war. An outraged protest would have arisen from Americans, British and Russians and in particular from the so-called liberals of the Western world if China had used her ex-enemies to help her reconstruct and rehabilitate her economy. Mr. Clarence E. Gauss, the former United States ambassador to China, now an official of the Export-Import Bank, was in fact reported in the Shanghai newspapers to have given as a reason for refusing a loan to China the possibility that some Japanese and German technicians might be employed to help build up China's industries.

The cost of vengeance is always high. China was forced to pay it in order to appear "democratic." One result is that some American military men now look on Japan as a better bet than China as a counterweight to Russia's aggressive imperialism in the Far East.

Although extraterritorial rights had been given up by the Western powers in 1943 the "Shanghai mind" had not fundamentally changed. The imperialist-minded members among the foreign community in Shanghai, although they had perforce to accept the new situation in which theoretically and legally the white man and the Chinese were equal, were no more willing than in the past to see China united, fully mistress in her own house, and helped by American capital and know-how to develop into a strong and independent nation.

Since the Communists were now the one element in China which could be counted on to prevent China from becoming united, independent and strong, it was perhaps not really surprising to find that many old China hands regarded them favorably.

The situation was ironical to anyone who remembered how, in 1927, the Shanghai taipans had hailed Chiang Kai-shek as their deliverer from the Communist menace. Their changed attitude toward the Communists and Russia could be understood only if one remembered how the die-hard racists, or simple seekers for easy profits, had at one time also been benevolently neutral toward the Japanese.

When the Japanese, in 1932, fought the Chinese Nineteenth Route Army in Shanghai, the prevailing sentiment among the foreigners there had been that it would be a "jolly good thing" if Japan taught China a lesson. They had made excuses for, or had no objection to, the rape of Manchuria and Japan's subsequent setting up of so-called autonomous regimes in the North, and encouragement of any and every separatist tendency in China. Their attitude had not changed until the Japanese started attacking Western interests, privileges and treaty rights. Why, therefore, today should one expect them to worry about what Russia and her agents were doing to China?

The really remarkable transformation which had taken place was in the attitude of foreign liberals.

In the twenties all who called themselves liberals had demanded that China be freed, helped to reconstruct her economy and attain unity and national independence. Now, however, many self-styled liberals voiced strong disapproval of the American Government's support of China in its efforts to attain precisely these objectives. A decade earlier the liberals had condemned Japan for setting up so-called autonomous regimes in North China, and for using force and intimidation to encourage every separatist tendency which would prevent Chinese unity and render Japan's aggression easy. Now some of the very same individuals who had condemned both Japan and the "Shanghai-minded" foreigners who sympathized with her, were all in favor of the Communists setting up autonomous regimes, maintaining a private army and laying China open to Russian aggression. They failed even to condemn the manner in which Russia was taking advantage of China's internal difficulties to try to extort concessions in Manchuria which would have given Russia the same absolute control as Japan had enjoyed after 1931.

General Hurley had sensed the unity of outlook and aim between the reactionary foreigners and the Communists when he said in November 1945: "Professional American foreign policy sided with the Chinese Communist Party and the imperialist bloc of nations whose policy it was to keep China divided against herself."

The Russian newspapers also recognized that there was a limited short-term community of interest in the Far East between the old and new imperialists. Hurley had specifically exonerated the British Government from blame and obviously referred to British, American and other foreign die-hard opponents of Chinese unity and independence. The Russian press, however, spoke of "the disquiet in England over the intentions of American politicians of General Hurley's type to take advantage of the American dissatisfaction with British behavior in India, Palestine and the Dutch East Indies, in order to squeeze England out of those places and strengthen the American position there." (*Pravda,* December 1, 1945)

The curious similarity in the views of old China hands unreconciled to the loss of their imperialist privileges, and those of the Communist sympathizers who called themselves liberals, was continually apparent in conversation and in the foreign press. Like the Japanese before the war, the die-hard conservatives and the neo-liberals considered the Chinese Nationalists unfit to govern and damned them on all counts. The only difference between them was that the former thought all Chinese unfit to govern themselves while the latter thought that the Chinese who accepted Russian tutelage would rule wisely, justly and well. Both were equally convinced that there is something so rotten in the state of China, or of her government, that she is undeserving of support and sympathy. Anyone who remembered that Mr. Gauss had been United States consul general in Shanghai in 1926-27, when the Shanghai taipans had wished to crush the Chinese Revolution by force of arms, could not be but amused to find him warmly praised by the Left in 1945, when he urged the United States to "go slow" in giving loans to China.

If one viewed the situation in historical perspective the amazing thing was that so few foreigners saw the parallel. One might have expected that men without Communist sympathies, some of whom had themselves suffered years of imprisonment in Japanese camps, would by now have realized that they stood to lose as much by the overthrow of the Chinese Government by Russia's puppets as by the former Japanese conquests. Instead they wittingly or unwittingly gave aid and comfort to the Communists.

To me it seemed like an old play revived with a new set of actors under new management. In the years 1936 to 1940, when one spoke in favor of strong diplomatic action and economic measures to stop Japanese pressure or aggression, one was not only denounced and vilified by the Japanese, one was accused of "wanting war" between the United States or Britain and Japan. How often had I been told, both in the United States where I had lectured for the American Committee for Nonparticipation in Japanese Aggression, and in England where I spoke for the China Campaign Committee, that I ought not to "provoke war" by suggesting that action be taken to stop Japan! We should, one was told, continue to be friendly to Japan and continue to supply her with war materials with which to fight the Chinese, since any other course would lead to war.* Now it was argued that we

* In 1938 the United States supplied Japan with 90.9% of her copper imports, 90.4% of her scrap iron and steel, 65.6% of ferroalloys, 76.9% of her aircraft and aircraft parts, 65.6% of vehicles and parts and 45.5% of her lead. Following the outbreak of the war in Europe the percentages became higher still. Although finally in July 1941 Japanese funds in the United States were frozen, thus precluding further large purchases, no complete embargo had been placed on war-material exports to Japan when she attacked Pearl Harbor.

must avoid a clash with Russia at all costs and bring about peace in China by concessions to the Communists.

Cynics say that the only lesson history teaches is that mankind learns nothing from history. The reason is, no doubt, that in each epoch the roles of "villain" and "hero" are played by different actors. Moreover human beings are naturally inclined to condone actions taken by a seemingly friendly power, or an ally, which they condemn when committed by a hostile or rival country. Only a minority recognizes that in international affairs, as in society, there can be no lasting peace and security until universal principles of justice and rules of conduct are established and enforced.

All this is not to say that the American and British community in Shanghai did not contain many people who not only welcomed the end of extraterritoriality and other lost imperialist privileges in China, but also understood very well that their own and their country's best interests would be served by the emergence of a strong and independent China. There were not wanting businessmen, as well as Embassy and Consular officials and army and navy officers, who appreciated the difficulties of the National Government and sought to give aid in the solution of its well-nigh insoluble problems.

General Olmsted, Chief of G-5 at United States Army Headquarters, said to me in an interview that he divided foreign businessmen in China into three categories:

The old China hands who had never put anything into China but just taken out profits. These would like to have China still in effect a colonial territory, and did not wish to help her reconstruction. (He would like to see all these sent home.)

Those who had done business in China in the past but recognized that the old privileges and easy profits were of necessity gone forever. They hoped, however, to be able to enjoy the same profits as in the "good old days" because the venality of Chinese officials might be expected to enable them to enjoy as privileged a position in postwar China as in the days of extraterritoriality.

Those whose first approach to China had not been through the prewar residents in Shanghai and other treaty ports: businessmen and others who had entered China through the back door, so to speak, in Chungking during the war years—these, he said, were ready and willing to treat the Chinese as equal partners and friends. A good example was the CNAC which was a profitable undertaking. The Pan-American Airways people had been willing to have Chinese as chairmen and vice-chairmen but had themselves supplied, or helped to train, the technicians, and had given the Chinese the know-how so badly needed. C. V. Starr, although an old China hand, was another example of enlightened foreign business interests since he had built up a huge insurance business before the war by taking in the Chinese as equal partners.

It was General Olmsted's opinion that the Chinese Government had acted eminently fairly as regards foreign property. It was willing to restore it in the former Japanese-occupied territory, only insisting that an end be put to the old privileged status of foreigners in China.

Many Americans did not agree with General Olmsted. There was in particular much bitterness on the automobile question. The Japanese had taken possession of every automobile they could lay their hands on. After the surrender these had come into the possession of the Chinese Army. The former residents of Shanghai coming out of internment or returning to China from abroad were indignant when they failed to obtain possession of their property. Most of them eventually got their cars back but it often took a long time, and there was great indignation when a certain United States Army colonel said that the Chinese Army had greater need of the automobiles than the foreign businessmen and should be allowed to keep them.

Since new cars could not be bought, and transport in the huge city of Shanghai with its streetcars filled to overflowing was a real problem, the automobile question caused a lot of ill feeling. According to the conception of the rules of war as applied by the Russians in Eastern and Central Europe the foreigners in Shanghai would have lost much more than a few old automobiles. Everything ever in Japanese possession, however acquired, would have been accounted Chinese "war booty." Every building, business and factory formerly owned by foreigners and taken over by the Japanese during the occupation would have become Chinese property.

The Chinese, unlike the Russians, were scrupulous in this regard. Only such properties as, for instance, the towering near-skyscraper Broadway Mansions sold to Japan by the British before Pearl Harbor, were taken over by the Chinese Government. Properties seized by Japan after she was at war with Britain and America were recognized as belonging to their former owners. Yet the foreigners in Shanghai were far more voluble in their resentment over the loss of their automobiles than the American investors who have lost factories and mines, buildings and equipment in Rumania, Bulgaria, Poland and the Russian zone in Germany. As usual a different standard was applied in dealing with China and Russia. The very same journalists who persisted in adopting a friendly attitude to the Soviet Union and the Chinese Communists wrote angry diatribes against the Chinese authorities on the automobile question.

On the bigger question of the administration of Shanghai, the foreigners had much more serious matters to complain about than the restitution of a few old automobiles. It would have been better for China if the transition from foreign to Chinese control of the International Settlement and French Concession could have been gradual. Shanghai is one of the largest cities and ports in the world, and China's main industrial center. It was by no means a simple task to administer it, and the few Chinese who had the necessary qualifications were not fully made use of. Those who had stayed in Shanghai through the occupation had little chance of getting jobs in the administration. And the type of official sent down from Chungking after Shanghai's liberation was too often of the carpetbagger type. Many regarded their jobs as an opportunity to make up for the lean years in the interior at the expense of those they considered as having failed to sacrifice for the nation by their failure to come to Free China.

The better part of Shanghai had formerly been the International Settlement and the French Concession. Since extraterritoriality had been abolished the former international police force was now replaced by Chinese police who were inadequately trained, poorly paid, and unable to cope with the gangsters and robbers of the city. Foreign merchants complained with justice of the serious robbery and pilfering of their goods in warehouses. UNRRA officials were often dismayed at seeing stolen supplies in use or on sale in Shanghai.

On the other hand some of the horrible sights one used to see in Shanghai were absent. I never saw Chinese policemen beating the rickshawmen and coolies as the Sikh police of the International Settlement had been used to do. There seemed to be less bullying of the poor and favoritism of the rich, even if there were more robbery and thieving than in the past. Many foreigners who complained loudly concerning conditions in Shanghai were in reality expressing their resentment at the loss of their former privileged status as men and women of the white race. They considered it intolerable to have to ride in streetcars together with the Chinese, and they would not willingly adapt themselves in any way to the new conditions of equality of race.

It must, however, be admitted that the transformation of Shanghai from a foreign city on Chinese soil into a part of China showed up as under a neon light the shortcomings of the Chinese Government. In the old days foreigners, secure in the foreign-administered "Treaty Ports," had not cared much what went on in the interior of China. Now the state of China as a whole was their immediate concern since there were no more foreign enclaves of security, order and good government. If China were in disorder the foreigners suffered with the Chinese. And few foreign businessmen had the tolerance and wisdom to be patient and to take into account the tremendous problems faced by the Government of China. Instead they gloated over China's failures as demonstrating the unfitness of the Chinese to govern themselves, and as a proof that the old and dead "unequal treaties," giving foreigners special privileges and the right to their own settlements on Chinese soil had been justified and should never have been annulled.

As John Kullgren of the United States Military Intelligence said to me, "The Chinese Government should have realized that Shanghai is China's great show window. Many foreigners judge China entirely by Shanghai. If a great effort had been made to put on a good show there, few people would have cared what was happening in the interior."

Morally, as in France, the war and foreign occupation had left deep wounds. A people who have lived long in conditions in which there is no respect for law because the government is an alien tyranny, naturally take time to come back to law-abiding habits and regard for the interests of the community. Shanghai, which used to share with Suez the reputation of being the most immoral city in the world, had always had more than its share of gangsters and racketeers; and the Chinese had never had much respect for government or national obligations. Small wonder that speculation, illegal deals, corrupt practices, black markets and robbery under the guise of patriotism flourished even more luxuriantly than in France.

It had always been a Chinese contention that the foreign concessions fostered and encouraged gangsters and prostitution, and that the evil example of the West destroyed "the law-abiding nature of the Chinese." It would have been more correct to say that the impact of the Western world on China had destroyed the old morality of her people without giving them a new one in exchange.

It was too much to expect that the Chinese, after having for so long been the underdog in their own country, should suddenly be able to take over and administer a Western-created metropolis, which ranked among the first half-dozen cities of the world in size and as a port and industrial center. As one of England's wise old China hands, Mr. Findlay Stuart of Butterfield and Swire, said to me in Shanghai, it would have been far better for the Chinese, as well as for the foreigners, if the process of abolishing extraterritoriality had been gradual, as had been planned before the Sino-Japanese War. The Western Powers had then been prepared to abandon their special rights and privileges as the Chinese became ready to administer Shanghai and other Treaty Ports. Now, instead of a slow transition from foreign to Chinese control, the difficult problems created both by liberation and by the change-over from foreign to Chinese administration confronted a government whose main energies were engaged in seeking for a solution of the Communist problem, and on recovery of its Northern provinces.

The National Government was also far less capable than in 1937 of administering Shanghai and other former Japanese-occupied areas. Its cadres of experienced administrators had been destroyed or dispersed during the war. Those who remained had lost their contacts and influence, since in some places the Japanese, in others the Communists, had broken the web of government by executions and expulsions of both patriots and "collaborators."

The Chinese Government would have lost face but it would undoubtedly have gained materially if the foreigners who had formerly administered Shanghai and the Chinese Customs Service had been asked to do so again until such time as the National Government was prepared to take over the task. Shanghai might then have become an enclave of security and good administration into which capital could flow instead of seeking shelter abroad or in British-administered Hong Kong. Trade would also certainly have been easier to revive.

It was no doubt politically impossible for Chiang Kai-shek to leave Shanghai temporarily under partial foreign administration. But his government could at least have employed some of the foreigners emerging from Japanese concentration camps at their old jobs in the customs, police and other services until there were enough qualified Chinese personnel to take their places.

That Chiang Kai-shek realized the difficult tasks created by the abolition of extraterritoriality was shown by the speech he made in Shanghai in February, in which he stressed the responsibilities which freedom brings equally with his satisfaction that the Kuomintang had at long last fulfilled the first principle of the *San Min Chu I:* national independence.

Shanghai was an example of the paradox that the war for China had lasted both too long and ended too quickly. The well-nigh insoluble economic problems which face China today are the legacy of the long war which imposed too great burdens and of the Japanese occupation which weakened the moral fiber of the nation. At the same time Japan's sudden collapse so soon after Germany's defeat was a disaster for the Chinese.

If the war had ended in a series of victorious campaigns, driving the Japanese out of China and re-establishing the authority of the Central Government over the lost provinces one by one, there would have been time for gradual recovery under the stimulus of victory. All the economic and political problems of a great but poor country suddenly liberated would not have been dumped into the lap of the Central Government at once.

China, it seemed to me in the winter of 1946-47, was like a man wounded and starving and long confined to prison who was suddenly required to stand up and cope with the responsibilities of a free life and faced at the same time with a new enemy seeking to put him in another prison.

Both politically and economically there was no transition period from war to peace. Economically China would have benefited enormously if the breaking of the blockade had come many months before victory instead of immediately preceding it. For her Lend-Lease of necessity never constituted more than a trickle of supplies.* It came to an end at the moment when it was about to turn into a flood. Consequently the country which fought first and longest against the common enemy faced the future with incomparably less accumulated American supplies than Britain or Russia.

To take only China's greatest need, transport: She received a mere fraction of the hundreds of thousands of trucks given to Russia and England. True, she was now getting UNRRA supplies, but in view of her huge population they contributed only a drop in the bucket of her misery. UNRRA allocations to China amounted to only about $1.25 per capita, as against $20.70 to Poland; $27.50 to Yugoslavia; $6.40 to White Russia, and $4.60 to the Ukraine.

Greece with a population about equal to that of the city of Shanghai had received a toal of $700,000,000 of UNRRA and British aid by the end of 1946 as against China's total of $535,000,000. Little Czechoslovakia which neither fought in the war nor was devastated received $270,000,000 from UNRRA—half of what was given to China.

The unexpected manner in which the war ended was also politically disastrous. For years China had been leaning all her weight to hold back a pressure now suddenly removed. Small wonder that she toppled over and moved perilously close to disintegration! The expectation of a great land campaign against Japan in the south had caused the concentration there of China's best troops and left the North open for the Communists to flood following Japan's surrender.

Even if the administration of Shanghai had been all that could be desired many foreign businessmen would still have been hostile to the National Government. For a hundred years the white man, backed by his governments, his banks and the treaty privileges wrested from China by force, had reaped the main profits from China's foreign trade. Now he had to compete with the Chinese on something less

* Following the Quebec Conference Winston Churchill said in Parliament that "after all the lavish aid which America has given to China, these defeats in China are most disappointing and vexatious." This singularly unfair and ungracious remark was made at a time when about 98% of American supplies were going to Europe and the Chinese were receiving only two-tenths of 1% of Lend-Lease. The Chinese could rightly ask whether the British Isles would not have been conquered by Hitler if England had rceived as little help as China from America.

than equal terms. Conditions which would have seemed natural in South America or Europe were considered an outrage in China.

During 1946, when little control was exerted over trade and exchange and China's imports rose above the 1936 level, there was profitable business for all, but many foreigners already felt the keen competition of Chinese traders. By the end of the year, when China's adverse balance of trade, depletion of foreign-exchange reserves and ever mounting inflation forced the government to ban luxury imports and institute import quotas and licenses for all imports, many foreign firms found themselves squeezed to the wall. Whether or not they were right in saying that licenses to import were unfairly allocated, there was not nearly enough trade to go around among old and new, foreign and Chinese importers.

Moreover China's scarcity economy was inevitably leading to increasing state control of her economy. Such controls were in fact even more necessary than they had been in America during the war, but it was not to be expected that many foreigners would see the matter in that light. Before I left China loud complaints were already being raised against the unfair competition and "monopolistic tendencies" of the Chinese Government agencies set up to buy commodities abroad and distribute them in China. The Chinese Universal Trading Company in New York was likened by some Americans to Russia's Amtorg and accused of supervising and controlling the whole China trade. As early as February 1946 the American National Foreign Trade Council and the China-American Chamber of Commerce and Industry appealed to the State Department to concern itself with "the drift toward increasing State control of industry and trade in China."

Of course, if the Chinese Government had not instituted such controls and had let Chinese and foreign merchants buy and sell as they pleased, there would have been no less of an outcry from the Left at home and abroad that the government was doing nothing to check profiteering, stabilize exchange and prices, and ensure the use of available foreign exchange for the import of necessities for the people and capital goods for reconstruction.

Since China had neither a free economy nor a competently and honestly administered controlled economy her government was, as usual, blamed by both conservatives and "progressives," capitalists and Communists, advocates of *laissez faire* and advocates of a planned economy. And the least prejudiced observer had to admit that the remedies instituted by the government with the aim of restoring China's disintegrating economy often proved worse than the disease. The venality of public officials, nepotism and the tremendous power and influence of the Soongs and Kungs and other financial magnates and their clients, combined with the lack of a competent civil service, balked even the best meant efforts to revive industry and exports, stabilize prices and ensure that China's small foreign-exchange resources be used as economically and usefully as possible.

The net effect of stringent exchange controls and the licensing of imports was not to curb speculation, divert capital into productive enterprise and halt the rise in prices. Precisely the reverse effect was accomplished. Merchants and government officials, who had previously speculated in foreign exchange and imported luxury goods, now speculated instead in the necessities of life, thus pushing prices ever higher. The insecurity created by the civil war and the runaway inflation naturally discouraged productive investment and encouraged the use of capital in hoarding of commodities and speculation. Nor did the rich and powerful find much difficulty in circumventing the foreign-exchange regulations in order to export capital for investment in the United States or South America instead of in China.

On February 16, 1947, Chiang Kai-shek announced that all individuals and corporations with holdings abroad must report them and at once sell them to the government or to the Chinese banks. But no one seriously believed that top-ranking government officials would be forced to obey this order. Chiang Kai-shek might tell them that "the survival of the nation is at stake" and call upon "all patriots" to join him in "working out the salvation of the nation," but he did not, or could not, give the new Premier Chang Chun the power to compel them to liquidate their huge foreign holdings and bring their capital back to China. If he were to do so Chiang would inevitably be forced to rely more than ever on the Kuomintang "reactionaries," since, generally speaking, it is Westernized "liberals," not the so-called reactionaries and land-owning classes, who have accumulated fortunes abroad.

Nor could it be expected that confidence in the security of investment in China would be restored by exhortations or decrees promising that hoarders and profiteers would be "punished as severely as the crisis requires." The flight of capital abroad or to Hong Kong, or its use in harmful speculation, would continue until the civil war ended, until revenue commensurate with expenditures could be raised, the printing presses cease to be the main source of government revenue and the government's credit restored.

While lack of confidence precluded the possibility of raising revenue through the sale of government bonds, lack of competent and honest administrative personnel made it impossible to raise enough through direct taxation in the cities. Chiang Kai-shek, when announcing in February 1947 that "rough and ready justice" would henceforth be applied in the collection of taxes, admitted that "since we have not developed a modern accounting system, collection of income and other direct taxes has proved very ineffective."

It seemed to me doubtful whether the disapproval of the Chinese National Government voiced by the foreign business community, and its opposition to a United States loan to China, was due to its disapproval of the corruption and ineffectiveness of the Chinese administration. In days gone by foreign businessmen in China had not worried themselves about the shortcomings of the Chinese Government, provided it left them a clear field for profit-making. The real grievance of both old and new China hands was state interference and participation in trade on the part of both the United States and Chinese Governments which cut out the foreign middleman's profits. This was evidenced by the attitude of Shanghai businessmen toward UNRRA.

True that CNRRA, the Chinese distribution agency for UNRRA goods, was not without the usual failings of Chinese Government agencies. But the real complaint of American businessmen was that UNRRA was giving away goods to the Chinese which they would have liked to sell to them. This was demonstrated in April 1946 when the American Chamber of Commerce at Shanghai submitted to UNRRA proposals of ways in which nonrelief goods could be marketed through commercial channels. It may also be suspected that the tender solicitude for the Chinese Communists in the distribution of UNRRA goods, displayed by many American capitalists in China, was not unconnected with their desire to see noncommercial imports to China distributed as far away as possible from their own hunting grounds.

Incidentally it should be noted that a quite different standard was applied by UNRRA officials themselves in dealing with the Chinese and with the Russians and their satellites.

No one ever suggested that the Polish Government should be required to distribute UNRRA supplies to the underground opposition, or that the Soviet Government should see to it that a due proportion of UNRRA goods be allocated to the millions of political opponents of the Soviet regime in Russian concentration camps. But in China it was insisted that the government should send UNRRA goods to the Communists who were fighting against it. Moreover, in Yugoslavia Marshal Tito's government was permitted to sell UNRRA relief supplies in shops at prices so high that the people, unaware that they were buying American gifts, complained of the high prices charged by the United States. Tito was thus able to accumulate huge profits to maintain his antidemocratic army as well as obtaining the use of UNRRA trucks and construction goods for military purposes. Similarly in the Ukraine and White Russia UNRRA supplies were sold to the people by the government. But in China the practice of selling UNRRA goods through commercial channels, followed in other UNRRA countries, was banned. The reason given was the impossibility of establishing a rationing system and price controls,* but this explanation hardly holds water. The very fact that China has no rationing system and effective price control made it the more necessary to allow sales to bring down prices by natural economic processes. In countries where rationing was in force, it would have been both more practicable and fairer to allocate UNRRA supplies free.

But when China, in February 1947, asked permission to convert her remaining UNRRA allocation into consumer in place of durable goods and to be allowed to sell cotton and grain to bring down prices, rectify the unfavorable trade balance and promote an industrial revival, an outraged protest was raised in the American press which accused the National Government of wanting to sell relief on the

---

* Statement by General Lowell W. Rook, Director General of UNRRA in China, on February 19, 1947.

"black market." And the UNRRA office in China protested that since UNRRA was a "nonpolitical agency" it should give no direct aid to the National Government's efforts to bolster China's shaky economy.

I have not so far mentioned the British in Shanghai, although I met more English people than at any time since leaving England to become an American.

No longer the lords of the universe, now resigned to taking a back seat and to the shrinking of their Empire and their influence, but also happily absolved from responsibility in the Far East, the British in China are not doing so badly. For one thing they are satisfied with small profits and no longer expect to make a fortune in a few years as some Americans still do. For another their goods arrive to be sold, while no American can be sure whether strikes or gifts to the world will hold up his shipments. Lastly old China hands who know the old ways, while ready to adapt themselves to the new, are to be found mainly among the British.

The British, never having expected the people of China to stop being Chinese, are less disillusioned than Americans and more realistic in their dealings. As one of them said to me in Shanghai: "We can sit back and wait for the Americans to break their necks. Some by now want only to clear out. And the Chinese who expected miracles from America will turn to us when trade ceases to depend on politics and handouts. Moreover we understand finance and trade much better than the Americans, and are also less conservative.

"Funny how the Americans who are so up-to-date in industrial techniques, are rigid conservatives when it comes to finance and banking. There's still life in the old British lion, and he is better at learning new tricks than the American eagle."

It was perhaps a symptom of the changing times that the British *North China Daily News* was more realistic about China's economic and political problems, and far less inclined to exonerate the Chinese Communists, than the American *Shanghai Evening Post.* My association with the one American daily paper in Shanghai had come to an abrupt end when its former editor, Randall Gould, came back to China in late December. Although personally friendly he had no liking for the views I had been freely expressing while the paper was edited by Charles E. Miner. Not that Charlie Miner agreed with me either—like the GI's in Kunming he wanted to leave China to the Chinese, but he was a Midwestern American without Communist sympathies and with old-fashioned ideas about free speech.

I thought that the course of events would soon change Randall Gould's tune. He was not a Communist and he would be sure to change his views once he realized that Russia threatened America. He was typical of the kind of liberals who consider that to be progressive you must be kind to Communists. Also he was a good journalist who went with the tide. Later on, as I relate in a subsequent chapter, Randall Gould began to take a different line following the revelations concerning the Red Army's reign of terror in Manchuria.

The British-owned *North China Daily News* asked me to write for them as soon as my column stopped appearing in the *Shanghai Evening Post.* But I was anxious to get back to Chungking while the Political Consultative Council meetings which followed the January 13 truce were proceeding. Moreover I was by this time the accredited correspondent of *Reader's Digest* and could now travel free on U. S. Army planes to visit the several other places I had in mind.

Although I had enjoyed Shanghai's cosmopolitan cocktail parties and excellent Chinese food, and had made some good friends there, I had had more than enough of the metropolis on the Yangtze. It seems to me to combine the worst features of both Chinese and Western civilization, with an admixture of the less pleasing characteristics of all other cultures. The massive buildings along the Bund, the luxurious hotels, great department stores and elegant shops, the innumerable prostitutes of all races—the largest number of any city in the world, they say—night clubs, dance halls, cafés and restaurants, gangsters, pimps and speculators, all side by side with a starving, ragged, overworked or unemployed mass of coolies, workers and the human flotsam and jetsam which pours in from all over China as a river flows into the sea, are an ever-present reminder of man's inhumanity to man. As my French friend Claude Rivière said: "Shanghai before, during and after the Japanese occupation always presented the most terrible combination of civilization and barbarism, culture, cruelty and indifference. Children die of hunger in the streets and men work like horses dragging heavy loads, while the rich, the prostitutes and other hangers-on feast and dance, indifferent to the condition of humanity."

Although no longer the citadel of Western power and privilege on Chinese soil, Shanghai is a monument to the white man's greed, aggressiveness, arrogance and racial pride. And nowhere are the unpleasing characteristics of the Chinese more in evidence. All races threw off the restraints of their codes of behavior in this city of corruption, which is neither European nor Chinese, and where fortunes were made in a few years by the few while the masses lived in squalor.

CHAPTER V

Last Days of Chungking

CHUNGKING in its last days as China's capital was not unlike Hankow before the fall. For a few weeks there was, if not a united front, at least a free intermingling of all parties and an ephemeral hope of peace. The truce of January 13 was being observed and the Political Consultative Council appeared to be hammering out an agreement for a coalition government.

The atmosphere was charged with optimism, and even the weather, about which I had heard so much ill, had evidently decided to reform shortly after V-J Day. After Shanghai's bitter cold the climate of Szechwan seemed mild and benign. The sun shone on most days in January and February 1946, and only occasionally was the city wrapped in damp mist or drenched with rain and its streets deep in mud. Victory weather they called it and already there was a hint of spring in the air.

In spite of the lack at the Press Hostel of the usual amenities of a mechanized civilization I felt happy. My arm still pained me a little but I rested better on my springless bed and rocklike pillow than in Shanghai's luxurious Broadway Mansions.

To my great joy I found two of the "Hankow Last Ditchers" at the Press Hostel. Arch Steele of the *New York Tribune* and Till Durdin of the *New York Times* were back in the city whose long agony they had experienced in the days when the Japanese planes bombed it at will.

The thin and scholarly Durdin, in whose company I had experienced my first air raid long ago, was considered by his Chinese friends to be practically one of them, so well did he understand their thought processes and their problems. Oddly enough he was also a great favorite with the marines as I discovered later in Peking. In the years since I had first known him he had been in Burma, India and the Pacific and had accompanied the Doolittle fliers in the first bombing of Tokyo. But he had returned to China as to his home.

Steele, with whom I had walked many a weary mile visiting the front in 1938, had also traveled far and wide in the intervening years. Since he had spent nine months in Russia our political views were not dissimilar. An adventurer and a thinker whose cynicism is mixed with humor and pity, Steele's respect for truth and energy in seeking it out have justly given him the reputation of being the most accurate and best informed correspondent in China.

Renewing old friendships I also made new ones. George Weller, of the *Chicago Daily News,* was probably more responsible than anyone else for the friendliness and good humor which now prevailed among the Chungking correspondents. A Pulitzer Prize winner for his Pacific War reporting, Weller was not an old China correspondent, but he had that rare quality of understanding and sympathy for all mankind, combined with intelligence and a knowledge of history and philosophy, which enable a man to get to the heart of a problem and make fair judgments.

Witty, good-natured, and always ready to share information or even to write another correspondent's dispatches for him if he wanted to leave Chungking for a few days, Weller made it difficult for anyone to display a meanly competitive spirit. He also prevented our frequent political discussions over breakfast, lunch and dinner from degenerating into personal wrangles.

The only woman correspondent, Charlotte Ebner of the I.N.S., had acquired a looking glass and a cupboard, but for the most part the correspondents lived in monastic surroundings. Each "rabbit hutch," as Steele called our rooms furnished only with a trestle bed, a desk and a couple of chairs, had a window onto the connecting veranda, or covered way, as well as to the outside. So everyone knew, more or less, what everyone else was doing.

If you wanted a wash you hailed the Chinese "boy" who brought you a tin bowl of water. For a shower you walked, rain or shine, across the central garden courtyard hoping that there might be hot water, but never certain whether the primitive apparatus would be working. Every bit of water at the Press Hostel, as in most other places in Chungking, had to be carried on men's shoulders. You saw the rows of coolies or soldiers with their wooden buckets waiting in line at the bottom of the hill morning and evening. There were, of course, no flush toilets.

The greatest drawback was the poor electricity supply. Chungking's power plant had been constructed to service a small backward provincial town. It could not supply enough current for the swollen population of the capital. From sundown to about 10 P.M. the lights were so dim one could hardly read or write.

We were all within hailing distance of one another and met regularly for meals and almost as frequently for parties. It was a gregarious life, luxurious in comparison with that of most Chinese, but primitive as compared with Shanghai or Peiping, where the correspondents lived in Western-style hotels and ate in their rooms or in restaurants. The camaraderie and good-fellowship and our close and frequent contacts with the Chinese inside and out of the Press Hostel gave the life there a quality all its own.

Probably not one American in ten thousand had ever heard of the Political Consultative Council. But we became so absorbed in the efforts of the Chinese to work out a solution of their political problems that we tended to forget how little interest there was in them at home. It was as if we imagined that millions of Americans when they opened their newspapers at breakfast would anxiously scan the pages to find out what had happened the day before in the P.C.C. Had the government given way as regards the proportion of votes in the State Council required to override its veto? Had the independent members sided with the government or the Communists on this or that particular issue? Had the political barometer risen or fallen in respect to the prospects for unity in China? "My God," said the newly arrived *Time* correspondent, John Walker, "even when you go to the movies you talk P.C.C. all the time!"

Chungking, in its last days as the capital of China, had become a vast forum for the discussion of political and economic theory and constitutional principles. Nowhere else in the world can people of all parties have mingled so freely. One met representatives of every faction at its parties. I even found myself talking to Soviet embassy officials.

At first I did not accompany the other correspondents when they visited Communist Party Headquarters for news, since I feared I would be turned away or cause embarrassment to my colleagues. But

I soon found that even the Communists were not averse to talking to me.

I had been on friendly terms with General Chou En-lai in 1938 but in those days I was known only as the author of *Japan's Feet of Clay*. The books I had written since had been published in China as well as in England and America, so I had no doubt that Chou En-lai was now well aware of my attitude toward Soviet Russia and Communism in general. Moreover, my articles in the *Shanghai Evening Post* and the attacks on me by the Soviet press and radio could have made my views emphatically clear to him. I was therefore astonished and somewhat embarrassed when at the first press conference I attended at Communist Headquarters, he advanced with hand outstretched and a broad smile. His cordial greeting disarmed me and made it impossible for me to question him in anything but friendly tones.

I could not but admire Chou En-lai's masterly conduct of his press conference. Standing in the middle of the small crowded room he turned to face each questioner, never hesitating in his replies, correcting his interpreter when the latter failed to convey his exact meaning, thrusting here and there in verbal repartee like a skilled fencer.

There could have been no greater contrast between this dynamic man arguing the Communist case and the poker-faced government spokesman who stalled off the reporters with meaningless replies, or a curt "no comment," at the dreary weekly press conferences at the Ministry of Information.

"Well, what do you think of him?" my friends asked after they had waited while Chou En-lai fixed a time for an interview with me.

"What do you expect?" I replied. "All right, I admit it. Even I was impressed. It is hard not to believe that he means what he says. I understand better now why so many foreigners believe that the Communists mean what they say when they talk about democracy."

"When Chou En-lai came to town," said George Weller, "I knew what would happen. It started with tea parties. By now he has us all eating out of his hand. How could it be otherwise since poor Wordless Wu and the other government representatives are so afraid of saying too much that they don't tell us anything."

Although Tillman Durdin's political sympathies are Leftist, it was he who was least impressed by Chou En-lai. "At the beginning," he said, "Chou overwhelms you by the force of his personality and his clever arguments. But after hearing him month after month and year after year, you realize you can't trust what he says. He has contradicted himself too often."

Timeo Danaos et dona ferentes. All that I knew and had experienced had taught me to beware of all Communists, even as Aeneas distrusted the Greeks. But Chou En-lai is hard to resist. He is witty, charming and tactful; he avoids Communist clichés and you find it hard not to believe in his sincerity and good intentions. His handsome countenance, intelligent eyes, still youthful figure, well-groomed appearance, vitality and apparent candor, all predispose you in his favor.

The morning fixed for my interview was cold and raw. Chou En-lai, dressed in an immaculate white sweater and American-style brown leather windbreaker, was plainly very tired. He had been up working most of the night and he shivered as we sat down in the unheated, barely furnished reception room at Communist Headquarters. I had an irrational feeling that I ought not to make him waste his energies on an unconvertible heathen like me. Soon, however, I was entirely absorbed taking notes on his replies to my questions. I was trying at the same time to watch his face and catch the real meaning behind his words.

I began by asking if he considered that Chiang Kai-shek's willingness to make concessions to the Communists was, in his opinion, due to American pressure. In reply he paid a tribute to the Generalissimo which few men have ever received from a political opponent.

"Partly, yes; but Chiang would never have met us halfway on account of any external pressure if there had not been in his heart a real desire for unity and peace."

Although he hastened to add that the Communists also had made great concessions, this did not detract from the Communist leader's substantial admission concerning Chiang Kai-shek's motives and character.

"What concessions," I asked, "has the Chinese Communist Party made?"

"We have compromised on matters of vital importance. In the first place, we have agreed to terminate the civil war, which has been going on for eighteen years, and to let our army be nationalized. Secondly, as regards the reorganization of the government we have abandoned our original proposal based on our experience in the liberated areas. We no longer insist on the 3:3:3 system—a one-third Kuomintang, one-third Communist and one-third nonparty administration. We have agreed to let the Kuomintang have a majority in the Executive Yuan (Cabinet) of a coalition government. We have agreed to a draft constitution similar to the British and American systems. Moreover, we have gone so far as to agree to tolerate the validity of the old elections to the National Assembly although this means it will be dominated by the Kuomintang."

"Are you really, then," I asked, "prepared to give up your private army once a coalition government is set up?"

"As a matter of fact," he replied, "not only the Communist armies are led by a party, the Kuomintang Party similarly controls the government armies. Do you agree?"

As the interpreter finished speaking, and before I could reply, Chou En-lai broke in to say in his own halting English: "If I were in the government, I also could control armies in a more mellow way."

Then he spoke again in Chinese, which was translated for me as follows:

"The reorganization of China's armed forces must be accomplished by both sides simultaneously, in order that there may be a complete separation of army and party on all sides. All armed forces must be placed under control of civil organs of government. In order to reach this aim both parties must do the same. Whatever the Kuomintang can and will do, we also can do, and will excel.

"The Chinese Army system," he continued, "should be modeled on the American and British systems. Restrictions should be imposed. The movement of troops should not be ordered by any individual, only by the government. Then no party would be able to promote civil war. In the interim period of coalition government prior to the constitutional period to follow, the Army should be under the control of the State Council, and thereafter under that of Parliament.

"In this way, which is the American and British way, the utilization of the troops by any party for purposes of civil war will be prevented."

General Chou next proceeded to outline the scheme for the amalgamation of the Communist and National armies then being worked out by a special committee presided over by General Marshall. In the first stage there was to be a parallel reorganization of both armies and the Communists had agreed to limit the Red Army to twenty divisions if the government limited its forces to ninety. In the second stage, then being discussed, the objective would be the gradual elimination of the "line of separation" between the armies. This, he stressed, "must be done gradually in a unified way so that no difficulties or confusion should arise." How this was to be accomplished he could not specify, as the question was still under discussion.

"But," he added, "in order that the two opposing armies may be fused together educational work is very important. The fusion of the educational plan should begin at once. Both armies should enjoy a democratic and national education. Once we have introduced a new system of enlistment—when the old soldiers have been replaced by new recruits—it will be possible to wipe out all trace of the present lines of demarcation."

All this made it perfectly clear that the Communists were not for a moment considering the submission of their army to the government. Chou's whole argument was based on the assumption that the Nationalist and Communist forces were to be treated as equals. He continually stressed the word "fusion" and regarded the problem as one of amalgamating two party armies, not of negotiating the terms and guarantees on which the Communist Party would give up its private army.

I inquired whether the government had its own reservations about the desirability of "fusing" the armies.

Chou smiled broadly and said, "The Kuomintang is in fact just as averse as we are to immediate fusion; they are afraid of their soldiers being converted into Communists if the armies are immediately merged into one. The government wants to use the Kuomintang armies as the cadres of a National Army, fitting in our soldiers as individuals. This would be unfair to us. We insist on the fusion of the armies on an equal basis, maintaining our own units as at present constituted. The Kuomintang does not like this idea at all. It says there would be confusion on both sides if such a scheme were adopted before the educational problem had been readjusted. It is true there would be a lot of quarrels. Somehow we have got to work out a method and decide on the concrete steps which must be taken."

All this did not sound very promising. The situation obviously gave the Communists the opportunity to stall indefinitely. There could be no unity as long as both sides distrusted each other so much that no scheme of amalgamation of the armies would ever be agreed on. So I asked, "When will you consider the National Government to have become sufficiently democratic for you to trust it and to give up your private army?" Chou En-lai's reply was open to the interpretation that the Communists would postpone recognition of the "democratic" nature of the government until it agreed with them as to the meaning of the word. He said, "The reorganized coalition government which we are now discussing in the Political Consultative Council would constitute only a start in China's democratic development. It would have to be gradually tested in its practical work before we should trust it. Nothing can be predicated beforehand and everything would depend on how the democratic process was implemented after the constitutional government is set up.

"As regards our army, our attitude and policy would be determined not only by proof of the government's truly democratic nature, but also by the character of the army system in peacetime. I cannot answer your question in a mechanical way. We should need to have proof that no single individual controlled the National Army in peacetime. A lot would depend also on the kind of education given to the soldiers.

"China is in a stage of transition and it is of little use to discuss principles and theories—actions are what count. But the present reorganization of the government and the armies is moving toward our goal."

"How long," I asked, "do you think it will take for the nationalization of China's armies?"

"It may take years," he replied. And again he repeated, "We shall have to be satisfied as to the truly democratic nature of the government before we give up our army."

In spite of all the hopes aroused in China during this period of the P. C. C. negotiations Chou En-lai's remarks made it abundantly clear that there was no real prospect of an end to the civil war. "Democratic" in the Communist lexicon, as we have learned in Europe, does not mean free election, representative government and civil liberties. It is an adjective used to describe only such governments as are dominated by the Communists or are "friendly" to the Soviet Union. Chou En-lai was, in effect, informing me that the nationalization of the Communist Army would, in all probability, be postponed until China has a Communist-dominated or Russian puppet government.

I tried to draw him out on the subject of Russia, saying, "I want to understand what you mean by the word democratic. Do you consider that Soviet Russia has a democratic government?"

Chou spoke rapidly and emphatically in Chinese to his interpreter who then said to me, "General Chou asked me to tell you that we have not met here to talk about Russia. Please confine your questions to Chinese affairs."

I lighted a cigarette and self-consciously sipped my tea. They were making me feel that my question had been in bad taste, and that it was outside the unwritten terms on which the interview had been given me to bring up the question of their attitude to the Soviet Government.

Chang Wen-ching, who was acting as interpreter, was a thin scholarly young man dressed in a long Chinese gown. He had an excellent command of English, perfect manners and an air of studious detachment. He rarely smiled and never raised his voice or gesticulated, unlike Chou En-lai whose expressive hands help him to convey his meaning. I had met Chang Wen-ching before, but I don't think he knew that his aunt, Mary Chen, was a good friend of mine, and that I knew all about him and his family. His grandfather Chu Chi-chien, whom I was to meet a few weeks later in Peking,* had held high office at the Manchu court but had joined with Yuan Shih-kai to overthrow the Dragon Throne in 1911. Yuan Shih-kai had become the first Premier of the Republic of China, and died when he failed to make himself Emperor. The grandfather of Chou En-lai's young colleague had become Minister of the Interior and had continued to be so loyal a member of the Kuomintang that when Chiang Kai-shek visited Peking in 1946, he chose the venerable Mr. Chu Chi-chien to sit at his right hand at the state banquet held to celebrate the liberation of China's ancient capital.

Mr. Chu's ten daughters had all married well and his grandson in the Communist camp had relatives in almost every political faction. One of his uncles was a close friend and associate of T. V. Soong, another was the brother of the "Young Marshal" Chang

---

* Both names, Peking and Peiping, are used in the text, since, although the city is now called Peiping, the old name of Peking is more familiar to the Western reader.

Hsueh-liang and another a prosperous Shanghai businessman who had lived there comfortably all during the Japanese occupation. One of Chang Wen-ching's cousins was the Vice-Minister of War, Yü Ta-wei, who in 1947 became Minister of Communications. Chang Wen-ching was himself the son of the ex-comprador of the Chase Bank in Tientsin, now assistant manager of a Chinese bank.

Chou En-lai himself is also the scion of a great Mandarin family, so it was not surprising that the two aristocratic Communists I was talking to were able to make me feel gauche.

Nevertheless I returned to the attack, although not again alluding to the forbidden subject of Communist Russia. I asked instead whether the Chinese Communist Party desired that the proposed coalition government should continue after a new constitution had been promulgated by a National Assembly and elections held.

His answer made it clear that the Communists had no liking for the idea of a popularly elected majority government and sought a more or less permanent coalition government. He said, "As the second party in China we are prepared to maintain this status during the initial period of reconstruction. We don't want quarrels or alternative governments according to popular vote. We propose long-term co-operation in a coalition government. We expect to be in a minority position for a long time. A coalition government would be the Chinese democratic way."

When I asked how a coalition government could function in view of the basic differences between the Kuomintang and the Communist Party, Chou said there was no difference in principle and aims since both adhered to Sun Yat-sen's Three Principles of the People. "The difference lies in the implementation of these principles."

Later in our conversation when I asked what economic policy the Communists would stand for when they entered a coalition government, Chou En-lai gave me an answer which constituted an admirable exposition of the fallacy of considering state ownership an improvement over capitalist private enterprise so long as there is no political democracy in the Western sense.

"The point is," he said, "that if the state enterprises were really in the hands of the nation—of a democratic government—they could be effectively operated by the Chinese people, with perhaps some assistance from foreigners. We could then get quicker and better results than through private enterprise. But, in practice, so-called state-owned enterprise is run by government officials who do as they like and are usually both inefficient and corrupt. Some consolidate their own personal economic power under the cloak of state ownership. Thus in some respects the Communist Party and the independent capitalists now make common cause against the practices of the government.

"Even if the state enterprises prove to be a success they should not monopolize industry. China is too backward. The government can't do everything. We need competition and free enterprise at this stage of China's development.

"Besides, I know from experience how stultifying bureaucratic management is. Why, I, when I used to be in the government in the days of the United Front, found myself affected by it. Save us from government control of everything!"

At the end of this interview I could well grasp that many foreigners and some Chinese believed in the sincerity of Chou En-lai's democratic professions. I almost believed in them myself after hearing him dissert upon the evils of bureaucratic administration of industry, and listening to his kindly sentiment towards capitalists.

But once removed from his presence I remembered that this soft-spoken, attractive, intelligent Chinese had at one time been a Communist official when dissidents in the Party were shot. I also reflected that whether or not he believed his own arguments made little difference. Let him once arouse suspicions in Moscow that he had really been converted to democratic principles, and he would be excommunicated if not executed.

Whether or not Chou En-lai in fact represented a liberal element in the Chinese Communist Party, he convinced many foreigners that he did. It seems probable that General Marshall was thinking of him when, in January 1947, the Secretary of State announced his conviction that besides the "dyed-in-the-wool Communists" there "is a liberal group among the Communists which would put the interests of the Chinese people above ruthless measures to establish a Communist ideology in the immediate future."

As stated in an earlier chapter, not only Americans but some Chinese Government representatives believed in Chou En-lai's sincerity. Certainly the Nationalist Government at this time was acting on the assumption that the Communists were negotiating in good faith and that unity could be achieved with American aid provided the Kuomintang agreed to a coalition government and made concessions to democratic demands.

The government negotiators in the Political Consultative Council were almost all liberals. They were led by General Chang Chun, the most prominent member of the Political Science clique, who became Premier in 1947, and who has always favored the solution of the Communist problem by political, not military means. The government's eight representatives in the P. C. C. also included Sun Fo and Shao Li-tse, who might be described respectively as China's Henry Wallace and Joe Davies. Sun Yat-sen's son, Sun Fo, like his stepmother Madame Sun, was known for his friendly attitude toward both the Soviet Union and the Chinese Communists. Shao Li-tse, who once attended a Comintern Congress as the Kuomintang's fraternal delegate, and who more recently was China's ambassador in Moscow, is so pro-Soviet that he was nicknamed the Russian ambassador to China.

It was clear that as long as there was any hope of achieving unity by compromise Chiang Kai-shek was holding the Right Wing members of the Kuomintang in check. Chen Li-fu was also a delegate in the Political Consultative Council, but he was outnumbered by those prepared to make every possible concession to the Communists for the sake of peace.

The Communists had seven representatives in the Political Consultative Council as against the Kuomintang's eight. There were besides: five representatives of the Youth Party, two representatives each of the Democratic League, the National Socialist (subsequently rechristened Social Democrat) Party and the National Salvation Association, and a representative each for the Vocational Education Association, the Rural Reconstructive Society and the so-called "Third Party."

The Youth Party, whose members are no longer youthful, but which is the third largest party in China, usually, but not always, sided with the government. The Democratic League always, and the National Salvation Association usually, sided with the Communists.

The remaining nine members of the P. C. C. were nonparty men of various shades of opinion, drawn in the main from among the most eminent scholars in China. Among them were Fu Ssu-nien, acting president of Peking University; Mo Teh-hui, a Manchurian and a friend of the Democratic League; Wang Yun-wu, founder and head of the renowned Commercial Press of Shanghai; and Kuo Mo-jo, the Left Wing dramatist and poet, who had formerly been a Communist. I had known Kuo Mo-jo in 1938, when as a returned exile from Japan he was prominent in the National Salvation Association and a friend of Chou En-lai's. I had once spent a day picnicking with them both and other Communists and Left Wingers in the halcyon time of the United Front. The fact that he and Mo Teh-hui were representatives in the P. C. C. was a proof that the nonparty representatives had been picked impartially from among China's best-known public figures or learned men.

In an interview he gave me during the negotiations, Chang Chun convinced me that the government was ready to risk a great deal on the slender hope for internal peace held out by the Political Consultative Council Agreements. "There is a chance," he said, "that the Communists will now compete only politically and economically. We believe that the truce may be the first stage in the agreement."

General Chang Chun, who was to become Premier of China early in 1947, is a large, amiable and patient man with the reputation of being a "fixer" in domestic politics—a Chinese Jimmy Byrnes. It had been his thankless task, as Foreign Minister from 1935-1937, to negotiate with the Japanese and stall for time; to hold them off from swallowing all North China while avoiding war, to take the rap when impatient students called for an end to appeasement before China was prepared to resist the aggressor. Like Byrnes in his dealings with Russia, Chang Chun finally took a firm stand and refused to budge, so that the negotiations collapsed. Later it had been Chang Chun who prepared the way for Chiang Kai-shek and the National Government when they were forced to retreat to the southwest following the fall of Hankow. The semi-independent war lords and landowners of Szechwan had not been at all partial to the establishment of the National Government's authority over them. Chang Chun, as Governor of Szechwan from 1940, had been successful in asserting the Central Government's control and transforming this fertile province into the main base of Free China.

Talking to him in Chungking, I realized that his experience in negotiating with the Japanese had fitted him for his present task. China's problem now is basically the same as before 1937: that of holding off their foreign aggressors while bending every effort toward weaning the Chinese agents or dupes away from their foreign allegiance. From 1935 to 1937 Chang Chun had managed to prevent the complete breakaway of the northern provinces under the "autonomous" regimes set up by Japan. Now he had to try to prevent the Communists, who held most of North China, from bringing these provinces into the Soviet sphere. To achieve this, it was worth while making great concessions to the Communists, as formerly it had been worth while treating the northern war lords or puppets with the utmost consideration in order to keep them at least nominally under the control of the Central Government.

Foreign Minister Wang Shih-chieh, who is also a patient man and one ready to bear the brunt of popular misunderstanding in carrying out a difficult policy, told me that the government was making "a real and dangerous test of Communist sincerity." What he did not say, but was implied in his conversation, was that the government had had no choice but to make the test, since the United States had exerted the necessary pressure by the double threat of withdrawing American forces from China and refusing a loan to China. When I asked him if he thought that General Marshall would now press the Communists also to make concessions, he replied:

"What pressure can the United States exert? In General Stilwell's day America still had the bargaining power of Lend-Lease, but today she no longer has it. Today the United States has no means to exert pressure on either the Soviet Union or the Chinese Communists."

The arguments in the P. C. C. centered around the composition and powers of the new State Council which was to supersede the National Defense Council in the proposed coalition government to be set up pending the convocation of a National Assembly to draw up a new constitution. The Communists and their allies in the Democratic League fought for the right of a one-third minority in the State Council to veto the actions of the President. After long debate it was finally agreed that on all important questions the acts of the Executive must be approved by a three-fifths majority of the State Council.

Since the State Council was to be composed of twenty Kuomintang members and twenty from the other parties, the Kuomintang had agreed to let itself be overruled by a minority. Chiang Kai-shek's powers as President would have been severely curtailed. Should the alliance between the Communists and the Democratic League continue they would together be able to hamstring the Administration.

The final agreements on these and other matters were announced to the public in a solemn final session over which Chiang Kai-shek presided. It was an impressive sight, and few of us present will ever forget hearing Chou En-lai shout, "Long live the *San Min Chu I!*" at the close of the meeting.

Had words meant what they said, the long conflict between those who had inherited Sun Yat-sen's mantle, and those who had formerly repudiated his principles in favor of Lenin's, had ended. China was, at long last, to know peace. Together they had brought about the annulment of the "unequal treaties" and fulfilled the first of Sun's principles. Now they had to implement the other two: livelihood of the people and democracy. For a moment that winter evening, in the dim light of the conference hall, with the rain falling steadily outside, one could almost believe that it was not a farce played out for America's benefit, but a solemn burying of hatchets and a true reconciliation.

Unfortunately for China, nothing fundamental had been settled. The really knotty problems had not been solved. The Communists still had their private army and their autonomous area, and the two sides still held entirely different views as to the path which China ought to tread. The coalition government which it had been agreed to set up would have been even more impotent than the present one. The strong minority position won by the Communists and their allies would have enabled them to cripple the administration, and the State Council would have resembled a United Nations Assembly. The real liberals, as before, would have been crushed between the upper and nether millstones of reaction and Communism.

The Kuomintang Government, although ready to let its powers be curtailed, would not relinquish them. So the Communists were not satisfied. They were uneasy concerning the continuance of their alliance with the Democratic League. They knew that its leaders, once they had acquired jobs in the government through the alliance with the Communists, might abandon their erstwhile allies. Thus the Communists were not at all confident that they had won a sufficiently strong position from which "to bore from within" a democratic government. It had not even been decided how the twenty non-Kuomintang seats in the State Council were to be allocated. In the months that followed the P. C. C. paper agreements the Communists accordingly started to insist on a minimum of fourteen seats for themselves in the State Council, since only thus could they be sure of their veto power in a coalition government.

Although the Communists were soon to show that they would not honor the P. C. C. Agreements it was the ruling Kuomintang Party which had made all the real concessions both in the military truce and in the political negotiations. The Communists had gained a great deal and given up nothing.

Previously Chiang Kai-shek had been adamant in insisting that the Communists give up their private army before being admitted into a coalition government. Now at Marshall's insistence he had agreed to let "democratization" of the government precede the nationalization of the Communist armies.

As one of the Chinese Central News reporters said to me at the time: "Thanks to the United States, the Communists have won their greatest victory to date at negligible cost. After two decades during which they tried to seize power by armed force they are to be installed in the government without it being required of them that they first abolish their autonomous 'Border Governments,' or their independent currency, or their private army; or that they cease suppressing civil liberties and liquidating all opposition in the territories they control. True that the Generalissimo said at the final meeting that the Communists would be expected to respect the rights of others to the liberties they claim for themselves. But who believes that any such assurance from the Communists is worth a nickel?"

Were the Communists "not real Communists;" were they the "liberal agrarian reformers" that they are pictured to be in innumerable American articles and books, there is little doubt that they would have settled down peacefully to exploit their gains and win power in China through the democratic process. Instead, at the end of February, they broke the truce and made their bid for control of Manchuria and North China.

In January and February 1946 the Chinese Government passed up a big chance to put its case before the world and counteract Communist propaganda. Most of the correspondents wanted to give the facts to the public, and were ready to judge the government's case on its merits. But they could get practically no information from the Ministry of Information or the Foreign Office or the Kuomintang representatives in the P. C. C. They were thrown back on the opposition as the only source of news.

The Democratic League, at least insofar as news was concerned, believed in democracy and did not worry about the supposed secrecy of the P. C. C. negotiations. Since it was in alliance with the Communists, this meant that the news available came almost entirely from antigovernment sources. It is a proof of the fairness of most of the American correspondents at that time that their dispatches were impartial, analytical, and by no means as one-sided as their sources of information.

On our way back to the Press Hostel after one of our nightly visits to Democratic League headquarters, George Weller said to me: "We don't want to get all our information from Lo Lung-chi and the Communists, but what can we do? The Ministry of Information won't, or can't, tell us anything."

I repeated this remark a few days later to Foreign Minister Wang Shih-chieh at a lunch I had with him alone.

"Surely," I said, "even if you can't speak out in public either about the negotiations with the Communists or about Manchuria and what the Russians are doing to you, you could give *some* information off the record. The American correspondents now are not Communist fellow travelers. They are honest men whose word you could trust. Wherever their sympathies may lie, they want to get at the truth and give it to the American public. Why don't you at least tell them the facts privately? That is what any other government would do. There are at the least half a dozen American correspondents whom you could trust not to quote you directly, men like Steele, Durdin, Weller, Spencer Moosa, and also Gordon Walker of the *Christian Science Monitor*. Your one hope to withstand Russian aggression is to let the American public know the facts. Why are you passing up this opportunity?"

His answer gave me an inkling of how the Chinese had felt about the flood of propaganda directed against them in the preceding years. "Yes," he said, "I suppose we are making a mistake in thinking that all American correspondents are biased against us and in favor of

Communism. But during the past few years it just seemed useless to talk to them."

My little speech had an immediate effect. For shortly afterward Wordless Wu actually did give out one bit of information to the correspondents. It had been reported a few weeks before that General Tu Li-ming, commander of the Nationalist forces in Manchuria, had said that the Russian general had forbidden American correspondents to come there. The Russian press had at once howled "lies" and "slander," and the Chinese had been forced to accept the blame for the refusal to let the Americans in. Now, at last, Wu admitted that General Tu Li-ming had spoken the truth.

Wordless Wu was a friendly, energetic and amiable man with an extraordinarily healthy appetite, as I discovered when I lunched with him in his office and we went through six courses of European food. He was a little dynamo who worked hard and always found time to talk to any correspondent who came to see him. Unfortunately for himself and us he was not allowed to talk about anything that mattered. All the correspondents liked him and sympathized with him to the extent of avoiding embarrassing him in public with questions he obviously could not answer. He was physically fearless, as shown by his behavior as mayor of Chungking during the worst bombings when he dashed around directing the fire fighters and relief workers. But as a diplomat he found discretion the better part of valor. I found him of less use as a source of information than other ministers and Kuomintang officials whom I reached by the simple method of calling and leaving my card.

K. C. Wu was too afraid of showing favoritism to render me much assistance. I secured my personal interview with the Generalissimo through other channels.

On this first occasion, however, I found that K. C. Wu had carefully arranged an "exclusive" interview of ten minutes each for every correspondent that same afternoon. So we naturally joined up and had a general press conference.

Two weeks later in Shanghai on my way north, I met the Gimo and Madame for an hour alone. Most of what they said to me was off the record, but, at least, it proved to me that Chiang Kai-shek is under few illusions. He certainly had not miscalculated the risks China was taking in throwing in her lot with America, and he is well aware of the subtlety of Russia's methods. It seemed to me that he did not fully appreciate the connection between United States foreign policy and American domestic politics, but it may be only that his extraordinary patience gave him the courage and self-control to wait for the turn of the tide in American public opinion, and that this explains why he expressed no resentment at American actions harmful to him and his government.

Before meeting her in Chungking I had feared that Madame Chiang would not be so friendly to me as she had been in Hankow when I met her frequently. For in *China at War* I had frankly criticized her and her closest friends in the New Life Movement. But, when I entered the room with the other correspondents, she greeted me warmly, although her first remark hardly pleased me. "Miss Utley," she exclaimed, "I did not recognize you for a moment, you have grown so much fatter!" In 1938 I had been thin from walking miles in the summer sun at the pace set by Chinese soldiers; also I was not then long out of Russia where food had always been short. Her remark was only too true and I knew also that in China her words would not be considered uncomplimentary. So I answered by telling her she looked lovelier than ever. It did in fact seem to me that the years of suffering which she personally, as well as China, had undergone had given her face a new beauty. Her eyes were kinder and although as elegantly dressed as ever she gave less of an impression of being a fashionable Shanghai lady or the chairman of a woman's club in the States.

She kept me behind for a talk after the Generalissimo's press conference and her conversation gave substance to my impression that she was now less hard and sure of herself and more like her sister Madame Sun. Not that she could ever let her heart run away with her, and be blind to political realities. She showed the keen discernment of old concerning both the international situation and Chinese politics, but she spoke of the death and suffering she had seen with feeling and in terms of humanity, not national pride.

She was in a soft mood and talked mainly of the moderating influence women could exert. She thought that men were more acrimonious and prone to suspect political attacks in the acts and words of their opponents.

Referring to the P. C. C. negotiations with the Communists, she said, "People should believe in one another until insincerity is proved. I have seen too much war and death not to want to try everything possible to avoid more bloodshed and suffering."

In 1938 she had been irreconcilably hostile to the Communists and more distrustful of them than her husband. Now she was all in favor of seeking an understanding with them on the assumption that they meant what they said.

I wondered how much her changed views and attitude were due to the failure of the West, to which she belonged in education and religion, to respond to her eloquent appeals for aid to China until too late and in too small measure. Or whether it was her personal troubles which had mellowed her.

Whatever the real reason for her separation from her husband for the best part of two years—whether it was personal or a political gesture repudiating her Western influence—Madame Chiang's illness in America had been real. Her overstrained nerves had caused physical disorders. She was now quite recovered, but she would never again be quite the same confident, ebullient First Lady of China I had known in 1938.

In Hankow days the difference in age between Chiang Kai-shek and his wife had been hardly apparent. Now he looks elderly beside her. He is as slim and erect as ever and his eyes still give an impression of intense vitality, but he is now almost bald and the bony structure of his face is more pronounced. In Chungking he was in military uniform, but the morning I talked to him in Shanghai he wore a black silk gown and looked more like a scholar than a soldier.

In his replies in Chungking to questions concerning the P. C. C. Agreements he emphasized that it was not a question of the degree of power to be relinquished by the Kuomintang, but of responsibility. The Kuomintang Party had not given up its responsibility for the reconstruction of China, but henceforth it would share it with other parties. Asked whether he would be a candidate for President in the elected government to be set up after the convening of the National Assembly, he replied that "as soon as the power to govern is restored to the people," he would have accomplished his task and ended his responsibility to China.

Some who heard Chiang that day wondered whether he meant he would take no responsibility for the situation which would be created if the Left opposition had its way and the State Council would be able to veto the acts of the Executive, or whether he was in fact anxious to relinquish the heavy burden of responsibility and duties he has carried so long. He gave an impression of being tired, as no doubt he was after the weeks of negotiation and discussion which had just ended. It may be that he is tired in a deeper sense: weary of the ungrateful tasks history has assigned to him.

In 1938 when I met Chiang Kai-shek for the first time I had written of his aloofness, his serene confidence and pride and the inscrutability of his lean countenance and firm mouth set in an almost sardonic half-smile. His deep black eyes had then seemed to me those of a man whose human feelings had been completely subordinated to his conception of his destiny; neither cruel nor sympathetic, almost unhuman and completely unrevealing of his personality.

Now, nearly eight years later, his smile was less tight-lipped and his manner easier. One no longer felt one ought to stand at attention in his presence. He seemed both more human and more melancholy. That dark winter afternoon in Chungking, seated beside Madame Chiang in their home and talking almost informally, he might have been trying to draw closer in understanding to us all.

Perhaps he longed to be able to penetrate the invisible wall between him and the foreigners who write about him; a wall erected not so much by the barrier of language as by background, traditions, history and values.

Very few people have ever become intimate with the Generalissimo, and it is to be doubted whether even they know the real mind of this enigmatic personage. But one thing is certain: he sincerely believes in his mission as Sun Yat-sen's heir and successor to unite China and make her strong and free.

Some of the statements which are interpreted by his enemies and critics to show his overweening arrogance and love of power are in fact the reflection of his belief that he is the symbol and the instrument of China's regeneration. In Hankow, he had said to me, "Wherever I am, there is the center of national resistance." Proud words, but also a correct estimate of what his name had come to symbolize.

Whatever his defects and shortcomings, Chiang Kai-shek must be accounted a sincere follower of Sun Yat-sen. His beliefs and actions are founded on the same belief in China's ancient traditions and ethical values. He became a Christian after marrying Mei-ling Soong, but his conversion seems to have been merely a recognition of the similarity between Christian teachings and the traditional ethics of the Chinese people. In moments of gravest danger, trouble and doubt, he turns to Confucius, as when just before the fall of Hankow he said:

> The men of old when they wished their virtues to shine throughout the land, first had to govern their states well. To govern their states well, they first had to establish harmony in their families. To establish harmony in their families, they first had to discipline themselves. To discipline themselves, they first had to set their minds in order. To set their minds in order, they first had to make their purpose sincere. To make their purpose sincere, they first had to extend their knowledge to the utmost. *Such knowledge is acquired through a careful investigation of things. For with things investigated knowledge becomes complete.* With knowledge complete the purpose becomes sincere. With the purpose sincere the mind is set in order. With the mind set in order there is real self-discipline. With real self-discipline the family achieves harmony. With harmony in the family the state becomes well governed. With the state well governed there is peace throughout the land.

At the same time that he calls upon his people to drink at the ancient founts of wisdom, Chiang always emphasizes the "revolutionary" character of the Kuomintang Party which he leads. In the days of doubt and despair when Hankow was abandoned he said:

> We have been resisting in order to complete the task of our revolution, and our fighting power will remain unimpaired if our revolutionary principles are kept intact. Foreign opinion attaches too great importance to the defense of the Wuhan cities; the experiences of this year of resistance show that our political and military center is in our people and not in territory.

Although America is China's best friend among the Powers, Americans are least fitted by their own background and history to understand China's situation. Educated Europeans all know that no nation in the modern world came out of medievalism to national consciousness without strong rulers who were the fulcrum of unity, and allegiance to whom was the earliest form of patriotism. In England the national anthem is still "God Save the King." Although the King is powerless and the British Government as democratic at home as that of the United States, the King is still the symbol of the nation and love of country.

The overthrow of the Manchu dynasty in 1911 and the birth of the Chinese Republic did not lead China to democracy but to war-lord rule. Sun Yat-sen knew that a period of "tutelage" was essential before the Chinese people could rule themselves, and also a necessity if China were to win her independence as a nation. He did not foresee that endless wars and dangers would prolong the period of party dictatorship so long that the Kuomintang would lose its reformist savor. Circumstances, not will, are responsible for Chiang's unenviable position of being a dictator without the power to dictate; having less real power than the elected President of the United States, while yet having to bear all responsibility in a country still medieval in organization, economic development and thought.

Since every American who has become at all intimate with the Generalissimo is convinced of his sincerity, I see no reason to doubt that he meant what he said to General Hurley:

> If when I die I am a dictator I will certainly go down into the oblivion of all dictators. If on the other hand I succeed in establishing a truly stable foundation for a democratic government, I will live forever in every home in China.

It would nevertheless be difficult for Chiang personally to become the leader of a democracy. He is too aloof and austere and cannot make speeches with human appeal. One of the few foreign diplomats in Chungking who had come exceptionally close to intimacy with him, told me how he had urged Chiang to make a few speeches of the kind which would endear him to Americans. But he cannot act out of character. His qualities are of the order of the great figures of European medieval history who united their countries and made them into nations, not those of a popular leader in the modern world. He has more in common with Edward I or Henry VII of England, or even with Cardinal Richelieu of France, than with a Roosevelt. On the other hand, he is not in the least like the European dictators of our era. His integrity and his inability or unwillingness to make demagogic appeals to passion, prejudice and stupidity, and the fact that he never rants or boasts, mark him off from Hitler, Stalin and Mussolini. His Puritanism and his emphasis on virtue are more reminiscent of Cromwell.

The tortuous methods by which Chiang Kai-shek has pursued his aims, his ability to keep silent even when misunderstood, his unhuman patience in playing for time against Japan, his simple and unostentatious manner of living, and his loyalty to his friends are all Chinese characteristics. His ability to concentrate on vital issues, his energy and swiftness of action and his ruthlessness and determination in pursuit of his aims distinguish him from most of his countrymen. Exceedingly stubborn, he yet knows when he must bow to the popular will. He has condemned thousands to death, as when he massacred the Communists and their allies in 1927, but he is also capable of a statesmanlike forbearance, and in his later years has sought to reconcile his enemies instead of killing them.

Chiang's great weakness as a ruler would appear to be his reluctance to admit persons of individuality to office unless they are his personal friends, and his loyalty to old companions of revolutionary days which he carries to extreme lengths. He keeps them in office not only after they have outlived their usefulness, but when they themselves wish to retire. He is also too prone to believe that even a corrupt subordinate can be reformed by lectures on virtue.

Private virtues are often public vices. Chiang Kai-shek's loyalty to friends and associates leads him to intervene to protect incompetent or corrupt subordinates when it would be far better for him to let Chinese politics take their own course—to let obvious faults be corrected through public discussion and "impeachment" of his ministers. For instance, when in 1947 Dr. T. V. Soong, Wang Shih-chieh and Governor Chen Yi of Formosa (who had ruled his island abominably) were attacked, Chiang Kai-shek intervened, took personal responsibility for their acts and so hushed the public outcry. In some cases he may be throwing his mantle over a good man, such as Wang Shih-chieh, who has in fact merely been carrying out orders. But even so it would be far better if he let the cleansing wind of public opinion blow through his administration and eliminate the men who have lost public confidence.

Perhaps the truest estimate I heard of Chiang Kai-shek was the one pronounced by the learned historian Fu Ssu-nien, who was a non-party representative in the Political Consultative Council in Chungking.

"Chiang Kai-shek," he said, "is like the hero of a Greek tragedy. His strength is also his weakness. The qualities of character which brought him to greatness and enabled him to save China in the war against Japan, are the reverse of those required to set us on the road to democracy."

A liberal Chinese editor expressed a similar view. "The Generalissimo," he said, "has a great love for China and is eager to bring her to peace and greatness. But his background, his knowledge and his views prevent him from achieving his goal.

"Unfortunately there are few people who can ever convince him that he is wrong. It is difficult for anyone to convince him because he is so sure of himself. So he is surrounded by 'yes men' who keep him in ignorance of the true state of affairs.

"Moreover, Chiang considers that Sun Yat-sen's Three Principles of the People are all he needs to know; he believes them to be immutable and perfect. Actually the *San Min Chu I* are not perfect and should be revised. But it is heresy to say so.

"Mao Tse-tung," continued this critic, "is much better educated politically than Chiang Kai-shek but he cares far less about China. If only Chiang had Mao's political understanding, or if Mao had Chiang's patriotism, China would not now be wasting the best opportunity ever given to her to become free and strong and prosperous."

The most frequent criticism one hears in China, from both friends and enemies of the Generalissimo, is that he is surrounded by bad advisers who shut him off from knowledge of real conditions in China; that he too rarely meets those who are bold enough to speak to him as an equal; and that it is almost impossible for anyone outside the official hierarchy to approach him.

General Wedemeyer told me how, on the occasion of Chiang's first visit to Shanghai after its liberation, he had planned a dinner at which the Generalissimo should meet some Chinese whom the American commander thought to be among the best men he knew. When his list of guests was submitted, General J. L. Huang of the New Life Movement struck out the names of all who were not in Chiang Kai-shek's inner circle.

Nevertheless General Wedemeyer paid the following high tribute to Chiang Kai-shek in a speech delivered months after he left China. On October 10, 1946, he said in New York:

> There are few people who could speak more authoritatively than I do this evening, concerning the sincerity, high moral purpose and Christian humility of Generalissimo Chiang Kai-shek. I had frequent, practically daily, contacts with him for approximately two years. I can attest to his unselfish devotion to the Chinese people and to his earnest desire to provide a democratic way of life within China. I am confident that if he were given our realistic and continued support during this critical period of postwar readjustment he would evolve a solution to the political and economic problems, and implement a program of political freedom, social reforms, and sound economy.

CHAPTER VI

The Fascination of Yenan

THE flight from Peking to Yenan in the early morning of a winter's day was sheer beauty. Passing swiftly over endless ranges of hills and mountains without sign of human habitation, the sky above pale blue and the banks of clouds ahead rosy in the dawn, one found it easy to imagine oneself flying over the top of the world to Shangri-la.

Perhaps the fascination of Yenan is partly due to the universal longing which made James Hilton's *Lost Horizon* popular. His vision of a haven of wisdom to the west of China may have prepared the mass of Anglo-American readers for a real-life lost valley of virtuous and happy men in the Chinese hinterland. Is not the dream of an El Dorado beyond the oceans or the high mountains as old as civilized man?

My fellow passengers were all Chinese Communists, returning to their homes from duty with Executive Headquarters and its truce teams. The plane was, of course, a United States Army one, placed at the disposal of the Communists as part of America's effort to bring peace to China through reconciliation and conciliation. It was loaded with bicycles and packing cases containing other products of capitalist civilization. The man next to me, a smiling broad-faced general, took off his two gold stars and put them in his pocket just before we landed. In Peking the Communists put on the insignia of military rank, but not in Yenan.

With the Communist capital in sight below, I experienced a growing sense of embarrassment. I was not afraid, but I was nervous. It was awkward to come as a guest among those whom I had criticized and denounced as agents of Moscow.

I ought to have known better. I might have guessed that Chinese courtesy would prove equal to the occasion. Indeed the combination of Celestial good manners with Communist mastery of the art of propaganda, and the visible evidence of good works, might have overwhelmed anyone who had never lived in Russia and learned into what a valley of despair Communist materialism can lead a people.

I had not been in Yenan twenty-four hours before I began to understand why so many American correspondents have fallen for the Chinese Communists as the hope of unhappy China. Although the city was to be captured by the Nationalists a year after my visit, it is still today the symbol, if no longer the capital, of Communist China.

After Chungking Yenan seemed a primitive paradise—the contrast was similar to that between the slums of New York and a sunny valley in Arizona. In Chungking it is hot in summer, rainy and foggy in winter and comfortable never. Sweating coolies toil up its steep streets, bending under endless loads human and inhuman. In Chungking, Nanking and Shanghai there is the ever present contrast between extreme and comparative wealth. The air is shrill with factional controversy. Men are forever debating, wrangling and railing against the government.

In Yenan, in the wild and mountainous northwest, the skies are blue and the air is sweet to breathe. It is a lovely place, a remote valley set among high hills honeycombed with caves. An ancient pagoda and the crumbling walls of the original city bombed into nothingness by the Japanese in 1938, are the only reminders of the past. Nearly everyone dresses alike in gray padded cotton or in sheepskin coats. All live in caves or in huts built of mud and straw. There are no rickshaws and no automobiles; no ladies dressed in silks or men in long gowns. Mongol ponies and mules, instead of coolies, carry the loads, or climb the mountain paths with healthy-looking peasants on their backs.

Smart Red Army men in khaki guard the homes of the Communist leaders, but the latter live almost as sparsely as everyone else. The austerity of the landscape and the clean dry air fortifies the impression of simple living and high endeavor.

"You have come," was the sardonic greeting of an American attached to the Yenan Observer Group, "to the largest boy scout area in the world." Everyone is doing good or thinks he is. Everyone praises the government instead of cursing it. Nobody argues. The structure of life is simple, primitive and seemingly equalitarian.

Superficially the comparison seems all in favor of the Chinese Communist area. One has to look deeper before pronouncing a fair judgment.

Yenan was as shut away from the outside world in thought and knowledge as it is geographically. The circle of hills which surrounds it is no higher than the political wall which prevented the people of this so called "Border Region" from hearing any news or views except those which their rulers wished them to hear. There was one newspaper; one radio station; and one party; and they all said the same thing. If anyone disagreed his voice was extinguished.

In Kuomintang China there are almost as many factions as in France; there are nearly six hundred newspapers, including Communist dailies, and at least half the press opposes the government half the time. In Communist China there is no opposition. The reason was explained to me by Chiang Lung-chi, the president of Yenan University. I had asked him what would happen to a student who questioned the basic policies of the Chinese Communist Party or argued that it was betraying China's interests to Russia.

"Would you put him in a concentration camp or merely expel him from the University?"

Chiang smiled. "We should do neither—we should reason with him and explain to him that his views are incorrect."

"And if he still disagreed?"

"There is only one truth and since youth is always on the side of truth there can be no disagreement."

Here I thought is the root of the matter. These people for all their claim to be liberals are just the same as the Russian or other Communists. They believe that they, and only they, are in possession of absolute truth. From this belief all the subsequent curses of totalitarian tyranny eventually must flow. In Communist China there is fraternity but no liberty. Anyone who opposes Communist policy on major issues, or denies its fundamental tenets, rejects "Truth." A heretic is *ipso facto* a "fascist" or an "enemy of the people."

No doubt President Chiang Lung-chi is a good man and a sincere man, but so, I suppose, was Torquemada. So also was Charles the First of England who preferred to be beheaded rather than to deny the Divine Right of Kings to order what is best for the people, whether the people liked it or not.

Some of my friends back in Chungking and Shanghai had thought that I would never be allowed to visit Communist China. Others had feared for my safety. As it turned out the Communists made great capital out of my visit. At once they went on the radio to proclaim that in contrast to Chungking which had refused to let the Left Wing Edgar Snow back into China*, they were welcoming the anti-Communist Freda Utley.

In Chungking a little while before, when there had been a last-minute hitch in my securing a permit from the Communists to visit Yenan, George Weller had remarked, "No. I can't believe it. If they refuse to let you in, Freda, I shall begin to be as sorry for the Communists as I am for K. C. Wu. But I just can't believe they will be that stupid; I am sure you will find there has been some mistake and you will be allowed to go."

As regards my safety, I was treated like a piece of porcelain. Every time I climbed the steep hillside to visit one or another cluster of the cave dwellings in which most institutions were housed, my guide and interpreter would take me by the arm lest I stumble and fall. One day I protested that after all I was not so very old; that I really needed no help.

"But," was the reply, "we have to take special care of you."

"You mean," I said, "that you are afraid that if I slip I might accuse the Communists of trying to make away with me?"

My relationship with my Communist hosts was by this time established on such personally friendly terms that we both laughed.

On this occasion we were leaving Yenan University on a gray and chilly afternoon. The path was muddy and very slippery and I was in fact a little tired after the long climb up to the "battlements" where the students' dormitories opened on a ledge high up on the hillside. I had inspected many rows of caves, whitewashed and clean, each with its six or eight plank beds set close together. The bedding was clean and neat, and there was no sign of personal possessions save a shirt or two hung on the walls. Students reading. Students writing. Students playing cards. Boys and girls hardly to be distinguished from one another since they all wore the same trousers and tunics. The girls had bobbed hair and their faces were rosy and happy. In

* Edgar Snow was readmitted to China a few weeks later.

one cave there was an old man with a beard—not a teacher—a peasant come from his village to study accounting. The caves were very cold and rather dark although their flimsy wood and paper doors stood open.

As I walked along, the whole student body left its books or its games to follow me. They talked but I could not understand. Feeling a little shy I stopped to ask my interpreter to tell me what was written on the big blackboard at the end of the row of caves. It was the text of the truce agreement with the National Government signed the previous month. There followed an exhortation to the students to study all the harder now that the Communists must prove their superior worth in a new and united democratic China. In the past, it was written, most Communists had been engaged in armed struggle. Now they must learn peaceful methods for advancing their cause—as for instance how to make speeches in the National Assembly.

Yet the university was half empty because many students, I was told, were "at the front." This meant that they were either still fighting the National Government forces or helping to organize new Communist regimes by military occupation.

Next day I visited a nursery school given over to some seventy tots, aged two to seven, sons and daughters of Red Army men at the front and of party officials. All were warmly clad, well fed and happy. They were also very bright and very charming. They put on quite a show for me and for the United States Army sergeant who had driven me over. They dressed up and fought mock battles with wooden guns. They danced, and they sang:

> Today we are only children.
> Tomorrow we shall be the masters of China.

They sang:

> We are little Eighth Routers.
> We love liberty from birth.
> To anyone who oppresses us
> We show a fist.

And they all shook their little fists with a sweet belligerency

They sang also a song about a poor little boy who could not study because he was so starved in Kuomintang China; and of how he came to Yenan and is now happy with the other children and well up in his grade.

Afterward the children clustered around their teacher. They loved her and they would obviously have been just as happy singing songs about flowers and fairies. I photographed them together with Sergeant Brooks, who was enchanted by their performance. For him there were no shades of the Russian prison house to mar the fascination exerted by a group of happy, clean and clever, well-cared-for babes, whose condition contrasted so sharply with that of the waifs and beggars of China's big cities. Yet I had seen children just as happy and well cared for in Madame Chiang's orphanages. With my memories of the Soviet Union, I also realized that show places in the Communist world are only for a minority of favored children.

It was in this children's home that I first heard of Hollywood's contribution to Yenan. Above the gates were the letters "L. A." The head teacher explained to me that since 1943 the school had received clothing and a substantial annual money contribution from Los Angeles. This was the source of the pretty pale-pink flannelette underwear which had been used for fancy dresses in the children's play. Later I was to learn that the donations of Hollywood's wealthy Communist sympathizers constituted a considerable item on the credit side in Yenan's over-all budget.

Most authors and correspondents who have visited Yenan say little or nothing about Communist finances. It had puzzled me how the Communists had maintained an army which they claimed to be fighting the Japanese more vigorously than anyone else was doing, without burdening the peasantry with its upkeep. The afternoon and evening I spent shivering in Yenan's Guest House talking to an official of the Finance Bureau, the mystery was explained. He frankly admitted that prior to 1941 seventy percent of the revenue of the Chinese Communist administration had been contributed "from outside." "From foreign friends, in particular in Los Angeles; and from the National Government which supplied the pay of the Eighth Route (Communist) Army."

It should be noted here that the impact of a single American dollar was tremendous in the bankrupt pauperized chaos of the wartime Chinese economy. One United States dollar provided exchange between Nationalist, puppet, Communist, Russian, Manchukuoan, and

Japanese territory far beyond its purchasing value in the United States. At the low point of the war, in the fall of 1944, the United States dollar was equivalent to 200 C. N. (Nationalist currency) dollars, and one C. N. dollar was exchangeable for eight Communist (Shan-kan-ning) dollars. Hence an American contribution of $10,000—a mere bagatelle in Hollywood—meant 16,000,000 Chinese Communist dollars and was a huge contribution in the rustic, policed economy of Yenan.

It had always been obvious to the impartial observer that the heavy burdens placed on the people of Free China by Chiang Kai-shek's government were due to the huge expense of maintaining large armies in the field against Japan. Here I found the Communists themselves admitting, by inference, that their agrarian reforms and the better condition of the peasantry in their areas had been made possible for several years because the people in Kuomintang China were paying for the upkeep of the Communist Army. The admission was all the more significant if one remembers that the Japanese never launched a major offensive against the Communist Northwest after 1939.

On other occasions I had been glad to see my little interpreter, Ling Ching, enjoying the sweets, peanuts and fruit provided for visitors. Evidently he did not belong to one of the higher categories in food allocation and he had a healthy, youthful appetite. That afternoon I was so interested that I got irritated at his halting translation between mouthfuls. My informant, who spoke no foreign language, was a mine of information, and was too absorbed in his subject to realize the political implications of what he told me.

"Until 1941," he said, "it had not been necessary to tax the peasants heavily. The 'Public Salvation Grain Levy' in 1938 had amounted to a mere 10,000 piculs and in 1940 to 90,000. But in 1941 with no further aid from outside of any kind, on account of the blockade, we had to double the grain levy. That year it was set at 200,000 piculs. But this was too heavy a burden on the peasantry."

Evidently the peasants had objected very strongly indeed. For the Communist Party had "listened to the voice of the people" and reduced the levy to 100,000 the following year. The Communist administration could not rely on taxation. It had to expand production.

At this critical time Mao Tse-tung had issued a new slogan: "Everyone work with his hands."

The army, the schools and all other institutions were put under the necessity of working to supply at least a part of the food they consumed.

Every possible inducement was offered to the peasants to increase production. Much wasteland was utilized. Cotton was planted and household spinning and weaving encouraged. Salt was "exported" and cloth "imported" through the blockade into and out of Kuomintang China.

The falsity of the picture of an "inhuman blockade" of the Communists by the Nationalist forces painted by Communist sympathizers in New York was here being admitted to me in Yenan itself. Actually there was so much trade that the National Government customs stations all along reported quite heavy revenues on a wide variety of goods passing between Nationalist and Communist China. The "blockade" pertained only to weapons, military supplies including machinery and radios, and subversive literature. But, of course, those who were shouting loudest about the wickedness of the Kuomintang could not read enough Chinese to follow the financial news in Chinese economic journals or daily papers, and would not have troubled to do so if they could.

When I inquired whether trade was also carried on with the Japanese-occupied areas to the east of the Border Region, I received an astonishing reply: "Very little, because the army of Yen Hsi-shan was between us and the Japanese."

Here again was a curious side light on Yenan whose soldiers were supposed by many Americans to have done nearly all the fighting against Japan in North China. Actually the army to the east, which recognized allegiance to the National Government, had constituted a buffer between the Communists and the Japanese.

Today, I was told, only fifty per cent of revenue is derived from taxation. The rest is supplied by the army's production and that of other government institutions. "The army is seventy per cent self-sufficient and some brigades have even produced a surplus for the government."

From the detailed account I was given of the economy of the Border Region I got a picture of a small self-sufficient community, left very much to its own devices while the Japanese and the government of Chiang Kai-shek fought their big war. Here was a little country which had turned in on itself and won a "battle of production" while its soldier farmers, like the Scottish border raiders of medieval Britain, had engaged, in the period between planting and harvesting, in forays into enemy territory which netted them arms and booty.

During the years 1941 to 1945 the greatest efforts were also made to win over the peasants, artisans and merchants of the Communist-controlled areas. Mao Tse-tung told the party members that they must on no account antagonize nonparty people and must be patient with them when they opposed the orders of the government. There had apparently been a great deal of honest self-criticism and fair dealing with the peasants. As one of the Yenan Communists said to me: "A political party which seeks to win over the whole nation cannot adopt dirty methods or tricks. It is impossible to deceive the people for long."

If he had added, "unless you have control of the radio and the press and have placed an iron curtain between yourselves and the rest of the world," I should have agreed with him.

Even as things are there was some truth in his statement. The Chinese Communists, being a minority in China battling to win power against the established government, have in fact been forced to seek and retain popular support by reforms and a clean administration. The "margin of corruption" compatible with survival is very narrow in their case; very wide in that of the legitimate government.

It was clear from all I learned in Yenan that the Communists had never been confronted with any such insoluble economic and social problems as the National Government. Having neither a large standing army nor city populations to feed, their land-reform program had been easy to carry through.

They created a chain of primitive economic areas run on autarchic lines and used all surplus production for local needs. Since the Japanese held most of the cities, the cutting off of supplies to the urban population could be regarded as a patriotic duty. Nor did the Communists, of course, offer to feed the starving Nationalist professional armies fighting the Japanese in or near Communist-controlled areas.

As Dr. Paul Linebarger has written*: "The resulting surplus gave the Communists local prosperity, while such segmentation brought bankruptcy to the Nationalist economy, wherever it operated at or behind the Japanese front lines, because the Nationalist mercantile

* "The Complex Problem of China," *Yale Review*, Spring, 1947.

and urban system was predicated on China-wide relationships. And the Communists, unlike the Nationalists, had no non-Japanese foreign trade or credit to maintain."

Alternating long conversations and the search for knowledge of the inner workings of the regime with sight-seeing, next day I visited the International Peace Hospital.

At this hospital, where I spent an entire day, I had the impression of being among men wholeheartedly devoted to a humanitarian ideal. I also felt that the doctors there longed for contact with the outside world. Their warm welcome, the almost pathetic efforts they made to show me how sanitary and up-to-date were their methods, their interest and sympathy when I spoke of Bobby Lim and his helpers in Kuomintang China, their desire for books from outside, all moved me profoundly. Most of them were Western-trained and spoke German or French or English, so I could converse with them without an interpreter. With one of them, in particular, I felt completely at ease. A slight, vivacious man, with one of those almost classically beautiful faces one sometimes sees in China, he won me completely with his ready wit, his warm smile and his intense absorption in his work and the well-being of his patients. He had been educated at the Sorbonne in Paris and since I also speak French fluently we could really talk to each other. Moreover he seemed to know me only as the author of *Japan's Feet of Clay* and to be unaware, or not to care greatly, about my political views.

I was reminded of the best men and women I had known in Russia—those who, whatever their inward opinions concerning Soviet tyranny, devoted themselves to their immediate tasks and hoped by their selfless labor for the common good to deny, or compensate for, the evil deeds of the regime they served. I was aware that day, as I had also been in Moscow in years before, that the strength of the Communists lies largely in their ability, even today, to hold the allegiance of men who hate their tyranny but regard it as a passing phase and spend their individual lives laboring to create the good society Lenin dreamed of.

The sun shone brightly that day. The caves where the patients lay on their wooden plank beds were dark and cold but outside it was almost warm in the sun and the sky was blue and cloudless. The walls of the "wards" were whitewashed and clean, and the up-to-date apparatus, supplied by friends abroad, contrasted with the primitive surroundings. There were a number of visitors inside the caves and on the paths all along the steep hillside.

I remember the babies in a row in the maternity caves, and a woman in bed with her baby at her breast and her soldier husband sitting beside her, both of them radiant with happiness. Here was a hospital run entirely by Chinese where the people of this remote mountain region were receiving if not the best care that modern science could give them, at least as good nursing as could possibly be provided in such primitive surroundings.

I climbed up and down and saw everything. It was late afternoon before we had finished the inspection. Before I left, it had been arranged that a nurse would ride over to massage my arm, which I had neglected since leaving Shanghai and which was still far from capable of normal movement. I was also presented with a bottle of liquor, the first I had seen in Yenan. It was pretty awful stuff, probably the same kind of alcohol as specimens are kept in, and a small glass or two produced a terrible headache. But it was a symbol of good cheer and friendship in the austere atmosphere of Yenan.

At sunset I was fetched home in a jeep. "Home" for the time being was the United States Army post where Colonel Ivan Yeaton commanded the American Observer Group composed of three officers and eight enlisted men. Either the personality of the colonel, or the atmosphere of Yenan, or a combination of the two, had dispelled any "morale" problems here. Soldiers enjoying the comforts, amusements and temptations of Shanghai clamored to go home. In Yenan where there were no dance halls, cafés, theaters or shops worthy of the name, there had been two re-enlistments, and everyone seemed happy. Officers and men ate the same simple food side by side in the same mess hall; hunted wild pheasants or climbed mountains together in their liberty hours; and every evening sat down with any Chinese who cared to come to see a movie in "Whittlesea Hall." When the plane bringing mail and supplies twice a month from Shanghai failed to arrive on account of bad weather, they saw the same movies over and over again.

Inside the post compound lived a number of Chinese either working for the United States Army and being trained as mechanics, drivers and radio operators, or acting as interpreters and liaison men between the Americans and the Communist Government. The conditions of living were the same for everyone and hardly differed from those outside. Whitewashed cabins made of mud and straw, trestle beds, and of course, no running water. But we had electricity and showers and our diet included such luxuries as coffee, cocoa and canned fruit, bacon and occasionally meat.

I was told when I arrived that I was the only woman who had ever stayed at the United States Army post. I was in fact the first woman correspondent to come to Yenan since Anna Louise Strong in 1938. Agnes Smedley had gone to stay with the Communist New Fourth Army in Central China when Hankow fell, but had not been in Yenan since the first year of the Sino-Japanese War.

I was afraid I should be a nuisance, but except for the necessity of stationing a sentry outside the bathhouse when I took a shower, there was no inconvenience. It was very much like the Press Hostel in Chungking except that bugles called us to meals and one had to get up early in the morning. The rooms or cabins were smaller, newer, cleaner, and somewhat better furnished than in Chungking. One might better call our habitations cells, for this word conveys something of the monastic atmosphere of Yenan, both in the town and inside the United States Army compound.

Ling Ching, guide and interpreter to visitors, lived next door to me. He was the son of a landowner in Chahar and had studied at Peking University, but he had joined up with the Communists when the Japanese invaders came. Short, thin, with large glasses, and not particularly intelligent, he was a nice earnest conscientious boy, happy and rather naïve. His room contained only a bed, a charcoal brazier, a large desk and some bookshelves. These were filled with Chinese Marxist literature and a very large quantity of American publications. He had accumulated piles of *Life* magazines and many novels in the United States armed forces pocket editions. Maybe he was in process of being corrupted by this "bourgeois literature" and by his nightly attendance at the movie together with the members of the English-language school.

I think I puzzled Ling Ching. He had, no doubt, been told that I was a wicked reactionary and an enemy of progress and peace. Perhaps I did not quite tally with his conception of a fascist warmonger, for I often found him looking at me curiously but not unamiably, and sometimes he asked me questions which displayed a real interest in my opinions. He was obviously not happy about Manchuria for this was the one subject in which he displayed interest after my many interviews.

Ivan Yeaton, who had formerly been United States military attaché in Moscow, was just the right man for his job, which required an expert on Communism, not on China. He was determined that under him the United States Army Observer Group should not show any political sympathies or prejudices one way or another. He forbade all political discussion in the mess and never expressed his political views. Discipline on the post and relations between his men and the local population were alike excellent, but under his command there was no such political fraternization as under his predecessor in General Stilwell's day.

I had known Ivan Yeaton and his wife in Washington but I never tried to ascertain his views on Chinese Communism. I understood that it would embarrass him even to be seen talking to me alone and that the performance of his duties required that he take no one into his confidence. I respected the extraordinary self-control of this exceptional soldier and intelligence officer, whose sole recreation was the ten-mile walk he took alone every morning.

It was, however, clear that apart from the other duties, Ivan Yeaton considered that it was a function of his small command to "sell" American democracy to the people of Communist China. Every man on the post was taught to treat the Chinese with respect and courtesy. There was no drunkenness and no whistling after women. After having witnessed the brutal disregard of pedestrians shown by American jeep and truck drivers in Shanghai, I was pleased to find the GI's in Yenan stopping to let the wild Mongolian ponies pass and getting out to walk rather than drive through the narrow main street of the "town."

It must have been hard for the Communist leadership to convince any of the inhabitants of the "Shensi-Kansu-Ningsia Border Region" that the American Army is an instrument of reactionary imperialism. Whatever the radio and the newspaper may be telling them today, they have seen the comradely relations between officers and men and the polite and considerate behavior of the Americans toward the people of Yenan.

Ling Ching was very conscientious and did not like me to waste a single afternoon or evening without its quota of sight-seeing or conversation. True, there seemed to be certain matters difficult to arrange. When I asked to see factories I was told they were all too far away outside the town, and had to be content with visiting some handicraft shops. Another excuse was made when I wanted to visit the prison. The day I was to have driven over to visit Wu Men-yu, Yenan's "labor hero" of agriculture, the weather was so bad and the snow so thick, everyone said the roads were impassable. On the whole, however, I was given plenty of opportunity to observe and question and look for any rotten wood there might be beneath the socialist veneer.

I saw the Red Army soldiers drilling on the sunlit plain beside the frozen River Yen. I attended a mass meeting of women where, after a report had been given of the party's success in establishing Communist administrations in formerly Japanese-occupied areas, a bespectacled and earnest woman gave a lecture on socialism in the home. Each member of the family, she said, should have his due share of the family income justly apportioned. The hundreds of women present, young and old, ugly and pretty, but all dressed alike in gray padded tunics and trousers, listened attentively, made notes and applauded.

At the end of a week the pattern had become a trifle monotonous. I already knew what I would see and hear at every institution. I had inspected countless identical cave dwellings and heard how everyone, whether he were doctor, nurse, teacher or party worker, received food, clothing and lodging, but no salary. Money was for the undedicated—for the peasants and artisans and shopkeepers.

Americans like Gunther Stein* have commented on the American soldier's surprise at finding Chinese who "ain't interested in money." This seems a remarkable phenomenon until one reflects that in a society where there is almost nothing to be bought, it is natural not to bother about money. How could the average American properly understand a society in which the ruling class got what it needed without paying for it?

Only when I walked through the little town which has sprung up

---

* *The Challenge of Red China.*

outside the walls of the ruined city did I sense unease. In Chungking even the most miserable coolies and street vendors smile. There are color and noise, laughter, quarreling and bargaining, misery and comparative opulence; all the infinite variety of unregimented life and an atmosphere of freedom in spite of all the poverty.

Yenan was like an iceberg in comparison, simple in structure, silent and cold. The storekeepers and the peasants who passed you by looked dour and grim. There was little conversation among the people in the streets. In the shops stocked only with the simplest necessities, and in the huts where artisans ply their trades as in days gone by, one received the barest answer to questions. This could be due to the difference in temperament as between the people of the warm, fertile but overpopulated South and those of the barren Northwest. But perhaps it also reflects the fear which always abides in men's hearts under an authoritarian regime. Having lived in the Soviet Union I know that no foreigner can get to know what people are really thinking under a Communist Government. Where dissatisfaction is regarded as treason who will complain to a stranger? Everyone knows about the "traitors' camps" in the Border Region where so-called "enemies of the people" are imprisoned. This was the shadow over Yenan which otherwise seemed so bright and hopeful.

Tillman Durdin who speaks Chinese, and who is far from being an apologist for the Kuomintang, after he visited Yenan remarked on the contrast between "the frightened people and the confident commissars" in Communist China.

In 1938 I had met that gallant old lady, Mrs. Chao, nicknamed "grandmother of the guerrillas" for the resistance movement against Japan she had led in Manchuria. Her son, who had fought the Japanese ever since 1931, had been shot by the Communists. I had heard of Wang Shih-wei, the Communist writer condemned as a Trotskyist because he had written some articles critical of the Yenan regime, saying that the youth of lower rank were dissatisfied and complained about such matters as "the five categories of food" between the various grades of Communist elite and the mass of the people.

I remembered Lao-shê, author of *Rickshaw Boy,* whom Durdin had taken me to visit in Chungking. In his little earth-floored shack, piled with books and cold as a tomb, he had said, "It's just about the same for a liberal writer in Chungking and in Yenan; maybe a little worse in Yenan. Both sides just want you to do propaganda and obscure realities."

I thought also of Chang Kuo-san, the young Chinese Central News reporter who was a friend of Till Durdin's and with whom I had had long conversations in Chungking. He had graduated a little time before from the Northwestern University, exiled in Kunming. His English was excellent and he had a knowledge of politics and economics which was both theoretical and practical. His qualifications and intelligence in any other country would have assured him a comfortable living. In China he was barely able to support his wife and child and their second baby whose arrival we celebrated just before I left Chungking. Nevertheless he was as anti-Communist as I was, and he told me the contents of letters received by his classmates from their relatives in Communist China. To them Communism was far from signifying the do-good, be-good atmosphere of Yenan. It meant murder and pillage and terror. When I suggested to Chang Kuo-san that he accompany me to Yenan as my interpreter, he had said he would be glad to, but first he must have some guarantee that he would be able to return to Chungking. "Few who have gone there," he said, "ever got out again. A message is sent to your family saying you like it so much in Communist China that you intend to stay. I just daren't risk being held there because of my wife and children."

In Yenan I wished I could speak to the people, alone and in their own language. Not that it would have helped much to understand Chinese. I knew from my Russian experience that no one dares to speak freely under a police regime. Even if the terror in Communist China is far less acute than in Russia, even if the Chinese Communist regime had become comparatively liberal in recent years, the peasants and merchants could not have forgotten the executions and expropriations which marked the arrival of the Red Army in the Northwest.

Already from beyond the "model state" centered in Yenan reports must have come of the forced grain deliveries, executions, and impressment of villagers into the Communist armies fighting the National Government for the control of North China and Manchuria. Even if the Communists had improved the lot of the peasants of the Yenan area, they were vastly increasing the misery of the great mass of the Chinese people by their refusal to stop the civil war.

Many a naïve foreign journalist has accepted as genuine the Chinese Communist claim to have established a democratic government and "free" elections. Two thirds of those elected to public office, they point out, must not be Communists. What they have failed to see is that where only one party is allowed to exist, the electors have no chance to oppose the ruling minority. The power of the people is even weaker than that of unorganized workers trying to bargain with a big corporation. For in Communist China, as in the Communist-dominated states of Eastern Europe, anyone who opposes the Communists is called "antidemocratic," or fascist and loses his liberty or his head.

When I argued with the Communists in Yenan that theirs was a spurious democracy, since neither the Kuomintang nor any other non-Communist party was allowed to function, they replied, "We do not forbid other parties to exist, but, of course, we don't allow Kuomintang 'spies' to come to Yenan."

"In 1944," I was told by the editor of the *Emancipation Daily*, "we had a cleanup of spies of the Japs and the Kuomintang who had tried to corrupt our program."

"Did you shoot them," I inquired, "or give them a trial?"

"No we didn't kill them. Sometimes we gave them a trial."

How simple it is to call a dictatorship a democracy when all who disagree are labeled enemies of the people, spies, traitors, fascists or otherwise undeserving of rights or liberty!

It was impossible for me to judge how great a part was played by fear, and how great a part by faith, in the regimentation of life in Communist China. But it is certain that the individualist Chinese, with their hatred of government interference in their private affairs, cannot easily have adapted themselves to the Communist regime.

The correspondents who have been fascinated by Yenan have accepted the popular, but false, assumption that liberty and equality are twins. Human society is not naturally equalitarian, and without compulsion it cannot be made so. Nor do human beings all think alike and desire the same things, or believe that there is only one Truth—one certain way to create the good and just society which men throughout the ages have longed for.

Few people would themselves like to live regimented, frugal lives possessing nothing that their neighbors do not also possess and striving always for what the government tells them is the common good.

But many people think such a society admirable. This is particularly true not of the worst, but of the best, Americans who have a vivid sense of guilt in foreign lands because they are so much better off and live so much more comfortably than other peoples. In Kuomintang China they feel better after they have denounced the government for the ills which are in fact mainly due to China's scarcity economy and the laissez-faire prejudices of the Chinese people. In Yenan they can reverence a way of life they would find intolerable if they were participants instead of visitors. The temptation to ascribe all the misery in China to the National Government is all the greater because of the Western world's large share of responsibility for China's plight. Emotional young correspondents are glad to forget, if they ever knew, the lasting effects of former European and American oppression and exploitation of China.

In an earlier chapter I have referred to the insidious and wholesale forms which corruption takes in a developed Communist society, in which the ruling class through its monopoly of political power owns everything in the country and can allocate to itself any share it pleases of the national income. In Communist China, however, society is still in too primitive a stage for the weeds of corruption to have stifled the flowers of original intention. Until Japan's surrender the Communists controlled no cities, had practically no industry and were so isolated that money had little value. The members of the Party still set an example of hard work and frugal living. They have not yet been corrupted by power because of their precarious situation and the necessity of retaining popular support. Seeking to win control over the whole country, they are still at the stage of advocating democracy in order to destroy it.

The rank and file have no idea of what the rest of the world is doing and saying and thinking. They never get the chance to read a book or a newspaper or hear a voice on the air, other than those approved of by the Communist Party. They know nothing of the terror, the concentration camps and the gross inequalities of Stalin's Russia. They are unaware that they themselves are but pawns in Soviet Russia's game of power politics.

The sincerity and decency of many of the Chinese Communists were unmistakable. I liked them and respected them all the while that I was conscious of their tragic destiny and the use made of their self-sacrificing lives by forces of whose existence they were completely ignorant. They put me in mind of the unwordly monks of Mount Athos who in the years of grossest corruption in Rome and Byzantium, when Popes fought Emperors for domination over the earth, continued to render an allegiance long since betrayed by the Church itself.

Here in Communist China was the embryo of what Russia might have become had not external opposition, hunger, lust for power and the frailty of man, unsupported by anything but a materialist philosophy, led the Bolsheviks and the people they dominated to the gates of hell instead of to paradise on earth.

Because I was once a Communist who believed that the overthrow of capitalism and imperialism would enable the human race to create the good society of the free and equal, I could not hate the Chinese Communists. I could only pity them. Here in the primitive Northwest, where Chinese civilization began in the dawn of history, the Communists had been trying to re-create in a modern pattern the life of primitive innocence which may, or may not, have existed before "man's first disobedience" condemned humanity to strive forever against one tyranny only to create another. As Goethe once said, Humanity is like a man on a sickbed turning continually from right to left and finding no ease on either side.

When I asked what guarantees there were against future abuses of power, it was suggested that I read a pamphlet by Wang Yen-pei of the Democratic League. The author had been told by Mao Tse-tung that he was confident of the "ability of the people to control the Party." "The Party," said Mao, "was always willing to listen to the criticisms of the masses."

I was told how undisciplined Communist soldiers had been reported by non-Party peasants and taught thereafter to behave themselves, also that when officials had been found "too hasty" or dictatorial in their dealings with the peasants they had been removed or reprimanded. "The difference between us and the Kuomintang," said one of the Moscow-trained and American-educated elite of Yenan, "is that we never squeeze the people in order to enrich ourselves. When we use compulsion it is because some comrades are too eager for the common good."

This statement unfortunately echoed all too loudly in my ears what I had heard in Russia years before. The peasants sent to Siberian concentration camps for resisting collectivization had not been victims of self-seeking corrupt landowners, capitalists or officials. They were supposed to have been sacrificed on the altar of the welfare of the Common Man although in reality they toiled and died to satisfy the insensate ambitions of a man and his party.

When I visited Yenan in February 1946 it was in process of becoming, like Chungking, only a secondary capital. The main activities of the Communists were already directed elsewhere. Their armies and their administrative personnel were spread out through North China setting up other "border governments" in other "liberated areas." They admitted that the control of large cities was producing new problems and required new methods. It was expected that salary payments would soon be substituted for payments in kind. The simple egalitarian society of Yenan seemed doomed to become only a memory even before it fell to the Nationalist Army in 1947. But Yenan remained the symbol of man's hope and man's illusions.

It is a profound mistake to assume that because the Communists of recent years have advocated agrarian reform, free enterprise and "democracy" they are not "real Communists." As the editor of their newspaper in Yenan said to me: "We Communists know how to make turns to reach our goal."

We were sitting talking by candlelight in his small mud cabin, huddled around a charcoal brazier after having dined adequately but not too well. My host, Chien Chun-su, was a small, vivacious, bespectacled intellectual who had been educated in America and spoke excellent English. He welcomed the "new era" about to begin. "The habit of keeping time," he exulted, would be enforced, and "interminable discussions" curtailed. From now on he thought it would be easier to "maintain a united will" than in the years "when the Communist forces were split off from one another."

"Our situation in 1941 and 1942 was precarious," he said. "We were blockaded and the Chungking Government no longer supplied the pay of our army. We had not previously produced enough food in the Border Region to be self-sufficient. It was imperative to increase production. Speeches and theoretical arguments were of no use. We had to teach the people practical things, such as how to increase the yield of the land, how to weave and how to make chickens lay eggs. Comrade Mao Tse-tung told us we must not antagonize the non-Party people. That we should be patient with them even when they disagreed with us. That we must give the masses some rein and convert them by democratic methods. He told us that when you go away from the people, however excellent your intentions, you will lose."

It was clear from his conversation that it was circumstances, not conviction, which had led the Chinese Communists to adopt a more or less liberal policy.

Chien himself had little patience with the people who disagreed. "Sometimes," he said, "we had meetings lasting two months. In the future that will be impractical; in cities, hours, and even minutes, count. We have got to learn the habit of keeping time. Very few of us here even have watches. When we make an appointment, we just say 'after breakfast' or 'in the forenoon.' We have only one newspaper so there is no competition. We are not worried about getting out the news on time. All this has got to be changed. Also these past eighteen years most of us have been engaged in armed struggle either in the army or in underground activity. Now we must learn new methods of advancing our cause."

As I stumbled down the hillside in the dark on my way back to my own mud hut at the United States Army post, I recalled Mussolini's boast about the trains running on time. I also remembered that in Russia there had been a period when the peasants were encouraged to increase production for their own profit and allowed, together with the artisans and small industrialists, to trade on a free market. This N.E.P. (New Economic Policy) period was ended by Stalin in 1929 when the Bolshevik Party considered itself strong enough to crush all internal opposition, force the peasants into so-called collective farms, liquidate all "capitalist elements" and suppress all opposition. After 1929, also, the Russian Communist Party completed its metamorphosis from a group of intellectuals vowed to poverty into a ruling class enjoying not only power but riches. So true it is that without liberty equality soon also disappears.

Lenin wrote of the unequal development of capitalism, contrasting the differences between the young period of free enterprise and liberty and the later period of monopolies and imperialism. The unequal development of Communism has been insufficiently recognized.

In Russia you already have a society of privilege and great inequalities in standards of living. In Communist China you find a society whose rulers have not yet been corrupted by power. Although the Chinese Communists have their own army and since Japan's surrender have begun to rule over large territories, they are still a minority party in China. They could not have existed without popular support and without making concessions to the desires of the people. But there is no guarantee and no likelihood that they, unlike other men, would not be corrupted by power.

All this was in my mind the day I dined with General Chu Teh, commander in chief of the Communist armies. We had spent the forenoon on a set of questions which he answered from a written text in the correct Marxist-Stalinist manner. I had been told to submit my questions in writing, and I was helpless when he skirted around the true content of the awkward ones. In particular he would not be drawn out on Manchuria. I wondered what he really thought but knew there was no chance of finding out and there was no sense in badgering him. Moscow's eagle eye was on him, and there were several high party officials present.

I sensed his relief once the ideological formalities had been disposed of. Now at last we could speak of Yenan, his bailiwick, his domain. Had he and his people not done well? And he eyed me with curiosity, as, with Chinese courtesy, he used his chopsticks to place a few choice morsels on my plate.

I said, "I have been much impressed by what I have seen in Yenan. If only you would cease to play Moscow's game by disrupting Chinese unity, and be Chinese, you would be able to give a lead to all China in the matter of agrarian reform. I cannot forget that Lenin too hoped to establish a society of the free and equal, but look at Russia now—a country of tyranny and terror and concentration camps, bent on imperialistic expansion; with the Communist Party living in luxury while the masses are desperately poor. How can one not fear that you too will take the Moscow road?"

Chu Teh did not argue. He simply stated that the Chinese Communist Party is Chinese and China would follow her own path. But the editor Chien was very angry and said with a sneer, "That's what you think!" I said it was what I had seen and experienced. "Some of us too have been to Moscow," he replied. The concluding remark was unnecessary. It was all too obvious in his case.

I then asked Chu Teh to define the meaning of democracy. He said that it meant free elections, free speech, no secret police or arbitrary arrests.

"How then," I asked, "can you call Russia democratic? There is no free speech; the press is one hundred per cent government-owned; there is an all-powerful secret police; no freedom from arbitrary arrest, and no party besides the Communist Party allowed to exist."

The general was not a good Sophist. The argument was taken over by Yung Hsiung-kuan of the Political Bureau:

"In the Soviet Union all other parties have been liquidated because they were enemies of the people, and the people wanted them to be destroyed. No other party is required because the Communist Party represents the will of the people."

This unequivocal definition of the "New Democracy" shows it to be simply old tyranny writ large. Instead of a king you have the Communist Party claiming to represent the will of the people. Instead of the belief that "the king can do no wrong" you have the axiom that the Soviet Union is always right.

The answer I had been given showed all too clearly that whatever the intentions of battle-scarred veterans like Chu Teh and Mao Tse-tung, their party was headed along the same bloodstained path as Russia and all her satellites. I would have been only too glad to find that the Chinese Communists are democrats, but obviously, like all other Communists, they had merely usurped the word and reversed its meaning.

The road to hell is usually paved with good intentions. My liking for some of the Yenan Communists could not change the fact that Moscow's ideology ruled their thoughts and actions. Once in power in China there was every likelihood that they would become a brutal, tyrannical ruling class. Those who kept their primitive faith would be liquidated as Russia's old Bolsheviks had been.

Those who take to the sword may not always perish by the sword, but after my six years in Soviet Russia I am convinced that social justice cannot be insured by violence, injustice, lawlessness and dictatorship. Not only is there abundant evidence that the Chinese Communist Party leaders have wholeheartedly adopted the same philosophy as the rulers of Soviet Russia; not only do they believe that the end justifies the means and that lying, cheating, political chicanery, cruelty, even murder are the means which must be adopted to win and retain power for the Communist Party, they have already advanced some distance along the same road to tyranny as the Russian Communist Party trod long ago.

In the closing months of 1946 the Chinese Communists started to throw off the democratic mask and to withdraw the iron hand of terror from the velvet glove worn in Yenan. They now no longer appear as reformers or seek to win popular support by moderate policies. As Tillman Durdin reported on February 3, 1947, the Communist land policy in its latest phase represents a sharp departure from the principles which were being propagated by the Yenan leaders during the Japanese War and for a period afterward. This land policy, says the *New York Times* correspondent, "has been carried out with the accompaniment of cruelties and other excesses such as the 'Settle Accounts' trials, executions and some cases of slaughter such as the recent massacre of the residents of the little Catholic village of Tsungli in Chahar."

In a later dispatch, sent from Yenan on March 8, 1947, Durdin reported that in the one third of China they claimed to control, the Communists were proceeding relentlessly with their program of land division, and that they expect to eliminate tenantry completely. "Information available here," he wrote, "indicates that the Communists are effecting the most extensive change of landownership brought about anywhere in the world since the early years of Bolshevik rule in Russia."

The editor of the *Yenan Emancipation News,* my old friend Chien Chun-su, gave Durdin a detailed account of how the process of liquidating landowners is being carried out. It is evidently done by means of the same process as in Eastern Europe. The landlords are "hauled before 'People's Courts' " and charged with some past action harmful to a tenant or a small landholding neighbor.

"When found guilty—and there is no record that any landlord has ever been found innocent—the landlord has properties taken away from him sufficient to meet the demands of his accusers and of the land-division regime."

However, "if a landlord has been 'good,' if he has co-operated with the Communist regime," he gets a "favored status." The mayor of Yenan gave Durdin, as an example, the relatives of Professor Chang Shen-fu of the Democratic League. Since the League is pro-Communist this family had been allowed to retain a large estate of between 200 and 300 acres.

In other words you can ensure yourself possession of your wealth if only you toe the Party line.

According to the claims of the Communists 60,000,000 peasants in North China and Manchuria have acquired farms through the forcible expropriation without compensation of a multitude of small landowners and richer peasants. The Chinese Communists, like the Bolsheviks before them, have already started to solve the agrarian problem by the mass murder of "kulaks."

Hundreds of thousands of refugees from Communist-held areas, the majority of whom are peasants, have flocked into Nationalist territory.

For instance the Reverend Wilfred McLaughlin, an American mission worker from Haichow in Kiangsi, when visiting Süchow in June 1947 reported that 100,000 refugees from near-by Communist territory had come to his district where famine conditions already prevailed largely as a result of confiscation of food stocks by the Communists when they occupied the area.

Many correspondents and authors have stated that they saw no evidence of any link between the Chinese Communists and Moscow. Of course you do not see couriers running back and forth between Moscow and Yenan. But it is glaringly obvious that the Chinese Communists, like Communists everywhere else in the world, steer their course by Moscow's star.

It was while I was in Yenan that the storm broke in China about Russia's looting of Manchuria and failure to hand the territory back to the National Government of China, as she had undertaken to do in the Sino-Soviet Treaty of August 1945. Chungking had for months kept silent concerning Russia's breaking of the treaty, knowing that China was too weak to force the Russians out. Hoping against hope that eventually the Red Army would go home, the Chinese National Government had not even protested Russia's refusal to let its troops land in the port of Dairen.

In February came the breaking point with great student demonstrations in Chungking and Shanghai demanding that Russia give back Manchuria.

This was the first clear test for the Chinese Communists. So long as it was Japan who bullied China, despoiled her and fostered disunity, it was possible to appear to be both a Communist and a patriot. Now with Russia stepping into Japan's shoes, it would be easy to see whose estimate of the Chinese Communists was correct. Were they or were they not Moscow's quislings?

The Yenan newspaper and radio left one with no doubts. The student demonstrations were described as "fascist-inspired" and no single word of censure or complaint was uttered concerning Russia's removal of machinery, rolling stock and food from Manchuria.

One quickly remarked the difference in reaction to the subject of Manchuria as between the "social workers" or "Boy Scout" leaders and the Communist elite. The former were embarrassed, tried to change the subject or showed that they were completely ignorant of what was going on. Not so Chien Chun-su, the editor. Here was a perfectly trained Moscow-orientated twister of words and confuser of issues. One can meet his like in all the Communist Parties of the world. They believe that you can fool a large number of people, for a sufficiently long time to gain your ends, so long as you can confuse your listeners by using words they like for things they hate.

Whenever I tried to pin him down with a clear question on a specific issue, he always eluded me.

"Do you approve," I said, "of the Yalta agreement which enabled Russia to regain all the Czarist privileges in Manchuria lost in the Russo-Japanese War, or voluntarily given up by Lenin?"

"Ah," he said, waving his thin scholar's hand, "you cannot consider something up in the air like that; you must not distort facts by considering them in isolation; you should always grasp what is the essence of a situation, its historical setting and its content. The essence of the Yalta agreement was that it paved the way for the Sino-Soviet Pact. Without Yalta there might have been no pact. Without the pact perhaps no victory. Leave aside meaningless talk of 'Czarist privileges.' That is nonsense. Your whole premise is wrong since the Soviet Union is not an Imperialist Power but a workers' state and has always been our friend. China and Russia must stand together against the danger of Japan's revival. That is the essence of the matter. It was very good of President Roosevelt as middleman to promote friendship between China and Russia. Chiang Kai-shek knew at

Cairo that Roosevelt was going to discuss Manchuria at Yalta, and he is not honest when he afterward expresses surprise."

He added significantly, "We had nothing to do with the pact. We are not in a position to negotiate."

From the final sentence in this jumble of words one might perhaps conclude he meant that only a Communist-controlled China would be in a position to hold its own. A non-Communist China must submit to Russia lest worse befall her.

I pressed him to commit himself as to whether or not he also approved of Russia pressing China for even greater concessions than those provided for in the Sino-Soviet Treaty. He would only reiterate, "I don't believe Russia will do anything against what she signed."

When I remarked that Russia had already broken the treaty by not withdrawing her troops from Manchuria and by trying to blackmail China into giving Russia possession of half the resources there, he said, "We are for the withdrawal of all foreign forces from China."

As regards the looting of Manchuria by the Red Army, he simply said he had no information that this had occurred. If consideration of the "essence" of a fact cannot transmute it into something different, your true Communist will deny the fact's existence.

I was not surprised, two months later, to read that the Yenan radio was categorically denying that the Russians had removed any machinery from Mukden. In the face of all the evidence given by American and other correspondents this was a barefaced lie. But since the inhabitants of Communist China get no news other than that which their rulers wish them to hear they would have no means of ascertaining the truth.

However loyally the Communists might cover up for Soviet Russia it was impossible to believe that men like Mao Tse-tung and Chu Teh did not, in their hearts, resent the wrecking of Manchuria. They must have hoped to inherit its industries as good soldiers of the Red Czar, and have come to suspect that Stalin was no more anxious to see a strong Communist China than a strong Kuomintang, or any other kind of China.

I had no opportunity to form a personal estimate of Mao Tse-tung since an interview was denied me. But as I sat with the burly and amiable Chu Teh, whose name signifies Red Virtue, and whose kindly eyes regarded me with what seemed a questioning, even sympathetic and certainly not hostile regard, I could not believe him to be without inner doubts concerning Moscow's leadership. Here was a man of such strength of character that he had not only given up a life of power and ease and pensioned off his wives and concubines when he joined the Communist Party, but had also cured himself of the opium habit when already in his forties; a man who had come to be a Communist through his sympathy for the downtrodden and by way of Marxist study in Germany and Russia in the early twenties. He belonged to the now almost extinct generation of old-vintage Communists. In Soviet Russia he would undoubtedly have long since been liquidated along with almost all Lenin's old Comrades. Chu Teh, it seemed to me, could not easily accept the role of a Stalin yes man however subservient his replies to questions might sound.

I would have given a great deal to know his real thoughts. Did he think that he had no choice? That he was committed and could not draw back? The Moving Finger had long since written and moved on. The hopes and ideals of twenty years before were dead on both sides. Chu Teh and Mao Tse-tung, even if they wished it, could never be reconciled with Chiang Kai-shek to join with him to save China. Too much blood had been shed, too much hatred and mistrust created. The Kuomintang as well as the Comintern had degenerated, and Chiang Kai-shek was committed to alliance with the Western Powers who still appear to the Chinese Communists as the implacable and cruel imperialists of the past.

Although I realized it was hopeless to expect Chu Teh to reveal his true thoughts, I questioned him closely on Manchuria, asking him to explain how the Chinese Communists, who had always stood for the first of Sun Yat-sen's Three Principles, the integrity and independence of China, could approve of the revival of Czarist Russia's imperialist privileges. His answers were as stereotyped and unconvincing as I had expected. He said that it was "insulting" to speak of the Sino-Soviet Treaty "in the same breath" as Czarist demands on China. Not only was it a vilification of the Soviet Union, but it was also a vilification of America since President Roosevelt had himself sponsored the Sino-Soviet Treaty. He also, no doubt with an inner chuckle, said that he remembered that the world's press had acclaimed the treaty as a "defeat for the Chinese Communist Party." His party, he continued, "had not had the slightest knowledge about the negotiations" but had approved because the treaty was "a safeguard against the recurrence of Japanese aggression and for the promotion of the common welfare of China and the Soviet Union. . . .

"If we compare the close relationship between China and distant America with the provisions of the Sino-Soviet Pact the latter does not seem at all extraordinary."

"You mean," I said, "that the Chinese Communist Party no longer disapproves of exclusive rights in any part of China for any Power?"

Chu Teh dodged the question and replied only that if negotiations were on the "basis of equality" China should sign commercial pacts with other nations.

When, during lunch, I taxed Yung Hsiung-kuan, a leading Communist theoretician, with the fact that the Communists had broken the January truce in which they promised not to contest the occupation of Manchuria by the Nationalist forces, he slipped out from under with more "dialectical" arguments.

"We do not object," he said, "to National troops coming to Manchuria to take over. But the settlement of the method of reoccupation is a matter of internal politics. The National Government's idea is to do away with all the people's forces and popular administrations set up there. The local popular forces in Manchuria recognize the Central Government but the latter must also recognize their status."

In effect this meant that, so long as the Communist forces arrived in Manchuria out of uniform (as they had in fact done) to organize local Communist administrations, they had not broken the truce.

The *Emancipation Daily* and the Communist News Service, as might be expected, did a good job of confusing the issue. Reading the excerpts translated into English and circulated among us in Yenan, I realized that it must be well-nigh impossible for the inhabitants of the Border Region ever to get at the truth. Their knowledge of events and facts is comparable to what an American would know if he never read anything but the *Daily Worker*.

The great student demonstrations in Chungking and other cities were represented as a wicked plot by "fascist elements in the Kuomintang" to "stir up feeling against the Soviet Union in order to sabotage the P. C. C. Agreements." The students were warned that one day they would appreciate "that they had been duped by these fascist elements, and come to understand that real love of country lies not in being anti-Soviet or anti-Communist but in joining hands with the Soviet Union and the Chinese Communist Party."

The general argument ran something like this: to oppose Russia is to be a fascist because the Soviet Union is the "main antifascist force in the world." There would be no question of the Red Army not vacating Manchuria if Chinese "democratic," *i.e.,* Communist, forces were in control there. ("If democracy were realized there would be no problem.") Chungking should therefore let the Communists run Manchuria.

"This kind of demonstration," said the Yenan News Agency, "is a hundred per cent antinational and antidemocratic in character. In other words it is counterrevolutionary, and is no different from Hitlerite demonstrations, although the motives of the bulk of the student demonstrators may be patriotic in intention."

Another day it circulated an ingenious and equally illogical argument to the effect that, since the National Government had not fought Japan when the latter took possession of Manchuria and had suppressed those who clamored for war against Japan in 1931, it had no right now to appeal to Chinese patriotism in seeking to regain Manchuria.

A week later in Peiping I met George Weller just out of Chungking. He told me that neither he nor the other foreign correspondents had ever seen the like of these demonstrations. They were terrific and could not possibly have been staged; it was a real mass popular protest. Moreover the government leaders clearly had not wanted them; they were far too frightened of Russia. The demonstrations were as embarrassing to them as the similar ones against Japan in the early thirties.

All in all Yenan's reaction to the popular outburst in China, which followed the American revelations of Russia's looting of Manchuria, was sufficient proof that the Chinese Communists are no different from Communists everywhere else in the world. They are as certainly the puppets of Moscow as Marshal Tito, or the Polish Government, or the American Communist Party.

The day I left Yenan the Red Army was lined up at the airfield rehearsing its reception for General Marshall who was at that time held in the highest esteem in Communist China. The general was not then aware that the truce he had arranged was enabling the Communists to hold their gains in the Northwest provinces while moving their best forces into Manchuria to take over as the Russians withdrew. He was royally received in Yenan. Not till many months later did the Communists start including him in their diatribes against "American imperialism."

Marshall plodded on believing he could unite China by fusing the best elements in the Kuomintang with the moderates, or Right Wing, of the Chinese Communist Party. Had he studied the history of other Communist Parties, he might have realized that whether or not such elements exist among the Chinese Communist Party, makes little difference. The German Communist Party, before Hitler, when it held the proud position now occupied by the Chinese—that of being the largest and most influential Communist Party outside Russia—had also had its "conciliators." The German Communists who disagreed with the Comintern line of silent collaboration with the Nazis to overthrow the Weimar Republic were either thrown out of the party by order of Moscow, or disciplined into impotence. So, in China, there can be no hope that those who take the present democratic pretensions of the Communists seriously, can ever swing the Party as a whole.

I flew back to Peking fully conscious of the reasons why so many liberal, sincere and decent, but politically naïve or ignorant Americans have been fascinated by Yenan. I reflected on my journey out how in the old medieval legends the Devil knew that to tempt mankind he must assume a disguise; his success was assured only if he appeared in the guise of a beautiful woman or a fair youth. The totalitarians who, like Hitler, plainly display their tail and horns, have no chance of succeeding. It is the totalitarian tyranny which, like the Communist, appears in democratic trappings and appeals to the best and most generous instincts of mankind—it is this that can destroy us. Men are often led to perdition by their best, not their worst, instincts and desires.

CHAPTER VII

Are They Real Communists?

THE popularity of the Chinese Communists in America is no doubt largely due to the unpopularity of China's National Government. Yet it is quite illogical to assume that because Chiang Kai-shek's government is not democratic, its enemies of necessity must be. The choice before us is not one between black and white. The real question we have to decide is which side in the civil war might, conceivably, with American aid, create a strong, independent and democratic China.

Unless the Chinese Communists are in fact a totally different species from all others—unless it can be proved that they have no political affinity with the Russian, European, American and other "real" Communist Parties, are not inspired by the same philosophy and do not follow Moscow's dictates—we know that they neither can nor will establish a democratic government in China. If they are "real" Communists we know that the kind of government they would establish in China would be the same type of totalitarian dictatorship as the ones which have been clamped down on Poland, Yugoslavia, Rumania and other countries within the Soviet sphere. On the other hand we know that however reactionary and corrupt the Chinese National Government may be, no regime constitutes so great a threat to liberty and progress as a Communist regime backed by Soviet Russia.

The slogans and immediate policies or pretensions of the Communists do not affect the issue. We know well enough from our experience at home and in Europe that "democracy" in the Communist lexicon has an entirely different meaning from the usually accepted one. The "democratic" governments set up in Eastern Europe by Moscow's agents allow neither freedom of speech nor freedom of the press, nor free elections, nor freedom from arbitrary arrest, nor respect for minority rights, nor the right to strike or organize in trade unions to protect or improve the workers' standard of living, nor any of the other liberties which our forefathers fought to win.

We also know that what the admirers of the Soviet Union call economic democracy is not only the opposite of free enterprise, but also has little in common with democratic socialism.

We are not confronted with a problem of language or historical background as writers like Edgar Snow have argued, but with a deliberate effort on the part of the Communists to confuse us by using words we like for practices we hate.

I am not concerned here to argue with those who consider Russia's economic and political system the best in the world, and who represent it as a higher and better form of democracy than our own. Unless and until they themselves experience the "blessings" of the Soviet system it is hopeless to argue with them. What seems to me of vital importance is that the great mass of Americans who have already seen the true face of Communism in Europe and turned away from it, should also cease to be deluded by the democratic masquerade which the Communists have carried on so successfully in China.

It must be determined, by studying the record, whether or not the Chinese Communist Party has changed its policy over the last quarter of a century according to Moscow's orders. Does the history of the Chinese Communist Party prove that it has been a loyal and obedient member of the Communist International? Are the basic beliefs and philosophy of the Chinese Communists the same as those of the rulers of Soviet Russia? Does the word democracy mean the same thing to them as to Stalin, Tito and the Moscow-sponsored government of Poland?

In order to judge whether or not the Chinese Communists have consistently followed the Party line as laid down in Moscow, we must be clear what that line has been. For there is a popular misconception that a Communist is a man or woman whose primary aim is socialism, and who works always for revolution everywhere to establish it. This has not been true for at least two decades. The basic thesis on which Communist policy has long been based is that, since Soviet Russia is the only socialist state in the world, Communists the world over must subordinate themselves, their party, the working class of their own country and the world's welfare to the interests of the Soviet Government.

Those who do not agree that Soviet Russia is the hope of the world, those who are convinced that social justice cannot be obtained by violence, the abolition of civil liberties, government without law and the subordination of the individual conscience to an all-powerful state, reject the Communist thesis once they come to understand it. But one must always remember that sincere Communists, however abhorrent their methods and philosophy may seem to us, believe that all means and every means are justified by their aim, which they still conceive as the emancipation of mankind from capitalist "tyranny," inequality, poverty and imperialist war.

Communist aims, having been identified with the interests of the Soviet Government, may, at different times and in various places, require the support of Hitler or of Roosevelt, of Peron or Chiang Kai-shek, of Henry Wallace or Kemal Ataturk, of Zionism or of Arab nationalism, of fascism or democracy. The only test is "friendliness," which in the Communist lexicon means subservience to Russia or willingness to give her what she wants.

In Finland Moscow allows a "capitalist" economy to function provided the people continue to work desperately hard supplying enormous reparations to Russia. In Rumania a king is allowed to continue on the throne so long as he remains obedient to Moscow. In Poland, Hungary, Bulgaria and Yugoslavia, Communist or Communist-dominated governments are required by the Kremlin, since these satellites are required to play an active role in Russia's interest.

Thus in its international relations the Kremlin's world aims may necessitate good will either toward a conservative or a fascist or a socialist government. The only criterion is the advantage of the Soviet State. Were Stalin to embrace Franco for the sake of a Spanish alliance, it would be no more surprising than Molotov's 1939 statement to Ribbentrop that Nazi-Communist friendship had been "cemented with blood" in the Russo-German partition of Poland. Nor is there much doubt that Stalin would sacrifice the Chinese Communists today, as he did from 1925 to 1927, if only he could induce Chiang Kai-shek to cut China's ties with America and become the Soviet Union's ally. The present National Government of China would undoubtedly find itself washed clean in the eyes of Communists all over the world, if only it would team up with the USSR.

Put in religious terms, in Communism's secular religion the sinner who belongs to the true church is welcome, but the upright and just man who is an unbeliever can never be forgiven.

Today there should be no difficulty at all in recognizing Communists anywhere in the world. People who are always ready to reverse themselves on any issue according to what is the immediate interest of the Soviet Union are Communists whether or not they go under their true colors.

It was not always so. In the first years of the existence of the Soviet Government and the Communist International the aim was world revolution, and the criterion the supposed interests of the "toiling masses" in all countries. The Communists were originally internationalists, and Lenin denounced patriotism and nationalism as incompatible with Communism. But gradually, after Lenin's death, the Comintern ceased to pursue the ever receding chimera of world revolution. It abandoned the concept of the international community of interest of the workers of the world for a Russian nationalist policy, or rather for one whose primary aim is the maintenance in power of Stalin and his party. Thereafter any Communist who questioned the correctness of the Moscow-dictated policy of the Comintern was liquidated or excluded from the Communist Party in every country. The Communist Parties everywhere became mere adjuncts of the Soviet Foreign Office.

The history of the Chinese Communist Party is of particular interest since the turning point in Comintern history was its failure in China in 1927.

Following the destruction in China of the last hope of spreading Communism by revolutionary upheavals in other lands, Russia turned in on herself. Stalin's slogan of "socialism in one country" came in time to signify that Communists in all countries should work only to preserve the Soviet Union and extend its power. Once this thesis was accepted it followed as night the day that Communists should become the greatest opportunists the world knows, with no fixed principles other than the advantage of the Soviet Union.

Today the Kremlin aims at world conquest, not primarily through Communist revolutions, but by the military strength of Russia aided by her satellites. The role of the foreign Communists in countries not yet subject to Soviet Russia is that of quislings or Fifth Columnists boring from within to weaken Russia's opponents before the battle is joined.

Socialism in one country naturally became National Socialism and the Soviet Union has even to some extent adopted racial concepts. The people of Germany whom Lenin viewed as political allies, once they should have been emancipated by the destruction of their government, have been treated by Stalin as collectively guilty for the sins of their rulers and punished accordingly by murder, rape, pillage and enslavement. Even within the Soviet Union, minorities such as the Volga Germans and the Tartars of the Crimea have been collectively punished by banishment to Siberia or condemnation to forced labor.

Nothing more clearly reveals the complete abandonment by the Bolsheviks of their original ideals than the contrast between Lenin's and Stalin's attitude toward Germany and the other defeated nations. Lenin said that he would risk all the gains of the Russian Revolution for the sake even of the hope of revolution in Germany. Reparations from the vanquished are the chief aim of Stalin's policy. Far from believing in the "Unity of the Workers of the World" which Lenin proclaimed, Stalin keeps millions of German prisoners of war working as slave laborers in Russia, and demands that the whole German people should toil for the profit of the Russian state. Whereas Lenin worked for the emancipation of all colonial peoples, Stalin refuses to the Koreans the independence which the United States wishes to give them, demands imperialist privileges in China, and, if not prevented by the United States, would force the Japanese as well as the Germans to spend their lives producing reparations for the enrichment of the Soviet Union.

Unfortunately the metamorphosis of Communism, and the Comintern's abandonment, not only of its original aims, but of the honesty with which it once proclaimed its purposes, has deluded many simple people whose Christian or liberal upbringing and environment have unfitted them to understand the depths of perfidy and deceit to which men can descend, in what they believe to be a good cause, once they accept the thesis that the end justifies the means.

The disguise assumed by all the Communist Parties of the world since 1935 has already worn so thin in Europe that most Americans are no longer deceived by it. But camouflage is naturally more successful at a distance and the Communist democratic masquerade has therefore been most successful in China.

The explanation lies not only in America's disgusted reaction against the National Government of China. The Chinese Communist Party, although it is a spearhead of the expanding Russian Empire, also leads a peasant revolutionary movement endemic in Chinese history. The Chinese Communist Party retains more of the original spirit of Communism than other Communist Parties. It includes a high proportion of men and women who, in the words of a Belgian Catholic priest I met in Tientsin, "are really Communists in the simplicity of their lives and their personal disinterestedness in riches."

It is indeed China's tragedy that what should have been a native revolutionary or reformist movement—a cleansing fire to destroy all that is corrupt, decayed and rotten in Chinese society—has degenerated into a tool manipulated by a foreign Power. What might have been a progressive force invigorating the Kuomintang and pushing it forward became instead a brake on China's development, a Fifth Column preventing unity and helping to keep her backward, miserable and in constant disorder.

In General Marshall's words, the Chinese Communists "do not hesitate at the most drastic measures to gain their end as, for instance, the destruction of communications in order to wreck the economy of China and produce a situation that would facilitate the overthrow or collapse of the government, without any regard to the immediate suffering of the people involved."

The Chinese Communists not only contribute positively to preventing reconstruction. The fact that they have been able to represent themselves as the champions of agrarian and administrative reform weakens the real liberal forces in China. The reactionaries are able to identify reform with Communism and treason, and the real liberals are rendered impotent.

To understand the present situation as well as in order to judge whether or not the Chinese Communists are real Communists who have followed every turn and twist in the party line laid down in Moscow, one must study the history of the past twenty-five years in China. Unfortunately, few American writers on international affairs ever trouble to do so.

Even eminent statesmen, such as Sumner Welles, have written that the Chinese Communist Party "commenced its independent political life when the Kuomintang party, as it had been created by Sun Yat-sen, split in 1927 into two parts." The fact is that the Chinese Communist Party was founded in 1921, along with others all over the world, as a branch of the Comintern *and was not allowed by Sun Yat-sen to affiliate with the Kuomintang.* Dr. Sun permitted Communists to join the Kuomintang only as individuals, and only if they pledged themselves to be loyal to its aims.

It should be remembered that Sun Yat-sen did not accept Russia's aid in the emancipation of China until after he had despaired of help from the West. The liberal concepts of the West were not applied in their relations with Asiatic peoples. The European Powers and America showed themselves unwilling to free China from the shackles they had placed on her sovereignty and they treated the Chinese as an inferior race. It seemed therefore to Sun Yat-sen that military force alone could enable the Chinese to escape the ugly reality of Western privilege and power, and the only powerful ally available was the Soviet Government, which had voluntarily renounced all imperialist privileges in China.

In accepting Russian aid Sun Yat-sen nevertheless rejected Communism and continued to be influenced by the liberal philosophy of the Western Powers even while fighting against them for China's liberation. As one of the best of his Marxist critics has written: "He hoped to evolve means of transforming Chinese society peacefully and without convulsions after securing power for himself and his followers by purely military means. *There was nothing in common between Sun Yat-sen's concept of democracy and the idea of the direct conquest of political rights and liberties by the people.*"*

In the joint statement issued by Sun Yat-sen and Russia's emissary A. Joffe, in January 1923, Communism was specifically rejected for China. The alliance between the Kuomintang and Russia was clearly stated to be one only for the achievement of national unification and independence.

Sun Yat-sen was under the illusion shared by many Americans

* Harold Isaacs in *The Tragedy of the Chinese Revolution.* This is the best, indeed the only detailed historical account of the Communist-Kuomintang partnership and break in the twenties. Isaacs was a Trotskyist when he wrote his book, but it is so well and thoroughly documented that no student of Far Eastern history can dispense with it.

twenty years later: that you can ally yourselves militarily with Russia without danger of Communism seeking to destroy you from within. Like the United States in the Second World War he ignored the old adage that when you sup with the devil you need a very long spoon.

By the alliance with Russia the Kuomintang received not only the help of Russian military and political advisers, but also the powerful support of the Chinese Communists and the unions of workers and peasants they had begun to organize. Hitherto a small party of intellectuals and patriotic military men, the Kuomintang now acquired the backing of a great mass movement of "common men" who believed they would both free China as a nation and emancipate themselves from servitude to landlord usurers and foreign exploiters. The almost bloodless victories which the Kuomintang under Chiang Kai-shek won from 1925 to 1927 would have been impossible without the support of the millions of Chinese peasants, workers and coolies, in face of whose mass pressure the armies of the war lords melted away, and even the Western Imperialists trembled.

There was Kuomintang-Communist unity as regards the primary aim of freeing China from the domination of the Western Powers. There was unity against the war lords who then ruled most of China. But there could be no unity as regards what should be done when face to face with the power of the West, or following success in uniting and freeing China.

Sun Yat-sen's Three Principles of the People although egalitarian were not Marxist and he had abjured class war. The Kuomintang Party included capitalist and landowning elements as well as liberal intellectuals and other radical elements.

The split was inevitable. It came as soon as the triumphant armies of the Kuomintang-Communist Coalition, sweeping up from Canton, reached Shanghai, the citadel of Western financial and political influences in China, and also of Chinese banking and merchant interests linked up with the Western "exploiters." The Right Wing of the Kuomintang, led by Chiang Kai-shek, hoped to avoid a head-on clash with Britain, the United States and France and to obtain treaty revisions by negotiation. The Communists wanted to chase the foreigners out of China by violence and feared that Chiang might compromise with the Imperialists, as he did, and "stabilize the revolution on a bourgeois basis."

Realizing that the Soviet Union and the Chinese Communists

wanted war, the British Government, followed by the United States, cut the ground from under the feet of the extremists by offering treaty revision and recognition to the Kuomintang moderates, or, if one prefers, to the Western-oriented elements in the Chinese Nationalist movement. Before the arrival of Chiang Kai-shek and the Kuomintang Army, the Shanghai Chamber of Commerce had offered to admit Chinese to participation in the administration of the International Settlement. The British had agreed to give up their concession in Hankow. A promise of tariff autonomy had been made. On its arrival in Shanghai, the alliance with Russia was broken by the Kuomintang in favor of compromise with the West and gradual negotiated annulment of the unequal treaties.

If it is impossible to say how far Chiang Kai-shek, and the majority of the Kuomintang which followed him, were influenced by fear of Britain and America and hopes of Western support, and to what extent by fear of a *Jacquerie* and anarchy, it is equally difficult to estimate whether external or internal causes were mainly responsible for Moscow's contradictory policies.

What Trotskyists call with some justice the betrayal of the Chinese Revolution by Moscow was almost certainly due partly to fear of British and French retaliation in Europe to the Chinese Nationalist-Communist assault on their Asiatic position. But the available evidence suggests that the Comintern's blunders in China were mainly the result of the internal Stalin-Trotsky struggle to which the Chinese Communists were sacrificed.

Battles fought long ago and ancient controversies have little interest for the present-day reader unless they can throw light on modern problems. It would be wearisome to recount in detail the involved and tragic story of Kuomintang-Communist collaboration in the middle twenties. It is however important today to remember that for a brief period the Soviet Government ordered the Chinese Communists to submit themselves entirely to the Kuomintang, in the hope that the latter under Chiang Kai-shek's leadership would expel the British, Americans, French and other Westerners from China for all time. Bolshevik Russia by 1923 had abandoned hope of revolution in Europe in general and in Germany in particular, but still retained the hope of weakening the "capitalist imperialism" of the West by an attack on its flanks: colonial and semicolonial Asia. Hence the aid given to Nationalist "bourgeois" China, and the orders given by the Comintern to the Chinese Communists to submit themselves entirely to the Kuomintang.

Those were the days when Shao Li-tze (who was to become a Chinese Joe Davis following his appointment as ambassador to Moscow from 1939 to 1942) was received with enthusiasm in Russia, and could shout "Long live the Comintern and the World Revolution!" in Moscow where he came as a "fraternal delegate." Stalin at that time said publicly that the "bourgeois" character of the Kuomintang was unimportant. The only thing that mattered was that its forces were directed against "world imperialism." But in the same period he made it clear that this community of interest between Nationalist China and Soviet Russia would be short-lived, that it was purely a temporary expedient and that the Nationalists were doomed to extermination when they had ceased to be useful to the Comintern.

No one should have been surprised that Chiang Kai-shek turned against the Communists in view of Stalin's speeches, as for instance that of April 5, 1927, delivered to the Communist Academy in Moscow in which he said:

> Chiang Kai-shek is submitting to discipline. . . .
>
> The peasant needs an old worn-out jade as long as she is necessary. He does not drive her away. So it is with us. When the Right is of no more use to us, we will drive it away. At present we need the Right. It has capable people, who still direct the army and lead it against imperialists. Besides this, the people of the Right have relations with the generals of Chang Tso-lin and understand very well how to demoralize them and to induce them to pass over to the side of the revolution, bag and baggage without striking a blow. Also, they have connections with the rich merchants and can raise money from them. So they have to be utilized to the end, squeezed out like a lemon, and then flung away.*

Chiang Kai-shek, apart from all his other claims to fame, can go down in history as the one man who ever bested Stalin. He became the squeezer instead of the lemon. Stalin's scheme to use the Chinese Nationalists against Britain, America and France while at the same time preparing to deny them the fruits of victory by a subsequent

---

* Quoted by Harold Isaacs in *The Tragedy of the Chinese Revolution*, page 185.

"proletarian revolution," backfired. He had hoped to use Chiang Kai-shek and then discard him. Instead, Chiang used the mass movement of peasants and workers organized for him by the Communists to sweep victoriously from Canton to Shanghai. Once in sight of supreme power, he turned round and destroyed his allies. Having utilized the mass movement led by the Communists to frighten the Western Powers sufficiently to force them to come to terms, he checked its revolutionary momentum.

In view of Stalin's announced intention of destroying him when he had served Russia's purpose, it is absurd to accuse Chiang Kai-shek of having "betrayed" the Chinese Revolution. The betraying was done by Moscow which wanted both to eat its cake and have it. The Chinese Communists were sacrificed to Russia's self-defeating policy of trying to be the ally of the Chinese Nationalists, led by Chiang Kai-shek, while at the same time directing a Communist revolutionary movement against him. The Communists, of course, have a word for this kind of double-dealing. Whenever in Moscow I pointed out contradictions and inconsistencies in Comintern policy, I was adjured to think "dialectically."

The price for Moscow's inept attempt to double-cross Chiang Kai-shek was paid by the workers, the peasants and the sincerest, most idealistic Communists in China. When Chiang Kai-shek, at the gates of Shanghai, ordered the Communists and their working-class supporters within the city to surrender their arms, the Comintern representatives told them to bury them. Having been forbidden either to surrender or to fight, they were massacred in thousands, first in Shanghai, then in Wuhan, and subsequently in Canton. The trade unions were smashed for a generation, to the acclaim of the foreigners who were ready to compromise with the rising force of Chinese nationalism, if only Chiang Kai-shek would stamp out the Communist-inspired revolt of the working classes.

Chiang Kai-shek, in those days, had not developed the qualities of statesmanship and restraint which in his later years have led him to try to conciliate his enemies instead of exterminating them. The whole history of China in our era might have been different if, in 1927, he had been less brutal and had not alienated many true liberals as well as the Communists. But he may have had no choice. One has to remember that the young Nationalist Movement was menaced by powerful foreign foes who could, and would, have drowned the Kuomintang Revolution in blood and fire, in the same manner as they had crushed the Taipings and the Boxers, if Chiang had not compromised with them. And he could not compromise unless he destroyed the Communists and their influence over a section of the Kuomintang.

Whether or not the foreign imperialists could have been driven out if the Kuomintang-Communist alliance had continued, is a moot point. Certainly Russia, in those days, had insufficient industrial and military strength to save China if she had become involved in a war with Britain and America.

The fundamental issue was whether China was to take the Moscow road of autarchic economic development under a dictatorship which would transform her into a replica of Soviet Russia, with peasants, workers and everyone else sacrificed to the need of capital accumulation, industrial development and military strength; or whether she would seek friendship and credits and technical aid from Western Powers convinced that she could not, and should not, any longer be treated as a colony.

Chiang Kai-shek chose the latter course. Had it not been for Japan, he might have been able to fulfill the aims and pledges of the Kuomintang by lifting China out of poverty and disunity with Western aid and gradual reforms carried through without violence and expropriation.

Chiang Kai-shek may have been wrong in thinking that the Imperialist Powers were too strong to be defeated in 1927. He may have been too strongly influenced by fear that the Communists would unleash a civil war which would deliver China to Russian hegemony. But to say with Teddy White and Annalee Jacoby that "the alliance of Chiang Kai-shek and the Communists . . . had broken over the basic question of the peasant and his land"* is to ignore the international situation at the time. Had the Kuomintang stood for agrarian revolution, there would have been a civil war which would have laid China wide open to further foreign encroachment. The Nationalist Revolution would almost certainly have been crushed by the Great Powers andall hopes of Chinese unity and independence destroyed.

For a few months in 1927 Left Wingers in the Kuomintang and the Chinese Communists maintained their own government in the Wuhan cities (Hankow, Wuchang and Hanyang) under the presidency of

---

* *Thunder Out of China,* page 44.

Wang Ching-wei (who twelve years later was to become Japan's puppet in Nanking). This government controlled the provinces of Hupeh and Hunan where peasant revolts against the landowners broke out which the Communists, under Moscow's orders, refused either to lead or suppress. Similarly the Communists restrained the Wuhan trade unions, then a powerful revolutionary force. Moscow at that time hoped that the Wuhan Government could make an alliance with the "Christian General" Feng, the most powerful of the northern war lords. Hence the orders given by the Comintern forbidding the alienation of landowners and capitalists.

The Comintern had not even now learned its lesson; it still hoped to get the best of both worlds by being and not being the leader of a social revolution in China. Again it fell between two stools: Feng went over to Chiang and barred the way to Peking.

In July 1927 the Wuhan Government capitulated to the government established by Chiang Kai-shek at Nanking. Borodin fled back to Russia across the Mongolian desert, and a reign of terror blotted out the peasant rebellions together with the majority of the Communists. Henceforth the "Nanking Government" was recognized by the Powers as the National Government of China, and the Communists became an isolated dissident group without a mass movement behind them.

Now when all was lost, when the ranks of the Chinese Communists had been decimated and they had lost the confidence both of the workers and the peasants, Moscow reversed its policy and called on them to start all-out civil war against the Kuomintang. To confuse them further the Chinese Communists were at first instructed to continue membership inside the Kuomintang, by now intent on exterminating them. Moscow demanded that they sacrifice their lives to no other purpose than the maintenance of Stalin's reputation as a true Bolshevik revolutionary.

Chen Tu-hsiu, the founder and leader of the Chinese Communist Party, resigned the chairmanship, saying that he saw no way out in a situation in which "the International wishes us to carry out our own policy on the one hand and does not allow us to withdraw from the Kuomintang on the other." Two years later he was expelled from the Communist Party when he broke a long silence by appealing for a Chinese united front against Japan, just beginning her encroachments in Manchuria.

In 1938, when I was in Hankow, Chen Tu-hsiu was dying in poverty in a remote village, and the Chinese Communists were demanding that he be executed by Chiang Kai-shek.

Chen Tu-hsiu was replaced as leader of the Chinese Communist Party by Li Li-san who was more Trotskyist than Trotsky and envisaged the Russian Army marching in from Mongolia to support the resurgent Chinese Revolution. Under his leadership and that of Stalin's two favorites, the German Heinz Neumann and the Georgian Besso Lominadze, a futile insurrection was staged in Canton in December 1927. It had no prospect at all of success since the Communists had lost their trade-union support and become a small isolated minority. But the Chinese were by now no more than cannon fodder in the battle between Stalin and Trotsky. The Canton insurrection was drowned in blood after three days. But Heinz Neumann was able to send a telegram to the Russian Communist Party Congress in Moscow, announcing a "glorious revolutionary uprising" of the Chinese proletariat at the moment when Stalin needed ammunition against the opposition who blamed him for the fiasco of the Chinese Revolution. Trotsky and his followers were sent into exile as the Chinese Communists died to help Stalin.

No one who studies the history of the Russian Communist Party and the Comintern can doubt that the Chinese Communists were sacrificed all along to the exigencies of Stalin's fight for supremacy in Russia. Nor is it ever possible to understand the Comintern's swings from Left to Right and back again without reference to Soviet Russia's internal situation as well as Stalin's foreign policy.

Prior to 1928, in trying both to collaborate with Chiang Kai-shek and prepare to overthrow him, Stalin was endeavoring to gain the support of the right wing of the Bolshevik Party while not alienating all those who were inclined to follow Trotsky. Trotsky had been against the policy of collaboration with the Chinese Nationalists and had wanted Russia and the Comintern to go all out for a Communist revolution in China. Bucharin and the right wing of the party were for the policy of collaboration with Chiang Kai-shek. Stalin, intent on establishing his personal supremacy, rode in both directions.

By 1928, having got rid of Trotsky, he turned on his opponents of the Right. This necessitated a sharp turn to the Left, which at home meant the agrarian policy of forced collectivization and Five-Year Plans, and for the Comintern a distorted version of Trotsky's revolutionary policies. In France, Germany and England, the Communist Parties were ordered to cease collaborating with Social Democrats or the Labor Party; in China they were told to fight the Kuomintang.

Li Li-san lasted until 1931 when he in his turn was made the scapegoat for the Comintern's failures.

It was not only the Chinese Communist Party which suffered disaster as a result of Stalin's personal ambitions. The Chinese nation lost heavily in the Kuomintang-Communist split. The youth who died, or lost heart, or became timeservers or cynics or nonpoliticals in the days of wrath and vengeance, torture and death, were the flower of the nation. Never again would there be such high hopes, such self-sacrifice and patriotic fervor as had been displayed in the brief period when men of all parties and classes had joined to raise China from the abject state into which she had fallen in the nineteenth century.

Twenty years after, in Shanghai in 1946, my friend Aying Yung, daughter of a famous scholar and herself renowned for her learning, talked to me of those days of China's awakening with profound sadness. She knew as well as I did the harm the Communists are now doing to China. But she mourned for the fine men and women she had known in her youth who had been masascred in those terrible months of 1927.

To understand the strength of the Comintern in China, one must recognize the power of attraction of its anti-imperialist professions and its pretensions to seek the welfare of the poor and oppressed. Even today the ideals and slogans which created so mighty a popular movement in China in the twenties still attract the youth of the nation. They know little or nothing of the realities of Stalin's Russia and are bitterly disillusioned by the self-seeking Kuomintang officials and the seemingly hopeless inefficiency or stupidity of the National Government. Having myself seen the inept diplomacy and lack of patriotism of many of the wealthy or well-connected Chinese appointed to represent her abroad, having also seen the incapacity of many government officials in China, I cannot but sympathize with the impatience of the Chinese youth who turn Communist. Disastrous as I know this reaction must be to all the hopes which now and in the past inspired the best of the Chinese intellectuals, I can understand why, once again, some of them listen to the siren voices bidding them take the Moscow road.

CHAPTER VIII

Success of the Democratic Masquerade

FOLLOWING the 1927 debacle, the remnants of the Chinese Communist Party, and of the few soldiers in the Kuomintang Army who followed them, established themselves in the south of Kiangsi province and in eastern Honan where they were joined by revolting peasants. In time these mixed forces, held together by Communist discipline and ideology, became the "Red Army." From the point of view of the peasants into whose villages they came, the "Red partisans" were little distinguishable from the bandits who from time immemorial have troubled China. The poor tenant farmers might at first welcome them when they killed off the landowners and redistributed the land, but the Red Army had to be fed by the peasants and this naturally made it unpopular.

The borderline between "rich" and "poor" is too close in China for the Communist armies to be able to remain popular by burdening only the "rich." The real problem in China is always the scarcity of land, and general poverty, and cannot be solved by shooting the few comparatively rich landowners and kulaks. Controlling no cities, the Communists could give the peasants nothing in return for the food they had to take from them. Thus the Red Army remained as great a burden on the people as any other army.

After years of fighting against the National Government, during which they retreated from one district to another, the Communists were finally driven out of Central China in 1934. The ensuing "Long March" of the remnants of the Red Army to the Northwest is better known to American readers than the Chinese Communist Party's earlier or later history, thanks to the graphic description in Edgar Snow's *Red Star over China.*

After their arrival in what was to become the Shensi-Kansu-Ningsia Border Region, the policy of executing or driving out all landowners, gentry and missionaries was abandoned for a reformist policy. In these remote, unfertile and thinly populated regions there were in any case few people who could be called rich even according to Communist standards. Mao Tse-tung, who had become the leader of the party following Li Li-san's disgrace in 1931, seems never to have favored the indiscriminate massacres which alienated the peasantry as a whole. And the Chinese Communist Party's geographical isolation from Moscow, and its possession of a territorial base and army of its own, rendered it a little less subservient to Stalin than the Communist Parties of Europe and America. Nevertheless the switch over to a policy which conciliated the peasants did not occur until the *volte-face* of the Comintern which followed Hitler's acquisition of power in Germany.

Events in China cannot be understood without reference to Europe, since the switches in the Communist Party line during the last twenty years were determined in the main by Moscow's European policy.

From 1928 onward the Comintern "line" had been ultra-Left. The Social Democrats in Europe had been denounced as "social fascists," as the main support of capitalism and imperialism and as more dangerous enemies of the working class than either fascists or Nazis or conservatives. In England in 1929 and 1930, when I was a member of the British Communist Party, we were instructed to "explain" to the workers that democracy was nothing but the disguised dictatorship of the capitalist class, kept in power by the "social fascist" Labor Party.

I can still remember the pitying glances of a crowd of unemployed outside a North London Labor Exchange when I told them this from the top of a soapbox. They evidently thought I was touched in the head, and walked away.

In England the Communists merely lost what little influence they had by this line of talk. In Germany, with its huge and influential Communist Party, the results were tragic. Here it was the official Comintern policy to tell the workers that if Hitler came to power it would be the turn of the Communists next. Their task was therefore primarily the overthrow of German democracy, and to accomplish it the Communists did not scruple to collaborate with the Nazis on more than one occasion.

Stalin was convinced that if Hitler came to power he would direct his hostility against France, then regarded as Soviet Russia's main enemy. Since the German Social Democrats wanted a reconciliation with France Stalin desired to destroy them at all costs. Hence his cynical but miscalculated refusal to allow the German Communists to join hands with the Social Democrats to save Germany and the world from Hitler. The German Communists and the whole German people were to pay the price of Stalin's and the Comintern's stupidities in this phase, as the Chinese had paid in the previous period.

Had the French Communist Party been as strong as the German it too might have brought fascism to power. As late as February 1934 the French Communists called for demonstrations against democracy at the same hour and place as the Action Française and, together with the fascists, forced the resignation of the government.

Moscow came to its senses just in time to reverse the Comintern line in France and call for unity with the socialists and radicals instead of continuing the fight against them.

For months after Hitler came to power the Soviet Government had gone on hoping for an understanding with Nazi Germany against France and England. I remember Jack Chen (son of the Eugene Chen who had been the Kuomintang's Foreign Minister in 1926 and 1927) complaining to me in Moscow, where he earned a living as an artist, that the publication of anti-Nazi cartoons in the Russian press was forbidden.

Only after Hitler had made it abundantly clear that he was intent, not only on destroying the German Communist and socialist parties, but also on an anti-Soviet policy, did Russia join the League of Nations, make an alliance with France, and order the Comintern to abandon its antidemocratic line and make a sharp turn to the Right.

The Seventh Congress of the Comintern in 1935 finally announced the new line called for by Russia's precarious international situation. The hitherto hated and reviled socialist, labor and liberal forces in Europe and America were now to be sought as allies. Dimitrov, appointed secretary of the Comintern following the Reichstag fire trial, told the delegates they must henceforth seek to establish alliances with all anti-Nazi forces. The Communists were not to give up their ultimate aims. But they were to don sheep's clothing for the duration of the German-Japanese menace to the Soviet fatherland, or until such time as opportunity offered to seize power in their own countries.

They were reminded by Dimitrov of the legend of the Trojan Horse and instructed to make their way within the wall of the capitalist citadel by means of the same tactics. They were ordered to get into key positions within the democratic governments by pretending to be liberal democrats, in preparation for the days of economic crisis to come when they would throw aside their disguise and seize the state power.

Of all the many changes in the Comintern line none proved more successful than the one inaugurated in 1935. Lenin's honesty in admitting that the Communists stood for dictatorship, and despised democracy, had got the Comintern nowhere. But since Communists, everywhere in the world, have taken possession of the magic word democracy and equated it with Communist dictatorship they have gone from strength to strength. Although in England and America they were unable to get into key positions in the government, they have been able by posing as democrats and liberals to exert enormous influence over the press and radio. In the United States their influence over the government was obviously considerable in the Roosevelt era.

In China the change in the Comintern line brought about by the German-Japanese menace to Russia called for a cessation of the civil war and an anti-Japanese united front. Mao Tse-tung, hitherto not regarded too favorably by Moscow, was appointed a member of the Comintern's Executive Committee in 1935. That same year the Chinese Communists began to represent themselves as liberal reformers as well as modifying their agrarian policy.

The change in the Comintern line from ultra-Left to Right was most easily effected in China, where the Communists had long since lost their working-class support and been transformed by the logic of history into a party whose only hope was leadership of a movement for peasant emancipation. In fact the Chinese Communists had become little more than the dissident rulers of sections of three remote provinces near the Russian border. Had it not been for the Japanese threat, to Russia as well as to China, they would have remained an insignificant and powerless minority.

In August 1935 the Chinese Communist Party announced that it would no longer liquidate any but "parasitic" landowners; that merchants, artisans, and even priests would not have their lands confiscated; that rich farmers would be allowed to keep a portion of their holdings; that "commercial and industrial development by individual capital" would be encouraged; that "excessive demands on the part of workmen and hired peasants that cannot be fulfilled or that increase bankruptcy and unemployment" would be stopped; and finally that non-Communist political parties and organizations would be given "democratic rights and freedom" provided they "struggled against imperialism" or participated in the "racial revolutionary movement."

Following the conclusion of the German-Japanese "Anti-Comintern" alliance in 1936 the Chinese Communists redoubled their efforts to induce the National Government to call off the civil war. They offered more and more concessions, denied that they wanted a social revolution, recognized Chiang Kai-shek as the only man to lead the nation in repulsing Japan, and offered to subordinate themselves and their armies to the National Government.

The Communists were back where they had been a decade earlier. Once again they wanted to collaborate with the Kuomintang while preparing to destroy it after victory over the common enemies of China and Russia.

The imprisonment of Chiang Kai-shek at Sian in December 1936 was the dramatic incident which marked the temporary cessation of a decade of Kuomintang-Communist civil war. Junior officers of the Manchurian forces exiled from their homeland by Japan and sent by Chiang Kai-shek to fight the Communists under the "Young Marshal" Chang Hsueh-liang had instead fraternized with the Red Army. Upon the Generalissimo's arrival in Sian to quell the mutiny they took him prisoner, threatened him with death and endeavored to force him to promise to stop the civil war and fight Japan. The Communists, realizing that only under Chiang Kai-shek's leadership could China hope to resist Japan, exerted their influence to have the Generalissimo released. Chiang promised nothing and showed his readiness to die rather than submit for fear of death. But the incident apparently convinced him of the sincerity of the Communist offer of collaboration against Japan. At the February 1936 meetings of the Kuomintang resistance to Japanese aggression took the place of the old slogan of "unification first" as the program of the government.

The Communist's proposals laid before the Executive Committee of the Kuomintang at this time, and accepted, were as follows:

1. The Chinese Soviet Government shall henceforth be known as the Government of the Special Area of the Republic of China, which shall be under the control of the National Government and of the National Military Council.
2. In the territory of the Government of the Special Area a democratic system of Government shall obtain.
3. All activities designed to overthrow the National Government shall cease throughout the country.
4. The policy of land confiscation shall be discontinued.

In the late spring of 1937 the Red Army assumed the Kuomintang uniform and, under the name of the Eighth Route Army, became nominally at least part of the National Army. From that time until the United Front was broken in 1940 the Communist forces received pay from the Central Government. As late as 1946 when I visited Yenan the soldiers still wore the Kuomintang insignia on their caps.

However, the Communists never intended to honor their agreement with the National Government. In a series of lectures for party workers entitled *Present Strategy and Tactics of the Chinese Communist Party,* printed in Yenan in 1937 and marked "very confidential," it was clearly stated that the agreement was only a maneuver and that Communist aims had not changed. The following passages from pages 49-51 of the original are given from the translation made by Dr. H. T. Chu.

> To establish a democratic Republic is the present strategy of the Communist Party and its tactic is to cease civil wars and co-operate with the Kuomintang. . . . Many of the Communist Party members seeing the abandonment of agrarian revolution, class struggle, and the Chinese Soviet, and the change of the Red Army's insignia began to doubt the wisdom of the Chinese Communist Party. These attitudes are erroneous for the present circumstances require a temporary compromise with the Kuomintang. Such a compromise is not capitulation; nor is it to sell the proletariat down the river. . . . Only by co-operation with the Kuomintang can we resist Japanese aggression. . . . In the minds of the Communist members there should be no doubt as to the wisdom of this policy which has the following bases:
>
> 1. It is politic to give up a dead-end policy for a passable road which will enable us to reach proletarian dictatorship.
>
> 3. The present tactic adopted by our Communist Party is really a revolutionary one. It is to be the weapon for destroying the power of

the capitalists and for consolidating and strengthening the revolutionary forces.

4. *Our present tactics are for the very purpose of protecting the growth of our secret programs,* and of co-ordinating the secret with the open work in order to win the support of the masses for the future overthrow of capitalism.

5. Our present retreat is to provide a period of recuperation for the proletariat so that we can prepare for their future tasks with more vigor.

6. To give up the policy of direct attack temporarily for retreating tactics is really adopting deviating tactics of attack.

8. To change the name of the Red Army to the National Army is not reorganization but merely a change of insignia. Actually the independent status of the Red Army will not only be maintained but also its strength will be consolidated and increased.

For the present the organization of the Communist Party should still be kept secret while the members of the party should openly participate in all patriotic organizations, forming a nucleus in them. It is important to assign certain Communist Party members to work as representatives of the party, but they should be under the direction of the secret organs of the Communist Party in that place.

The same booklet (pages 63-66) analyzes the lessons of the Russian Revolution for the benefit of the doubting Thomases in the Communist Party who objected to the temporary cessation of civil war. They are told how after 1907 the Bolsheviks entered the Duma in order to bore from within and finally overthrow the Czarist government, and that similarly "our present compromise is for the purpose of winning a legal status for the Communist Party . . . to weaken the Kuomintang and to overthrow the National Government . . . by utilizing the name of a Democratic Republic. . . . All these [compromises] are aiming at the goal of proletarian revolution. . . . The success of the Democratic Republic will mark the beginning of the second proletarian revolution and the realization of proletarian dictatorship."

These lectures on Communist strategy and tactics contain other frank admissions (as valuable today as when they were first written) that the Communists demand democracy in China only in order to establish their own dictatorship:

For our benefit in the near future as well as for the realization of the socialist society, it is necessary to have political freedom. . . . Under the present circumstances, in order to establish the Chinese

Soviet it is *necessary first to create a capitalist Democratic Republic which will be the foundation of, and key to, proletarian dictatorship.* . . . Under such conditions the Chinese Communist Party can send its delegates to the National Assembly and carry out its program in and out of the Assembly. Thus the Chinese Communist Party can be sure of success. One of the factors of success is the loose organization of the Kuomintang. . . . The Chinese Communist Party can eventually destroy the Kuomintang.

It is only by supporting the creation of a Democratic Republic that the Chinese Communist Party can . . . sharpen the conflict of class interests and quickly bring about a Soviet regime in China.

Although so many innocents abroad have concluded that the Chinese Communists are not "real" Communists, you can find no Communist Party anywhere in the world which has better understood and applied the Trojan Horse tactics laid down by Dimitrov at the last Congress of the Comintern. Nor can you find any party which has more faithfully carried out Moscow's orders. Yet, in face of all the evidence, even the authors of the Book-of-the-Month Club's choice, *Thunder Out of China,* assert that by 1935 the ties between the Chinese Communists and Moscow had become "nominal."

Having worked in Moscow up to the summer of 1936 in the Pacific Ocean Cabinet of the Institute of World Economy and Politics, I know that the Chinese Communists never ceased to be under Moscow's orders. It was our task, in conjunction with the Comintern, to study the economic and political situation in the Far Eastern countries and lay the theoretical foundations for policy decisions. Of course these decisions were not really made with reference to the objective situation in China, Japan or elsewhere. Emphasis would be laid on Japan's wickedness, or the Kuomintang's, or on the "revolutionary situation" engendered by the misgovernment of their colonies by Britain, France or Holland, according to the degree of hostility or friendliness displayed toward Soviet Russia by the various governments concerned. There was never any question but that the Communist Parties would do what they were told.

The Kremlin was in a better position to help its friends and discomfit its enemies in the Far East than anywhere else, thanks to the Institute of Pacific Relations. The Institute where I worked was a branch of the Communist Academy (now the Academy of Sciences) and was also the Russian branch of the I.P.R. It was we who received its American delegates when they came to Moscow for help and advice. To hear these Americans submit themselves to our dictates on theory and policy was amusing, if sad. In the spring of 1936 one of them, Owen Lattimore, attempted to argue with the theoreticians of our Institute on questions concerned with Mongolia but he was overborne by the prestige of these high priests of Communism. Mr. E. C. Carter, the Chairman of the I.P.R., did not seem to be troubled by theoretical questions but made a friendly speech in the evening to the "party actives," as the leading members of the Russian Communist Party were called.

There were few Chinese left at the Institute of World Economy and Politics by the time I left Russia shortly after the visit of the American I.P.R. delegates. Some had "escaped over the frontier" and joined up with the Kuomintang. Others had disappeared into concentration camps or obscure employment in the provinces. The most zealous Chinese Communists were those who never came to Moscow or learned anything about the Soviet Union.

The Chinese Communist Party, although comparatively immune from the purge which decimated the servile parties of the West in the last year of my residence in Moscow, never denied that it took its orders from Moscow. Indeed it affirmed and glorified the fact. Its secretary, Wang Ming, wrote in the *Communist International,* in December 1937, how the Communist Party of China, in its appeal in 1935 for a united national front against Japan, was "guided by the new line of tactics of the Seventh Congress of the Comintern and the historic report made by Comrade Dimitrov."

In the same article Wang Ming made it clear that in "abandoning the policy of the violent overthrow of the Kuomintang Government" and embracing the Three Principles of the People of Sun Yat-sen, the Chinese Communists had not "ceased to be true disciples of scientific Communism-Marxism-Leninism. . . . The cessation of the movement for Red China," he continued, "was only a tactic since, when the Chinese people should have conquered the Japanese aggressors through a united front, the slogan of 'Sovietizing China' would be revived." To warn any backsliders who might imagine that the Chinese Communist Party had really changed its spots, Wang Ming wrote: "Any other interpretation of this formula of the Communist

Party of China, as meaning that the Chinese Communists give up their political and organizational independence, or give up the propaganda of Communist principles, is the deliberate intriguing of pro-Japanese and other elements, or else, at best, a complete misunderstanding." He concluded his article with a paean of praise to the Soviet Union and the words:

> They [the people of China] regard the USSR as the country which in actual practice has shown China how it can and must transform the country . . . into one mighty and capable of defending itself, from a country poor and backward into one rich and cultural . . . into the most democratic country in the world under the banner of the Stalinist Constitution.

In 1937 and 1938 the Chinese Red Army fought bravely and effectively against the Japanese defending both China and the Soviet fatherland. In spite of their secret aims the united front was a reality when I was in China in 1938. Indeed in those days the Communists had seemed to be leaning over backward to avoid giving offense or arousing the misgivings of the Kuomintang. As I wrote in 1938 in *China at War,* the Communists seemed ready to accept every rebuff and restriction of their activity, considering that only thus could the united front be maintained and China kept fighting Japan.

How misleading my impression, like that of others, was at the time is shown by the directive given by Mao Tse-tung to political workers of the Eighth Route Army when, in October 1937, it left Yenan to fight in North Shansi:

> The Sino-Japanese war affords our party an excellent opportunity for expansion. Our fixed policy should be seventy per cent expansion, twenty per cent dealing with the Kuomintang, and ten per cent resisting Japan. There are three stages in carrying out this fixed policy: the first is a compromising stage, in which self-sacrifice should be made to show our outward obedience to the Central Government and adherence to the Three Principles of the People [nationality, democracy and livelihood, as outlined by Dr. Sun Yat-sen], but in reality this will serve as camouflage for the existence and development of our party.
>
> The second is a contending stage, in which two or three years should be spent in laying the foundation of our party's political and military powers, and developing these until we can match and break

the Kuomintang, and eliminate the influence of the latter north of the Yellow River. While waiting for an unusual turn of events, we should give the Japanese invader certain concessions.

The third is an offensive stage, in which our forces should penetrate deeply into Central China, sever the communications of the Central Government troops in various sectors, isolate and disperse them until we are ready for the counteroffensive and wrest the leadership from the hands of the Kuomintang.*

Following the Stalin-Hitler Pact of August 1939, the Chinese, like every other Communist Party, reversed itself. Mao Tse-tung announced that Russia's understanding with Nazi Germany "strengthened the confidence of the whole of mankind in the possibility of winning freedom." Lend-Lease was denounced in Yenan as in Union Square as a wicked device for "embroiling" the United States in the "Second Imperialist War."

The Chinese Communists now began to refuse to take orders from the National Government, started calling Chiang Kai-shek a fascist and declared that the Chinese Communists "are always social revolutionaries, never reformists." In 1940 the united front in China was broken when the "New Fourth" Communist Army tried to occupy the triangular area between Nanking, Shanghai and Hangchow and came into head-on conflict with the Nationalist forces.

By the end of 1939 Mao Tse-tung had also begun to prepare the minds of his followers for the possibility of a Russo-Japanese understanding on the model of the Russo-German Pact. In an interview with Edgar Snow in December 1939, he stated that it was "not inconceivable" Russia might decide to save part of China in the same fashion as she had "saved" half of Poland when she partitioned it with Germany.

The days when foreign writers friendly to the Communists paid glowing tributes to the valor of China's National armies led by Chiang Kai-shek were gone forever.

In his account of his interview, published in the *China Weekly Review* on January 13 and 20, 1940, Snow quotes Mao as saying that "with the liquidation of the Nazi anti-Soviet, anti-Comintern policy,

---

* *Documents on the Problem of the Chinese Communist Party*. Presented to the People's Political Council, March, 1941. Published in Chungking, 1944, by the Supreme National Defense Council.

the distinction formerly drawn between fascist and democratic countries lost its validity; the period of attempting to win over the capitalist class and their governments" had become a thing of the past. Mao further stated that "the center of the anti-Soviet movement is no longer Nazi Germany. It is among the so-called democratic countries with Britain in the lead."

Asked by Snow whether he meant that he saw no difference between fascism and the cause of the democracies, Mao replied, "No, there is no difference in their positions in this war." Snow also reported Mao as having said that President Roosevelt was hoping "to win the leadership of the capitalist world and wants Chamberlain for a Secretary and Japan as his rear guard, with Hitler and Mussolini his vanguard."

When Russia and Japan signed their first pact in April 1941, the Communists announced that since "it strengthens peace on the eastern frontiers of the USSR and guarantees the security of the development of socialist construction," this treaty "is in keeping with the interests of the working people and oppressed nations of the whole world."

True to their principle of Russia first the Chinese Communist denounced as "craven tricksters" all Chinese who expressed dismay at Russia's recognition of Japan's puppet state of "Manchukuo."

After Germany attacked Russia in June 1941, the Chinese Communists as suddenly as every other Communist Party discovered that the war in Europe was, after all, not an imperialist war but one in which England and America were the children of light. Roosevelt was no longer called a "warmonger," Willkie no longer figured as "a fascist"; even Winston Churchill received some Communist bouquets.

However, in China, the breakup of the Nazi-Soviet alliance was not followed by the re-establishment of a popular front against the national enemy. For Japan was not at war with Russia. The Chinese Communists could direct their main war effort against the Chungking Government instead of against the Japanese, without immediate fear for Russia's safety.

For their part the Japanese naturally continued to exert most of their strength against Chiang Kai-shek's armies. The Chinese Communists were both Russia's protégés and a thorn in the flesh of the Chinese National Government. Throughout the duration of the Russo-Japanese Pact the Japanese refrained from launching an offensive against the Communist capital although Yenan was only about a hundred miles away from their lines.

According to the testimony of General Okamura, the Japanese commander in China, in his report to America after V-J Day, the Japanese during the whole course of the Sino-Japanese War lost only 50,000 men to the guerrillas—and not all the guerrillas were Communists by any means.

Germany's attack on Russia did not even necessitate the withdrawal from circulation of *The New Democracy* in which Mao Tse-tung described Americans as the "sons-of-bitches Western Imperialists."

This book was written originally in 1940, when Britain, France and the United States, not National Socialist Germany, were regarded by Communists the whole world over as the enemies of mankind. But it has continued until now to be the bible of the Chinese Communists, only slight text revisions being found necessary through the years.

By the middle of 1946, when the Communists were announcing on the Yenan radio that there was no difference between Japanese and American imperialism except that the latter was stronger and more hypocritical, the unexpurgated original edition again became entirely suitable as the statement of basic Communist views, since, as in the period when Stalin and Hitler were allies, the Western democracies were once more the villains on the international stage.

The English translation of *The New Democracy,* issued in 1944 with an introduction by Earl Browder, was carefully edited to expunge or obscure its anti-American thesis. But the complete subservience of the Chinese Communist Party to Moscow's dictates could not be hidden. Indeed one must do the Chinese Communists the justice to admit that they have been far franker, and considerably more honest, than other Communists in announcing their aims and their views.

Again and again in his book the venerable leader* of the Chinese Communist Party states that "China's revolution is a part of the world proletarian-socialist revolution," that it depends on the assistance of the Soviet State, that its aim is the "overthrow of capitalism"

---

* Mao Tse-tung is chairman of the Central Executive Committee of the Chinese Communist Party; chairman of the Party's secretariat and of the Presidium of the Politbureau. From 1935 until its ostensible liquidation in 1943, he was a member of the Executive Committee of the Comintern.

and "the establishment of a New-Democratic Society," which will not be "democracy in its general sense," but "the dictatorship of revolutionary classes."

The following quotations are taken from Lin Yutang's direct rendering from the Chinese text of the fifth edition, published in Yenan in 1944. The words in italics are those omitted by the American Communist Party editors in their endeavor to draw wool over the eyes of the American public and keep alive the legend that the Chinese Communists are simply agrarian liberal reformers.

> This [Chinese] Republic of New Democracy is different on the one hand from the old Western-style capitalist republics *under the dictatorship of* the capitalists which are already out of date. On the other hand, it is also different from the newest, Soviet-style, Soviet Socialist Republic under the dictatorship* of the proletariat. *This kind of republic has already arisen and grown strong in the Soviet Union and furthermore will yet be established in the different capitalist countries, and will undoubtedly become the type of government of all progressive countries through the Union of Nations and of political power. . . .*
>
> *According to their social character, the forms of government of all the countries of the world fall fundamentally into three categories: a) republics under the dictatorship of the capitalist class, b) republics under the dictatorship of the proletariat, and c) republics under the joint dictatorship of several revolutionary classes.*
>
> *The first category comprises the countries of the old democracy. Today after the outbreak of the second imperialist war, the breath of democracy has already disappeared from all capitalist countries. All have become, or are about to become, blood-smelling, military dictatorships of the capitalist classes. Certain countries under the joint dictatorship of the landlords and the capitalist classes can be grouped under this heading.*

Thus while their American admirers have been representing the Chinese Communists as democrats in the Western sense, they themselves have all along proclaimed that capitalist democracy is a sham, that Russia is ruled by a dictatorship, and that the Second World War was not a conflict of "peace-loving" democratic peoples against the

---

* The American Communist Party's translation substitutes "ruled by" for dictatorship throughout the text.

wicked war-loving dictatorships, but an "imperialist struggle for power."

The New Democracy is equally explicit concerning the Chinese Communist refusal to become allies of America and "go the road of a capitalist society." "Such a way," writes Mao, "is a dead alley" because *"the present-day international environment is that of a struggle between capitalism and socialism, one in which capitalism is going down and socialism going up."*

He continues:

In this world all imperialists are our enemies. We cannot be separated from the Socialist State (Russia) . . . if we wish to seek for independence. That is to say we cannot separate ourselves from the assistance of the Soviet Union or from the victory of the anti-capitalist struggles of the proletariat of Japan, Great Britain, the United States, Germany and France. Their victories help us. . . . This is especially true of the aid of the Soviet Union, an indispensable condition for the final victory of China's war of resistance. . . .

The world now depends on Communism *as its star of* salvation, and so does China. . . . *If we do not adopt the policy of allying ourselves with the Soviet Union, then we have to adopt a pro-imperialist policy, have to ally ourselves with imperialist powers, and . . . Great Britain and the United States might ask us to join up against the Soviet Union. If we go along with them, we shall at once line up ourselves in the counterrevolutionary camps of the imperialist powers, and our national independence will be over.*

In another passage Mao clearly and unmistakably refutes the thesis propagated by many American writers who believe the Chinese Communists could be America's friends and allies. He writes:

You may say, *"There is a difference between Eastern and Western Imperialists. I will ally myself with the sons-of-bitches, the Western Imperialists. That sounds indeed brave! Unfortunately the Western Imperialists will be anti-Soviet and anti-Communists. If you join them, they will ask you to strike northward. Then good-by to your revolution."*

If we forsake the policy of allying with the Soviet Union and co-operate with the Imperialists the *San Min Chu I* will become a reactionary doctrine.

Here we have the thesis clearly stated: any Chinese who wants to co-operate with the United States is a reactionary. Chiang Kai-shek's government is friendly to the United States, therefore it is reactionary. "The genuine *San Min Chu I,*" says Mao, "has to be one allying itself with the Soviet Union" and can never be one that allies itself with those who "oppose the Soviet Union." "No matter whom you follow, so long as you are anti-Communistic, you are traitors."

Mao Tse-tung does not even trouble to hide his contempt for the Western liberals whose propaganda on behalf of the Chinese Communists has been so useful to him. In his book, *Battle for Asia,* Edgar Snow, who is better acquainted with the Chinese Communist leaders than any other Western writer, admits that it is impossible to reconcile the popular view of the Chinese Communists as "only a peasant reform party" with its loyal adherence to the Comintern and says:

> Mao Tse-tung . . . would not be bothered about these aspersions cast upon his Marxism. He would chuckle and say that if it would solve the contradiction in the sentiments of liberals who want to be known as pro-China but anti-Stalin they might call him anything they liked.

It is true that Edgar Snow at other times has written precisely the contrary, telling his readers that "there has never been any Communism in China, even in Communist areas"; and that "long before it became defunct, the Comintern ceased to have much direct contact with the Chinese Communist Party."

These contradictions in his testimony could no doubt be "dialectically" explained, or attributed to semantics, by the author whose articles and books on China are so widely known. However, both the historical record and the sacred writings of the Chinese Communists afford sufficient proof that they *are* "real" Communists. There is no reason to doubt that their conception of democracy is the same as that of Stalin and his stooges in Eastern Europe. Given the chance the Chinese Communists would undoubtedly establish the same kind of new democracy as that at present enjoyed by the people of Poland, Yugoslavia, Hungary, Bulgaria and Rumania.

The apparent discrepancy between tributes to the Communist exploits against Japan on the one hand, and the charges on the other side that they did not fight Japan, is partly to be explained by a confusion of dates. Men like Congressman Judd, who himself lived for a time in the Communist areas as a medical missionary, testify that the Communists were all out against Japan for the first two years of the war, but not after 1939. Snow's personal knowledge also relates to this early period and this gives greater weight to the admission in his earlier books that they are real Communists under Moscow's orders than to his recent attempts to represent them as independent Chinese liberal reformers. Agnes Smedley last visited the Communist area eight or nine years ago, during the period when Japan was Public Enemy Number One to the Communists throughout the world, and repeated Russo-Japanese clashes along the frontier of Manchuria were occurring.

Most of the foreign correspondents who visited Yenan during the war had no means of ascertaining the truth of the statements made to them. Few of them spoke Chinese and few, if any, had the necessary experience of totalitarian techniques to understand the setup there. Anyone who has seen how foreign correspondents in Moscow are deceived need not have been surprised when Brooks Atkinson, Harrison Forman, Teddy White, Gunther Stein and others came home to write glowing accounts of Chinese Communist democracy and Chinese Communist military prowess.

It was not the Japanese, but the Chinese, who suffered wherever the Communist guerrillas operated. The Japanese retaliated for Communist depredations by burning whole villages, and the Communists killed all those not willing to help them and labeled them "collaborators." The Communist forces could not defend the people against the Japanese, and the Japanese had no particular interest in defending them against the Communists. Caught between two fires the Chinese people often had no choice but that of who was to be their executioner.

One of the few Christian missionaries who remained in the Northern occupied areas from 1937 to 1942, the Reverend Wallace C. Merwin, wrote in the *Christian Century* that the Chinese Communists had undoubtedly killed far more Chinese than they had Japanese. He said:

> The common method of dealing with a traitor was burial alive, and a traitor was anyone who remained in occupied territory or was caught coming out of a town with Japanese-sponsored puppet money on his person, even so little as ten cents.

Another missionary, the Reverend Reinbold, wrote in 1940 that in the province of Shensi:

> . . . the Japanese invasion was short and the population did not suffer much, but many have been killed since by the Communists for not having evacuated the place.

The testimony of this Norwegian is particularly valuable since he was highly praised in *Twin Stars over China* by the late Colonel Evans Carlson of the United States Marine Corps, who was a warm admirer of the Chinese Communists.

The great advantage of the Communists, both during the war and following V-J Day, consisted in their irresponsibility for the fate of the Chinese people. The National Government was trying, however ineffectually, to defend what was left of Free China. The Communists were engaged simply in raiding into Japanese-occupied or Kuomintang-controlled areas.

There were no Chinese Communists fighting in any of the major engagements of the Sino-Japanese or World War; neither at Shanghai in 1937, or at Taierchwang in the north in 1938, nor defending the Wuhan cities, nor in the four battles of Changhsha, nor at the Tungting Lake, nor in the battles on the Salween and Burma fronts.

According to the testimony even of those kindly disposed toward the Chinese Communists, they could not and did not challenge any important Japanese garrison post or Japan's control of the North China railway system. Theodore White says that Communists fought only "when they had an opportunity to surprise a very small group of the enemy. . . . During the significant campaigns it was the weary soldiers of the Central Government who took the shock, gnawed at the enemy and died."

The many engagements the Communists boast of having fought against Japan were in reality minor guerrilla skirmishes. They fought only when they came across small isolated Japanese detachments, and many of their "victories" were won against Chinese puppet forces who never wanted to fight their countrymen but were just earning a living as Japanese mercenaries.

Communist "victories" were often won against small Nationalist forces already weakened by fighting the Japanese. The Communists adhered to the line laid down by Mao; seventy percent of their efforts were expended in extending the area of Communist control. They took over regions abandoned by the Japanese when the latter withdrew their forces to launch attacks on the National Government armies. Since the main efforts of the Japanese were always directed against the Chinese National armies, the Chinese Communists could wait and attack one side or the other when it was exhausted. Lin Yutang, who was sympathetic to the Communists in the early years of the war, has written: "For every Japanese they claim to have killed, the Communists have killed at least five Chinese. For every town they have captured from the Japanese they have captured fifty towns from other Chinese. Of the hundreds of 'clashes' per year they claim to their credit, a fair percentage must include those with the Chinese 'enemy'—half of their weapons have been robbed from other Chinese guerrillas and regular units.*"

Perhaps this is an exaggeration. We may never know the truth of what went on in North China during the war. One cannot deny the bravery of the Chinese Red Army and partisans, or their readiness to fight, to starve, to march in the cold of winter and heat of summer, to sacrifice and to die. The tragedy is that all their courage and conquests were not utilized in China's interests or to advance the ideals the rank and file of the Communists believe in. Knowingly or unknowingly they were but pawns in Stalin's game of power politics. Of them it might be said as Tennyson said of Lancelot:

> The shackles of an old love straitened him,
> His honour rooted in dishonour stood,
> And faith unfaithful kept him falsely true.

There is little doubt that the prevailing sentiment in America encouraged the Chinese Communists to direct their main war effort against the National Government during the last year of the war with Japan. The Comintern's democratic masquerade was more successful in China than anywhere else. Many an American editorial writer, columnist and radio commentator was to continue repeating the old refrain, "The Chinese are not real Communists, merely liberal agrar-

---

* *The Vigil of a Nation*, p. 125. Many instances with names and dates are given by Lin Yutang to prove the truth of this assertion.

ian reformers," long after the falsity of Communist pretensions in Europe was plain enough to dispel all illusions.

The long-current misapprehensions as to the nature of Chinese Communism resulted partly from America's disgusted reaction against the National Government of China. But it also arose from the reputation achieved by Communist-sympathizing journalists posing as "experts" on China. During the early years of the Sino-Japanese War it had been the Communists and fellow travelers who had been most concerned, because Japan then appeared as a close and dangerous menace to the Soviet Union. Except for a few missionaries and one or two far-sighted Republicans like Mr. Stimson, few other Americans had cared what happened to China. Mr. Grew, as ambassador to Japan, had shown concern only for American interests in China and had favored the continuance of friendly American-Japanese relations until the Japanese menace to the United States became clear. President Roosevelt had never considered Japanese aggression against China as on a par of wickedness with German aggression in Europe and had not applied the Neutrality Act in the Far East.

Consequently, when the American public started to become interested in China, following Pearl Harbor, the writers already established as popular experts were for the most part inclined to the Communist point of view. Others got on the Communist band wagon once Russia became America's "gallant ally."

In the early stages of the Sino-Japanese War the influence of Communist-sympathizing journalists and "experts" in the American press was not harmful to China, since Russia's fears of Japan, and the existence of a united front in China, led them to represent the Chinese Government in a favorable light and pay tribute to the valor of the armies of Chiang Kai-shek. During the period of the Stalin-Hitler Pact, however, and in particular following the Russo-Japanese Treaty of April 1940, strong criticism of the Kuomintang was voiced in so-called liberal journals in America, and in such publications as the *Far Eastern Survey* and *Pacific Affairs,* published by the Institute of Pacific Relations.

Following Hitler's attack on the Soviet Union, China once again enjoyed a comparatively favorable press, but, following the Russian repulse of Germany at Stalingrad in February 1943, increasingly strong criticism of the Chinese Government began to be heard. Once it was clear that Russia was released from all fear of a Japanese attack the Government of China was belabored with abuse and her war effort minimized, not only in Communist publications but also in American magazines with a mass circulation.

This was the time when Edgar Snow wrote in *The Saturday Evening Post* that the situation in China was similar to that in Yugoslavia "with the Chinese partisans led by Generals Chu Teh and Mao Tse-tung corresponding to Marshal Tito and his following, and the policy of Chungking toward them being about the same as that which Mikhailovitch and King Peter tried to enforce toward the Yugoslav guerrillas." Snow, of course, urged us to transfer our support to the Communists, or at least threaten to treat Chiang Kai-shek like Mikhailovitch unless he knuckled under to the Communists.

The Institute of Pacific Relations followed the same line. Mr. Lawrence Salisbury, who had left the State Department to edit *Far Eastern Survey,* wrote an article on April 25, 1945 in which he also urged America to treat China like Yugoslavia, called the Communists "liberty-loving" and argued at one and the same time that unless Chiang Kai-shek would embrace the Communists, Russia would arm them against the National Government, and that America was in danger of "thrusting the Communists into the arms of the Soviet Union."

All in all, it is not the fault of the I.P.R., Edgar Snow *et hoc genus omne* that we are not today confronted with a bigger and more menacing Tito in the Far East than at Trieste.

At least three out of four books published on China were favorable to the Communists. Even the War Department was not immune from such influence. It issued a special Armed Forces edition of Edgar Snow's *People on Our Side.* When I visited Communist China, I was struck by the fact that the United States Army post library at Yenan contained not one of the books critical of the Chinese Communists, but every single one written by their protagonists.

The distorted view of China given to the American public by friends of the Chinese Communists was remarked upon by the unpolitical but intelligent Emily Hahn whose articles in the *New Yorker* gave a far more realistic picture of China. On her repatriation to the United States from Japanese-occupied Hong Kong, she remarked on the fact that everyone asked her only about three things in China: Communists, guerrillas and industrial co-operatives. Miss Hahn wrote in 1944:*

> The average American is full of hooey through no fault of his own. He thinks guerrillas are the only soldiers who do any fighting at all in China. He thinks the woods are full of them. Actually, the great burden of resistance has rested on the regular army. The situation is due to the peculiarity of most American newspapermen in China, who are nearly all of them inclined to be Leftist, out of a frustrated sense of guilt, a superior viewpoint of things as they are, and a tendency to follow the crowd—of newspapermen. Most newspapermen don't know any more about the Communists in China than you do. They hear rumors . . . but the chances of seeing what goes on among the Chinese Communists are even less than those of seeing the inside of Russia. If you live in Chungking, you can always interview Chou En-lai. That is what he is there for. But if you think he is going to give you all the answers you are as innocent as an American newspaperman.

The Communist inspiration for China's bad press in the United States was demonstrated with peculiar force following the Russo-Japanese Pact of March 1944. China's fortunes were at their nadir. She had ample reasons to fear that Russia had become benevolently neutral toward Japan. Not only had the Moscow radio followed up the pact by starting a verbal campaign against the Chinese National Government, but reports were coming in that Japan had taken seven divisions of her famous Kwanting Army from Manchuria to help launch a new offensive against China designed to get control of the whole Peiping-Hankow-Canton railroad and cut China vertically in half.

It was obvious that without the reassurance given her by Russia, Japan would not have dared to deplete her forces along the Russian frontier in order to launch her first big offensive in years against a Free China. Yet, one might have imagined from reading most of the newspaper reports and magazine articles published in America that Russia, not China, was our ally in the war against Japan.

Instead of reassuring the Chinese as to our future intentions at this

---

* *From China to Me*, by Emily Hahn. Copyright, 1944, by Emily Hahn, reprinted by permission of Doubleday & Company, Inc.

period of the lowest ebb in their fortunes and of their greatest fears of Russia as well as of Japan, it became fashionable in America to excoriate China, denounce the alleged fascist features of her government, and scorn her war effort. The fact that China had had to fight alone and unaided for many years before we entered the war was ignored. The maintenance of Central Government troops in the Northwest was represented as a proof of the "antidemocratic" character of the Chungking Government, without regard to the fact that the Communists were devoting a large part of their energies to fighting the National Government forces. Also, there was always a possibility that the Communists might open Free China's back door to the Japanese. The West had forgotten the Stalin-Hitler partition of Poland in 1939, but the Chinese Government naturally feared that the Russo-Japanese Pact of 1944 might lead to similar collaboration.

The accusation, so widely disseminated in the American press, that Lend-Lease supplies brought into China by the gallant United States Air Force flying over the Hump, were "hoarded" by Chiang Kai-shek for use against the Communists, was in any case a libel. An inquiry conducted by the United States Army Headquarters in China established the fact that none of the arms of the Chinese National armies around the Communist zone were of American origin. It was established that although these forces were well equipped according to China's low standards, their complement of arms was the normal one and resembled a military junk pile collected from all Europe.

General Stilwell appears to have been responsible for more "hoarding" of Lend-Lease supplies than the Chinese. General Chennault told me, in an interview in Shanghai, that in 1944 Stilwell had 100,000 tons of United States arms and equipment uselessly stored at Kunming while the Chinese were fighting desperately without benefit of Lend-Lease a short distance away from Kweilin to stem the Japanese onslaught.

The very same journalists and authors who denounced China for not being a democracy praised Russia to the skies and were silent concerning the totalitarian features of her regime. The fact that the Russians, armed and equipped with vast quantities of Lend-Lease supplies, were winning victories, while the unaided Chinese were unable to fight, was somehow held to prove Russia a "democracy" and China "fascist."* Never was so illogical a conclusion reached. If ability to wage war and fight bravely were a proof of democracy, Germany and Japan must surely have been full-fledged democratic states.

Our blindness to the help Russia and the Communists were giving to Japan was the more inexplicable in that both America and Britain had had experience of Communist aid to Germany in the period of the Stalin-Hitler Pact, when national defense measures were opposed, and the war in Europe denounced as an imperialistic struggle for which Germany was no more to blame than England, France and the United States. We ought to have understood why the leaders of the Chinese Government were suspicious of the Chinese Communists and insisted upon keeping blockaded in the Northwest those who took their orders from a foreign power which maintained seemingly friendly relations with Japan and adopted a far-from-friendly attitude toward the Chinese Government. Instead, we praised the Chinese Communists and nearly went along with General Stilwell in what would have been the suicidal policy of arming them, without any guarantee that they would not fight the Chinese Government instead of the Japanese with whom their masters were on friendly terms.

The Stilwell incident in 1944, which led to his recall, illuminated like a searchlight the deadlock in China which almost led to her being knocked out of the war half a year before Japan's total defeat. It highlighted the decay in Chinese morale, the effects of the Russo-Japanese Pact, and the influence of Communist sympathizers in the State Department on General Stilwell himself. It also illustrated the unfortunate convergence in view of American soldiers who neither knew nor cared what the war was about and hated serving in China where wine, women, good food and the amenities of a mechanized civilization were woefully lacking; of the imperialist-minded British who were happy to find "proof" in American disgust with China that no Asiatic peoples were fit for self-government and who wanted China's best troops to be used to defend British imperial interests in Southeast Asia; and of

* According to Donald Nelson's statement to the China-American Council of Commerce and Industry in January 1945, Free China had only 6,000 trucks running and they were from 3 to 12 years old. He also stated that the Chinese kept them running long after they had reached a state of disrepair in which Americans would have abandoned them. Russia, meanwhile, had received hundreds of thousands of trucks from the United States.

the Communist-sympathizing "liberals" who adored Stilwell, hated the Chungking Government and made no allowances for its need to defend itself from its internal, as well as its external, enemies. As General Li Tsung-jen, the Kwangsi general, said to me in Peiping in February:

> The American Army under General Stilwell concentrated all its efforts and ours on reopening the Burma Road and on building up forces south of the Yangtze for an offensive against Japan from that quarter. Thus North China was depleted of troops and the Chinese Communists had a field day. When the Burma Road was finally reopened it was too late to be of any use.

Japan's ultimate defeat owed nothing to the much-publicized Burma-Salween campaign to which General Stilwell sacrificed all other considerations. But it resulted in China's National Government finding itself on V-J Day with its main forces concentrated in the Southwest and unable to reoccupy, at short notice, all the Chinese territories liberated by Japan's sudden surrender. In other words, General Stilwell's strategy, while contributing little or nothing to Japan's defeat, materially aided the Chinese Communist postwar bid for power.

Chiang Kai-shek and his generals had not been alone in their opposition to the Stilwell strategy which utilized China's only properly equipped and Western-trained divisions for a campaign of greater benefit to the British Empire than to China. General Chennault, an advocate of air power and commander of the Fourteenth Air Force which had performed miracles with the little it had, considered the Burma campaign a waste and wanted to concentrate available supplies on severing Japan's sea communications, thus starving out her forces in Burma and South China. He told me in Shanghai that Stilwell had refused to allocate to Chiang Kai-shek enough American equipment to defend even the airfields in China. As Dr. Walter Judd told Congress in March 1945, he had been informed by Americans in China that "we did not give the Chinese infantry who had to defend those bases one rifle, or one machine gun, or even one bullet for the job." Yet Stilwell and his friends and protagonists damned Chiang Kai-shek and his government for China's defeats, ascribed her military reverses to the undemocratic nature of his government and wanted to arm the Chinese Communists instead.

General Wedemeyer, as Admiral Lord Louis Mountbatten's chief of staff in Southeastern Asia, had also opposed the Burma campaign; he favored a strategy which would have served both American and Chinese interests better. As he said to me, fighting the Japanese in the jungle gave them every advantage and prevented America's technological superiority from being brought to bear against the enemy. He had argued in favor of amphibious landings to recapture first Rangoon and then a southern Chinese port. Japan's forces could then have been cut off from their supply bases with less, or no greater, expenditure of lives than those sacrificed in the futile Burma campaign and in flying supplies to China over the Hump. Moreover, the opening up of such a port as Canton would have been of inestimably greater value to China than the trickle of supplies which could be carried over the Burma Road.

When I asked General Wedemeyer whether it was not the lack of landing craft which prevented the adoption of the strategy he favored, he replied that in wartime supplies become available when the need is obvious and a commander is using all he has. The Southeast Asia command, he said, had been deprived of what it had and also denied more ships in favor of the European theater, because it was not in any case making use of its naval forces.

Until the history of the war is written by those who have the necessary inside knowledge and military competence, it is impossible for the layman to pronounce judgment. It is at least certain that the Chinese had reason to distrust Stilwell's military judgment as well as his motives. "Vinegar Joe" made no secret of his dislike and contempt for Chiang Kai-shek and his government. He surrounded himself with Communist sympathizers. Any proposals made by Stilwell were naturally suspect in the eyes of the Chinese Command, since he had made it all too clear that he preferred the Communists and would not be at all sorry to see the National Government overthrown.

Stilwell, for his part, accused the Generalissimo of keeping many of his best divisions immobilized in the Northwest, blockading the Chinese Communists. In his judgment the disastrous defeats in 1944 were all due to Chiang's fear of the Chinese Communists, his inability or unwillingness to institute reforms in Free China and his general incompetence. The American commander freely expressed his views of the head of the Chinese State, calling him a "coolie," a dishonest man and a ruthless dictator. He carried his personal hatred of Chiang to such lengths that he avoided meeting him and communicated with him through Madame Chiang, whom he liked, or at least did not dislike so much.

The net result of mutual dislikes and suspicion was a total lack of co-operation which Japan turned to her advantage.

General Stilwell's own friends admitted that he was obsessed by the desire to return as a conqueror to the territory in which he had "taken a hell of a beating" in 1942. His warmest admirers also state that he was a "forthright soldier" for whom there was only one consideration: "to fight the Japanese with everything available." What might happen afterward apparently did not concern him. His typically American contempt for "political considerations" in wartime; his personal courage, endurance and readiness to share all the hardships of the men he commanded; his hatred of caste divisions—all constituted excellent qualities for a commander in the field and endeared him to newspapermen, but they were not the requirements of a statesman or a diplomat, or of a strategist in global warfare.

Nor were General Stilwell's virtues and qualities as a soldier of a kind to render him immune to Communist influence and intrigues. His lack of patience, tact and self-control prevented his even trying to make the best of things. He would curse and swear and pour out the vials of his wrath and contempt over the heads of Chiang Kai-shek and his generals, instead of endeavoring to establish a working partnership between allies.

According to the testimony of all his friends and admirers, he hated "paper work," was a poor administrator and was badly served by the men who did his staff work. Officers who served under both Stilwell and his successor told me that Stilwell had never worked out an over-all strategic plan for China. His tactics were opportunist and haphazard, and his feud with General Claire Chennault, combined with his hatred of Chiang Kai-shek, resulted in the lack of a common purpose even among the Americans, much less an American-Chinese plan either for defense or attack.

Stilwell, as George Taylor of the Office of War Information once remarked, treated Chiang Kai-shek like a tribal chieftain. Although a liberal, and although he spoke Chinese fluently, Stilwell had neither respect nor liking for those who represented a culture and a civilization alien to his own. The Chinese had damn well got to learn to do the right thing as represented by American desires and American judgments as to what was good for China.

As Fred Eldridge reports in *Wrath in Burma,* Stilwell was "psychologically incapable of humbling himself before a man he considered to have the mentality of a peasant, and grew to hate the Generalissimo."*

On the other hand, Stilwell loved the Chinese soldiers and vouched that, properly trained, equipped and led, they were second to none. In spite of his hatred of the British and all other imperialists, Vinegar Joe reminded me of the best type of British Indian Army officer who damned the Indian Nationalists but loved his Indian soldiers, just as Stilwell despised and hated the Chinese Nationalists but loved the Chinese "common man."

I had known General (then Colonel) Stilwell in 1938 in Hankow and had been friendly with the men and women who were to have so much influence with him when he became commander of the United States forces in China and Burma: Agnes Smedley, the faithful and singlehearted champion of the Chinese Communists; John Davies, of the State Department, who in spite of his intelligence and skeptical outlook came to believe that the Chinese Communists were liberals; and Evans Carlson, the gallant Marine colonel whose faith in the Communists was that of a little child—a man of religious temperament who stated that the Chinese Communists were true Christians; Jack Belden and other correspondents who "fell for" the Communists' democratic masquerade.

In 1946 in Chungking, I asked Jack Belden's old friend, Tillman Durdin, what had happened to turn Jack's sympathies toward the Communists, since in Hankow he had been a bitter misanthrope with Trotskyist inclinations but as anti-Communist as I. How had he been transformed from the unbelieving, sad and skeptical Belden of 1939?

"Chou En-lai," laconically replied Durdin. "Like so many other people, he came under his spell in Chungking. And, Freda, you must understand that it was easy to believe in the Communists in those

* Published by Doubleday and Company, 1946.

days. It was so utterly hopeless in 'Free China.' The graft, the misery, the lack of will to fight any more. Even I felt that it could not be worse, and must be better in Communist China.

"You missed the depressing hopeless years in China following the fall of Hankow. You have to get the feel of them, in order to understand why so many Americans fell for the Communists."

The incident which led to General Stilwell's recall in the fall of 1944 resulted in part from his own character and the open contempt he showed for Chiang Kai-shek, and in part from the influence in Washington of the friends of the Chinese Communists.

According to the account given me by a top-ranking civilian representative of the United States Government in China, a telegram was sent from Quebec to General Stilwell by President Roosevelt, instructing him to demand that the civil government as well as all China's armed forces be put under his orders, so that Stilwell should control all China's resources. Chiang Kai-shek had already agreed to put General Stilwell in command of the Chinese armies; now he was expected to let China be administered like an American colony. The telegram stated that in the event of Chiang Kai-shek's refusal, he should be threatened with the withdrawal of all American forces from China and the complete cessation of Lend-Lease.

Stilwell went off at once to the Generalissimo's house where Chiang was dining with Ambassador Hurley. When Hurley read President Roosevelt's telegram, he said to Stilwell that the substance of what was demanded could probably be obtained diplomatically if no threats were made. Stilwell, however, insisted on showing the telegram to Chiang Kai-shek.

Chiang, after it had been translated to him, said:

> Tell your President that I cannot abdicate the leadership of my people or the Presidency of my country. If he insists on withdrawing American forces and Lend-Lease, we will have to do the best we can. We have been fighting for seven years and except for Chennault's air force, we have received no aid from America to date. We will continue to fight to the end without any if we have to, but now I insist that General Stilwell leave China.

Chiang added: "I will accept another American general in his place but Stilwell cannot remain."

Chiang Kai-shek's boldness won the day—at least temporarily. General Stilwell was recalled and replaced by General A. C. Wedemeyer. Ambassador Gauss, who had also shown a partiality for the Chinese Communists and had been urging Chiang Kai-shek to come to "a friendly agreement" with Russia, thereupon resigned. General Hurley, who had been the President's special envoy, and who had become Chiang Kai-shek's supporter, was made ambassador to China.

Although rebuffed, the State Department advocates of all-out aid to the Chinese Communists continued to influence United States policy and were to win the next round when, a year after Stilwell's recall, Ambassador Hurley was compelled to resign.

At the time of Stilwell's recall, it appeared that Chungking itself would be captured and China's long war of resistance practically ended at the very time when American forces were advancing from triumph to triumph in the Pacific. Japan's advance, which reached its high-water mark in December 1944, was halted by bitter cold, her lack of supplies, and General Wedemeyer's intelligent strategy and success in infusing a new spirit into Chinese-American relationships and the Chinese Command.

The eleventh-hour repulse of Japan in the winter of 1944-1945 thus synchronized with the weakening of the pro-Communist elements which had come to dominate American policy. With the recall of General Stilwell and Ambassador Gauss, Chinese-American relations became sufficiently healthy for General Wedemeyer to establish a workable pattern of collaboration and to start building up a military force in China capable of taking the offensive against Japan. Almost everything which Stilwell had failed to do by bludgeoning, threatening and abusing the Chinese Government, Wedemeyer accomplished by his tact, his sincerity, his fair-mindedness and lack of personal vanity, his readiness to treat the Chinese as equals and his freedom from Communist influence.

As long as Russia was in danger, as long as America's defeat of Japan was not certain, the Chinese Communists did not launch an open full-scale attack on the Chinese National Government forces defending what was left of Free China against Japan.

The turn toward all-out hostility against democracy's battered, weak and corrupt ally, the National Government of China, began in the winter of 1944-1945.

The Communists had refrained from offering any resistance to the Japanese when the latter in 1944 moved their forces south from Manchuria and North China to launch their last and greatest offensive against China. Not a single troop train passing through Communist territory was derailed; no move at all was made by the Communists to stem the Japanese onslaught. But, in the hour of China's greatest disaster, when the Japanese were almost at the gates of Chungking, the Communists took the offensive against their own countrymen. Foreseeing Japan's early collapse at the hands of the American Navy and Air Force in the Pacific, the Communists came out of retirement to deprive China's National Government of the fruits of victory. From their bases in the North they launched their campaign for dominance of Central and North China.

When V-J Day came the Communists had great hopes of success. The best-equipped and trained Nationalist forces were in the Southwest preparing to launch an offensive to the southern coast. The sudden Japanese surrender seemed to afford the Communists a chance to win control of all North China and the Yangtze Valley.

They were checkmated by the United States, at this time represented by Ambassador Hurley and General A. C. Wedemeyer, who, as Commander in Chief of the China Theater, flew and transported by ship sufficient Chinese Government troops to occupy Shanghai, Nanking, Peking and other important liberated cities. The U. S. Marines arrived in North China; and the Japanese were ordered to surrender only to the National Government's representatives.

In the months preceding V-J Day Chiang Kai-shek had again and again invited Mao Tse-tung to come to Chungking to confer. The invitations had been rejected with vile abuse; but, following the signing of the Sino-Soviet Treaty of August 1945, when it seemed that Russia and China were to become "friendly," Mao came to the capital to negotiate an agreement.

The subsequent story of Kuomintang-Communist negotiations, truces and recurrent armed conflict has been told in other chapters. Here sufficient details have been given to prove that the Chinese Communist record shows beyond any reasonable doubt that the Communist Party of China is just as loyal and obedient a branch of the Comintern as any other. Indeed, it does not deny it except in speeches, interviews and articles intended only for a gullible American public.

Some well-known writers who admit that the Chinese Communists *are* real Communists nevertheless argue that the United States ought to support them.

It would be impossible for the United States to lead a Communist Revolution abroad while retaining a capitalist organization of society and a democratic government at home. The historical monstrosity of a Chinese Communist Revolution made in America would in fact mean imperialist intervention on the grand scale. The assumption that if America should proceed on such a course "we should not clash with Russia" is naïve. Moscow would most certainly object violently to seeing the Chinese Communists transfer their allegiance to America. Stalin would not hesitate to denounce them as Trotskyists, fascists and "running dogs of American imperialism"—the term now applied by the Communists to the National Government of China. Nor would Stalin scruple to switch over to support of Chiang Kai-shek. He would undoubtedly be as ready to kiss and make friends with Chiang as he was in 1946 to embrace Peron. He would be able to come forward as the champion of Asiatic liberty against America in the same manner as he did against "Yankee imperialism" in Latin America.

Chiang Kai-shek, who has known all along that he could get Moscow to curb the Chinese Communists if he were ready to break his ties with the Western democracies and bring China into Russia's sphere, would have no alternative but to call on Moscow for aid against an American-led Communist Revolution.

All in all, it was hardly surprising that when Major Robert B. Rigg and Captain John W. Collins of the U. S. Army were imprisoned by the Communists in Manchuria early in 1947 they were given *Thunder Out of China* to read while threatened by physical tortures.

The whole idea of American sponsorship of a Communist Revolution in China would be too fantastic to deserve consideration were it not advocated by some of the best-known and most influential American "experts" on China. Mr. E. C. Carter, until recently secretary general of the Institute of Pacific Relations, said in a speech in Cleveland in 1946 that the United States should shift its support from the

National Government to the Communists, both because the latter's way of life was closer to the American and in order that the Chinese Communists should take our side if we become involved in war with Russia. As Edgar Ansel Mowrer commented in the *New York Post,* "There is no more chance of the United States supplanting Russia as the first love of the Chinese Communists than there would be of the American Catholics taking Russia's side in a war between Stalin and the Pope of Rome."

Whether or not General Marshall originally believed that the Chinese Communists are not real Communists, he certainly had no such illusion when he left China. In his public statement on January 7, 1947, he said:

> The Communists frankly state that they are Marxists and intend to work toward establishing a Communistic form of government in China, though first advancing through the medium of a democratic form of government of the American or British type.

Nor did General Marshall fail to express his resentment at the "provactive" and lying propaganda of the Chinese Communists against America.

Although he also accused the Nationalist Government publicity agent of numerous misrepresentations, he added that they were "not of the vicious nature of the Communist propaganda."

Unfortunately General Marshall still clung to his belief that it should be possible to give China a better government by uniting the liberals in the Kuomintang with the liberal elements which form a substantial element among the Communists. (See Chapter X.)

While agreeing with General Marshall that many young people have joined the Communists in disgust at the corruption of the existing government, and that the Chinese Communist Party contains some people whose impulses and aims are liberal, this fact is not likely to affect the issue. The history of the Comintern affords many examples, in various countries, of Communists who joined the Party without understanding its aims and methods and subsequently rejected them. Such "liberal elements" never had any influence. They were always expelled from the Party if they failed to submit to the rigorous discipline imposed by Moscow. Usually they were also given whatever nasty label happened to be popular at the time in Moscow to designate the enemies of Communism—"rotten liberal," "social fascist," "fascist" or what not.

Moscow may have feared that General Marshall was correct in believing that the Chinese Communist Party contained truly liberal elements for, in 1946, the notorious Li Li-san returned to China.

After his fifteen years in Moscow Li Li-san was no doubt regarded as a more obedient and pliant tool than Mao Tse-tung and the other Chinese Communist leaders who had long commanded an army of their own and been governors of large areas. Li Li-san could be expected to instill a proper Stalinist spirit into the Chinese Communist Party should it show any signs of backsliding by taking its democratic pretensions seriously. The arrival of a man, long trained in Moscow, to share authority with Mao Tse-tung and Chu Teh and to spy upon them would ensure their continuing obedience to the Kremlin's orders, should they disagree with the line of policy laid down by their Russian masters.

If there ever was a chance of detaching the Chinese Communist Party from its Russian allegiance, it depended upon the degree of strength and firmness displayed by the United States in international affairs and in China. The greater the evidence of American appeasement of Russia, the more unlikely the Chinese Communists would be to break away from Moscow.

If, in fact, as Marshall believed, a substantial proportion of the Chinese Communists were really liberals driven into the Party by the corruption and misgovernment of the Kuomintang Government, how could they trust the United States? Russia is near and America far away. Russia protects her own while we have sacrificed millions of people on our side for the sake of "good relations" with Moscow. Our abandonment of the democrats in Poland and the rest of Western Europe, our signing away of Italian and other territory in order to get an agreement with Russia—all of America's futile and unnecessary sacrifices of principle and interest to Soviet demands in 1945 and 1946, must have convinced all Chinese Communists that if they broke with Moscow they could not rely on American aid.

CHAPTER IX

The Struggle for Manchuria

HAD Russia obtained from China the concessions demanded over and above those agreed to in the Sino-Soviet Treaty, the Chinese Communists would probably have honored for a time the Political Consultative Council Agreements reached in January and February 1945. In the truce effective January 13 they had specifically agreed that:

> The cessation of hostilities order does not prejudice military movements of forces of the National Army into or within Manchuria which are for the purpose of restoring Chinese sovereignty.

Russia had for months been demanding that China "co-operate" exclusively with her in Manchuria, this "co-operation" to take the form of joint ownership of all the natural resources and industries. Stalin must have calculated that China would not dare to refuse, however long she protracted the negotiations. The silence of the Chinese Government concerning the Red Army's looting of Manchuria; the lack of public protest at Russia's refusal to let Chinese forces land in Dairen and her other breaches of the Sino-Soviet Treaty; America's role in helping the Chinese Communists to win concessions from the Chinese Government—all indicated to Russia that she would be as successful in raping Manchuria as the Japanese had been in 1931. It seemed that Russia's Left hand, the Chinese Communists, could be withdrawn. Hence the Chinese Communists pledged not to interfere with the occupation of Manchuria by Nationalist forces.

The Chinese Government for its part may have had the illusion that, in coming to terms with the Communists and agreeing to share power with them in a coalition government, it had sufficiently appeased Russia and would be allowed to regain actual, as distinct from nominal, possession of Manchuria. Or it may have hoped that by doing exactly what the United States wanted, it could calculate on sufficient American backing to cause the Russians to vacate Manchuria. However, my conversations with Chinese Government leaders at the time led me to believe that they might have given way to Russia's demands in the new "economic talks" with the Soviet Government, which followed the conclusion of the P.C.C. Agreements, had it not been for an unforeseen occurrence.

In the middle of February the first group of American correspondents entered Manchuria. They practically forced their way in, determined to see for themselves in spite of the embargo imposed by the Chinese Government at Russia's insistence. Without permission from anybody these eight American newspapermen, one of them a woman (Charlotte Ebner of I.N.S.) and one English correspondent, took the train from Chinchow to Mukden. After a long and uncomfortable journey in unheated coaches, they were immediately taken into custody by the Red Army, and locked up for fifty-two hours in the Yamato Hotel, renamed "Intourist" by the Russian "liberators."

I was in Peiping at the time and there was a certain amount of discreet amusement at the idea of the U.P. correspondent, Reynolds Packard, who was distinctly anti-Communist, being incarcerated together with such others as Pepper Martin of the *New York Post,* Lieberman of the *New York Times,* Potter of the *Baltimore Sun,* and Fritz Opper of the Mutual Broadcasting Company, all of whom were more than a little inclined to sympathize with the Chinese Communists, blame the National Government for everything and believe in Stalin's good intentions. Lieberman and Potter had steadfastly refused to believe that the Soviet Government was responsible for the ban on American correspondents in Manchuria. Lieberman a month or so earlier had joined with McGaffin, of the *Chicago Daily News,* Spencer Davis, of the A.P., and Pulitzer-prize-winning photographer Frank Filan, in asking their home offices to protest to President Truman and General Marshall on the assumption that the refusal to admit foreign correspondents into Manchuria was the fault of the Chinese Government. If it had not been for the detention of others with them one could have rejoiced at an example of poetic justice when the Russians locked them up.

Eventually this first group of foreign correspondents was allowed out of the hotel and told they would be permitted to move around. Touring the desolate industrial section of the city they saw American Lend-Lease trucks loaded with looted machinery being taken away for transshipment to Russia. The Chinese manager of the biggest aluminum plant showed them a penciled receipt given him by the Soviets after the place had been stripped bare. Everywhere they saw broken walls and debris and were told by the Chinese that the Russians had taken delight in setting off demolition charges after carrying off what they wanted.

Not only had all Mukden's heavy industries been dismantled or destroyed, but its weaving and dyeing plants were found stripped of all spindles, motors and dye vats. When questioned as to whether the Russians were responsible for all the ruin, the Chinese told the Americans that the Red Army was responsible for 80 or 90 percent of the looting but that, later on, when the Russians had taken everything they wanted, Chinese Communists and local residents had been let in to glean what was left.

Although the Russians had announced a month previously that they were handing Mukden back to China the correspondents found Chinese Army headquarters "like a haunted house" while Soviet headquarters were packed with soldiers and officers and were humming with activity.

Before leaving Mukden the American correspondents were fired at by Russian soldiers because they were not quick enough in getting off a truck in which they thought they would be permitted to ride. Fritz Opper said to me after he got out, "I have been through the whole war as a correspondent, but I have never felt so nervous as I did in Mukden." He had been appalled at the reign of terror in Manchuria. He said to me: "What Russia is doing to China is as beastly as the raping of a child."

In spite of their considerably less-than-friendly reception by the Russians in Mukden, some American correspondents dared to go on to Changchun and another small group went to Dairen. Meanwhile there had been a second invasion of Manchuria by the American press, and the total number there was now doubled.

The following are extracts from what they said when they got out of Manchuria into the safe haven of Nationalist China.

Since newspapers in the States published only short versions of the dispatches written by the Associated Press correspondents at the time, I quote here from the fuller versions published in the Shanghai English language press.

Richard Cushing of the A.P. reported from Tientsin on March 4:

The Soviets in Manchuria, caught off balance by the audacious invasion of 22 news correspondents, must think the Americans have more crust than a homemade pie.

Only the element of surprise could have enabled the coup. . . .

The Russians were startled that the Americans could enter the Red Army-controlled territory merely by stepping off the train. They were still suffering from the first shock when another group of a dozen correspondents arrived by the same method, bringing the total in Mukden to 21. A French newsman turned up later.

The Soviets must have been still frozen by surprise at the fast working, joking Americans, when they boldly managed to slip onto Soviet trains to drive the invasion spearheads north to Changchun and south to Dairen.

But by now the surprise has worn off, and undoubtedly any more foreigners showing up in Soviet territory will be in for a rough time unless they have proper Russian papers, especially when word gets back of what the boys have been writing about.

The first wave of eight Americans including a woman, and one British writer, had been waiting weeks to get into Manchuria to cover what was considered a legitimate news story within the jurisdiction of Lt. General A. C. Wedemeyer, commanding general of the China Theater, which includes Manchuria.

Angry at being stalled by Chinese and American red-tape, they took the simple expedient of boarding a train bound for Mukden. . . .

The correspondents tried to sound out the Mukden commandant on whether he would permit them to travel to Changchun, the capital of Manchuria. He obviously was unhappy at the prospect, especially since his boss, Marshal Rodion Malinovsky, Soviet Far East commandant, is there. He strongly urged them not to go, but the first wave, spurred by a renewed wanderlust, climbed aboard a train by night, and somehow reached the capital, where they were promptly—as happened to them at Mukden—detained. . . .

While the first wave is still in Changchun, the second wave, sensing that the Soviets were unhappy over their presence in Mukden, entrained for the long cold ride to Chinchow.

They were given a rousing send-off in the form of a trigger-happy Soviet guard and his henchmen, who stopped the Chinese truck and ordered all off at the point of submachineguns, firing one burst of four shots over their heads to show that they meant business.

The Soviets are now stopping trains south of Mukden, searching for foreigners.

On arrival in Changchun the A.P., U.P., I.N.S., *New York Times, New York Post, Chicago Sun, Baltimore Sun* and *London Daily Express* correspondents received the same "frigid" reception as in Mukden. A Soviet officer and eight soldiers with Tommy guns escorted them to the "Intourist" Hotel and interned them. This time they spent 53 hours in captivity before being released with "limited freedom" and a warning not to try to see or write about the Red Army in Manchuria. Although Manchuria was supposed to have been given back to China, the correspondents were told that Changchun was "the frontier" and permission to go north to Harbin could be obtained only in Moscow.

Spencer Davis, of the A.P., wrote:

Throughout the interview with Major General Karlov, we were treated with cold formality and forbidden to smoke in the General's presence. We were denied use of Soviet machines for return to our quarters, some two miles distant through snow-banked streets. For the remainder of our stay we walked or rode "droshkies" through the streets where the sight of American Lend-Lease jeeps, weapon carriers and six-by-six trucks was only too common.

The correspondents were themselves told by General Karlov that the Red Army would quit Manchuria no later than the Americans left North China. What they heard in Changchun convinced them that Russia regarded China as a Russian-American battleground. A few days before their arrival at a Red Army banquet before high Soviet officials, Marshal Malinovsky, Commander in Chief of the Russian armies in Manchuria, had made a speech in which he warned the United States that there must be no interference with Russia's "friendship" for China, and Russia's "efforts to help China in Manchuria."

He had also said:

China and Russia are real friends. We don't want any country to harm this friendship, especially those people wearing white gloves and carrying gold in their pockets. If anybody puts out a hand to interfere we will cut it off.

The Russians have come to Manchuria not for money nor banking interests but because of ideals and friendship. Russia helped China early in the war while others only came in later when their own interests became involved.

The few Chinese officials who had come to Changchun to take over the city from the Russians were virtual prisoners. They hardly dared venture in the streets since the Soviet occupation forces warned them that they could not guarantee their "protection." A short while before Chang Hsin-fu and six other representatives of the National Government had been brutally murdered when they went to the Fushun collieries to take them over.

One of the bitterest critics of the Chinese National Government said to me later in Shanghai that he had to admire the guts of the Chinese officials in Changchun who preserved their equanimity and stayed there in spite of the constant danger of assassination by the Red Army.

No Chinese planes could leave without Russian permission and, when the Americans left for Peiping, Russian fighter planes "made a pass" over them when engine trouble caused their return to Changchun. They spent the night at the municipal hospital under Chinese auspices to avoid being imprisoned again by the Russians, who thought they planned to "sneak into Harbin"; next day they took the train south "to avoid further misunderstanding." Sung Chu-hsieng, manager of the British-American Tobacco Company in Mukden, who had dared to speak freely to the Americans, was murdered by the Russians a few days later.

The three American correspondents who went off to Dairen had an even worse reception. They were given "the bum's rush" out on February 27 after first being locked up in the hotel and then told that if they ventured abroad their "health" might be endangered. When, in spite of this warning, they walked in the city, a Red Army colonel accompanied them wherever they went to make sure they didn't see anything that shouldn't be seen, and didn't talk to the wrong persons.

When they produced their China Theater credentials the Americans were told that they were no good because "Dairen is the same as Russian soil"—this in spite of the Sino-Soviet Treaty of 1945 in which it was specifically stated that Dairen, unlike Port Arthur, was to remain a Chinese city and a free port.

Richard Cushing wrote:

The Soviets finding I had vanished sent a carload of secret police after me, and in a surprisingly short time knocked on the door of a frightened Scandinavian family which was serving me tea. Whisked back to headquarters, the Commandant, beet red with rage, said he was sorry we would have to leave; that we were going on the 2 P.M. train, just two hours off. . . . In the train three tough guards sat facing us and permitted no one to talk to us.

The *Stars and Stripes* correspondent had also managed to elude his guards for a short while, so a little knowledge was gleaned concerning conditions in "liberated" Dairen. "Worse than under the Japanese" was what he was told by the frightened inhabitants. Some foreigners there who had been in Europe said the Russian Secret Police were more efficient than the Gestapo, and they were mortally afraid of being seen talking to Americans. Soviet notes with a stamp saying they must be accepted "under pain of punishment" were "legal tender."

It was also noted by the Americans that Japanese civilians were being treated more courteously than the Chinese in Dairen, as elsewhere in Manchuria. Wives of Red Army men had arrived to set up permanent housekeeping, and Dairen had not been stripped of its industrial and port equipment. The vast quantities of machinery being shipped thence to Vladivostok had been looted from other parts of Manchuria. Evidently Russia intended to hold on to Dairen.

Korean ports were also used to transport the machinery, food and other goods looted from the Chinese by the Russians. It was estimated that in the short period of September to November 1945 northbound trains carried a daily average of five hundred loaded freight cars to Dairen and North Korean ports to be conveyed by Lend-Lease Liberty Ships to Russia.

Edwin S. Pauley, the United States Reparations Commissioner, cooled his heels for weeks in Southern Korea waiting in vain for permission from the Russians to enter Manchuria. Finally he returned to America.

After the damage had all been done, Mr. Pauley was permitted by the Russians to enter Manchuria and the Russian zone in Korea. His report on Russia's "preventative wrecking" has not at this date been made public, but sufficient details were given to the press to establish the fact that Manchuria today contains little of the great industry built up by the Japanese with Chinese labor. Russia succeeded in depriving China of the only valuable compensation she might have received for her huge losses in her eight-year war against Japan.

The treatment given them by the Russians led even the most pro-Communist correspondents to change their minds and join with the others in telling the world what was going on in Manchuria. As Reynolds Packard said, it was quite illogical for them to be so prejudiced by their personal experience, but it was all to the good nevertheless.

Fritz Opper gave a series of broadcasts from Shanghai and wrote some articles so convincing and horrifying that even the *Shanghai Evening Post* changed its tune. The editor, Randall Gould, had previously soft-pedaled all reports and rumors about the goings-on in Manchuria. Just a few days before the first correspondents got to Mukden he had written a soothing editorial saying there was nothing to get excited about in Manchuria; that Russia would of course honor the treaty with China and that the Yalta agreements (made public a little while before) were just dandy. A little later he had tried to make a joke of the treatment of the American correspondents in an editorial, "Another Manchurian Mystery," in which he wrote:

> Nine foreign newsmen now visiting Manchuria are reported ensconed in Mukden's de luxe Yamato hotel, "under thorough Russian protection," but going out very little. Their seclusion is said to be disappointing to curious residents of the city. Just why they venture forth so seldom is not precisely stated and there is an underlying suggestion that they are being restrained by their Soviet hosts. Yet at the same time it is stated that they are "consuming a considerable amount of Japanese beer to kill the long hours."
>
> Here we have another Manchuria mystery which ought to be gone into. Are the correspondents actually in durance vile, forced to a desperate swilling of ex-enemy beer as their sole recourse? If so there should be prompt action by the W.C.T.U. or some similar temperance organ. Maybe it is a case for the U.N.O. It is intolerable that nine men of normally abstemious habits should be so literally driven to drink.
>
> But perhaps it is the beer which is the attraction after all. There may be correspondents from Chungking, whose whistles have been dry for many a long month. Perhaps it is the availability of beer which is detaining the newshawks (or newsducks) indoors. Maybe it is not the correspondents who are desperate, but the victimized

> Russians whose stock of seized Japanese property must by now be running low.
>
> Anyway the whole matter should be exhaustively gone into. We suggest a rescue and investigation party. If necessary, we're prepared to volunteer in person.

On March 6, 1946, however, the *Shanghai Evening Post* completely reversed itself saying there was an "outrageous" situation in Manchuria and there was "nothing funny" at all about it. "Mukden," it quoted the *Stars and Stripes* correspondent as saying, "is the victim of one of the most scientific and thorough looting and stripping operations in history . . . and is living in a state of constant lawlessness and terror."

At long last recognizing the truth of the reports and rumors it had formerly disregarded as merely anti-Russian propaganda the *Shanghai Evening Post* continued:

> We are told that the Soviet authorities have cleaned out Mukden's vast industrial establishment, shipping hundreds of thousands of tons of machinery to Siberia. Acts of violence are daily occurrences. Soviet authorities are charged with giving direct aid to the Chinese Communists as against the National Government with whom they are in treaty relation. And that the National Government, whose sovereignty over Manchuria has been confirmed by Soviet Russia, is held off from exercising any real authority whatever in Mukden.
>
> It is a grim picture. Neither Chinese nor any friends of China, such as Americans, can view it without dismay. The *Stars and Stripes* correspondent additionally portrays "tough, arrogant Red Army troops, flushed with victory in a war they do not consider ended," busy building a mighty arsenal in Manchuria and tightening a military and political stronghold on a vital portion of Asia. . . .
>
> Nothing like this was contemplated by the United States at any stage of relations with the Soviet Union. Of that we are sure. . . . The question is, what to do? Someone had better take a strong position in more than a merely verbal way soon, unless we are willing to put our tacit seal of approval upon a clearly outrageous situation.

This reaction was typical. For a few weeks the American press was shocked into awareness of the real situation in the Far East. The National Government of China ceased temporarily to be the villain of the piece. The futile policy of silence concerning the Red Army's looting and the Soviet Government's brazen disregard of the pledges it had given in the Sino-Soviet Treaty was brought to an end by American correspondents, who, even if they had formerly been prejudiced in favor of Russia or the Chinese Communists, were honest reporters who described what they had seen.

Fritz Opper, whose long residence in the disheartening atmosphere of Chungking had formerly inclined him to give the Communists the benefit of the doubt, was now completely disillusioned and hot with indignation at China's treatment by Russia. "To think," he kept on saying back in the comparatively free atmosphere of Nationalist China, "to think that I used to call for a second front."

In talking to Fritz Opper and to Phil Potter of the *Baltimore Sun* in Shanghai I reflected how different a course history might have taken if more correspondents had known the truth about the Soviet Union sooner. For the influence of the fourth estate on American public opinion and government policy is incalculably great.

The following are extracts from what Opper wrote at the time and said over the radio:

A five day stay here brings these conclusions:

1) The Soviet authorities have cleaned out Mukden's vast industrial establishment and have shipped hundreds of thousands of tons of machinery to Siberia.

2) Mukden's citizens are fearful of almost daily acts of violence.

3) *The Soviet authorities have given great indirect assistance to the Chinese Communists and trustworthy witnesses declare they have cooperated directly, as well.*

4) The Chinese Central Government has no more real authority in Mukden than it has in Moscow.

Shops are boarded up here on every street and what business is being conducted is chiefly confined to tiny sidewalk stalls, in most cases handling looted Japanese knicknacks while the 8 P.M.–6 A.M. curfew makes Mukden's nighttime streets deserted and dangerous. Gunfire is heard nightly and looting, theft and murder are common.

The Japanese built up a great industrial section on the western outskirts of Mukden, containing an estimated 60 percent of all Manchuria's industries but today this is a deserted, looted area. *The destruction in Tokyo and Osaka is dramatic; the destruction in Mukden is more thorough and efficient.*

For mile after mile, factories have been denuded of machinery and today stand bare and gaunt. Window frames, telephones and light fixtures went first—to Chinese mobs that got out of hand after the Jap surrender.

Then the Soviet authorities came with trucks and Japanese prisoners of war as coolies, tore out the equipment, knocked holes in the walls to permit the removal of bulky machines and shipped the equipment to the Soviet Union. In some cases, demolition charges were set off in the empty buildings; in other cases they stand with their four walls and roofs only.

An engineer who was forced to participate told me the Russians have done the same elsewhere. He said that 70–80 percent of the great Anshan steel works have been stripped, taken to Port Arthur, Dairen and Korean ports and shipped to Vladivostok, some of the shipments being carried in Russian-manned American Liberty ships.

The extent of the Soviet stripping is shown in the fact that some generators have been removed from the power plant on the Yalu River that supplied most of southern Manchuria and that today Mukden is frequently without electric lights and running water.

This latter fact also presents possibly serious complications for refuse and filth is piling up in the streets here and if the present cold weather should break and warm weather set in there is real danger of wide-scale epidemics. Already tens of thousands of persons are reported to have died from disease in Manchuria, chiefly from typhus, and city authorities are worried.

Opper told me that he had been moved by the affection shown for the American uniform by Chinese under the Red Terror who "halted us to pat the China Theater shoulder emblem, and to enquire anxiously when Americans would bring Chinese forces here." He wrote:

Even the Japanese seemed glad to see us, asking when they would be repatriated.

People speak guardedly in Mukden and are careful to ask that their names are not used in stories. Many refuse to be interviewed at all and one report says that a Chinese who talked with correspondents was later shot at his own doorstep.

This sense of uneasiness, if not outright terror, seems to affect the White Russian emigrants as well as the Chinese and Japanese. In fact the Nazi Germans appear to be as little affected by the Soviet entry as any group. They are living unmolested and one eyewitness told me he saw the Nazi flag flying over the German club for two weeks after the Red Army arrived here.

Sergeant Dick Wilson, a young and intelligent soldier without political prejudices, gave a vivid account in the *Stars and Stripes* of the looting and terror, and went on to supply evidence of Russia's co-operation with the Chinese Communists:

Tough, arrogant Red Army troops, flushed with victory in a war they do not consider ended, today are building a mighty arsenal in Manchuria and tightening a military and political stranglehold on a vital portion of Asia.

While Russia's dreaded secret police spreads terror throughout this new Soviet occupation zone, battle maneuvers are under way in the strategic Dairen-Port Arthur area.

From Harbin to Dairen the Russians have virtually completed stripping of factories to build up Russian war industry strength and, according to the fears of competent observers, to leave no plants that could be utilized by potential enemies should China's northland become a battleground.

"Worse than Germany under the Nazis" and "terror rule as bad as the Nips" are expressions used by non-party residents of this once rich industrial area in describing their life under the Russians.

. . . .

Writing behind doors locked against imminent Russian intrusion, we correspondents are convinced we have seen and heard enough evidence to support these conclusions:

1) The so-called Kwangtung leased territory—the Dairen-Port Arthur sector of the Liaotung Peninsula—is being transformed into the Red Army's Manchuria arsenal.

2) *The Russians have no intention of leaving the areas they now hold in Manchuria unless they get costly economic and military concessions from China. The conviction is growing that they do not plan to relinquish control of Dairen and Port Arthur for any price.* [Italics in this and following paragraphs of this account are mine.]

. . . .

4) The all-seeing NKVD which has held a tight rein of fear on the Russian people since the revolution, has moved into Manchuria with the Red Army to launch a program of espionage, intrigue and intimidation of anybody who does not see eye-to-eye with the party.

5) The Russians are completing a systematic stripping of Manchuria's heavy industries. They are shipping materials to Russia via Vladivostok, using, according to reliable sources, some American Lend-Lease Liberty ships to haul away the booty. Japanese soldiers were forced to help in the stripping job, after which they mysteriously

disappeared. Indications—including a damning tongue-slip by Maj. General Andre Kovtun-Stankevitch, Mukden commandant—are that they are being sent to Siberia and Russia to work for the Soviets.

6) *The Russians are cooperating with the Chinese Communists, arming them and using them as propaganda tools. The Russians also are rumored to be enlisting Jap Army officers and technicians to create friction between the Japs and the Chinese.*

Each of these conclusions is supported by eyewitness observations or statements from authentic sources who cannot be identified while they live under Russian rule.

In another dispatch written in Mukden and also published later, he reported:

The Red Army has supplied the Eighth Route Army with weapons and ammunition and is using the Chinese Communists as a propaganda agency and as an occupation and administrative force in areas already stripped by the Russians.

This was revealed by captured Communist officers and residents of areas turned over to the Eighth Route Army after the Russians moved on to greener pastures.

In Anshan, Fushan, Yinkou and reportedly Dairen, administration of the cities now is in the hands of a civil government set up by the Communists. In all except Dairen, the cities are garrisoned by Eighth Routers, residents revealed. . . .

Even the Chinese Communists appear to be enlisting the aid of Japanese. On January 10th a technical commission of the Eighth Route Army arrived in Anshan to ask Japanese engineers to come to Honkeiko, on the Korean border, to help the Communists build up war industries for their own use there.

Some former Japanese army officers held in a camp north of Dairen are allowed to visit their families over week ends, reportedly because they had promised to cooperate with the Russians in spreading anti-Chinese and anti-American propaganda.

In Eighth Route army-held areas, anti-American posters and slogans are appearing, and residents are convinced the Communists were urged to spread such propaganda because the Russians—allies of the Americans—could not do so. *English no longer may be taught and matter may not be printed in English.*

Evidence that the Russians have armed Eighth Route army units came from captured Communists. In one a captain said *Russian interpreters with his unit contacted the Soviets to secure the arms. No Russian ever visited his unit, he said, but through interpreters the*

Russians sent them Japanese rifles, machine guns, mortars and even specially-made Eighth Route uniforms.

It has seemed necessary to quote at some length from these eye-witness reports, not only because the American public's memory is short concerning happenings far away, but because so many writers ignore the evidence concerning Russia's aggressively expansionist policy in China.

In March on arrival back in Peking from Yenan I tried to get to Mukden but the Marines would not permit it. General Worton, Chief of Staff to General Rockey, having read some of my writings and knowing about the Russian radio and press attacks on me in Peiping as well as Shanghai, told me I would be mad to go and that he would not take the responsibility of giving me air transport to Chinchow.

I feared that I might be liquidated or quietly bumped off, since I was not yet an American citizen and the Russians might think up the excuse that since I had been married to a Soviet citizen they had the right to send me to a concentration camp or otherwise dispose of me. I could have gambled on the local Russian commander not bothering to find out my name or never having heard it, but I knew I would be taking a chance. George Weller offered to come and rescue me if I should not return in a week's time, but I told him I had a healthy fear of the Russians and that although I wanted to see for myself what they had done in Manchuria I was not too sorry the Marines had refused to let me go there.

I may have been cowardly but I have a son and, having once escaped with him from Russia, I did not want to tempt Providence by putting my head back into the noose.

A few weeks later, while waiting in Tientsin for the Marine plane which was to fly me to Hawaii, I got the chance to pay a flying visit to South Manchuria already liberated by the retreat of the Red Army. Dr. Logan Roots, who was head of the UNRRA medical services in North China, told me one evening that three L5's belonging to the Army Liaison group (OSS) were leaving next morning for Chinchow. I secured permission from Colonel Kellis to be taken as a passenger, together with an English UNRRA worker called Menzies, who was going to Manchuria to investigate the reports of plague in the cities evacuated by the Russians.

Flying in an L5 was a thrilling experience, not to be compared to traveling in large planes. There is room for just one passenger and the pilot and there are only a cellophane hood and windows you can open if you wish. It was bitter cold but Colonel Kellis had lent me his flying boots and I had a navy parka. The pilots of these "flying jeeps" were all young volunteers who loved their work and had been specially trained to land almost anywhere and in all weathers. We flew low over the Great Wall of China where it comes down to the sea, and I learned what it means to "buzz the town" when we arrived at our destination. I felt I was really flying for the first time in my life. I enjoyed it immensely but I hadn't the nerve to lean 'way out of the plane window to take photographs as Menzies did.

I spent the evening at Chinchow with the Chinese Chief of Staff, General Chao, who took me home to dine. From him I heard further details of what the Red Army had done, and of the difficult situation of the Chinese National forces in an area supposed to have been returned to China, but still controlled by Russia. In the morning I walked round the town with Colonel Stewart, an Australian volunteer in the Chinese Air Force, whom I had met earlier in Shanghai. He showed me the gutted buildings left behind by the Russians as the monuments of their liberation of this Southern Manchurian town.

To me, however, the story of the Red Army in Manchuria was already an old one. I had heard months before from the Chinese what was happening. I had old friends among the Chinese generals and ministers who had taken me into their confidence and given me the details while the hush-hush policy was still in force. And I did not need to learn what terror means since I had lived under it for nearly six years in Russia.

Of course, other correspondents whom the Chinese trusted had also known the facts long before their revelation burst like a bombshell in the foreign press. But silence had been the official policy and silence had been kept.

One of China's leading generals whom I had known at the front in 1938 had come to visit me in the hospital in Shanghai early in November and, trusting me as an old friend of China's, had told me the facts about the Manchurian situation, which were only now being revealed to the world. Not only were the Russians removing all the machinery, they had taken away foodstuffs, cotton and even livestock. (This fact was subsequently confirmed to me by the UNRRA official who flew with me to Chinchow.) Locomotives and rolling stock and motor vehicles had also been seized by the Red Army. There was no rolling stock left for the Chinese Nationalist forces to use. Supplies and transport constituted the main difficulty for the government forces. Supplies had all to be brought from Shanghai and Tientsin by ships since the Communists had destroyed the railways. Hence China's dependence on the American Navy. Chinese officials who had gone to Changchun had been confined to their quarters like prisoners and had therefore left.

When I asked him why China kept all this a secret, he replied that it was because they hoped to "maintain peace and have friendship" with Russia. Diplomatic negotiations were proceeding and it was hoped that eventually Russia would honor her pledged word.

When I insisted that China gained nothing by keeping the facts hidden, since she had no other hope than American backing, he evaded a direct answer and said he hoped I would recover soon and go to Peiping and Manchuria. This I took to be tantamount to saying that he personally agreed with me.

He went on to speak of the Communist problem which "looks like an internal one but is really external politics on account of Russia."

"Have the Russians given arms to the Communists?" I asked.

"The Communists certainly must have received arms. There were no Communist troops in Manchuria when the war ended. Now there are 100,000. They now have some heavy artillery which they could have got only from the Russians. They are not yet powerful. They are organizing and training but our progress against them is easy because they have not yet learned how to use the arms supplied to them by the Red Army."

"But," I said, "they can continue destroying communications and making reconstruction impossible."

He agreed and said it would be easier if the Communists met the National forces in pitched battle.

"Do you," I queried, "hope that Russia will order the Chinese Communists to stop fighting?"

"Do you," he replied, "think it probable or possible? We don't hope for the impossible."

"Why then do you make concessions to Russia; what good can it do you?"

"Well, we were obliged to make concessions to Russia in the Sino-Soviet Treaty, because America had already made them at Yalta without consulting us."

"But Russia has already broken that treaty."

"China is like a poor man. Finally there is nothing more we can give and still live."

"Russia is acting just as Japan used to!" I exclaimed.

"Maybe even worse" was his laconic reply.

"If Manchuria is lost to us," he went on, "the eight-year war will have been fought for nothing. But we still hope to regain possession of her by peaceful means."

He was confident that America would supply transport to enable the Chinese Nationalist forces to regain Manchuria. In this he was mistaken. America denied sea passage for the Nationalist forces into contested ports that November, and by January it was too late since Hulutao was frozen and Yingkow had been captured by the Chinese Communists with the aid of Soviet tanks and artillery.

If the American policy implemented by Generals Hurley and Wedemeyer at the time of Japan's surrender had been continued the Nationalist forces would have been able to regain control of Manchuria. In those decisive weeks the National Government's troops had been rapidly moved in American planes and ships to occupy and control the areas formerly in Japanese hands and to facilitate the surrender of all Japanese forces to Central Government authorities. But General Wedemeyer was now being attacked by the Communists in the press and on the radio. Communist-contrived incidents were resulting in the ambushing of United States forces and the killing of some Americans. Certain officers in the State Department were placing obstacles in General Wedemeyer's way. He found himself restricted in the use of American ships to aid the National Government. Shipments of ammunition and other supplies to China were soon to be cut off by the refusal of the State Department to O.K. them. The net result was that America gave tacit acquiescence to the Communist occupation of Manchuria.

In Chungking, the Minister of Economics, Dr. Wong Wen-hao, whom I knew from Hankow days, had discussed the situation with me more frankly than anyone else. A man of science with a reputation for absolute honesty, he is one of the best administrators in the government. He also had a particularly thankless and difficult task, and was typical of the unfortunate liberals caught between two fires. He detested and distrusted Communism but he had no love for the Chinese tycoons who made fortunes during China's difficulties. He never said anything against T. V. Soong but I sensed his distrust when he told me that he had not agreed to the "nationalization" of ex-Japanese and puppet cotton mills in Shanghai, until he had received T.V.'s personal promise that they would be given back into private hands after two years. Having heard in Shanghai that one of T.V.'s henchmen was running the mills, I thought I understood this minister's troubles and misgivings. He told me, that evening in Chungking, how he longed to get out of it all and once again become a geologist.

Diminutive in stature, very energetic, fearless, with brilliant eyes and a plain but intensively expressive face, and even more expressive hands, Wong Wen-hao's gestures were eloquent of his despair in the situation China faced. He said:

Not only have the Russians carried off from Manchuria every bit of machinery they could move and destroyed the rest of its productive capacity, but they are now demanding that we pay back 30,000,000 gold dollars for the arms they supplied us at the beginning of the war. According to the contracts Sun Fo signed in 1937-1938 payment has to be made this year in minerals and other raw materials. Of course we calculated that we would have Manchuria back and could pay out of its resources. But Russia still occupies Manchuria and has stripped it bare.

"Stealing?" No, of course not, say the Russians. All property in Manchuria is "war booty" and theirs by right. But, they say, the Soviet Government is *so* friendly to China, that she wants to "sacrifice" some of her legitimate war booty for the sake of "co-operation!"

Abandoning sarcasm he continued:

Malinovsky has told us frankly that Russia is preparing for the next war and will brook no "foreign interference" in Manchuria—meaning, of course, America. The Russians have indicated all too plainly that they will never let us develop Manchuria into an industrial base until we break our ties with the United States. They have actually said that until Siberia is well developed into a strong industrial and military base Manchuria must remain backward and undeveloped. That is the reason why they not only looted it but destroyed what they could not remove.

"But," they say, "if you will co-operate with us, it is the policy of the Soviet Government to help us reconstruct China. Manchuria is the first field for such co-operation."

It is the Japanese all over again; the same hypocritical talk about "co-operation" when domination is what is really meant.

But what can we do? We are poor, weak, disorganized. We cannot fight another war. Stalin knows we cannot resist alone, that we dare not even protest. And the United States is only halfhearted in helping us to resist Russia's demands that we abandon the American connection. The United States tells us to "unite" with the Communists whose aim is to force China to abandon her friendship with America and come into the Russian orbit.

The terrifying thing in the world today is this awful accumulation of power in the hands of one man. Stalin's one aim seems to be the accumulation of more and more force at the expense of his own people and other nations. All his policies, all his moves and actions, aim at one thing only: the accumulation of overwhelming material force. It is inhuman, terrible, terrifying, not only for us but for the whole world.

And he threw up his hands in a gesture of despair.

In Peiping a few weeks later General Li Tsung-jen, one of the famous Kwangsi generals whose agrarian and administrative reforms in their province had been as far-reaching as those of the Communists, but far less bloody, said to me:

The Russians have told us, in effect, that so long as they are hungry, we must starve, that we must wait to be fed until they are satisfied. They have told us that they removed or destroyed all the machinery in Manchuria for the express purpose of keeping us weak. That they will not allow us to develop Manchuria until after they have developed Siberia. They don't say in so many words that what they are afraid of is the United States. It is not clear whether they mean they will not allow us to develop Manchuria under any condition or whether they will not permit it while we are friendly with America, whom they fear.

Russia is insatiable; she is never satisfied. This too is barbaric and uncivilized. China has been thinking that if she herself were very restrained Russia would begin to behave better. This has been a false assumption. The more Stalin gets the more he wants.

Of course, Russia is bluffing, trying to get away with all she can in preparation for the war with America which she envisages.

On the surface the Soviet Union pretends to be friendly with us.

She invites our officials to come to Manchuria, then interns them as "confined guests". They just have to listen to what the Russians tell them. If they don't do what they are told there is a lot of unpleasantness. We have absolutely no power, even in the cities which our officials are supposed to be allowed to take over. While they stall us, the Russians are trying to create a Communist Army in Manchuria and they have told us we had better not come to Harbin.

The brutal murder of Chang Hsiu-fu at the Ashan mines was intended as a warning to other Chinese officials. We had negotiated with the Russians and they had agreed to let us take over the mines. But when our officials got there from Mukden and tried to assume authority they were rebuffed and had to leave. On the way back they were brutally murdered in the train. The only ones who escaped were two who had been so happy and excited that they got out of the train at a wayside station on the way to Anshan to buy a Chinese flag. It took them so long to find one that they missed the train. So they escaped being killed with the others. The Russians pretended they had been murdered by "300 armed bandits." This was absurd since the only armed forces in the vicinity were Russian, and Russian guards were on the train in which they were killed.

Of course, we want American correspondents in Manchuria, but they create a grave problem for us. They will not be allowed full liberty and Russia will only increase her pressure on China if we let them in. American officials have all along known what was happening in Manchuria even if the American public had no information. So it can't help us much for the American public to be informed and Russia will only make it harder for us.

Of what use is it to protest, since we are weak? Some incidents of the Russian outrages on the common people of Manchuria have been reported in our press. Protests are unavailing. When we protested at the wholesale raping and robbing by the Red Army, the Soviet Commander replied that his troops were "very tired"; that they had worked and fought so hard that they were entitled to "a little relaxation." Thus, in Russian eyes they should not properly be blamed for taking our women off the streets, raping them and, when they were through with them, forcing their families to pay a ransom to get them back!

As regards the looting, the Russians would first go to a factory or warehouse and remove everything of real value. Then they would spread rumors to encourage the mob to come in and take what was left. Russian photographers would be at hand to take pictures so that they could say afterward that it was the Chinese who had done the looting.

The Russians regard everything in Manchuria as "war booty" belonging to them. Yet Russia risked little or nothing in the Pacific war. She entered it when it was already over. And Russia defeated Germany only because of the Second Front and Lend-Lease. Without this she would not have been so successful. By what right can she claim priority in seizing everything as her war booty? We fought Japan for eight years.

The idea of letting sleeping dogs lie is not good. Look at what happened in the past. In 1931 Japan was not strong, nor was Italy when she attacked Abyssinia. Now Russia is following the same path. Will the world again wait until it is too late to avoid war?

Equally, the American correspondents' "invasion" of Manchuria was an advantage to China. It was instrumental in causing the Communists to renew the civil war, but it led to at least a temporary stiffening in the United States' attitude toward Russia. The United States continued to strengthen Stalin's Left hand by insisting on "unity" in China, but at least Russia was unable any longer to bludgeon China with both hands, once the United States had protested her actions in Manchuria.

An incautious remark made by Major General Kovtoun-Stankevitch to the American correspondents who got to Changchun put the fat in the fire. He had said that the Russian "evacuation" of industrial equipment from Manchuria had been agreed to by the Big Three. Coming on the heels of the revelation to the Chinese public on February that President Roosevelt had agreed at Yalta to give concessions to Russia in Manchuria—a disclosure which had caused much popular indignation—this Russian assertion had to be squashed, if even the patient Chinese were not to lose all faith in the United States.

On March 1 the State Department made a declaration denying that Russia had any right under any allied agreement to remove machinery from Manchuria; and saying that the U. S. Government "does not accept any interpretation of 'war booty' to include industrial enterprises or components thereof such as Japanese industry and equipment in Manchuria." The U. S. Navy at the same time protested the Soviet Union's attacks on its planes which had occurred ten days before but had not been revealed to the American public. A few days earlier Byrnes in a speech to the Overseas Press Club in New York had given the first indications that the United States was abandoning its appeasement of Russia, and had given China some comfort by stating that "no power has a right to help itself to alleged enemy properties in liberated or ex-satellite communities before a reparation settlement has been agreed upon by the allies."

The Chinese Government could no longer prevent an "official crisis." Even if it had wanted to give Russia what she asked for in Manchuria in order to prevent a recurrence of civil war this was no longer politically possible. The Chinese public had been roused to bitter protest. Vast student demonstrations occurred in Chungking, Shanghai and other large cities demanding that Russia quit Manchuria. The Communists, of course, said that these demonstrations were organized by the government. This was manifestly untrue. The demonstrations were the largest any correspondent had seen since the old days before the Sino-Japanese War, too large to be so inspired, and the government did its best to allay popular indignation on account of its fear of Russia. It was caught in much the same dilemma as in the years 1931 to 1937 when public opinion demanded strong action against Japan's continual aggressive acts which those in responsible positions dared not take. The situation now was even more difficult for the unhappy Chinese Government. How could it either resist Russia or tell its people that after eight years of war with Japan full sovereignty and control over Manchuria could not be regained?

K. C. Wu, the Minister of Information, was found almost in tears in his office by one of the American correspondents on the day of the big demonstration. He was fearful that it would only cause Russia to hit China harder. As he had said to me privately a month before: "We *can't* face another war. We can't again fight for years alone. We must give way to Russia unless the United States is ready to fight or take a strong stand against her." He had hastened to add that he did not blame President Truman and understood his position. The American people were not ready to take a stand against Russia. The American soldiers all wanted to go home.

The weak can least afford to be meek and turn the other cheek when injured. China's one hope was to let the American people know the facts. She benefited not at all from "behind-the-curtain" diplomacy and some of us strongly suspected that the United States was largely responsible for the hush-hush about Russia.

General Marshall certainly gave this impression, for he always refused to say a word when questioned about Manchuria even in off-the-record press conferences. Once, when Steele, and George Moorad of C.B.S. had both pressed him hard for an answer, he went into a long dissertation concerning Russia's peculiar conception of what constituted "spoils of war," but said nothing which could have offended the Russians if they had been there.

'Averill Harriman, passing through Chungking on his way to Washington from Moscow, assumed such a mask of ignorance that he denied even knowing anything about the grant of the Kuriles to Russia, two days after the Moscow radio had announced this additional secret Yalta concession. To see, hear and speak no evil was still American policy.

The perfect synchronization of Russia's moves and those of the Chinese Communists was displayed when the Communists at the end of February broke the truce and tried to take and hold possession of Manchuria. America's protests had made it advisable for Stalin to withdraw the Red Army without having succeeded in extorting from China the concessions which would have concerted Manchuria into an exclusive Russian sphere. But in withdrawing his Right hand, Stalin called upon his Left, the Chinese Communists, to take on the job of keeping Manchuria safe for Communism.

CHAPTER X

Why Marshall Failed

ONCE it became clear that the Political Consultative Council Agreements were not worth the paper they were written on, it was the liberals who reaped the whirlwind. Although many of them had doubted the good faith of the Communists and the wisdom of the concessions made to them in the hope of peace, the liberals were America's friends, and it was America who had insisted on concessions to the Communists and to Russia.

The Right Wing of the Kuomintang, which had never believed that the Communist problem could be settled by political means, now assumed the ascendancy in the government's councils. "Look," the conservatives said in effect, "we let you go ahead and try to win internal peace by concessions to Russia and to the Chinese Communists according to American advice. Your policy is utterly discredited. The civil war has been resumed, Manchuria is still not regained, and you have not even got an American loan."

The revelation concerning Russia's looting of Manchuria, and the simultaneous publication of the terms of the secret Yalta deal at China's expense further discredited the liberals. As the *New York Times* justly remarked on February 28, 1946, "the net result of Russia's current actions in Manchuria is to strengthen the reactionaries in Chungking and to reduce the prospect that there will be internal peace in China." It failed, however, to recognize that this was also the effect of American policy.

On February 25, 1946, eight members of the Control Yuan, the highest supervisory organ of the Chinese Government, publicly declared that the Yalta agreements "violated China's sovereignty and territorial integrity to a greater extent than Japan's demands clamped down on China after the Mukden incident (1931)."

Prior to 1937, it had been the Left which cried "traitor" at the members of the government responsible for trying to avoid or postpone war with Japan. Now the Right cried "traitor" at those who had tried to make a deal with the Russian aggressor. At the Plenary Session of the Central Executive Committee held in March 1946, Right Wing members of the Kuomintang proposed expulsion from the Party of four of the negotiators in the "unity talks." Foreign Minister Wang Shih-chieh, Chang Chun, Governor of Szechwan who had led the Government team in the P.C.C. negotiations, Shao Li-tse, secretary-general of the Kuomintang, and the "Christian General" Feng Yu-hsiang, were all accused of "disloyalty." Wang Shih-chieh was also under fire for his secret diplomacy regarding Manchuria. The attack was led by veteran Kuomintang diplomatic, military and political members, who said that to keep foreign relations secret was a "gross mistake." The men who held this view were by no means all reactionaries or conservatives. They were a miscellaneous group united by their concern with the Russian menace to China's sovereignty, and the belief that silence and appeasement would not remove it.

Bitter attacks on the financial and economic policies of the government also tended to discredit the liberals, since T. V. Soong as President of the Executive Yuan was held responsible for the inflation, graft, misgovernment and ever worsening economic conditions. The fact that T. V. Soong was as much disliked by the reformist and liberal "Political Science group" as by the conservatives did not help the former. T.V. had signed the Sino-Soviet Treaty; T.V. was responsible for the nation's finances; T.V. was highly regarded in the United States and considered a liberal. The liberals or Westernizers were therefore held responsible for his failures and bore the onus of his unpopularity in all camps.

Chiang Kai-shek, in his address on March 1, did his best to prevent his party from responding to the Communist breaking of pledges by refusing to implement the P.C.C. Agreements. "Let us of the Party first be sincere and have trust," he said. "I feel sure that such qualities will exert an influence on other parties and encourage growth of mutual trust, thus facilitating the task of National reconstruction."

The tide was too strong for him. The belief was growing that it was futile to honor agreements continually broken by the Communists. The latter had asked for war; they should have it, despite American pressure for peace at any price in China.

By April 1946 the civil war was again in full swing. While truce teams still flew out to various battlefields in North China from the Executive Headquarters established by General Marshall in Peiping, the armed struggle for possession of Manchuria raged unchecked.

The Chinese Communists, who are apt at confusing issues, and who for so long enjoyed priority in the American press in stating their case, have represented the renewal of civil war as the government's responsibility. They say that the Communists broke the truce only after the Kuomintang Congress had refused to implement the P.C.C. Agreements. The facts of the case are against them as a little consideration of dates will show.

The Communists had started taking over Manchuria *before* the Plenary Session of the Kuomintang Central Committee which temporarily established the ascendance of the "reactionaries." They had, in fact, been busy infiltrating their armed forces into the Northeast before the Red Army evacuated Mukden and Changchun at the end of February. (See Chapters III and IX.)

Russia, as we have seen, completely ignored the Sino-Soviet Treaty in which she had promised to give "moral support and military supplies" only to the National Government in China. It had long been an open secret that she was supplying the Communists with captured Japanese, Russian and American Lend-Lease arms. The American correspondents who penetrated the Iron Curtain to enter Manchuria in February 1946 had brought back information that advance guards of the Chinese Communist Eighth Route Army had reached Mukden as early as September 1945, and that there were thousands of Chinese Communists in the city performing police duties.

As Russia's armies finally withdrew northward from the lands they had ravished, they handed over the towns to the Chinese Communists. The Chinese garrisons installed by the Russians were reinforced by "Union Communists"—Korean, Japanese and Chinese exiles trained in Russia—by Russian "volunteers" and a considerable force of Japanese given the chance of fighting as an alternative to a Russian concentration camp.

The Chinese Government, still adhering to its futile policy of hiding the evidence of Russia's support of the Chinese Communists, kept silent. Some of the Nationalist generals were both more indiscreet and more intelligent than the Chinese Foreign Office. George Weller reported from Mukden on May 6, 1946, that he had been shown a captured document revealing a secret agreement between the Soviet High Command and the Chinese Communists.

According to this agreement, the Soviets had pledged to assign 5,000 men and officers to help the Eighth Route (Communists) Army with technical aid and also to leave a few army technicians behind disguised as White Russians. These technicians were to supply explosives and train the Communists how best to smash up the Tientsin-Shanhaikwan railroad guarded by U. S. Marines. The Soviets had also undertaken to supply twenty armed patrol boats to "monitor" ship traffic entering the sea between Chefoo and Dairen "with especial reference to American Navy transports bringing Chinese Nationalist forces" en route to Manchuria.

The date on which Chinese Communists pledged to begin "the joint defense of Manchuria" and to "subordinate the Eighth Route Army to the Russian Command during the period of their joint occupation" was January 19—nine days after they had signed the truce agreement in Chungking, and at the very time when the Communists in Chungking had evidently persuaded General Marshall of their current desire to end the civil war and help establish a united, "democratic China."

Apocryphal or not, the course of events demonstrated that some such agreement undoubtedly existed. The Russians evidently gave a great deal more military aid to the Chinese Communists than that provided for in the agreement which the Chinese Government claims to have found. According to Alsop's column of May 20, 1946, intelligence had reached Washington that ten percent of all casualties on the Communist side in Manchuria were Russian soldiers.

For a few weeks after they broke the truce in February 1946, it seemed that the Communists would be able to hold Manchuria against the National Government forces. They had every advantage of position and numbers, and their enemies were hampered by Russia's ban on China's use of her own port at Dairen and the railway leading from it. As it turned out, the Communists had vastly overestimated their own military capacities. The high-pressure advertising in the American press of the Communist armies' prowess against the Japanese may have distorted even the Kremlin's judgment, but it could not stop the victorious advance of China's National Army in Manchuria.

When the devil is sick the devil a monk would be. As soon as they found that they would be crushed unless saved by yet another "truce," the Communists once again proclaimed their desire for "peace and unity." Once again they reverted to the tactics of advocating democracy in order to destroy it. Having failed militarily they wanted another breathing space; another opportunity to get in a position to bore from within a coalition government or time to be trained by their Russian instructors in the use of the arms given them by the Red Army. Confident that if they cried "Uncle," America would once again save them from annihilation, the Communists in Manchuria announced in May: "It is up to Chiang Kai-shek to yield to Marshall and negotiate."

They did not appeal in vain. The worthlessness of Communist promises, agreements, "compromises" or truces, and the Communists' co-operation with Moscow had been amply demonstrated by the course of events. Their tactics and the purpose behind them were perfectly obvious. Yet the United States was still ready to do business at the old stand.

As soon as General Marshall returned from Washington in May he began urging both sides to "cease fire" in Manchuria. He did not denounce the Communists for wrecking the truce according to which they had agreed to the National Government taking over Manchuria unopposed. Instead he blamed both sides and urged the National Government to let the Communists keep the parts of Manchuria they held, by agreeing to let the truce teams operate there as well as in North China. Although the Communists refused even to discuss conditions until after an "unconditional truce," although they rejected a National Government proposal that the American officer on each truce team should have the power to break deadlocks, General Marshall continued to exert pressure on Chiang Kai-shek to halt his offensive. The United States was still, in effect, favoring the Communists by being "impartial" between the National Government which had observed the terms of the truce, and the Communists who had openly violated them. As usual, pressure was exerted on America's friends instead of on Russia's agents.

China desperately needed our credits and technical aid to halt the process of economic decay which breeds Communism. We continued to refuse her such aid until such time as her government should come to terms with those who profited by her distress.

The "veto" credits to China still held. The Communists who had publicly announced that they did not want an American loan made to China, were still to be assisted by America to blackmail the National Government in the interests of Soviet Russia.

On June 28, 1946, Acting Secretary of State Dean Acheson made a statement on China in which he said that America was "impartial" and stated that "too much stress cannot be laid on the hope of this Government that our economic assistance be carried out in China through the medium of a government fully and fairly representative of all important Chinese political elements, *including the Chinese Communists.*"

Acting as if the truce had never been broken and the plan for the amalgamation of the Nationalist and Communist armies was still practicable, General Marshall next agreed to a Communist request to have American officers assigned to train this army. Sixty-nine United States officers were actually detailed for this duty although most of them were marooned in Shanghai waiting for a lull in the civil war to enable them to get to their stations. Four hundred tons of American equipment were earmarked for this training program.

One recalls Stalin's words in 1939 concerning Anglo-French appeasement of Nazi Germany and Japan: "Incredible but true."

The projected American aid to the Chinese Communists was the more difficult to understand in view of the fact that by this time Communist hostility to the United States was no longer hidden. Formerly they had relied on America to exert sufficient pressure on the National Government to establish them in as strong a position in China as the Communists hold in France. Once it became clear that America either would not, or could not, give them the degree of power they demanded, they started anti-American demonstrations; they accused the United States of "propagating civil war" and demanded the withdrawal of all American armed forces from China. After refusing the National Government's proposal to let General Marshall have the supreme arbitration power to settle the basic issues in dispute, the Communists let loose a virulent campaign to discredit America and arouse popular hatred against her. On July 7, 1946, the Central Committee of the Chinese Communist Party stated that "the only difference between American and Japanese imperialism is that American imperialism is stronger and its aggressive methods appear civilized and legal on the surface."

Nor did the Communists confine their anti-American campaign to words. Some marines were shot and wounded and others temporarily imprisoned in North China.

Nevertheless, the United States continued to advise the Chinese to admit the Communists to a share of power. True that Dean Acheson intimated on June 28 that aid to China "to forestall a financial and economic breakdown might have to be given prior to the achievement of unity," but he also reaffirmed President Truman's December declaration of policy.

When the November 1946 Commercial Treaty between the United States and China was signed, a spokesman of the State Department hastened to assure the American public that this did not signify support for the Government of Chiang Kai-shek.

Had Chiang Kai-shek given way to American pressure for another truce prior to June 6, the Communists might well have succeeded at this early date in establishing a "Northeast Liberated Area": a Russian puppet state to replace Japan's Manchukuo, and to be similarly used as an industrial and military base from which to launch new attacks on China and, when the time came, on us.

Chiang had the courage and independence to disregard American "advice" and go ahead until he had re-established Chinese sovereignty over the greater part of Manchuria. He saw that the potential half-billion-dollar loan from the United States, denied to him unless he came to terms with Moscow's agents, was nothing compared to the vast resources of China's own Northeast, which would be lost if he acceded to General Marshall's demands.

Chiang agreed to give the Communists another chance "to demonstrate the good faith of their intentions to carry out the agreement they signed" only after the National forces had arrived at the gates of the part-Russian city of Harbin. There is little doubt that what the *New York Times* correspondent in Nanking called "the threat of a sharper clash of international interests" was the factor which General Marshall stressed when he finally persuaded Chiang Kai-shek to agree to another armistice on June 6, 1946.

On July 20, 1946, Chiang Kai-shek once again announced his desire to settle the Communist problem by political means, and said that in spite of the fact that the Communists had broken the Political Consultative Council Agreements the government was still prepared to carry them out. The National Government would be broadened by the inclusion of men from all walks of life, and a National Congress would be convened on November 12, 1946, to draft a new constitution, if, this time, the Communists would observe the terms of the truce.

The second truce was even less effective than the first. Fighting never stopped and Executive Headquarters in Peiping served mainly to provide free and convenient air transport to both Communists and Nationalists to the various "fronts." The truce teams occasionally quenched the fires in one place only to see them break out in another. By August they were beginning to find themselves caught between two fires and several Americans were killed or wounded.

The successive "truces" arranged by General Marshall were like patches on running sores. New abscesses were continually appearing on the ravaged body of China. The civil war ceased temporarily in one place only to break out in another. The Communists continued to destroy railways, mines and industries. Inflation proceeded unchecked. Channels of trade continued blocked. The number of the destitute and starving increased. Economic decay and despair drove more and more bewildered souls into the ranks of the Communists.

In the fall of 1946 the Nationalist forces seemed to be well on their way to crush the Communists and reunite China. Everywhere they went the Communists broke or faded away, thus finally dispelling the old myth of their fighting prowess against the Japanese. Some of the Nationalist forces had been armed and trained by the Americans, but by no means all. Generally speaking, they cannot have been as formidable an army as the Japanese. Yet the Communists hardly ever stood to fight even though in possession of the arms Russia had supplied them with.

In the fall of 1946 when the Communists had been driven to the north of Manchuria and government forces had recaptured Kalgan and other strategic points in North China, Chiang Kai-shek once again halted military operations in a final effort to settle the conflict by political concessions. In October he welcomed Chou En-lai arriving in Nanking for peace talks; and on November 8, following a two-day series of conferences with General Marshall and United States Ambassador Leighton Stuart, the Generalissimo ordered all government troops to cease fire at the height of almost year-long government successes. Once again the Communists were invited to attend the National Assembly about to open in Nanking. Once again they were offered positions in a coalition government. And once again they were given the opportunity to show that their democratic pretensions were sincere.

The Communists refused the offer with abuse and the civil war continued. Nevertheless, Chiang Kai-shek threw his weight behind the liberals in the National Assembly to insure approval of a democratic constitution. Although America had done little to help him acquire the necessary strength to oppose the reactionaries, the Nationalist victories over the Communists had strengthened Chiang Kai-shek's hands sufficiently to allow him at least to start trying to establish a democratic form of government.

The routing of the Communists in 1946 could not, however, give China peace. They remained to harass communications, wage guerrilla warfare and render reconstruction impossible, until such time as they could once again mount a military offensive. Time was on their side since Russia was behind them, and America's support of the National Government was grudging and uncertain.

Of what use to advance into one province to crush the Communist forces since they never stayed to fight but faded away and began their depredations in another place? And the cost of maintaining and moving Nationalist armies to chase after them is so high that the overtaxed and ruined peasantry finds relief only by joining the Communist forces, while the whole economy is stagnant or decays under the strain of continual civil war. Unless and until the Government of China should become "friendly" to Russia the Chinese Communists would continue to tear the country to pieces.

Destruction is easy and reconstruction difficult. The Communists, caring nothing for the welfare of China as a whole, are in the happy position of being able to increase their strength through destroying the livelihood of the people. But the government's very existence depends on its ability to restore law and order, rebuild communications and get the economy in working order.

Chiang Kai-shek continued to offer peace, but now only on condition that the Communists evacuate the railway lines and strategic centers. Chiang had not completely given way to the members of his government who had all along advocated solution of the Communist problem by force. But he was determined to clear the railways and make possible some economic rehabilitation. He had no choice for the economic situation had become so desperate that his government would lose all authority and China lapse into complete anarchy unless some order were restored. Moreover, even though American public opinion was still confused or indifferent about China, the conflict between America and Russia was by now openly displayed before the eyes of the world at the Paris Conferences and in the United Nations meetings. Whereas in the years preceding the Sino-Japanese War the most inveterate optimist in China could see no hope of American support being forthcoming in the near future, in 1946 there was hope that the United States might give aid to resist Russian domination of the world in time to save China.

Chiang Kai-shek could believe that if he and his exhausted people held on just a little longer, they would not have to submit to Communist or Russian domination.

The Marines remained in North China "because of the predatory policy of Soviet Russia," as the Army and Navy Bulletin expressed it on August 24, 1946. Surplus army stores were sold cheaply to the Chinese Government. Just enough help and encouragement were still given to China to keep her from following the line of least resistance and entering Russia's sphere in despair.

By the late summer of 1946 General Marshall was already beginning to admit the failure of his mission. But neither he nor the United States administration could admit they had wrongly diagnosed the disease which was wasting China away. Dr. Marshall continued to prescribe more of the same mixture as before. In December 1946 President Truman issued another statement on China practically identical with the one he had issued a year previously. China was still told she must be cured of her disease before we would help her. "Unity" was still insisted upon as the *sine qua non* of American financial aid long after it was apparent that submission to Moscow was the price of internal peace.

Although the American people had begun to wake up from their dream of one world, happy and peaceful, to be established by "trusting" the Soviet Union and allowing it to wreak its will on its weak neighbors; although in Europe we had begun to say, "thus far and no farther," in the Far East the same self-defeating, face-saving policy was not only continued but intensified.

From European experiences we had observed that coalitions which include Communists can never establish democratic government; that such coalitions simply enable Moscow's agents to insert the wedge for securing their own despotic power. But this lesson, learned by what the Chinese call the hardship of error, was not applied in China. In China we continued to believe, or to pretend, that the Communists are liberals anxious only to reform China along democratic lines and owing no allegiance to Moscow.

General Marshall continued to insist that "unity" could be achieved long after it was demonstrated that the Communists would never be satisfied short of a predominant position in China. He himself cannot be blamed unless one considers that it was his duty to resign in protest of the dangerous futility of the policy he was ordered to implement. Had he done so there is little doubt that his enormous prestige in America would have caused a change in United States policy. But he seems to have believed that the Chinese Communists could be "weaned away" from Russia. Either Chou En-lai's blandishments or the influence of the Stilwell school in the State and War Departments, or his own loyalty to the late President Roosevelt's peculiar view of Communism, prevented General Marshall from facing up to the realities of the situation.

Like the State Department's Far Eastern Division headed by John Carter Vincent, General Marshall continued to act on the assumption either that the Chinese Communists were not under Moscow's orders, or that they could be detached from their Russian allegiance.

One of General Marshall's aides in Chungking assured me with charming naïveté that the Chinese Communists, being Chinese, and therefore individualists, were "different" and could be relied upon never to establish a totalitarian tyranny on the Soviet model.

One also heard the argument that the stronger their position in China, the less the Communists needed to depend on outside support; the more responsibility they acquired within China, the less they would be inclined to put Russia's interests above China's national interest.

The more extreme form of the argument used by the protagonists of the Chinese Communists in the State Department ran something like this:

A Chinese Communist-dominated government would have to turn to America for capital and would therefore not disturb capitalist property relations. The Russians would have to accept a certain degree of orientation toward the United States on the part of the Chinese Communists since this would inevitably result from the aid and influence flowing to China from the United States.

The State Department "experts," who argued that the Russians would have much to gain if the situation in China were stabilized, since they would have an opportunity to compete on equal terms, showed an equal ignorance of the nature of Communism, East or West.

When General Marshall finally left China and drew the remaining United States forces out after him, America's Far Eastern policy was left suspended in the air while the new Secretary of State concentrated his attentions on Europe. The alarms and excursions, discussions, negotiations, accusations and counteraccusations of the war of words with Russia in Europe caused most Americans to forget all about Marshall's signal failure in China.

It is as yet too soon to say whether his China experience taught General Marshall a lesson in Communist strategy and aims which will save him from a similar failure in Europe. Certainly in Moscow it took him only weeks, as against months in China, to learn that you can't get an agreement with Communists by just talking to them. But it is too soon to say that the United States has definitely abandoned appeasement even in Europe.

As regards China, General Marshall continued to act either as if he had learned little from the course of events in Europe and from his thirteen months of futile endeavor to mediate the civil war; or as if America had decided to put no obstacles in the way of China's being dragged behind the Iron Curtain.

On leaving China he did not admit that his failure was due to a mistaken policy. His parting statement, issued on January 7, 1947, was predicated on two premises which events all over the world have disproved: that a coalition government including Communists is the way to establish democracy and peace, and that those who oppose the appeasement of Communists at home or abroad are "reactionaries." Explaining his failure he said:

On the side of the National Government . . . there is a *dominant group of reactionaries who have been opposed, in my opinion, to almost every effort I have made to influence the formation of a genuine coalition Government.*

These "reactionaries," complained the present United States Secretary of State, "were quite frank in publicly stating their belief that co-operation by the Chinese Communist Party in the government was inconceivable and that only a policy of force could definitely settle the issue."

One wonders whether, a few months later, in his negotiations with Molotov in Moscow, Secretary Marshall still believed that only "reactionaries" find it impossible to "co-operate" with Communists.

Marshall admitted in this same statement that the "dyed-in-the-wool Communists" were equally to blame for the continuing civil war and went so far as to admit that:

> . . . they do not hesitate at the most drastic measures to gain their end as, for instance, the destruction of communications in order to wreck the economy of China and produce a situation that would facilitate the overthrow or collapse of the government, without any regard to the immediate suffering of the people involved.

He further complained of the "provocative" propaganda of the Communists, saying that:

> . . . in the deliberate misrepresentation and abuse of the action, policies and purposes of our government this propaganda has been without regard for the truth, without any regard whatsoever for the facts, and has given plain evidence of a determined purpose to mislead the Chinese people and the world and to arouse a bitter hatred of Americans.

Lastly Marshall testified to the fact that the National Government had honored the P.C.C. Agreements. He said:

> In fact, the National Assembly has adopted a democratic constitution which in all major respects is in accordance with the principles laid down by the all-party Political Consultative Council. . . . It is unfortunate that the Communists did not see fit to participate in the Assembly, since the constitution that has been adopted seems to include every major point that they wanted.

Secretary of State Marshall, however, failed to draw any lesson from the facts he stated. He apparently still clung to the illusion that the Communist Party is just an ordinary political party composed of men of varying views. The rest of his statement was obviously based on this fallacy and his consequent belief that the Communists could be detached from their allegiance to Stalin. For he said:

On the side of the Chinese Communist party, are, I believe, liberals as well as radicals, though this view is vigorously opposed by many who believe that the Chinese Communist Party discipline is too rigidly enforced to admit of such differences of viewpoint. Nevertheless, it has appeared to me that there is a definite liberal group among the Communists, especially of young men who have turned to the Communists in disgust at the corruption evident in the local governments—men who would put the interest of the Chinese people above ruthless measures to establish a Communist ideology in the immediate future.

Since he refused to listen to those whose experience or study had taught them that Communist Parties allow no opposition or liberal backsliding, it was not surprising that General Marshall still "hoped" that "the door will remain open" for the Communists to participate in a coalition government.

Shortly after my return to the United States, Chen Chih-mai at the Chinese Embassy, who had returned from a visit to Switzerland and France, said to me:

Well, bad as things are in China it is worse in France. In France the Communists have obtained a dominant position in the whole economy of the country through their control of the trade unions, and they also have the whip hand over the government through the ministries they occupy. They have veto power over the whole of France. It seems to me a little better in China since the Communists are not in the Government. Better to let them control some territories in China than admit them into a coalition government as America desires.

Yet it seemed that the United States was determined to force China to become a second France if not a second Poland.

Had it not been for the extraordinary patience of Chiang Kai-shek and his unswerving loyalty to the United States and the Western World, China would long since have been driven, in despair, to enter Russia's totalitarian orbit. The odds against China's development on democratic lines, and against her ever being able to become united, strong, free and independent, were rendered impossibly long by America's policy of giving aid and comfort to the Communists and of rescuing them by a new truce each time they broke the previous one and subsequently found themselves in danger of liquidation. It was in fact something of a miracle that the Chinese Government did not say, "What's the use? Even our American friends are pushing us into Russia's arms. The only way we can get peace is to give in to Stalin and be friendly."

The tragedy of the situation lay also in the fact that the United States could have used its influence and its pressures to aid the liberals in China instead of the Communists. Instead of insisting on a unity which could never be achieved without Stalin's permission, America could have urged and assisted Chaing Kai-shek to replace the corrupt and reactionary elements in his government by liberals and efficient administrators. Loans and technical assistance could have been given or withheld, not as a lever to hoist the Communists into a coalition government, but to bring about democratic administrative reforms and to cure abuses. We could have helped the liberal-minded elements in the Kuomintang to win the ascendancy, instead of ruining them through their identification with our own discredited policy. In a word, our criterion for a democrat should not have been the degree of his friendliness to Communists or willingness to yield ground to an armed Communist. It should have been opposition to all forms of totalitarianism, a willingness and ability to reform China along democratic lines.

Like the die-hard isolationists in the United States, the reactionaries in China gained strength through the barrenness of a victory which had merely substituted one totalitarian menace for another. They themselves might not go so far as to say that it would have been better for China never to have fought than to come out devastated, torn by civil war , threatened by Russian, in place of Japanese, domination. The people of Manchuria had no doubt that Russian tyranny would be even worse than Japanese, and said so.

It could be argued that China's loyalty to the Western democracies had been but poorly rewarded. At Yalta President Roosevelt had given away Chinese resources to Russia without consulting China and put Russia into a strategic position in Manchuria from which to conquer the whole of China. Since V-J Day the United States had bent its efforts to make of China what John Carter Vincent, Director of the

Far Eastern office in the State Department, called "a buffer, or a bridge, in America's relations with the Soviet Union in the Far East." To be a buffer between two express trains is not an enviable position. Although the "reactionaries" in China and the former so-called pro-Japanese elements had not joined hands with the "liberals" of the Sun Fo school, they very well might have if America refused sufficient support to China to enable her to resist Russia.

Sun Fo and his group had always argued that China could make a better bargain for herself by being friendly with Russia than by clinging to the American connection. Wang Ching-wei, who became Japan's puppet in 1939, had once been the main ally of the Communists inside the Kuomintang, siding with them against Chiang Kai-shek in the stormy year of 1927. He had changed sides always according to his calculation of relative strength. Why should not at least some of the reactionaries who had opposed war with Japan in 1937 similarly advocate appeasement of Russia? It would be only logical since now, as then, China was too weak to fight, and the support of the West was uncertain.

Even Japan's collaborators would have no need to fear that Stalin would refuse to clasp their hands if he got the chance. Was not Soviet Russia in Europe taking the line that anyone who was anti-American was a friend, whatever his past, and did she not welcome even ex-Nazis into the Communist Party? Stalin was obviously willing to accept the most reactionary elements as friends against the liberals and socialists in Europe. In Manchuria the Communists were enlisting Japanese to fight the Chinese Nationalists. Obviously the Chinese conservatives would have nothing to fear if they switched over to a policy of Sino-Soviet collaboration.

Americans were left in unawareness of the danger because Chiang Kai-shek's influence, combined with the basically antitotalitarian attitude of nearly all the Chinese, including conservatives and reactionaries, prevented any such course being taken.

Chiang Kai-shek was reported to be bitterly resentful at General Marshall's failure to see that the Communist problem could be settled only by American backing of the National Government with ammunition and credits, and at America's continued insistence on "unity" through concessions to the Communists, but he continued his endeavors to keep China on our side of the Iron Curtain.

Kuomintang leaders, such as Chen Li-fu and others popularly

known in America as "reactionaries," helped the Generalissimo to keep China in the Western democratic camp, while Sun Fo, Madame Sun Yat-sen and others labeled as liberals by General Marshall and the State Department's Far Eastern Division tried in vain to pull her into the Soviet sphere.

In the final outcome, however, Sun Fo, whom I have described in a former chapter as the Chinese Henry Wallace, showed himself possessed of deeper insight and intelligence than the former Vice-President of the United States.

In his interview with Tillman Durdin, of the *New York Times,* Miles Vaughn, of the United Press, and others in Nanking on June 20, 1947, Sun Fo, Vice-President of the Executive Yuan, spoke out as boldly against Soviet Russia's aggression as he had formerly done against Japan, saying:

That the Chinese Communists were "absolute instruments" of Soviet policy.

That Communist control of Manchuria would be the same thing as control by the Russians.

That Russia was directly helping the Chinese Communists.

That Korean troops from Russian-controlled North Korea were fighting with the Communists, and that the government had unconfirmed information that the latter were being trained by the Russians in a school in Eastern Siberia.

That China, having paid her price for the Sino-Soviet Treaty, had obtained no benefit, since the Soviet Government had violated the treaty by obstructing China's taking over of Manchuria, by helping the Communists and by "snatching away" Chinese sovereignty over Dairen.

That, with the Communists ruling Manchuria, the Soviet Union would have access to areas so rich in material resources that with its 40,000,000 inhabitants, it would be built up in conjunction with Siberia into a major military base.

That the only difference between Japan and Russia is that while the Japanese placed large amounts of industrial equipment in Manchuria, the Soviet removed them totally therefrom.

That, if Manchuria is lost to the Chinese Government, it will become "an appendage of the Soviet power and in five or ten years could be built up as a base from which to conquer the rest of China.

"Who doubts," said Sun Fo in the same interview, "that Dairen has been maintained for the benefit of the Communists? The port has served as a supply base for them. The Russian refusal of entry to our troops there is tantamount to a denial of sovereignty to the recognized government of the country."

Finally, Sun Fo charged the Soviet Union with being "more imperialist than Czarist Russia" and urged America to give immediate large-scale economic aid and military supplies to his government to halt the march of Communism and Soviet aggression. "If this is not done," he concluded, "the ultimate outcome might be a Communist China and subsequently a Communist India."

Unfortunately General Marshall took longer to learn his lesson than Sun Fo. Immediately following his appointment as Secretary of State, China ceased to receive even the limited amount of backing given her in 1946. Before he went to Moscow, General Marshall ordered the return of all United States forces from China. On April 2, 1947, in Moscow, he assured Molotov that American forces were being removed from China "as rapidly as shipping becomes available" and that by June 1 only 6,180 United States military and naval personnel would remain in China. General Marshall was apparently still under the spell of President Roosevelt's illusion that Stalin could be mollified by unconditional American concessions. Even if, as it seemed at the time, the United States Secretary of State had decided to anbandon China and save Europe, he should at least have used the sacrifice of China to obtain Russian concessions in Europe. Instead he laid China wide open to Soviet aggression without obtaining either a *quid pro quo* in Europe or the withdrawal of Russian forces from Manchuria.

It was a little surprising, except to those without any belief in the rationality of mankind, that in spite of all the fashionable talk about "one world," and although the United States had been brought into the Second World War by attack across the Pacific, General Marshall and most Americans still cared little about China's fate. Stalin's high-handed disregard of his treaty commitments in Germany, Austria, Hungary, Rumania and Bulgaria seemed to Americans worth at least a protest. But they regarded Russia's acquisition of Manchuria as hardly worth a thought. Just as formerly the United States had helped and encouraged those who fought Nazi Germany while continuing to supply Japan with war materials, so now, in 1947, the United States poured out her wealth to save Europe from Soviet domination while refusing to help the enemies of Communism in China.

Those whom the gods wish to destroy, said the ancient Greeks, they first make mad. In the spring of 1947, the United States gave Greece $400,000,000 to keep the Communists out while refusing the Chinese Government a similar sum until she would take the Communists in.

Since the new United States Secretary of State was evidently far more benevolently inclined toward the Communists in China than toward Communism in Europe, it was hardly surprising that in the spring and early summer of 1947 the Soviet Government was emboldened to give more open support to the Chinese Communists and that the latter launched a new and far more successful offensive in Manchuria.

The Chinese Communist forces were now reinforced by large numbers of battle-wise Japanese and Russian-trained Korean forces with a convenient base in Russia's Korean zone. Moreover, since the United States Government was "neutral" now, as in the thirties when Japan attacked China, we refused to let the National Government buy arms in America. The Nationalist forces were becoming weaker in fire power as the Communists, generously supplied by Russia, became stronger. The guns of the New First Army, originally trained and equipped in Burma by the United States and sent to Manchuria in 1946, were reported in June 1947 to be worn out, with the barrels of some machine guns so burned that "bullets fell through them to the ground."* But the Communist forces could count on continual replenishment of their equipment from Lend-Lease stores supplied to Russia for the war against Japan which she never fought.

The Communists by this time seemed to have been so well supplied with everything they required that they refused UNRRA relief and medical supplies, rather than allow American personnel to enter their territory. According to a *New York Times* dispatch from Peiping dated June 21, 1947, Cornelius Bodine, of Philadelphia, the UNRRA director for the Changchun area, was twice refused entry to Communist-controlled areas of Manchuria. The Communists evidently desired to prevent at all costs foreign observers from learning how much help Russia was giving them.

Had American or United Nations investigators been able to con-

---

* *New York Times,* June 22, 1947.

duct the same type of investigation in Manchuria as in Greece, they might have become convinced of the truth of Chinese reports.

According to the Chinese Central News Agency, 30,000 Japanese "prisoners" and ninety tanks were backing the Communist offensive in Manchuria. Its Mukden correspondent reported early in June that "a special bureau" of "a certain nation" had supplied the Communists with equipment for twenty divisions, and that citizens of that "certain nation"—the usual designation for Russia in the Chinese press—or Japanese manned the tanks spearheading the Communist offensive. The eventuality feared all through the Sino-Japanese War had become a reality: the Communists were fighting together with the Japanese against China under Russia's orders.

In March 1947, General John R. Hodge, United States commander in Korea, had stated that Chinese Communist troops were participating in the training of a Korean Army of 500,000 in Russian-held North Korea. The Chinese Central News Agency stated in June that more than a 100,000 Russian-trained Koreans plus a cavalry division from Outer Mongolia were in action against the Chinese National forces. As General Wang Yao-wu, the government commandant in the Tsinan area, said in April 1947, the Shantung War could be shortened by six months if the government had control of Dairen.

Nor was the help given to the Communists in Manchuria and North China the only example of overt hostility which the Soviet Union displayed. In June 1947, troops from Outer Mongolia (which is as integral a part of the Soviet Union as the Ukraine or White Russia) supported by planes marked with the Soviet emblem, attacked the Altai district of Chinese Turkestan.

In June 1947, it seemed that there was little or no hope that the Nationalist forces would be able to save Manchuria from becoming a Russian puppet state. The odds seemed too heavy against them. A U.P. dispatch from Nanking on June 22 stated that neutral sources estimated that 200,000 Nationalist troops were up against 300,000 armed Communists, and that the Communists already had control of more than three-quarters of Manchuria.

Chiang Kai-shek's persistent attempts to "solve the Communist problem by political means" had not only been unavailing, but by halting its military offensive time and again to negotiate, the government had denied itself victory while the Communists were weak and enabled them to grow strong enough with Russian help to attack in greater force than ever before.

As General Pai Chung-hsi, the Minister of Defense, stated on May 1, 1947, the government's military progress had been blocked by the truces and peace talks of the preceding year. "Immediately after the recovery of Kalgan [October 1946]," said the Kwangsi general, who is regarded as China's foremost strategist, "we could have blasted open the whole Peiping-Hankow Railway, but our actions were deferred by intervals of negotiation. The government has suffered from an irresolute policy."

By June 1947, when prophecies were already being made in the American press that Manchuria would be lost to China, the National Government at last realized that its long silence concerning Russia's hostile acts had merely emboldened the Soviet Government to increase its aid to the Chinese Communists and that United States help was unlikely to be forthcoming until the American people were informed of the true facts of the Far Eastern situation.

On June 25, the Chinese Ministry of Foreign Affairs issued a communiqué detailing for the first time the long record of Soviet obstruction to China's attainment of her rights under the Sino-Soviet Treaty.

"Sources close to the Generalissimo" were reported by American correspondents to be saying that Chiang Kai-shek and his advisers were framing a new policy calling for a stronger stand against Russian aggression. The policy of appeasement was being abandoned, but the extent to which China would go toward a diplomatic showdown with Russia would depend upon United States support.

General Chen Cheng, the Chinese Chief of Staff, charged on June 24 that at least thirty-one Russian advisers were known to be with the Communist forces fighting at Szepingkai, the important railroad point seventy miles from Mukden.

The Chinese Nationalist commander in besieged Szepingkai said that the Communists had battered the city with 100,000 artillery shells (which they obviously had not manufactured themselves), and that Russian-trained Koreans manned the Communist guns.

Following the lifting of the siege by Nationalist forces at the end of June, the Chinese Central News Agency accused Russia of having shipped 56,635 tons of military supplies to the Chinese Communists in June, twelve Soviet ships having unloaded supplies for them at

Dairen, while others ran a shuttle service between the Manchurian port and Cheefoo, the Shantung port occupied by the Communists.

Even those who chose to disbelieve Chinese reports of Russian assistance to the Communists could not deny that the Soviet Government was giving aid and comfort to the Chinese Communists by its continued refusal almost two years after V-J Day to evacuate Dairen according to the terms of the Sino-Soviet Treaty. The denial to the Chinese Government of the use of Manchuria's principal port and the railway leading from it not only created a difficult supply problem for the National forces in Manchuria; it also put the Chinese Communists in an advantageous strategic position. As in the days when they had to fight the Japanese operating from an untouchable base in the International Settlement at Shanghai, so in 1946 and 1947 the Chinese Nationalist commanders found themselves unable to crack the Communist line north of Dairen for fear of encroaching on Russia's newly established extraterritorial rights on Chinese soil. In the fall of 1946, according to Christopher Rand of the *Herald Tribune,* two Communist regiments had taken refuge at Port Arthur from Nationalist attack, and sheltered there until they emerged in the spring of 1947 to take part in the Communists' greatest offensive.

As Tillman Durdin reported in April 1947, the Communist forces were backed up against the Russian "defense zone" running from Port Arthur in back of Dairen, and the Chinese Government feared the "complications" which would arise if the Communists retreated into Russian-occupied territory.

On July 4, the National Government, after rallying its forces for a successful counteroffensive in Manchuria, announced its abandonment of all hope for a political solution of the Communist problem and denounced the Communists as "armed rebels" who could be dealt with only by force.

Vice-President Sun Fo, so long the darling of Communist sympathizers in America, was reported to be one of the leading advocates of this resolution, which marked the end of China's Coué diplomacy and placed her unequivocally in the world anti-Communist camp.

Meanwhile some small encouragement had been given to the anti-Communist forces in China. A loan was still denied to the National Government, but on June 27 it was announced in Washington that we were permitting China to buy 130,000,000 rounds of surplus rifle ammunition. True that it was also stated that this ammunition had been released partly because it was of a special caliber used only by the Chinese, and the United States could therefore find no other buyer. True that the embargo on Chinese purchases of arms had probably been lifted too late to affect the course of battle and Manchuria might still be lost to Russia. True also that General Marshall on July 2 denied that the United States Government was now supporting the Chinese Government. True that according to Washington dispatches, China could expect no economic help until the civil war ended—in other words, until her need for it became less desperate.

But the Chinese are a rational as well as a patient people. They could hope that eventually the logic of facts would cause the United States to recognize that there is no sense in stalling Soviet aggression at the front door, in Europe, while leaving America's back door, across the Pacific, wide open.

CHAPTER XI

General Wedemeyer in China

HAD I not broken my arm and been forced to spend two months in Shanghai I would not have had the opportunity to know the man who did more than anyone else to counteract the effect of the State Department's muddleheaded meddling in China. General Albert C. Wedemeyer constituted for a time a counterweight to the forces impelling China toward chaos or Communism. Even after the Communists had succeeded in getting him withdrawn from China,* his influence remained in the cordial, sincere and mutually advantageous relations he and his staff had established with Chiang Kai-shek and the best elements in the Chinese Army.

Arriving in China to succeed General Stilwell in October 1944, when it seemed that nothing could stop Japan's last and greatest offensive against Chungking, General Wedemeyer had achieved what seemed a miracle at the time. By re-establishing Sino-American relations on a basis of mutual trust, and by his masterly strategy, he had prevented China's being knocked out of the war on the very eve of Japan's defeat in the Pacific.

The evacuation of Chungking had begun. Wedemeyer wanted to concentrate on the defense of the nearest supply point. Chiang said he would stay and die in Chungking. Wedemeyer cabled to Marshall to ask whether he, too, should stay and die. Happily, the choice never had to be made. Not only did bitter cold and lack of supplies force Japan to stop and recuperate on the Liuchow-Tushan line, but Wedemeyer flew in two Chinese divisions from Burma to defend Kweiyang, and the Chinese agreed to let him bring several divisions from the Northwest to reinforce the hard-pressed forces fighting at Kweilin.

The Chinese had originally demanded that all the Chinese divisions

---

* General Wedemeyer was to have been appointed ambassador after his return in 1946 on sick leave from command of the China Theater. But his appointment was canceled at the last moment.

in Burma should be brought home to stem the Japanese offensive. Wedemeyer persuaded them to agree to only two, instead of five, being withdrawn from Burma, but compensated for this by a master stroke of psychological warfare. He arranged for the Chinese Secret Service (under the much-maligned Tai Li) to sell to the Japanese the false information that four, not two, American-trained and equipped Chinese divisions had been brought from Burma. Wedemeyer then posted the two divisions at a point whence they could block Japan's advance if she took one road, or cut her forces off from their supply base if she took the other. Thus Chungking was saved and Japan's last great offensive rendered abortive.

The Japanese, instead of advancing, fell back. Free China was saved. Wedemeyer's relations with the British became less friendly, since the latter were furious at his removal of two Chinese divisions from the Burma front, but American-Chinese relations were established on a new basis of trust and collaboration.

I was told by United States officers, who served under both Stilwell and Wedemeyer, that when the latter took over, relations with the Chinese Command were so bad that his first and one of his most difficult tasks had been to break down the wall of mistrust and dislike. The Chinese generals at Chungking Headquarters had not only been treated with open contempt by General Stilwell and his aides, but they had never been allowed to know what the Americans were doing or what supplies were available. Aggrieved, humiliated and distrustful, the Chinese were so touchy and difficult that joint staff meetings had become purely formal and quite useless.

Wedemeyer managed to change the whole atmosphere by inviting the Chinese to discuss and criticize American tactics and strategy, while frankly discussing Chinese shortcomings himself. In time he established a real alliance; a working partnership which enabled him to persuade the Chinese to do the right thing, because he convinced them that he was fair-minded and did not disregard China's interests.

According to the same testimony, it was General Wedemeyer's great contribution to the war in the Far East to insist on the concentration of available air power on a few important objectives and teach the Chinese to aim at cutting off the enemy from his supply bases, instead of futilely endeavoring to resist attacks everywhere with their inadequate fighting power. He also taught the Chinese not to be lured into a premature advance after a small victory—a mistake which had often cost them dearly—but instead always to wait to attack until their supplies had caught up with them.

General Wedemeyer himself attributes his success in large part to the repercussions of the Stilwell incident in China. Chiang Kai-shek and the National Government were well aware, he told me, that if the new American commander were to pronounce as adverse a judgment upon them as Stilwell had done, they would be deprived of American aid.

"Wedemeyer changed the spirit of everything," General Odlum, the Canadian ambassador, had said to me in Chungking. "Whereas Stilwell and Gauss were inclined to build up both sides in China, thereby weakening her and preventing her from ever becoming strong and united, Wedemeyer has given America a logical role and a consistent policy in line with American interests and the maintenance of world peace."

Victor Odlum had also said to me, "When you get to Shanghai try to find out how Wedemeyer did it; how he managed to win back the trust of the Chinese and accomplish so much more than Stilwell in the reorganization of the Chinese Army into a real fighting force."

My first interview with Wedemeyer and the press conferences I attended gave me some idea of the answer. Wedemeyer struck me at once as a democrat as distinct from a demagogue, a man who respected others whatever their race or rank. His tact, intelligence and patience never failed him and he kept his mind always on principles and nonpersonal issues. Sometimes he reminded his questioners that "it is personal liberty we fought for," but he neither swore nor preached, and I never saw him lose his temper although he often had plenty of provocation.

The pro-Communists among the correspondents continually tried to put him on the spot at the regular weekly press conferences. This should have been easy since he had the impossible assignment of supposedly being in China only to "repatriate Japanese prisoners," while actually, as everyone knew, the United States Army and Navy were giving some help to the National Government in recovering its sovereignty over its liberated territories. Wedemeyer, being not only the American Commander in Chief but also Chief of Staff to Chiang Kai-shek, was in an awkward and ambiguous position. A lesser man would have been driven to administer a sharp rebuke to those who, week after week, needled him concerning the help being given to the Nationalist forces and asked questions which they knew he was precluded from answering. But Wedemeyer never treated their questions as if they were meant to embarrass him, and disarmed them by his amiability and honesty. He frequently reminded us that as a soldier he carried out orders but did not inaugurate policies, and he never gave rude or smart or lying answers. In general he escaped from being drawn into political controversies in which he might have become as identified with anti-Communism as Stilwell had been with pro-Communist policies.

Being able to meet the correspondents in any game of wits, Al Wedemeyer won their respect, while his natural and unpretentious manner, courtesy and reserved friendliness made him generally popular.

Very tall and slim with prematurely gray hair, blue eyes, and a Byzantine cast of features, this soft-spoken, self-controlled man seemed as free of personal vanity as he was well-informed and intelligent. Far from "hating paper work" like his predecessor in China, Wedemeyer had been the brains of the Operations Division of the War Department and been responsible for the planning of the Normandy invasion. In conversation with him, one was aware that he had read and thought a great deal. He is a student of history, fully conscious of the connection between economics and politics, and well aware that the sacrifices of war are meaningless unless the aims for which they are fought are consistently pursued. He was also too wise to think that he has all the answers to the problems of China and the world.

One American officer said to me, "Do you notice that everyone associated with Wedemeyer tries to protect or shield him? From his chauffeur to his Chief of Staff they all fear that advantage will be taken of his kindness and his trustful nature."

Another, a colonel, said, "Trouble with the old man is that he thinks there is good in everybody."

His friends had no real reason to be afraid. The general was not a fool, and although it might be his philosophy that belief in a man or nation calls out the best that is in them, he was not easily deceived. Once anyone had betrayed his confidence he never trusted him again, and he could be mercilessly outspoken to friends as well as opponents.

The important thing in China was that his attitude and behavior were exactly what was required to win the trust of Chiang Kai-shek and the better elements in the Kuomintang. The Chinese took strong criticism from him and accepted his advice because of his unmistakable integrity and lack of personal vanity. Whereas the admonitions and insults of Stilwell had but rendered them more obstinate and set in their ways, Wedemeyer's frank and friendly approach disarmed them.

Wedemeyer was never superior or contemptuous but instead approached the Chinese saying, in effect: "We are Americans and you are Chinese. We are different but we are friends and equals. I want to help you for the sake of both our countries. I cannot help you unless we are frank with one another and speak plainly. I see and appreciate your difficulties and doubt if I could have done better in your place. But if we co-operate the situation can be greatly improved."

In spite of all the elaborate politeness and ceremonious circumlocution of the Chinese, they appreciate truthfulness and plain dealing. Thus Wedemeyer was able to get changes made and reforms instituted in the Chinese Army, where Stilwell had failed to make any impression.

Even the Communist sympathizers among the correspondents liked the general and never labeled him a "reactionary." In conversations with me and others he said he understood, and had sympathy for, the aspirations which the Chinese Communists voiced. But he was too intelligent and analytical not to understand the real purpose behind the democratic slogans which deluded the followers and sympathizers of the Communist Party. He knew that Communism is a world conspiracy against democracy and above all against America. He had read enough and seen enough to know Russia's purpose and, while recognizing the good side of what the Chinese Communists had done in the Northwest, he saw them as the obstacle to Chinese unity and knew they were Russia's puppets.

As he said to me early in December 1945:

We did not fight the war in order to permit the Russians to ravage and plunder the land of an ally as they are doing in Manchuria; nor to allow the Communists to create chaos and confusion in China in order to preclude the possibility of unification and democratization under the National Government.

It was clear that Wedemeyer for his part was in favor of giving the Chinese Government the necessary moral and material support to prevent her "crashing down" according to Japanese prophecies. But, as I have already related, obstacles were already being placed in his way by the State Department.

Leaving United States Army Headquarters in the Development Building one afternoon I was held up by a long column of trucks full of Chinese Sixth Army men on their way to the docks to take ship for Manchuria. I had never before seen Chinese soldiers like these and I stared at them in amazement. Each man was warmly clad in woolen khaki uniform and greatcoat. They all had steel helmets. They had gloves. They even had leather boots. Bronzed, lean and hardy, obviously well fed and alert, in both their equipment and their appearance they offered a striking contrast to most Chinese soldiers.

Here was visible proof of what American help had done for some units, at least, of China's National armies. To the Communists and their sympathizers the sight of this division was, of course, an outrage. Wherever one's political sympathies lay one realized how little chance the Communist forces up north would have against such soldiers as these. China had never before had such well-equipped soldiers to fight for her. Had the United States in 1946 and 1947 not refused to let the National Government have the ammunition and replacement supplies required, these American-trained divisions would almost certainly have saved Manchuria from the Communists. But we wasted our investment by refusing to supply working capital.

Wedemeyer would not talk about himself but I obtained the answer to Victor Odlum's question in interviews with members of his staff.

General Paul Caraway, who enjoys the unique distinction of being the son of two United States Senators, since both his mother and father were elected to Congress from Arkansas, gave me a graphic description of the situation in China when Wedemeyer arrived in October 1944:

Everything was going to hell, he said. The Chinese armies were melting away, the Japanese were advancing. Chiang Kai-shek was extremely depressed. Everything seemed hopeless.

General Wedemeyer told us he had decided on three things: First, on a plan to hold our supply bases at all costs. Second, on a way to improve the fighting effectiveness of the Chinese Army. Third, he said, we must at all times act like Americans. By this he meant that we must be honest and straightforward with the Chinese. He said that the old China hands or experts who had hitherto handled things had stayed too long in China to be objective in their judgments. There was no middle ground as between the group who considered the Chinese hopeless and those who thought China could do no wrong.

Wedemeyer said no Chinese was to be spoken, and we should not try to imitate the Chinese by bowing, clasping our hands together and generally pretending to be like them. We must always speak through an interpreter, thus making sure that we were understood. We must keep our own customs and entity and always act like Americans. Above all we must never promise what we could not perform or produce. We must always keep our word and never deceive the Chinese or withhold the truth from them.

Under Wedemeyer we always did what we had undertaken to do. When it was impossible to supply something the Chinese asked for, we frankly refused, but at the same time we explained why it was impossible. Unlike our predecessors in Stilwell's day, we did not keep secret from the Chinese what supplies were available. So they knew just as well as we did what could or could not be done.

Then also Wedemeyer showed a real interest in the Chinese armies. He did not regard them as a pawn to be used by us, irrespective of China's interests in any campaigns we decided upon.

Studies were made on how to improve the soldiers' rations in the actual supply conditions which existed, and on how to decrease the size of the Chinese Army while increasing its fighting power. We worked out a merit system. We worked on the basis of the existing pattern of handling Chinese troops, instead of imposing our own pattern.

Wedemeyer reorganized the Chinese Combat Command and the Chinese Training Center. Under the latter we set up an Artillery School, an Infantry School, an Ordnance School, a Heavy Mortar School, and a Command and General Staff School. The Chinese Combat Command, on the other hand, undertook the figuring out. It advised and assisted the Chinese commanders on how to distribute their supplies and how to fight.

The results were gratifying. Forty miles northeast of Kweilin the Chinese gave the Japs bloody hell.

We helped with supplies. The Chinese soldier is brave enough. Our S.O.S. started deliveries and put liaison men in the Chinese S.O.S. We got a terrific trucking system going in South China.

None of our success in improving the efficiency of the Chinese armies would have been possible had it not been for Wedemeyer's personality. His sincerity, modesty and patience won the admiration and affection of Chiang Kai-shek. The two men respected and appreciated each other, for the Generalissimo has some of the same qualities which distinguish Al Wedemeyer.

Never have I seen a time when, harassed as he may have been, Chiang Kai-shek was not honest and did not take remarks in the spirit in which they were offered. When he refused to do something we suggested he always explained the reasons why.

On one occasion when things were most difficult, the Japanese continually advancing, and disaster imminent, we submitted a plan to the Generalissimo on how to beat the Japanese offensive. He came to our headquarters to listen to it, never letting his attention wander. The plan was approved.

We never tried to double-cross or outsmart the Chinese. Nor did we look down on them or their efforts. Always we told the Chinese just what supplies we had.

We established a parallel system with Chinese and American opposite commands sitting together from the lowest level to the highest. Then if, for instance, the Divisional Command American and Chinese representatives could not agree, the situation would be reported to the next higher level. Usually the matter was settled lower down. But Chiang Kai-shek gave the order that in the event of disagreement at the highest level the American view should prevail. He so completely trusted Wedemeyer that he was ready to take his word as final.

Colonel Logan worked out a ration for the Chinese soldier including meat and peanut oil. This Logan ration was adopted for all the American-sponsored units in the Chinese Army.

We raised heck about the recruiting system in China. We took the big shots to *see* and impress them with the terrible condition of the recruits. Thus we managed to get improvements made.

I asked Caraway about Wedemeyer's earlier history. He replied simply: "When he graduated from West Point Al Wedemeyer was designated as the cadet who in his conduct best exemplified the motto: Duty, Honor, Country."

Captain MacAfee, another officer who served under Wedemeyer, said to me: "He is distinguished in particular by his power of analysis and ability to carry things through; by his determination. He never throws up his hands in despair or tries to place blame on others. Desperate as the situation was when he arrived in China, he remedied it by those qualities."

General Caraway and Captain MacAfee are young men. General Stratemeyer, who commanded the U. S. air forces in China, was

Wedemeyer's senior in age and permanent rank, and was regarded by the press as something of a martinet and a man of little warmth and humanity. Nevertheless he too was Wedemeyer's staunch admirer. He said:

Too many Americans judge the Chinese by Shanghai. They don't know the Chinese and they don't understand what appalling difficulties they had to face during the war. As Chiang's Chief of Staff, Wedemeyer too had to cope with these problems. No one was better fitted to do so, because, under Tom Handy in the War Department, he had been the brain power back of the Operational Division.

Wedemeyer was the staff strategist of the whole war. Marshall gives him the credit. You ought to talk to Marshall about him, for Marshall believes in giving credit to his subordinates. It was Wedemeyer who gave Marshall the Normandy invasion plans for the Joint Chiefs of Staff.

Wedemeyer is air-minded. He believes in air power and sacrificed supplies and ammunition for the ground forces to give them to us in China. When he came to China he said that the only reason for military offensives was to get back our air bases, protect them and advance them. He never dillydallied. He always made clean-cut rapid decisions: yes or no.

He gave me the authority and the means to set up flying schools in China: primary, basic, advanced, operational, and training schools for Chinese fliers. He pushed the composite Chinese-American Air Wing backed logistically by Americans. The great difficulty was maintenance and supply. The Chinese can be trained to be excellent fliers. This American-Chinese composite wing had half Chinese and half American personnel. Gradually we built up an integrated Chinese-American force. If, for instance, there were nine planes, five would be commanded by Americans, four by Chinese. To bolster up the Chinese we dispersed our base forces.

Wedemeyer accomplished much with little because of his personality. He is convincing, thorough, hard-working and straightforward in all he does. He put his cards on the table and everyone, Chinese and Americans, got behind him and pushed. He accomplished wonders with the army, the air force and the Chinese Government by his patience, tact and honesty.

I think he just sold himself and his ability to everyone. When he came there was chaos. He is both a smart strategist and a reader of human nature. That is a rare combination and makes him a great general. In southeast Asia where he was Mountbatten's Chief of Staff before coming to China, the situation with the British was also very difficult. By speaking his mind but always remaining courteous and never becoming self-important Wedemeyer did a lot of good. I think his success is due to his always keeping himself in the background and always showing consideration for others, whether Allied commanders or American junior officers and enlisted men. He does not push himself forward and is never personal.

Before he came to China he had had to sell the British the right way of doing things. Then he had to sell it to the Chinese. His lack of vanity and his sincerity enabled him to do it. He succeeded in convincing the Chinese that the best plan would be to agree upon a reasonable number of divisions to be fed and clothed and equipped. He collaborated with the Chinese in improving the pay, food and medical care of these selected Chinese divisions. In particular we wanted to improve the treatment of the wounded. If Japan had not surrendered before the projected offensive in South China had come off, we should have evacuated the Chinese wounded by air in a planned campaign.

Personal contact of the kind which Wedemeyer inaugurated was of greater importance than Lend-Lease. Ninety percent of our boys now have a warm spot in their hearts for China. Earlier they had only contempt or dislike.

General Stratemeyer seemed to me too optimistic. I fear that few American GI's had much, if any, affection for the Chinese. United States Army Headquarters contained a high proportion of personnel with an understanding of Chinese problems. Besides the generals I have quoted, and such men as Colonel Don Scott and Colonel Linton of the Education Department, I might also mention Colonel Pendleton Hogan of G5 whose sensitive personality as a novelist in civilian life enabled him to appreciate and interpret an alien culture. As already related, I met junior officers who had served with Chinese troops and appreciated their qualities. But most GI's never got to know any Chinese but prostitutes, and had dealings only with coolies and barkeepers. I met one young corporal who had made friends with a college graduate. When he got to know her family, he conceived such a liking for the Chinese that he contemplated returning to China after the war. But the Chinese attitude toward social intercourse between the sexes, combined with the average American's color prejudices, prevented most GI's from being invited to Chinese homes.

There was, of course, also the Leftist politically conscious type of soldier who managed to have touch with Madame Sun Yat-sen. She entertains like a queen and likes bright young men. One of them I knew. He thought her so wonderful that he had naturally become a Communist sympathizer.

The United States Army Command received little or no help from either the *Stars and Stripes* or the United States Information Service (U.S.I.S.) in its efforts to establish good relations between the American armed forces and the Chinese. U.S.I.S. (formerly the O.W.I.) seemed to have an unduly large quota of Communist sympathizers. The Chinese press selections which it translated and circulated, although purporting to represent a cross section of Chinese opinions, were culled largely from Communist and Democratic League sources. Even their stateside news seemed to give preference to anti-National Government expressions of opinion. But here it must be admitted that U.S.I.S. was hardly to blame. A large number, if not an actual majority, of American newspapers at this time represented the civil war in China as one between a "reactionary" government and the "progressive liberal" forces led by the Communists.

General Wedemeyer had practically no control over the *Stars and Stripes* which seemed intent on exacerbating Sino-American relations and encouraging the agitation to be sent home. Rarely did this organ of the United States Army publish anything which might have taught the GI's the why and wherefore of their presence in China, or enabled them to judge the Chinese more fairly. Of course, any real discussion of the world situation, or of the danger Russia constituted to America as well as to China would have been taboo since we were still practicing Coué diplomacy. But it was hardly necessary to angle the news in favor of the Communists, and something could have been done to inform Americans in China as to the causes for the poverty and material backwardness of China, and make them aware that an alien civilization is not necessarily contemptible.

Naturally the bored American soldiers and sailors in Shanghai, longing to go home and seeing no valid reason for their presence in China, failed to present the Chinese with any striking evidence of the superiority of American culture. Some treated the Chinese as badly as or worse than Negroes are often treated in the States. There were also incidents of drunken brawling and of actual physical violence done to Chinese civilians. And, as everywhere else, some Americans engaged in black-market operations, selling goods obtained at the PX stores at a huge profit.

Either because many Marine officers had been in China before tne war, spoke the language and understood and respected the Chinese, or because the Marine Corps is the best disciplined of the United States armed services, there was a striking contrast between the behavior of the Army and Navy in Shanghai and that of the Marines in North China. Discipline certainly counted for a great deal, as also the better "indoctrination" of the Marines. There was no *Stars and Stripes* to play up their grievance and incite them to hatred of the Chinese Government. I was surprised to find how many enlisted men and sergeants as well as officers understood very well why they were in China. Their minds had certainly not been corrupted by Communist propaganda, and several of them told me that their officers had explained to them that their presence in North China was necessary to keep the Russians out.

Perhaps, however, the ancient culture of China, so evident in Peking, also had its effect. I do not, of course, mean to imply that the marines spent their time studying Chinese civilization, although a good many of them went on the sight-seeing tours arranged by the Red Cross. But I was struck by their politeness toward the Chinese in stores and restaurants, and on the streets, and by the number of young men who told me they liked the Chinese people. No one in Peking could consider the Chinese uncivilized or regard them with the ignorant contempt shown by many GI's and sailors in Shanghai.

The marines coming into China after Japan's surrender, never having been subject to the vitiating atmosphere of wartime Chungking or liberated Shanghai, and commanded by commissioned and noncomissioned officers with great pride in the traditions of the Marine Corps, did not publicly clamor to go home. They knew they had an important job to do. Sometimes they talked of the possibility of war, and I found them surprisingly well-informed. They knew, if the Army enlisted men did not, that Russia threatened America as well as China. And they had no affection for the Communists who sniped at them and occasionally made prisoners of men who went duck shooting in the countryside or were ambushed on patrol duty.

In Tsingtao, when I went to obtain a billet for the night en route to Peking, there was a notice on the major's desk saying, "We Too Want to Go Home."

"Does it mean," I asked, "that, like the Army and Navy, you want to get out?"

"No," he replied, "it means that we, in the personnel division, want to go home as much as the men who come to us."

"But you haven't had any demonstrations here?"

"No, of course not. *We* are marines."

I talked to many Marine enlisted men in the Peking Hotel where I was billeted and which, now called "Hostel Number 2," was full of them. Far from being the tough "leathernecks" of tradition, most of them were young and courteous and some of them surprised me by their views and their way of spending their liberty hours. There were, for instance, the three young sergeants who met me near Executive Headquarters one evening and asked me to have a drink with them, because, as they said, I "looked so American" as I walked down the street. I found they had spent the afternoon playing with the Chinese children at a Catholic orphanage, and they took me off to visit a Japanese family they were sorry for. All three were veterans of the Pacific War and when I expressed some surprise at their attitude one of them said: "There was a time and place for hatred; we don't feel that way now. These people are very decent and the war wasn't their fault."

The Marine Corps commanders seemed to be in an advantageous position in that they were evidently freer of control by either the War or State Department or less afraid of press censure than the Army. Whereas Army officers knew they might get into hot water at home if they spoke freely or acted according to their convictions concerning the Communist or Russian menace, the Marine officers I met could apparently afford to be realists. This was particularly true of General Worton, General Rockey's Chief of Staff, who went out of his way to help me make the most of my few days' stay in Peking and Tientsin because he saw the danger which the Communists constituted as clearly as I did.

Until General Marshall withdrew them from China in February 1947 the U.S. Marine Corps by its presence kept the Communists and the Soviet Government in check. The big Communist offensive in Manchuria, which endangered the whole Nationalist position in North China, was not launched until after the marines were on their way home.

General Wedemeyer had shown himself to be a statesman as well as a diplomat and a soldier in his late 1945 proposal for dealing with the Manchurian situation. He said to me in Shanghai:

China has not got the strength unaided to re-establish her authority over both her Northern Provinces and Manchuria against the strong Communist opposition. It is most improbable that American public opinion would allow sufficient aid to be given to the Chinese Government to recover and to hold both the provinces between the Yangtze and the Great Wall, and the Northeast. Moreover, a unilateral approach by the United States might involve us in a war with Russia. I have therefore personally advocated that we should invoke the machinery of the United Nations Charter.

The United Nations organization has been set up to solve international problems which might develop into a world-wide conflict. Action should therefore be taken through U.N. to stop the establishment of these Russian puppet governments in the Far East and in the Middle East. I have suggested to Washington that the United States propose a temporary trusteeship of the Big Four over Manchuria, under terms which envisage the return of Manchuria to China when, in the view of the Four Powers, she is in a position to establish her own control. Both the legal and ethnological right of China to possession of Manchuria would be specifically recognized. The same action should be taken with regard to Korea whose future independence was pledged by the United States, but which is at present split into a Northern Russian zone and a Southern American zone.

The correctness of General Wedemeyer's appraisal of the situation has been amply proved by the course of events. Yet it is doubtful whether Chiang Kai-shek could have taken his advice. Not only was it politically impossible for him to go before the Chinese people and say that after their eight-year war against Japan Manchuria could not yet be regained. Uncertainty as to the continuity of American policy made it an even more dangerous gamble to trust the United States to prevent a permanent partition of China, sanctified by a Big Three agreement. It seemed a lesser risk to endeavor to regain both Manchuria and North China by force of arms.

Having been for so long a victim of power politics China is sadly aware that she cannot count for certain on a square deal in any international conference or organization. Having been betrayed at Yalta, how could she be certain she would not again find her rights sacrificed to Russia's ambitions if she trusted to the United Nations to preserve her integrity and prevent Russia or her puppets from stealing Manchuria?

Other Army and Marine officers I talked to were equally aware that China was a sort of prewar Spain in reverse, with the United States backing the legitimate government and the Russians backing the rebel Communists, as the Axis had backed Franco.

Stalin had little need at this time to fight his own battles. Americans who called themselves liberals were busy fighting them for him. As already noted, Wedemeyer at his press conferences was being hauled over the coals by correspondents who opposed aid to the National Government and wanted us to transfer our support to the Communists. This was at a time when the Communists were already fighting a verbal campaign against "American imperialism." The Soviet radio station in Shanghai and the two Russian language newspapers there were carrying on a continuous subtle campaign to discredit and deride America. The Associated Press correspondent in the Communist capital of Yenan was already reporting on the extensive anti-American propaganda being carried on by the Communists. A Communist spokesman in Chungking, when welcoming the resignation of the "Imperialist" Hurley, regretted that General Wedemeyer had not been "removed from his command."

I used to reflect in Shanghai that if American economic advisers and government representatives only could establish the same relations with the Chinese as the American Army advisers had done, there would be a real hope of Chinese progress, of the emancipation of her people from poverty, and the elimination of graft and incompetence in the administration, without China's subjection to foreign domination.

The Chinese, after a hundred years of being bullied and looked down upon by Westerners, and after thousands of years of considering theirs to be the one and only civilization, are unduly sensitive. They are so afraid that they are being looked down upon, and so fearful of criticism, that it is hard to teach them anything. At least, so one is always being told. But I wonder sometimes whether the fault does not lie largely in us. Certainly, foreigners who have won their friendship and trust do not find it so difficult to advise or teach them. This was demonstrated in the case of General Wedemeyer and many of the officers under him, notably by General Robert McClure, who was in charge of the U.S. Army personnel training the Chinese Army. But such a task requires patience and tact and good will.

Personally it has been my experience that the Chinese do not resent criticism if they are convinced that one is a friend and sincerely trying to help them. In 1938 I had given utterance to the most scathing denunciation of the treatment of the wounded in China in interviews published in the Chinese press. My book *China at War,* published in 1939, was certainly no paean of praise. I had tried to understand the situation in China but I had pulled no punches concerning what I had seen, both at the front and in Hankow, and what I had heard. I criticized the government very strongly and I was not at all forbearing concerning Madame Chiang and her advisers in the New Life Movement. Nevertheless I continued to be regarded as a friend. My criticisms were even welcomed by many although some of my strictures were no doubt based on too superficial knowledge. It was recognized that I wanted to help China, not harm her. Even when I tactlessly blundered in social intercourse by a brutal or insensitive Western frankness I was forgiven.

The Communists have a distinct advantage in that their devotion to Moscow and their iconoclastic attitude toward China's old values and pattern of civilization free them from any such aversion to learning from the Russians, as hampers the Nationalists in their relations with the Americans and the British.

Back in the United States it seemed to me a tragedy that General Wedemeyer's appointment as Ambassador to China was canceled at the last moment for fear of annoying the Communists. Here was one of the few Americans who was fully trusted by the Generalissimo and could have influenced him in a truly liberal direction. He might have been able to lay the foundations for the same firm and friendly Sino-American relations in the political and economic field as he had already laid in military matters. For it seems to me that China has only two choices: one to become a part of the Soviet Empire; the other to accept friendly Western guidance until the material and political foundations have been laid for democracy. She cannot work her way to democracy if she stands alone; her enemies are too close.

Our demands for a strong *and* democratic China are incompatible at the present stage. China might become strong if she developed into a replica of the militarist-feudal-monopolistic-capitalist Japan we have destroyed. She might become strong if she followed the Moscow road and industrialized under a totalitarian dictatorship on autarchic lines. But if she is to become both democratic and strong we must help her, and we cannot do so unless we take account of the root causes of her difficulties and recognize that her problems are very different from our own. Co-operation between two peoples, one materially and politically backward and the other the richest and most advanced technologically of all nations, presents grave difficulties which can be overcome only by tact, intelligence, forbearance, understanding and sympathy. The pattern for effective Sino-American collaboration was set by the United States Army during the last months of the war. Unfortunately, since then, we have done little but affront Chinese susceptibilities, while also diminishing their confidence in our political sagacity by our clumsy pressure on behalf of the Communists. Because of all the bad advice we have given them since Yalta, they are by now perhaps impervious to good advice even when offered in a friendly spirit.

China badly needs friends who both understand her difficulties and are not afraid to tell her the truth; friends whom she can learn from, and listen to, without fear that they will take advantage of her weaknesses and faults. Such a friend, it seems to me, was Al Wedemeyer, and it was an ill omen for both China and America that he left China.

Whether or not it is possible to hope that the United States would help and guide China without dominating her is a moot point. But such tutelage would offer both countries a better hope for the future, and also be more profitable for the United States than the present halfhearted military and economic support coupled with curses and compulsions to set up an impotent coalition government.

CHAPTER XII

The Dilemma of the Chinese Liberals

THE double standard used in judging Soviet Russia and other countries by Western "progressives" is nowhere more apparent than with regard to China. Stalin's ruthless totalitarian dictatorship is excused as a necessity forced on the Communists by the "hostility of the capitalist world." This hostility, real a quarter of a century ago, has been a myth for at least two decades. The United States poured Lend-Lease into Russia to save her. Britain likewise supplied the Red Army with equipment. The leaders of the "capitalist world" allowed Soviet Russia to establish her dominion over more than half of Europe by the ill-omened Yalta and Potsdam agreements and the earlier betrayal of Mikhailovitch. Since the end of the war Russia and her satellites have been treated with greater generosity by UNRRA than most other countries.

On the other hand, no excuses for the lack of democracy in China are made by the same writers who give Russia every benefit of every doubt. Yet China was preyed on, oppressed, exploited and weakened by the Western Powers and Russia for a century; left to fight Japan unaided year after year; never received more than a trickle of Lend-Lease, and is today, unlike Russia, actually menaced by foreign conquest. Moreover although Chiang Kai-shek's so-called dictatorship is not even comparable to the iron tyranny of the Russian Communist Party, some of the same writers who condone concentration camps, terror, press censorship, hunger and servitude in the Soviet Union, label Chiang-Kai-shek's government the worst in the world.

The difficulties faced by the Republic of China since its inception, only three decades ago, have in fact been unequaled in the history of any modern state. It inherited both the evil legacy of nearly three hundred years of ultraconservative Manchu rule and the problems created by the aggressive European imperialism of the nineteenth century. The vast size of China, her enormous population, her backward economy and ancient cultural traditions, would alone have rendered the task of the reformers a colossal one. Their problems were immeasurably enhanced by the fact that almost all the Powers meddled in China's affairs.

From the outset forces within and without sought to stifle or destroy the New China to which the Kuomintang acted as midwife. The Republic was almost strangled at birth by its progenitors when Yuan Shih-kai, its first President, sought to make himself emperor with the backing of foreign Powers. It was kept in swaddling clothes by the unequal treaties which curtailed China's sovereignty and freedom and prevented a normal development. All the Great Powers sought to crush Chinese nationalism when it infringed on their "special rights" or commercial interests. No one of them would protect China from aggression by any of the others. It was this situation which led Sun Yat-sen to describe China as a subcolony, meaning that she suffered all the ills of foreign exploitation by a number of Powers, without the advantage of being a colony protected by one of them.

When finally, in 1927, the Western-orientated Kuomintang majority led by Chiang Kai-shek broke with the Communists and Russia and established its rule in place of that of the war-lord-dominated Peking Government, the reformed China they hoped to create was stunted in childhood by too heavy labors. True that the Kuomintang Government won customs autonomy by 1928 and was soon well on the way through negotiation to abrogation of all the unequal treaties with the West. But, as the West retreated and signified its willingness to relinquish imperialist privileges, to treat China as an equal and to help her to modernize herself, Japan was advancing.

Japan's young, confident and aggressive imperialism, built up originally by Britain and the United States as a counterweight to Russia, menaced Kuomintang China from the moment of its birth.

As if this were not a sufficient handicap for the Chinese seeking to reconstruct their country, the old Russian threat to her independence came alive again in a new form: the Communists constitute an unsurmountable obstacle to China's national unity, reconstruction and democratic development.

Never since its inauguration has the present National Government of China been free of the necessity to divert its main energies to war. The civil war on two fronts—against the Communists on the Left and for the suppression of the surviving war lords and other reactionary elements on the Right—occupied the government's main energies and burdened its finances for the whole of the first decade of its existence. When Japan, in 1931, struck her first great blow against China by the rape of Manchuria, Chiang Kai-shek's armies were busy fighting the Communists. It was not until 1935 that the Communist Army was driven into the Northwest and China could at last settle down to peaceful reconstruction. Meanwhile the Japanese had got into a position in which they expected to be able to detach North China under an "autonomous" government. Failing to do so, they struck at China again with redoubled force, determined to "beat China to her knees," as Prince Konoye expressed it in 1938.

The National Government of China was always between the Scylla of Japanese domination and the Charybdis of Communism, which in effect means Russian hegemony.

Chiang Kai-shek's endeavor to free China from her colonial status without her falling from the Western imperialist or Japanese frying pan into the Communist fire, has been rendered all the more difficult by the unawareness of most Westerners of what was at stake. During the Sino-Japanese War and since V-J Day, too many Americans failed to realize that the Generalissimo dared not trust the Communists since they were under Moscow's orders and might at any moment be ordered to betray China.

In the historical circumstances outlined above it is hardly surprising that the Kuomintang has so far failed to reconstruct China on democratic lines, and has been unable to eliminate the dead wood and corrupt elements in the government. One of the Chinese Central News reporters said to me in Chungking: "Chiang Kai-shek's hands have always been tied. He has been fighting continuously to save the life of the nation, and has never had time to clean up the administration."

The American demand for a strong *and* democratic China is totally unrealistic. China should not be expected to run before she can walk. We may have forgotten, but the Chinese remember that the premature attempt in 1911 to set up a parliamentary form of government resulted in anarchy and war-lord rule, with the so-called Republican Government at Peiping the puppet of whichever war lord in the vicinity happened to be strongest.

China is at about the same stage of development as England and France were in the fourteenth and fifteenth centuries when the greatest need was for a king who could insure some security and liberty for the people by curbing the feudal barons. This does not imply that China ought to have an emperor today; but it does mean that her greatest need is law and order, which can be enforced only by a strong government.

If security for private enterprise were assured, the basis for a subsequent democratic development could be created. But China is not only expected to telescope into a few years the developments which other countries have required centuries to achieve, she is also required to be all things to all men—to establish a government and an economic organization of society which will be pleasing both to the democratic West and to the Communist totalitarians. Pulled all ways at once she cannot move forward.

Secondly, few of China's critics see that, since even in the most advanced Western democracies war necessitates some curtailment of civil liberties, in an economically and politically backward country such as China it requires an authoritarian administration. Indeed, China's military failures in the war against Japan, in so far as they were not due to her lack of arms and her exhaustion after so many years of unaided struggle, were the result of the weakness of her government—not in its dictatorial nature but in its failure to dictate.

To call the Kuomintang Government "fascist" is the very reverse of the truth. Its powers are not limitless but far too limited. In war it lacks entirely the simian efficiency of the Nazi, Japanese and Soviet States. It interferes with the individual too little, not too much. Its sins of omission are far greater than its sins of commission. Its gravest fault is the ineffectiveness of its administration, and its failure to force through necessary reforms. It is too soft, not too hard. Whether or not any other government could have done better in the circumstances, the whole problem of China is distorted by those who paint a picture of a small group of wicked reactionaries maintaining a totalitarian dictatorship.

In their efforts to discredit the administration of Chiang Kai-shek, American liberals as well as the Communists endeavor to have it both ways.

As Counselor Chen Chih-mai said to the New York Shanghai Tiffin Club in May 1947: "In one breath the Chinese Government is described as both incompetent and fascist. Fascism, as we all admit, is a bad thing . . . but incompetence is certainly not one of its sins. The word fascist and the word omni-competence are almost synonymous, and if we are one [incompetent] we certainly cannot be at the same time the other [fascist]."

In the economic as in the political sphere the Chinese Government cannot do right in the eyes of its critics. If it were to allow free trade, free exchange and free enterprise, it might please foreign business interests but it would affront foreign and Chinese "progressives." When it endeavors to control the national economy in order to promote industrial development and curb the abuses of an uncontrolled capitalist society, it is labeled "fascist," not only by its Right Wing critics but also by those who approve of a regimented economy only if it bears the Communist label.

Nor is it easy to see how the National Government can at one and the same time reconstruct China for the Chinese and make her strong enough to maintain her independence, while also pleasing her Western allies.

The Chinese Government is in somewhat the same situation as Aesop's character, the man who was traveling with his son and his donkey. No matter what he did, he was abused by the public. If he rode and his boy walked, people said it was shameful; if his son rode and he walked this too was disapproved; when both rode, he was held to be abusing the donkey. Finally he and his son, in despair at the outcries of the public, carried the donkey.

Since it cannot do right in the eyes of its Western critics the Chinese Government wastes the energies and lives of its people trying to please everybody and thus fails to cope with any of the grave problems it faces. Nor is its situation rendered easier by the conflicting views of the Chinese themselves as regards what ought to be done.

Both the weakness and the strength of the Kuomintang lie in the diversity of the elements which compose it and in the mixture of Confucian and Western concepts which constitute its ideology.

Sun Yat-sen had hoped to unite China, make her independent and set her on the road to reconstruction and modernization by including all "good men" in his party. Since China needed all her strength for the gigantic tasks ahead of her he had emphasized nationalism and sought the support of all classes. The only internal enemies were conceived to be the war lords or other elements who opposed the National (Kuomintang) Revolution. Both on this account and because Sun Yat-sen clung to the Confucian belief that virtue, derived from understanding or knowledge, is the primary requisite of good government, the practical application of his Three Principles was left indefinite enough for all to subscribe to them.

Consequently the house of the Kuomintang has many mansions. It includes the most diverse elements, both socially and with respect to their conceptions of the desired image of a New China, and also in regard to the methods to be adopted to bring it into existence. Even the Communists now give at least lip service to the *San Min Chu I*—Sun Yat-sen's Three Principles of the People.

The heterogeneous composition of the Kuomintang Government constituted its strength when the primary problem was to maintain Chinese unity in face of the Japanese invader. However, when China's internal economic and political problems demand solution by positive action, this same heterogeneous composition becomes the government's weakness. During its triumphant march north from Canton to Shanghai in 1926–1927 the Kuomintang was transformed from a small party and army of patriots and revolutionaries into an enormous coalition. Men who could not agree on anything else could agree on the Kuomintang's primary aims: the national liberation of China; her freedom from the shackles on her national sovereignty imposed by unequal treaties with the Great Powers; an end to war-lord rule under the Peking Government and to the weakness and disunity which had allowed foreigners to dominate and exploit China.

It has always been a Chinese characteristic to compromise rather than to fight. So the war lords and other "feudal" or reactionary elements were not all exterminated, but were allowed to join the Kuomintang if they were ready to submit. The Communists were as much in favor of this policy as the Kuomintang in the days of their collaboration. In 1926 Stalin argued in Moscow, against the Trotskyists, that Chiang Kai-shek was a valuable ally because he knew how to demoralize the war lords and "induce them to pass over to the side of the revolution, bag and baggage, without striking a blow."

In 1927, before it had had time to digest the reactionary elements it had absorbed, the Kuomintang lost its extreme Left Wing, the Chinese Communists. The coalition broke when, on arrival in Shanghai, there seemed no longer any possibility of collaboration between those who wanted to compromise both with the foreigners and the "feudal" elements at home, and those who wanted to transform the National Revolution into a social revolution.

It may be argued that it was Chiang Kai-shek's initial and greatest mistake to break completely with the Communists in 1927; that he would have been able to win greater concessions from the West and ward off Japanese aggression had he retained in reserve the powerful weapon of a Communist movement with which to threaten the Powers. It is undoubtedly true that the fear of Communism in China was what brought Britain and America to terms in 1927 and 1928. Had a real Communist danger existed in subsequent years Japan might not have dared to fight the National Government which was the only bulwark against it. By massacring and fighting the Communists, Chiang Kai-shek was destroying what could have been his most potent weapon in his dealings with foreign Powers.

Had the Chinese Communists been a native revolutionary movement, instead of an arm of the Soviet State, this thesis would be tenable. But Chiang Kai-shek had every reason to believe that Stalin's promise to the Comintern to destroy him and the Kuomintang was not a bluff. The extermination of the Communists, which seemed the only way to halt the momentum of the extremist revolutionary movement, was the price China had to pay for collaboration with the West.

What Chiang Kai-shek could not possibly have foreseen was that less than twenty years after his Shanghai massacre of the Communists, America and Britain, whose good will the slaughter was expected to secure, should turn around and castigate him for his refusal to make sufficient concessions to the Communists to induce them to enter a "coalition government." Such is the irony of history.

Had China been left alone, the civil war might have worked itself out and led eventually to the establishment of a vigorous and progressive government. The Communists would not have won out, but in so far as they represent a native revolutionary peasant movement, their influence would have prevailed and allowed China to shed the old skin of medieval or primitive agrarian social and economic relationships. However, since foreign Powers were forever taking advantage of China's difficulties to further their own selfish aims, the conflict between Right and Left in China became irreconcilable. Each side hardened and the sap of liberalism dried up or dripped uselessly to the ground.

In expelling the Communists and seeking to exterminate them, the Kuomintang was inevitably led to rely to an increasing extent on the conservative forces. Yet it did not at once lose its character of a reform movement. In the years preceding the war with Japan the Kuomintang not only gave China a higher degree of unity and a stronger and a more effiective administrative system than she had known since the seventeenth century, but it started her along the road toward modernization of her economy and development into a Western-type democracy.

In the decade before the Sino-Japanese War, the internal weakness engendered by the civil war with the Communists was in part compensated by the National Government's increasing control over the war lords who had originally refused to accept its authority. The pressure of both the Communists and the Japanese helped to bring formerly independent provincial governments under the control of the National Government. For, once the local governments were compelled to call for Nanking's aid, they inevitably found themselves forced to accept its financial and administrative supervision. Bit by bit the Kuomintang Government was succeeding in establishing respect for its laws over most of China and creating the nucleus of an effective administrative apparatus.

During this period T. V. Soong, the outstanding representative of the Western-educated and orientated Chinese, performed near miracles in the organization of China's finances. A managed currency was successfully instituted, although the Chinese hitherto had regarded a coin as worth only the metal of which it was composed. Confidence was great enough for loans to be floated within the country, rendering China more independent of Western and Japanese financiers than she had been for a century. Britain and America, ready by now to aid the National Government in the reconstruction of China, helped institute the currency and other reforms which were laying the foundation of a modern state.

At the same time it must be recognized that Chiang Kai-shek, when in 1927 he decided to check the revolutionary movement and enlist the support of the compradors and their Western partners or bosses, gave the Treaty Port merchants and bankers a paramount voice in the settling of China's destiny. Chiang's marriage to Mei-ling Soong both consolidated and symbolized the alliance. Some writers have regarded it as a betrayal of the original aim of the Kuomintang Revolution, but since Sun Yat-sen had himself not only married another daughter of the Soongs, but also obtained financial aid from Western-orientated Chinese capitalists, this thesis is hard to maintain. That Chiang paid a high price is, however, unquestionable.

It was Japan who, in spite of her own ruin, succeeded in crushing the rising forces of liberal reformist Chinese nationalism represented by the Kuomintang. The National Government did not degenerate until the war with Japan had ruined China's middle classes, cut her off from foreign trade, thrown the government on the support of the backward Western provinces and vastly increased the power of the Chinese Communists.

Chiang Kai-shek had originally been able to balance himself, with consummate political skill, on the support of many diverse elements and political groups in China while yet leaning slightly in the direction of the liberals. Following the fall of Hankow and Canton, and with increasing difficulty after the Stalin-Hitler, and Russo-Japanese pacts, he had held China united in spite of her military reverses. But, as the long years of war dragged on, and particularly after the early defeats of the Anglo-American forces in 1941–1942 had enabled Japan to make the blockade of Free China practically watertight, the National Government in Chungking was forced to rely more and more on the quasi-feudal or reactionary forces.

It is as if Chiang Kai-shek had originally sat on a three-legged stool supported by Right, Left and Center. The Center (the Westernized middle class with its economic base in the cities of the lost coastal area) was desperately weakened by the war and Japan's occupation of China's coastal provinces. The Left (the Communists) broke away and was used as a club by his enemies. Even the third leg was pared down by Wang Ching-wei's defection to the Japanese in 1939. Unless he and his government were to collapse entirely, Chiang Kai-shek was forced to retain the support of the conservatives and reactionaries. He could not, until the war was over, even assert his authority over such pre-Kuomintang war-lord elements as "Tiger Lung," the Governor of Yunnan. Much less was it possible for him to alienate the whole provincial rural gentry by drastic land reform.

The influence of the Westernizers naturally declined once the National Government was driven to the backward interior provinces and had to depend in large part for survival on the support of what the Communists call the feudal elements. The Whampoa officers, trained in the Military Academy set up by the Kuomintang in the early twenties, constituted a professional caste personally loyal to Chiang Kai-shek. The loyalty of other generals and officers was more questionable, in particular that of the provincial armies. It had to be held through eight years of defeat and Japan's tempting peace offers, and these officers came in the main from the landowning classes. This alone made it practically impossible to institute agrarian reforms during the war. The government's dependence on the land tax as its main source of revenue during the blockade also forced it to rely on the village gentry to collect it. As Owen Lattimore admits, "It is simply impossible to collect the land tax without the goodwill of the landlords."

Americans like General Stilwell, who damned Chiang Kai-shek for not making a clean sweep of all the reactionaries and grafters in the administration, ignored political realities. Even President Roosevelt had been careful not to alienate the bosses who controlled the Democratic machine in several large American cities. It would have been far more difficult, indeed impossible, for Chiang Kai-shek to dispense with the support of similar types of Chinese politicians. Chiang was forced to retain in power men like his Chief of Staff Ho Ying-chin who, timid and inefficient as he might be, had the necessary connections and influence to hold China's heterogeneous armies together. The Generalissimo, I was told, would have liked to appoint General Chen Cheng in Ho's place long before he actually did so in 1946. But, although Chen Cheng was both able and incorrupt and held in high esteem by American officers, he is not a Whampoa graduate and this was too great a handicap in wartime for a chief of staff in China, where the ties between the graduates of China's West Point kept various armies more or less united under Chiang Kai-shek's command.

The Generalissimo was confronted with the same problem whenever he attempted to cleanse the civilian administration. Even if he had desired to replace H. H. Kung or T. V. Soong, he could not find anyone else with the necessary knowledge of finance combined with political connections. When in 1947, he made Chang Chun Premier, the latter was handicapped from the start by the tremendous financial power and influence enjoyed by the Soongs and Kungs, by then both excluded from the administration.

China's backwardness was both her strength and her weakness. Her primitive economy and quasi-feudal social organization made it impossible for her to win the war alone, but it also enabled her to survive in spite of her defeats, loss of territory and revenue, and isolation through blockade. The semimodernized Eastern provinces with their railways, roads and factories fell to the invader. The old primitive China in the West remained unconquerable.

The bright promises and hopes of the young Kuomintang Party died in China's unending struggle to survive as a nation. It was inevitable that the government should develop into a military dictatorship, since war was its constant preoccupation. At the same time, the traditions and philosophy of the Chinese people, their individualism, their age-old refusal to honor force above reason, their sense of humor, cynicism and laissez-faire philosophy—in a word, their rejection of both the militarist concepts which underlie Western civilization and the ruthless totalitarian concepts of Communism—prevented the National Government from becoming a streamline dictatorship on Nazi or Communist lines.

China got the worst of both worlds. Her government is not democratic; yet it has few or none of the advantages enjoyed by a fascist or a Communist dictatorship. Hence its failure to win the approval either of the West or of Russia. Hence its military failures. Hence the inability to mobilize the whole people for war, to force everyone to sacrifice for the nation, and to pursue an internal policy ruthless enough to squash all opposition. Hence also in large part its inability to cope with the postwar economic crisis.

China emerged from the war morally as well as economically exhausted. Internal moral decay and the withering of the Kuomintang's roots in the economic and political life of the nation rendered the

National Government incapable of rehabilitating the country fast enough to halt the insidious Communist infection. The Kuomintang, which had originally been the party of the National Revolution, had lost its functional cells in the economy and become in the main a party of officials and their hangers-on. It had been narrowed down into too close an approximation of a group of "ins" and their friends and relatives, divorced from the people as a whole. The government suffers from hardening of the arteries and badly needs new blood. Young men of promise either cannot get into office or are kept in subordinate positions.

The poverty of the country and the civil war gave little opportunity to the educated classes and the small merchants and industrialists to obtain an adequate income. Since the political problem seemed incapable of solution by political means a huge army still had to be supported. Only the printing presses could supply the required revenue. Inflation destroyed the initiative of private enterprise and the continuous rise in prices hit the middle classes hardest. Government service seemed the only road to security. Hence the greater and greater pressure from the "outs" to get in, and the strong resistance of the "ins" to get out.

All this, of course, plays into the hands of the Communists. Some of the disgruntled "outs" join them, or support them, without any liking for what they stand for, because they have no hope of winning position in, or influence with, the present government. The Democratic League is an outstanding example of a group of politicians trying to rise to high office through an alliance with the Communists. There are also individual examples, as for instance the former Tientsin comprador of an American friend of mine. In 1946, he joined the Communists in the hope that if they came to power he would have got in "on the ground floor" with a new government.

Loyalty to old friends and associates, which is a virtue in private life, has become a vicious hardening and narrowing influence in Chiang Kai-shek's government. Yet it may have been for a time the only cement which could hold China in the war, and may have caused her government to refuse Japan's tempting peace offers when there seemed no hope of victory. Some government members who had opposed the war at the start were held in line by their loyalty to the Generalissimo, even when they thought a peace should be negotiated.

There is a reverse side to most defects and virtues. The ramifications of the family system, and the adherence, even of radicals, to the old Chinese ethic which puts so much emphasis on loyalty to family and friends, are a great handicap in setting up a modern, efficient and incorrupt administration. On the other hand they soften political hatreds, offer a strong barrier to Communism and provide a sort of group insurance in times of anarchy or civil war. As regards the latter point I remember how many of the refugees arriving in Hankow in 1938 were fed and sheltered by their own clan organizations. The family system also operates sometimes as a political insurance in times of disorder and civil war.

In general, both the gulf between the "ins" and the "outs" and the chasm which divides the two sides in the civil war are bridged in places by the curious criss-cross of family relationships and old friendships. Many families have a foot in both camps. Some have connections with almost every faction, old and new. Relatives of the Communists can be encountered among the fashionable women of Shanghai, and the sons and daughters of some high Kuomintang officials have joined the Communists. One of the wealthiest Chinese bankers, Kang Hsin-chih, had a daughter in Yenan; her sister was married to the Chinese Consul General in New York, P. H. Chang.

Dr. Paul Linebarger told me of a talk he had in 1940 with a certain Kiang Kang-hu who had been a friend of his father many years before. Mr. Kiang was an old man who a long time ago had formed a Socialist Party of his own which was refused affiliation with the Second International because it had only a half-dozen members. In 1940 he had become an official of the Nanking puppet government headed by Wang Ching-wei. Linebarger was grieved but Kiang told him not to worry about him.

"My son," he said, "is an official of the Chungking Government. My daughter is at Yenan with the Communists, and when she speaks on the radio she tells the world what a horrible person I am. But both of them are good children who will not forget the duties of filial piety. Best of all there is my wife—she is in San Francisco with a bank account. Don't be too sorry for me."

Mr. Kiang Kang-hu was justified in the faith he had put in his children, at least in so far as his daughter was concerned. In 1947 she came to Nanking to try to save her father, in prison as a collaborator.

The Chinese press recounted how she went daily to visit him and was moving heaven and earth to save his life. Her husband, a Jewish doctor, famous in Yenan under the Chinese name he had taken, once gave me a lift in his automobile from the airfield in Peiping to Executive Headquarters, but he would not tell me from what country he came.

In an earlier chapter I referred to the young scion of the Chu family who worked with Chou En-lai at the Communist Party Headquarters in the capital and who, through his nine married aunts, was connected with the Soongs, with the "young Marshall," Chang Hsueh-liang, of Manchuria, and with some half-dozen other influential and wealthy Chinese families. My conversations with this young man's grandfather in Peking were among the most interesting I had in China. Mr. Chu Chi-chien had lived long and seen much and could find little evidence of progress in recent years either in China or the rest of the world.

One evening he spoke of Chinese lost hopes of what the revolution would accomplish, and of the decay of public and private morals today. He said:

Nowadays everything is upside down. In the old days government aimed at taxing as little as possible, and expenditure was based on income. Now the reverse is done: it is decided first how much to spend and then the necessary income is raised. Formerly the ideal was frugal living and many people were supported. Now our ideals have been twisted around. We have adopted the European idea that everyone should be independent. We no longer have the old sense of family obligation. But are things any better? The old family system had its merits as well as its faults. In general we seem to have discarded our old morality without acquiring a new one to take its place. Society is in dissolution, not only in China but also in the Western world. Society needs the cement of accepted ethical values and standards of behavior. When you destroy the old morality without creating a new one everything goes from bad to worse.

The ills of China are not the fault of the Kuomintang. If you try to reform too fast you make matters worse. The amalgamation of old China and the West is difficult enough, but our financial crisis makes matters infinitely worse.

It is sad for me to reflect at the end of my life that our National Revolution and our long war against Japan have not made conditions better; indeed they are worse than ever, not only on account of the dangers that threaten us from without, but because of the decline of our morals.

Mr. Chu was one of the old guard of the Kuomintang, although no longer active. His nephew, Yu Ta-wei, who interpreted for us, was not a member of the Kuomintang but was nevertheless Vice-Minister of War. Having studied at Krupp's in Germany before the war, he had done an excellent job setting up the arsenals in blockaded Free China which supplied the armies with about all the ammunition and arms they had. Shortly after I met him, Yu Ta-wei, who is regarded as one of the ablest administrators in China, became Minister of Communications. He is admitted by foreigners and Chinese alike to be doing an amazingly good job of restoring the railways. His work of reconstruction cannot, of course, keep pace with the Communist work of destruction, but in Central and South China he has accomplished miracles of quick restoration of destroyed communications.

The corruption, graft and nepotism, which constitute China's gravest weakness, are in large part the legacy of the past. They are rooted in conceptions of loyalty to family and friends which were socially valuable in a loosely knit agrarian society in which government played a minor role, but are a deadly poison in a modern, highly integrated state. They also stem, however, from the too-great trials and difficulties to which the Republic of China has been subjected and the terrible poverty which denies an adequate livelihood to the great majority of the people, under any system of distribution.

Most individuals whom life has treated too hard and too unjustly become demoralized in one way or another. The same may be true of nations. If no amount of striving and self-sacrifice and devotion to principle ever produces rewards, and the fates are forever confronting us with new difficulties, there comes a time when further effort seems futile and the easy path is chosen—it cannot lead to glory but will at least ensure a livelihood.

If it be true that the original essence and quality of the Kuomintang Party has been lost in China's unending wars, and the clear stream muddied by the accretion of too many alien elements, the same process of degeneration has affected the Communists also. On the one hand their subservience to Moscow has afflicted them with the same process of moral degeneration as other Communist Parties. They have changed their principles as the wind blew and now have only one unchanging aim: to win power. On the other hand, like the Kuomintang, they have of recent years accepted the services of anyone ready to give lip service to the party. Bandits, former Japanese puppet troops and collaborators, old war lords and compradors have joined with the Communists since V-J Day.

Many old branches on the Kuomintang tree are rotten. But there are some fresh green branches underneath. One can meet many younger officials who are personally incorrupt, efficient and qualified. In Communist China the position is exactly the reverse. The leaders are efficient, clever, energetic and personally incorrupt. But their followers are quite incapable of fulfilling the duties of administrators or technicians.

From all accounts the Communist administration of the territories they have "liberated" since V-J Day does not compare with that of the old model Border Region centering around Yenan. The Communists are finding it impossible to check graft and stop abuses of power now that the orginal Party membership is spread thin over wide areas. In some places they have been so short of personnel that they have installed in office former bandits who extort more from the people than the landlords and tax collectors and, in general, behave like the old war lords whose origins were similar. The inhabitants of Harbin, for instance, were reported in 1947 to be living under a reign of terror with no security of life or property.

It is not only the "rich" who flee when the Communists come. For instance, a *New York Times* correspondent on June 10, 1946, reported the presence of 40,000 refugees in Chinkiang who had fled there from the Communist-held northern half of Kiangsu. For the most part, they were peasants owning, at most, three or four acres of land, and they had become refugees in Kuomintang China to escape Communist exactions or conscription into the Communist armies. In May 1946, 120,000 refugees from Communist areas were reported to be in Shihchiachuan in southwest Hopei.

The capture of Kalgan by the Nationalist forces, in October 1946, illustrated most clearly how far the Communists have moved from their original position as the champions of the Chinese working classes. They had so little faith in the Chinese proletariat and so complete a disregard for their interests that, before surrendering the town, they deprived three thousand workers of their livelihood by dynamiting fifty-two factories (including those producing such necessities as flour, soap, matches and soybean sauce) and also destroying the workers' dormitories. They also dynamited the rail yards, the power station and all other public utilities.* It was hardly surprising that the people of Kalgan appear to have welcomed the Nationalist forces as liberators.

Nor are the peasants faring any better than the working class in Communist-controlled areas. Fighting more vigorously and continuously against the National Government than they ever did against the Japanese, the Communists, in order to supply larger armies, resort to methods of squeezing the farmers no different from those of the old war lords. At the height of the Communist offensive in Manchuria and North China, peasants in Hopei (near Peking) were complaining that the Communists had come three times within a month to collect "taxes."**

Just as formerly the Chinese "common man" was punished by the Japanese for not resisting the Communists and by the Communists for not resisting the Japanese, so now he is squeezed between the opposing Communist and Nationalist forces.

Neither the Kuomintang nor the Communist flood has ever possessed sufficient force to sweep away the old landmarks in China. When united, as from 1922 to 1927, they proved irresistible. But their unity could not possibly endure since each wished to follow different courses in reconstructing China, and in foreign policy. So the government has been forced continually to waste its revenue in trying to suppress the Communists; and the Communists have concentrated their efforts on destroying everything the Kuomintang built up.

Although unavoidable, the divorce between the two movements has been a tragedy for China. Each desired to destroy the other but had not the strength to do so. Each welcomed the support of alien elements in order to acquire the necessary strength. Each was corrupted in different ways. The reforming patriotic essence of the Kuomintang was watered down and almost lost. The Communists became a group out for power at any price, ready to lie and cheat to get it, and even to deny their own theories, betray their own precepts and pretend to be followers of Sun Yat-sen, not of Marx. At times they can hardly

* See *Time* magazine of November 18, 1946, for an eyewitness account of what its correspondent Frederick Gruin called the Communists' "political mistake rivaling their military failure."

** See *Time* magazine June 30, 1947, as well as Chinese Central News reports.

be distinguished from robbers and war lords. The leaders of the Party remained personally incorrupt in a narrow material sense but morally and politically they have lost their integrity by becoming Moscow's puppets.

The Chinese liberals who have been attracted to Communism by their disgust at the shortcomings of the National Government are usually quickly repelled when they come into close contact with the Communists. Dr. Fu Ssu-nien, the distinguished historian and philosopher who was one of the nonparty delegates to the Political Consultative Council, said to me in Chungking that the Kuomintang and the Communists actually support each other. "Those who are inclined to withdraw their support from the Kuomintang stick to it because the alternative, the Communists, is worse; those who are revolted by Communist practices as distinct from their professions nevertheless do not all repudiate Communism because the only alternative is the present Kuomintang Government."

Most Chinese are convinced that the National Government, weak and corrupt as it is, has at least the virtue of being for China, whereas the Communists are for Russia first. Few educated Chinese, after their country's experience during the past century, will pin their faith to a Party which takes its orders from a foreign Power. The unhappy liberals continue to support the government, hoping against hope that it can be reformed and purified.

The Chinese being an old and experienced people recognize the limitations of human nature. They are ready to tolerate a considerable margin of corruption—too great a margin in fact—in the established government. Years ago, when I remarked to Madame Chiang that one had to admit that the Chinese Communists were personally incorrupt in the material sense, she retorted at once: "Yes, of course; they aren't yet in power." The answer was typical of the Chinese view of government. The established government has more leaway for corruption and maladministration than in the West. And the Kuomintang has inherited the position of the emperors in the sense that it is "the government," accepted as such by the great majority of the people. The Chinese, however great their disappointment at its performance, are disposed to give it decades in which to reform itself and show what it can accomplish. The Communists, on the other hand, have only a small margin in which to operate. They would lose everything, including their lives, unless their leaders were incorrupt and able. They have no hope at all unless they set a better example than the established government since the cost of revolution would not be worth while unless the Chinese were certain that a change would be very much for the better.

The Communists, owing to the poor quality of their recent adherents, their terroristic measures and the anarchy they create, as well as their foreign ties, offer no guarantee that their rule would be an improvement over that of the present government.

The defeat of Japan and the support of America should have enabled the liberals to regain their strength. But America has given them little backing, and the civil war has prevented the economic recovery which could resuscitate China's middle classes and enable the liberals to regain the position they held in 1937.

China's primary need is not the installation in power of men who talk glibly about democracy, or of ineffectual dreamers who refuse to see the realities of China's situation. What the Chinese people desperately require is a clean, efficient and progressive government able to inspire respect for its laws, protect both capital and labor, encourage enterprise and carry through the immense tasks of reconstruction.

Had the United States exerted a fraction of the energy and effort it has used to force Chiang Kai-shek to share power with the Communists, in pressuring him to get rid of the dead and rotten wood in his government and give scope and opportunity to the men inside and outside the government who could and would reform the administration, the Chinese people would not now be faced with no alternative to reaction and misgovernment other than the Communist dictatorship and subjection to Moscow.

Such interference in the internal affairs of China would no doubt be labeled "imperialist intervention," but it would in fact constitute a real good-neighbor policy since it would liberate China from the double stranglehold of reactionaries and Communists which is ruining her.

In the statement he made on January 7, 1947, General Marshall recognized that the salvation of the situation in China "would be the assumption of leadership by the liberals in the government and in the minority parties" whom he characterized as "a splendid body of men."

He did not, however, specify who are the liberals who, "under the leadership of Generalissimo Chiang Kai-shek," would, he believed, be able "to unite China through good government." Moreover, by identifying liberalism with willingness to appease the Communists, he confused America's friends in China and emboldened the enemies of democracy.

How can any intelligent Chinese understand why America, intent on rooting out the Communist termites from public office at home, insists upon China admitting them into her government? Why, it is asked, do we insist that what is bad for America is good for China?

No Chinese has forgotten that, until a short while before Pearl Harbor, America supplied Japan with war materials while encouraging China to continue fighting Japan. Now he hears the Communists saying that "the essence of the policy of American imperialism is to colonize China." Although he may have no sympathy for the Communists he is uneasy. He asks himself: "Is this perhaps the reason why the United States seemingly backs both sides, thus perpetuating civil war? Is America deliberately seeking to weaken China?"

Thus our confused and vacillating policy adds fuel to the fire lighted by the Communists. We have made it easy for the Communists to inspire anti-American demonstrations and to convince many Chinese that they are speaking the truth when they say that "the only difference between Japanese and American imperialism is that the latter is stronger and more hypocritical."

The long war, Soviet Russia's determination that China shall know no peace until she submits herself to Moscow, and America's misguided China policy, have all combined to weaken the Chinese liberals. They continue to be ground between the upper and nether millstones of Communism and reaction. Many have given up all hope and attend only to their private affairs. Some escape to America. Others begin to believe that nothing could be worse than the present state of affairs, not even submission to Moscow, which would at least ensure peace. Yet, at least while I was in China, even the most pessimistic liberals still had a faint hope that Chiang Kai-shek would reform his administration.

It had not been forgotten that in the few years of peace which preceded the Sino-Japanese War the Kuomintang had given China the best government she had known for centuries and had won the confidence of the Western Powers in its ability to secure order and modernize China. The National Government, corrupt and inefficient as it has become, still has the prestige of having brought China through an ordeal which no one in 1937 would have believed she could survive.

Chiang Kai-shek's steadfastness in defeat, his cool and farsighted judgment and his unswerving loyalty to the democracies at the lowest ebb of their fortunes; the fact that he had maintained the fabric of the state and a high degree of national unity through the dark and dreary years when Japan occupied half of China; the abolition of extraterritoriality so long the objective of the National Revolution; and China's elevation, at least on paper, to Big Power rank—all combined to give the Generalissimo a stature which the worst abuses of his administration could not entirely obscure.

Anyone present when Chiang Kai-shek came to Shanghai in February 1946 could not fail to be impressed by the mood of the people. I am not referring to the huge mass meeting at the Race Course at which the Generalissimo and General Wedemeyer both spoke to the multitudes from far off over the heads of soldiers and police. It was an impressive sight with the innumerable banners of the demonstrators waving in the sunlight, and Chiang speaking, not of triumph, but of the responsibilities which the Chinese had assumed now that extraterritoriality and foreign privilege had after so long been done away with. But what really impressed me was the look on the faces of the crowd when next day the Generalissimo appeared on the balcony of the Municipal Building.

This was no organized demonstration, but an unheralded appearance after his first press conference in the city so long held by Japan. There were love and devotion in the eyes of the young men close to me in the street. There was only a handful of police and they did not try to prevent the crowd drawing close. Chiang and his wife stood fully exposed on the second-floor roofless balcony. Correspondents climbed up to take pictures close enough to touch him, and he would have been an easy target for anyone in the crowd below to which he spoke. Such a scene would have been unthinkable in Moscow where Stalin keeps the population at a more than respectful distance and would not dream of risking being shot at by his "loyal" subjects at close range.

Since then Chiang Kai-shek's prestige has undoubtedly declined. But still no intelligent Chinese liberal, however bitterly he may denounce the shortcomings of the government, wants to see it overthrown. The alternative he well knows would be anarchy or foreign domination.

As Christopher Rand, a correspondent by no means favorably inclined toward the National Government, reported in the *New York Herald Tribune* of April 12, 1947: "The fact is that non-Communist China without Generalissimo Chiang Kai-shek is a picture horrible for many thinking Chinese to contemplate. For better or worse, he is believed practically indispensable to its orderly existence. The political balance between its diverse regions, personalities and cliques is almost entirely in his hands."

The situation as some Chinese liberals see it was expressed to me by one of the editors of the *Ta Kung Pao,* China's leading independent newspaper, as follows:

China's primary problem is unity. Everyone agrees that democratic unity, political freedom and economic equality are the aim. The people want these things and both the government and the Communists say they believe in them. But neither the Kuomintang nor the Communists live up to their professions. There is a tendency toward an organized movement opposed to both the government and the Communists but it has not yet come into existence. The opponents of the government are by no means all Communists. I myself am non-Party.

The sad thing is that the international situation affords China a great opportunity, but it is doubtful whether we are capable of taking advantage of it.

Chiang has led China to victory and he brought China nearer to unity than at any time in her recent history. If I were in his position I would proclaim an end to the one-party rule of the Kuomintang as the first step toward democratic unity. I would hold a general election throughout the country for a truly representative National Assembly. I would try to give this assembly full powers like a Parliament or a Congress. On the other hand I would make no compromise with the elements who want to split up China.

I asked him how democracy could be established in a country with so high a degree of illiteracy. He replied that even a man who cannot read or write can vote. But he was vague on the system of voting in so huge a country with a population consisting mainly of peasants who would be unable to judge whom to vote for, and would be an easy prey to demagogues and easily bribed. Like so many Chinese liberals he tended to ignore the practical difficulties.

"If I were Mao," he went on, "I would become the leader of the Second Party in China. Mao ought to struggle for a democratic China instead of for personal prestige. In his place, instead of demanding that the Communists keep their arms and troops, I would insist on a democratic setup for everyone. I would abolish the autonomous Border Region and give up my private army. At the same time I would ask what the Kuomintang would do in return. Would they also give up one-party rule and their army? There is no real conflict of ideologies. Compromise is possible."

"But," I said, "don't you think that the Communists follow the Party line laid down in Moscow?"

"My personal opinion is that they do."

"What then? How can you believe in that case that Mao would ever do as you suggest?"

"That is the sad part of it. There is a deadlock in China."

The amount of criticism of the government one hears in China is itself both a healthy sign and a proof of the falseness of the charges leveled against it by foreigners who loosely use the word "fascist" as a term of opprobrium for any government which is either not democratic in the Western sense, or not "friendly" enough to Russian totalitarianism. The men one talks to inside the Chinese Government are as dissatisfied with its working and its achievements as the liberals outside. The reformist urge is there, continually pulsing below the surface. There is not, even in the higher ranks of the bureaucracy, any of the self-complacent hypocrisy concerning the condition of the people which one finds in Russia. In China, at least, when men starve they are not expected to pretend that life is glorious and joyous and happy. Men in high positions in the administration will discuss frankly with you its manifold shortcomings.

On the other hand, Chinese officials naturally are put on the defensive by those foreigners who approach them with an obvious Communist bias, or unwillingness to see or learn anything about the real causes of China's shortcomings. With them they put on a "front" or foolishly make face-saving statements which only give a weapon to their enemies.

To me the Chinese seemed refreshingly unhypocritical and honest in discussing their difficulties. No serious attempt is made to throw dust in the eyes of visitors. There is no Intourist to guide you so that you should see and hear only what the government is proud of. The secret police do not dog your steps. This is proved by the lack of fear with which anyone in China will criticize or damn the government.

American military observers who visited Kalgan, following its capture from the Communists in October 1946, reported that one of the main objections the inhabitants had to the Communist regime was the ubiquitous spy system which made them afraid to talk. In Nationalist China at least one important freedom exists: the freedom to grumble.

Nor has the Chinese Government ever tried to prevent the people from reading foreign literature. Such incidents as the shutting down of the British public library in Moscow, or the refusal of Marshal Tito to allow his subjects to read American magazines and newspapers in the reading room of the United States Embassy, are simply unthinkable in China. Foreign newspapers and books are freely admitted, and foreign journals and books published in cheap pirated editions give them a wider circulation than shortage of foreign funds would otherwise permit. In general it is quite absurd even to compare conditions in China with those existing in totalitarian countries with regard to freedom of access to news and knowledge, and freedom of thought and expression.

The following remarks, made to me by a liberal writer and former university professor who had taken service with the government on the outbreak of the war with Japan, are typical of the "self-criticism" freely voiced by members of the administration.

Our greatest weakness is the slowness and the cumbersome working of the administrative machinery. There is far too much "red tape," as the English call it. Even minor decisions cannot be made until they have been okayed by a multitude of departments. Also the various ministries are inclined to interpret their powers too liberally. As in the United States there are overlapping jurisdictions, but we are too poor to be able to "muddle through" as Americans can, and as Britain used to be able to do. We urgently need a simplification of the administrative machinery and a clear definition of the spheres of the various departments.

Our greatest lack is trained and efficient personnel. Most of our Chungking bureaucrats are incapable of adjusting themselves to their increased responsibilities. The same is even more true of our local government where the shortage of educated people is acute.

The National Government officials are failing to live up to the demands of China's new status in the world. They are inclined to go on doing things in the old traditional Chinese way, as if China were still fighting a lone battle with nothing to sustain her but her belief in her own culture. Moreover they fear to shoulder responsibilities and try to dodge issues, postpone decisions and shift their burdens onto others.

Wendell Willkie was right when he said that there was in China an equivalent of British "old school tie." Most of China's leading men were at one time fiery revolutionaries, but many of them have outlived their usefulness. They are too Chinese, so to speak, to be leaders of China now that we have become an integral part of a global community and are expected to play our part alongside the leading Western Powers.

It is unfair to classify these men as reactionaries, but it is a fact that they are out of date and have become obstacles in the way of China's development and progress. Just because in the past they played so important a role, and were so necessary to our survival as a nation, they are inclined to think that any innovation constitutes a reflection on what they have accomplished in the past. Men like H. H. Kung, for example, are not reactionaries, and perhaps only they and their methods could have kept China fighting against such great odds for so long. The trouble now is that although they favor reform they often miss the point on the most important issues; they are incapable of adapting themselves to the requirements of a new situation.

I used to sit in on most of the meetings of the Central Executive Committee of the Party which take place twice a year. You would be surprised at the frankness with which the Party leaders criticize those in executive positions, and also at the many propositions for reform which are made. The same is true of the People's Political Council instituted in 1938 to represent the provincial assemblies and professional associations. Although it is true that the members of the latter were, generally speaking, appointed by the National Government, this did not prevent them from acting independently and freely voicing their opinions. Appointed or not, they voiced the grievances of the localities they represented.

"Yes," I replied, "it sounds rather like England six or seven centuries ago when the first Parliaments were called by the King. The representatives of the people, although sitting at Westminster at the King's pleasure, did not always vote the way the monarch desired."

In this mixed-up era of ours the "liberal" label is too often tagged to those who in no respect deserve it but call themselves "progressives" because they are friendly to Communists. Conversely the designation, "a reactionary" has become a synonym for those who, in Winston Churchill's words, "react to the menace of an armed Communist."

Our own political terms are all confused and they are in any case peculiarly inappropriate to the Chinese scene. In a country composed largely of illiterate peasants, ruined by eight years of war against Japan and continuing civil war, threatened by anarchy or partition, desperately needing not a paper democratic constitution but a strong, clean and efficient government, what are the truly progressive forces?

It is rather like asking who were the liberals at the time of Magna Carta? Certainly they were not the wicked barons who forced a bad king to grant them the liberty to oppress their own underlings.

A free election in China today might well result in a repetition of what happened after the overthrow of the Manchu dynasty in 1912: unlimited war-lord rule in a divided country inviting foreign conquest.

A good example of confused Western thinking about China was presented in the first issue of *United Nations World* which put Sun Fo first on the list and included the following in its roster of liberals: Wang Shih-chieh; Shao Li-tse; Yu Ta-wei; Yen, the educator; Chang Lan, Chairman of the Democratic League, Lo Lung-chi, its spokesman and Mrs. Herman Liu, its foremost woman member; Wang Yun-wu, the publisher who is now Minister of Economics; Wong Wen-hao; Chang Chia-ngau, the industrialist, and brother of Carson Chang; Lu Tso-fu, shipping magnate; Lin Yutang; and Kuo Mo-jo.

A comparable American list would include Henry Wallace; Cordell Hull; Joe Davies (author of *Mission to Moscow*); Robert Young; Claude B. Hutchison; Claude Pepper; Marshall Field; Mrs. Roosevelt; Charles A. Beard; Henry Ford; Henry Kaiser; Walter Lippman and John Steinbeck. It might even include Al Capone since the veteran Chang Lan of the Democratic League included on the Chinese list is a former war-lord who made a fortune selling opium.

Thus the essence of the dilemma of the Chinese liberals lies not only in the impossibility of establishing a democratic government on Western lines at this stage of her development, and in the midst of civil war with the totalitarians of the Left. It lies also in the failure of the modern world to define liberalism in intelligible and noncontradictory terms. Does liberalism retain its original meaning of free enterprise, elected representative government and equality under law? Or does liberalism mean "progress" toward state capitalism, or state socialism, or whatever one chooses to call a state-controlled economy and government regulation of all the activities of the people?

Chiang Kai-shek is generally regarded as ignorant of economics and unaware of the social and economic forces which move mankind. Yet, in *China's Destiny,* he shows himself better informed of the tendencies of our era and the contradictions they pose than many liberals. He writes:

> People who favored democracy looked down at China's position, long suppressed under the unequal treaties, without considering that the economics of the world after the first world war, advanced from free competition toward monopoly and centralization. They praised themselves as being modern while applying economic theories of the first industrial revolution to fit a China facing the trends of the second revolution in Europe and America.*

Chiang Kai-shek puts his finger on the spot when, in referring to the 1927–1937 failure to develop economic rehabilitation according to schedule, he says that the cause was not only imperialist interference (Japanese aggression) and civil war ("counterrevolutionary influences") but also theoretical disagreements. "The economists at that time," he writes, "were equally divided between the theories of democracy and Communism."

Which way, indeed, should China develop? It is expected of her by her conservative American patrons that she apply nineteenth-century economic theories; while at the same time her voluble American critics of the Left demand that she institute "economic democracy" on Communist lines. To make confusion worse confounded, both schools of American "friends of China" demand that she institute a Western-type constitutional government, with sufficient power guaranteed to the Communists to bore from within to destroy it.

Chiang Kai-shek is eminently right in seeing that many liberals put the cart before the horse; that in "devoting their efforts to the articles of constitutional law and to creating a political system," with-

* A private rendering of this passage from the original.

out realizing that "a revolution of reconstruction" must come first, they opened the door "for the secret schemes of the war lords, giving the imperialists the opportunity to extend their exploitation." This is as true today, when "the imperialists" signifies mainly Russia, as it was following the overthrow of the Manchus in 1911 when "the imperialists" meant Britain, France, Japan, Russia and even America who all backed different war lords in order to try to establish paramount influence over the weak "Republican," "constitutional" Peking Government.

I think any unprejudiced historian has to accept the correctness of Chiang Kai-shek's dictum:

> We all know that political tutelage is the path to be followed in attainment of a democratic government by the people, that without this the foundations of a government of the people cannot be erected, and that otherwise the constitution to be framed in the future can only become a valueless piece of white paper with black words.*

The basic dilemma is how to ensure that those in charge of the tutoring are qualified and honest enough to do it. Undoubtedly the Kuomintang has lost most of its original savor as a reforming, revitalizing agency. Yet, perhaps it could be restored if America would use her friendly efforts to encourage, assist and aid the best elements inside the Kuomintang, instead of squeezing out the remaining salt in the body politic of China by pressuring the government to admit to a share of power democracy's worst enemies: the Communists.

---

* A private rendering of this passage from the original.

CHAPTER XIII

Poverty and the Land

MOST popular writers on China ascribe the terrible poverty of the Chinese peasant to exploitation by "feudal" landowners supported by a "reactionary" government; and they lead their readers to suppose that China has only to redistribute the land for her people to enjoy prosperity. This view is entirely misleading.

Backward as China is, the miserable condition of her farming population is not due to the same causes as those which made life brutish and short for the peasants of medieval Europe.

The feudal organization of society came to an end in China thousands of years ago. There is no hereditary caste of landowners; the peasants are not serfs tied to the soil; land is freely bought and sold. The law of primogeniture, which preserved large estates in Europe by entailing them on the eldest son, was abolished in China in the second century B.C. The hereditary fiefs of the nobility were subsequently divided up among all sons and thus disappeared. Dr. Hu Shih, the world-renowned scholar who was for a time Ambassador to the United States, has written:

> This tradition of the equal division of hereditary property among all the sons of a family was the practice among all classes of the population and tended to equalize wealth and landownership. Because of this practice no great estate could remain in existence for as long as three generations.
>
> This economic equalization has tended to create a social structure in which there are practically no class divisions, nor even enduring divisions between the rich and the poor.

In Lancashire, England, they used to say, "Clogs to clogs in three generations," meaning that the grandsons of workers who became capitalists frequently reverted to the ranks of the proletariat. In China estates and farms are continually being subdivided so that today's rich may be tomorrow's poor. Few landowners in any case own large estates.

Of course, some families enlarge their land holdings and make money as merchants, petty industrialists, usurers or government officials, remaining "rich" from generation to generation. It is not to be denied that the "rich" exploit the poor; but feudal, so beloved by the Communists, is not the correct word to apply to landlord-tenant relationships.

Communists in particular ought to know better since Marx made a distinction between feudalism and the "Asiatic system" of payment of rents in kind. This system is neither feudal nor capitalist. In some places it has already given place to a capitalist landlord-tenant relationship through the payment of cash instead of crop or share rents.

The problem in China is one of protecting the tenant from rack rents, high interest rates, the inequitable allocation of the tax burden caused by the landlords' political influence and of helping him to acquire ownership of the land he cultivates. But the Chinese peasants are not serfs as the Russians were before 1864.

The basic trouble in China, from which flow all the curses that afflict the farmers, is simply too many people and not enough land.

Until fewer people try to make a living off the land, no action by the government can be effective in curing agrarian poverty, or counteracting the play of economic forces which places the tenant at the mercy of the landlord and the small peasant proprietor at the mercy of the usurers and merchants. Nor are most landlords likely to cease squeezing their tenants so long as they themselves are only a little better off than those they exploit.

Exact statistics are not available. The government has never had the necessary respite from war to get as far as making a census or a land survey. In this respect China is still behind England under William the Conqueror who, in 1086 in his famous Domesday Book, surveyed every estate and farm and catalogued the livestock and implements they possessed. Surveys have, however, been made in various parts of China which supply an approximate idea of the number of people in relation to the cultivatable land.

According to the most recent estimates, China's population now totals 457,000,000, 331,000,000 of whom live off the land. The amount of farm land amounts to only about half an acre per head and to less than one acre per farm inhabitant. These figures compare with approximately eight acres per person in the United States and thirty acres for each American engaged in agriculture.

According to Dr. John Lossing Buck,* the number of farm persons per square mile of cultivated territory in China proper averages 1,500. Dr. Chiu** apparently including all the outlying territories under nominal Chinese jurisdiction, such as Manchuria, states that the density of population according to the estimated area of land is 104.4 per square mile, as compared with 41.3 in the United States, 453 in Japan, 365 in Germany, 197 in France, and only 19.8 in Russia.

The discrepancy between the figures per square mile of cultivated land and total area is explained by the fact that half of China has a mean annual rainfall of less than twenty inches, and by the mountainous nature of other areas. According to Dr. Wong Wen-hao, China's foremost geologist, less than 20 percent of China's land is suitable for agriculture. Her Northeastern provinces (Manchuria) are her only large thinly populated area. Prior to Japan's conquest it is estimated that a million Chinese emigrated there annually. Since V-J Day Russia and the Chinese Communists have prevented the resumption of such internal emigration.

Britain, with an acreage of 0.67 cultivated land per head of the total population, has to import half her food. Even the fertile land of France with only one person to each 1.29 acres has failed to feed herself since the end of the war. In Russia, with an estimated 2.01 acres of cultivated land per capita, and huge empty areas which could be made arable, collectivization and mechanization had not by 1939 substantially increased the total grain production above the level of Czarist times.† Millions of Russians, like the Chinese, are on the borderland of starvation. All in all, however, the primitive but skilled "gardeners" of China make a better showing with regard to the use made of the available land than semi-industrialized Russia.

---

* Buck, *Land Utilization in China* (Chicago, 1937), p. 364.

** Dr. A. Kaiming Chiu, *China*, University of California Press, 1946.

† Freda Utley, *The Dream We Lost*, page 156. The Soviet Government's figures of grain production give the "biological yield" which is the quantity of grain estimated in the standing crops with a deduction of 10 percent for harvest loss. On this basis, the total grain harvest in 1913 was 94.1 million tons as against 82.7 in 1936, 120.3 in 1937, 95.0 in 1938 and a similar figure in 1939.

Dr. Y. C. Koo, one of China's leading economists, said to me in Chungking:

> Increased production, industrialization and birth control afford the only solution for China's agrarian problem. Even the conservatives in the government admit the necessity for land reform. But liberals and conservatives alike know that this alone cannot solve our problem. At present there is not enough food and there are too many people. Western science and techniques and organization, soil conservancy, irrigation, reforestation and improved seeds and chemical fertilizers can very greatly increase the yield of the land. Combined with the industrialization which will decrease the pressure on the land, and village industries to give the peasants employment in their free time, this is the best solution. There is in fact no other solution for China's poverty. The redistribution of the land which the Communists want would not help much nor provide a lasting remedy. Most of China's landowners are small holders. We have few great estates. The pressure on the land and the acute poverty of the peasants would be only temporarily relieved by expropriating the landowners or killing them off.

How true this statement was is borne out by the findings of the American-Chinese Agricultural Mission. After a five months' investigation on the spot, it reported in November 1946 that overpopulation in relation to the available tillable land is China's fundamental problem. Claude B. Hutchison, Dean of the College of Agriculture of California University, who headed the American section of the mission, states that overpopulation is more important than the ills emphasized by political writers—landlordism, high rents and interest rates, heavy taxes and the "feudal" backwardness of Chinese agriculture. The Mission, while making constructive suggestions for coping with the political and social problem, declared that the benefits of agrarian reform, and even of industrialization, could not afford a solution for Chinese poverty unless population pressure decreases.

It is obvious that, with only half an acre of cultivated land per head of her population and the country split three ways by strategic stalemate, China could not under any system have avoided starvation for large numbers of her people. The large army and the refugee-swollen population of the large cities—both in Nationalist territory—could be provided for only by forcing the peasants to give up food they needed for themselves. The correspondents who blamed the Chinese Government for all the misery they saw around them should have studied the facts instead of letting their emotions run away with them.

Not only is most of the good land in China already settled, but there is far too much cultivation of marginal areas. The deforestation of mountainsides to carve out farms has resulted in soil erosion and in the silting up of many streams and canals, thus destroying or impairing large areas of good land.

The greatest pressure of population is on the most fertile rice-bearing lands of the South. The number of farm persons per square mile in Central, East and South China is estimated to be 1,700 as against 900 in the Northwest. But the average production per capita of the farm population in the former territories is 1,500 kilograms as against 800 in the Northwest where wheat is the main crop.

Outside of Manchuria and the Northwest, according to Dr. J. Lossing Buck, an additional ten percent of farm land could be made available for profitable cultivation by such measures as the removal of graves, elimination of land in boundaries after consolidation of fragmented holdings, and putting under the plow arable lands not now cultivated. The last measure requires a capital expenditure outside the range of individual farmers or landlords, but it can be noted that grave clearance has proceeded on a fairly large scale and amounts to a spontaneous reform which takes place without government compulsion.

It is generally agreed that the following measures are needed:

Improved water control to prevent floods and droughts.

Reforestation to prevent soil erosion and the clogging of streams and irrigation canals with silt washed down the mountainsides.

Repair and extension of the irrigation systems of the plains.

Improved seed and the use of chemical fertilizers.

Remedies for insect pests and plant diseases and, in general, the application of modern scientific knowledge to the improvement of soils, crops, livestock and farm implements. These could increase the quantity and quality of China's agricultural production and prevent the famines which frequently occur.

Co-operative marketing, credits and improved transportation are other measures essential if China is to feed her people and give the peasants a reasonably high standard of life.

But the basic problem remains: rural overpopulation which cannot be remedied by redistribution of the land. Nor would the collectivization and mechanization of farms on the Soviet model be an advantage. On the contrary, it would vastly intensify the problem by throwing millions out of work and diminishing China's total food production. For although her per capita production is very low the amount of food produced per acre is correspondingly high. In his *Land Utilization in China,* published in 1937, Dr. Buck showed that the average yield of wheat per acre was actually higher in China than in the United States—sixteen bushels as against fourteen. But the Chinese crop is harvested with sickles and, of course, requires many times more people to produce it. The total rice crop is twice as large as the wheat crop. Farms average only four acres in size and the density of population, according to Dr. J. Lossing Buck, is as high as 1,700 farm persons per square mile of cultivated territory in Central-East-South China. Production per farm worker is estimated at only one-fourteenth of that of an American farmer.

A general discussion of "feudal landowners" and the interpretation of basic geographic and demographic factors as "oppression" clearly does not fairly portray the Chinese agrarian problem.

Of course, the Communists have a simple remedy for overpopulation and the agrarian problem. It consists simply of liquidating the landowners—cutting off their heads or driving them out. Lin Tsu-han (Lin Pai-chu), the Communist Commissar of Finance, told Edgar Snow years ago that forty to fifty percent of the revenue of Soviet China was raised by land confiscation. This policy was abandoned in 1935 but, as we have seen, appears to have been resumed recently under the guise of "settle account" trials of landowners. However, Chou En-lai once admitted to Carl Crow that the confiscation of estates had worked hardships on a great many innocent people and created "wrong ideas" about the ownership of property.

Clearly the solution of the agrarian problem by violence was not popular among a majority of the peasants. It is extremely doubtful if a free vote in China would lead to the passage of a law for the confiscation of all land without compensation. Many of the poor are related to the rich, others are loyal to those they work for and every peasant hopes to become a property owner. Only a Stalinist dictatorship, hardened to the starvation or killing of millions and indifferent to the wishes of the people, would attack China's agrarian problem by wholesale expropriation of the landowners and kulaks—the Russian term for a prosperous peasant owner.

Even so, it would not be a lasting solution. The lack of enough land for all the cultivators would soon lead to a situation similar to the one which exists today.

The National Government is itself largely to blame for the readiness with which foreigners accept the oversimplified Communist version of the causes of Chinese rural poverty. Its information and propaganda agencies do not encourage journalists or authors to obtain such statistical and factual information as is available. The officials who come in contact with visiting foreigners are for the most part American-educated Chinese long since cut off from their ancestral roots in the villages and often themselves ignorant of the facts revealed by the economic and social surveys which have been made.

It was not until I returned to the United States that, thanks to Dr. J. Lossing Buck, I discovered that the University of Nanking's College of Agriculture, while in exile at Chengtu, had continued to make surveys and to publish its monthly journal *Economic Facts*. Dr. Buck has summarized much of the available information from this and other sources in a paper prepared for the 1947 Conference of the Institute of Pacific Relations. The picture he presents of agrarian conditions in China bears little resemblance to the popular American conception of China as a country in which rural poverty is the result of "feudal" oppression.

Dr. Buck does not deny the oppressive nature of the landlord system in many places, or the fact that rents are too high. But he shows the great variety of tenures, some good and some bad, and he points out that more farmers in China own the land they cultivate than in the United States—about 50 percent in China as against 42 percent in the United States.

Many tenants are also owners of a small plot of land of their own, and some tenants are more prosperous than owners. Taking China as a whole, he estimates that only a quarter of the farm population owns no land at all. In the most fertile rice-growing districts of the South, however, the proportion of tenants rises as high as 75 percent, as against only 25 percent in the wheat regions of the North.

According to a survey conducted by the National Agricultural Research Bureau, in a majority of the Southern provinces 40 percent of the farmers are tenants and 20 to 30 percent owners.

Since no land survey covering the whole country has been made in modern times the above figures are all only estimates and must be accepted with reservations. Moreover, the really important point is the amount of land held by those who cultivate it as compared with that owned by landlords.

According to an estimate made by the Sun Yat-sen Institute of Nanking before the war, 10 percent of the farming population owns a little over half the cultivated land in China.

According to an investigation conducted in 1926–1927 by the part-Communist Wuhan Government 43 percent of the cultivated land was owned by only 5 percent of the population. Another 20 percent of the land was owned by poor and middle-class farmers with less than 100 *mou*,* so that three-quarters of the farming population owned only a third of the land. These figures, however, relate to the central Yangtze Valley area where it is known that there are more large landowners than elsewhere.

These estimates are in any case all prewar and it is known that the inflation has enabled the peasants in many districts to become owners of the farms they formerly cultivated as tenants.

When visiting a textile factory in Shanghai in January 1946 I was told that the difficulty in obtaining skilled labor was largely due to the fact that workers who had returned to their villages during the Japanese occupation would not now go back to the factories because of the better economic position of their families. Many former tenants had become owners, thanks to the inflation.

In Free China during the war years, according to Dr. Buck, the situation of the farming population was generally better than before the war because the normal large surplus of man power on the farms minimized the effects of war on the supply of farm labor for crop production. In other words, the forced recruitment of soldiers from the villages improved the economic situation for those who escaped the draft by diminishing the supply and increasing the demand for agricultural labor and farm products.

In general, Dr. Buck concludes, costs of production in agriculture,

---

* One *mou* is 0.152 acre.

taxes, labor and interest rates and cash rents lagged behind the prices received by farmers for the products they sold. True that up to 1943 the prices received by farmers for their produce increased less than the prices they paid for clothing and other manufactured goods, so that they bought less clothing and spent less on recreation. But since the farmer's cost of production expenditures occurred prior to his sales the continual rise in prices put him in an advantageous position. His expenses were incurred at a lower price level than his receipts.

On the other hand, the institution of taxes in kind instead of cash naturally worked to the farmer's disadvantage.

As regards rents, Dr. Buck, basing his estimates on surveys made in Szechwan by the Nanking College of Agriculture and Forestry, finds the average to have been as high as 12.5 percent of the land value, as against a total of all taxes of 3.44 yuan for each 100 yuan of land value. Landlords, after deducting taxes paid from rent received, obtained 11 percent annual interest on the value of their land.

Rents are certainly too high. Conversely, interest rates are usually much higher, averaging 30 percent in the case of loans provided by landlords and between 21 and 28 percent when provided by relatives and merchants. The Farmer's Bank charges only 12 percent, but the credits it supplies are only a small fraction of the credits required by farmers. The natural working of economic laws in a country of terrific pressure on the land, dearth of capital, and undeveloped industries, makes it practically impossible to lower rents by law. Rather than die of starvation without employment the landless Chinese will accept the most onerous terms of tenancy, and even if he knows that the law is on his side, who will enforce the law?

There are many different kinds of land tenure: rents in kind amounting to a percentage of the crop, rents in kind of a fixed quantity per *mou* of land, and cash rents. Rents in kind are often higher than 50 percent of the produce. As might be expected, rack renting is prevalent in the most fertile districts where the pressure on the land is greatest.

The National Government, as long ago as 1936, passed a land law forbidding the payment of more than a third of the produce as rent. In 1946 a new law limited landlords to an 8 percent return on their investment. But little, if any, notice is taken of these laws. The tenant's lack of education is another factor enabling the landlord, merchant and usurer to cheat him. The lack of marketing facilities and poor communications further penalizes him and forces him to sell to the same person to whom he owes rent or interest.

Yet we cannot conclude that the renting of land is inherently wrong. At least, if we do we must also conclude that all private ownership of property, however acquired, should be abolished and we ought all to establish a Socialist order of society. It is certainly not logical to maintain that China should annul all property rights while America continues to believe in the capitalist order of society. What is wrong in China is the failure of the state to protect the rights of the tenant and restrain the landlord from taking advantage of his position to deprive the cultivators of the rewards of their labors. The landlord-tenant relationship should be an equal and just partnership with the landlord supplying capital and technical advice. In China there are instances of this, but too often the tenant's lack of education as well as his poverty renders the relationship more nearly that of master and servant. However, good landlords both assist the tenants and act as a buffer between them and the state by saving them from overtaxation.

The absence of a land survey works grave injustices and also diminishes the government's revenues. The Land Administration so far has surveyed only 600 hsien. Samples of these surveys indicate that perhaps a third of the cultivated area of China is not recorded. The owners of perhaps a quarter of the cultivated area pay no taxes, thus increasing the burdens of the others.

There is no doubt that land taxes are too high, averaging $1.79 (U. S. money) per acre in prewar days as compared with only $.91 to $1.15 in the eastern and northern United States, and imposing in many parts of China an intolerable burden. Nor is there any doubt that the big landowners are usually able to avoid paying as much as the poor because they are often themselves the tax collectors. Nor does the farmer receive from the government any benefits commensurate with the taxes he pays. In other words, the Chinese State rests on the back of the poverty-stricken and often starving farmers who reap little or no benefits from its expenditures. Since those expenditures are almost all for war, the farmer does not even indirectly profit as he would if industries were to be developed and communications improved.

It is, nevertheless, unfair to conclude that the government's paper schemes for land reform are just window dressing. Kuomintang China has model districts where rents have been reduced, and beginnings made in local self-government. Yenan is not the only region where land reforms have been instituted, but few journalists have been interested in viewing the National Government's show places.

As Dr. Buck remarks: "The Communist Government in the North has received a much better press than the National Government although its actual accomplishment in the field of technical agriculture is slight in comparison."

Nor is it true that the National Government represents in the main the "reactionary landowning class." The old civil service examinations which gave a monopoly of office to the "scholar gentry" were abolished in 1912 following the establishment of the Republic. Today government officials are recruited from all classes and are largely of bourgeois origin.

The landowners today are not an organized class. The trouble is that the ignorance of the peasantry and the weakness of the Central Government give the village gentry too much power in local affairs. As one district magistrate said in a meeting of the People's Political Council: "We need three things in order to reform local government: education, more education, and again more education. Only education can free us of servitude to the village gentry and from backwardness and corruption."

It must be written to the credit of the National Government that it has made a real effort to set up schools in the villages. Appropriations for education are the third largest in the Budget, although military expenditures, of course, are very much greater.

The Minister of Education, Chu Chia-hua, told me in Chungking that there are already two schools in existence for each *pao* (a *pao* meaning 500 families). The National Government provides free tuition and food in its universities—an example of the tendency to try to run before you can walk, since China is far too poor to afford this. The result is that the students don't get enough to live on, and consequently demonstrate against the government.

Also, one is always being told in China that the bright village lads who succeed in getting an education go off to the towns to get jobs. Hence the lack of educated people in the rural districts which forces the local magistrates to fall back upon the "gentry." Hence also the dearth of teachers.

The influence of the landowning class seems to be strongest precisely where the authority of the National Government is weakest, particularly in the provinces which have never been more than nominally under the Central Government's control, and where ex-war lords oppress the people.

As in so many other spheres the sins of the Central Government are those of omission rather than commission; they arise from lack of power, not from the exercise of tyrannical power.

The high rate of taxation levied on the landowning class is in itself a proof that it is not favored by the government. The city merchant and industrialist bear no such heavy burdens.

Sun Yat-sen said that "to the tiller belongs the soil" should be the aim of the Kuomintang. But he did not advocate expropriation of the millions of landowners who own the soil of China. He thought that equalization of landownership would come through an application of Henry George's theory of unearned increment. The landowner was to assess the value of his land, and the state should have the right to purchase it at the price set by the owner. The landowner would be prevented from placing too high a value on his land by having to pay a correspondingly high tax. Any increase in the value of the land should go to the community.

It is impossible to say whether or not this scheme if carried out could have brought to an end the present exploitation of the Chinese peasantry through high rents and usury. For up to now, war being the main preoccupation of the government, and obtaining the supplies to feed its armies its main concern, land reform has had to wait.

Yet if one looks, one can find men in the National Government who appreciate the fact that land reform is China's primary need. Unlike the demagogues, they realize the immense difficulties.

In a small bare room in a tumbledown house on a side street in Chungking I found the Land Administration office. I talked to a man there who was an enthusiast, but a tired one. The room was very cold, and he was elderly, thin and emaciated. Both Mr. Cheng Chen-yu and his surroundings seemed symbolic of the lack of attention being given by more prominent members of the government to the economic and social reforms which alone can save China.

Mr. Cheng told me that the government had a complete policy for the relief of the peasant but it had been impossible to carry it out in wartime. Nevertheless, in Free China something had been done even during the war. The policy of the Kuomintang, he insisted, has in view the protection of independent farmers and the creation of more of them. He said:

The registration of tenancy in all provinces is being carried out, and tenancies will be annulled when found to be illegal.

We want to create independent farmers. Those who cultivate should own the land.

We have experimented in almost every province. According to our land regulations rents should not exceed 375 per 1,000 of the produce of the land. A law to this effect was passed in 1936. Wherever our authority extends we try to enforce this law. In 1936 we tried to enforce it in Kwantung, Shansi, Kwangsi, Shensi and Kiangsu. The trouble is that the law cannot be generally enforced because in many hsien there is no effective administrative authority.

In the provinces where the Central Government authority has been long established, the law can be enforced. In others it is not possible to do so. For instance in Szechwan taxes are passed on to the tenant and we cannot stop it.

Our aim is to develop strong local government authorities with the ability to enforce the law. Since 1929 the Central Government has been trying to create a new hsien system which would create powerful local administrations. These administrations are usually elected. In some provinces, notably in Kiangsu and Kansu and Kwangsi, the work has been carried out more energetically than in others.

Basically our problem is the question of our ability to enforce the laws and regulations of the Central Government. But there are also members of the Central Government who oppose our reforms. There is always much opposition to the new laws we try to introduce. They are opposed at meetings of the Executive Yuan and the Supreme Defense Council. The opposition's argument is always that enforcement of the rules would create local disturbances and we cannot afford this in wartime. Also, China is so big and local conditions vary so greatly that it is impossible to lay down regulations from the center which will be applicable everywhere.

The majority of government officials is in favor of reform. The Generalissimo himself is. Unfortunately often someone gets between him and those who want to tell him the true situation.

A conversation I had in Chungking with Dr. Y. C. Koo, who shortly afterward became China's representative on the International Monetary Fund, illustrated most clearly the financial difficulties which are the stumbling block in the way of agrarian reform. I had met this youthful-looking, quiet-spoken, American-educated Chinese economist two years before at the Bretton Woods Monetary Conference and been impressed by his exceptional combination of theoretical and practical knowledge.

Dr. Koo was at this time still head of the Farmers Bank which uses its funds to give six-month production credits to farmers in the period before harvesting, and also grants five to ten-year loans for land improvement, irrigation and other capital expenditures.

"The Farmers Bank," he said, "can do no more than scratch the surface of China's agrarian problem. Its resources are infinitesimal compared with the needs of the Chinese farmers. During the war the whole of the government's revenue could not finance the war, hence the inflation. Every state institution in China clamored for funds and all of them had useful proposals. But there was simply no way of financing the most desirable projects."

The Farmers Bank's depositors are mainly government institutions which are required to put some of their funds in it. The Bank is not able to issue bonds because the public would not buy them. So it has to struggle to get deposits in competition with the commercial banks.

In March 1946 the Farmers Bank had a total of 6,400,000,000 yuan in loans outstanding, of which sixty-four percent were for irrigation. But the inflation was already rapidly diminishing the value of its funds.

Dr. Koo was of the opinion that the peasants had suffered relatively less from the inflation than other sections of the population. This was indicated by the statistical tables he showed me comparing the price rises of the goods they bought and the produce they sold. Loans, at least those repayable in cash like the Farmers Bank loans, had of course been lightened by the inflation. But local usurers' loans were almost always in kind and the interest rates were terrific; often one hundred percent. The peasants had suffered most through the loss of men to the army. Also, their taxes in kind had been greatly increased.

Dr. T. F. Tsiang, at that time head of CNRRA, said to me in Chungking:

The war taught us the importance of solving that great problem of the common man in China—partial unemployment. In the long winter months the peasant has little to do and his land is insufficient to maintain him. Contrary to reports abroad, the war improved the condition of the peasantry because labor was in such great demand. The wives and daughters of the peasants made money in local industries, in public work and as servants. As regards the public works, such as road building, even if little or nothing was paid to the laborers, they were at least fed. Unemployment almost disappeared during the war and the peasants acquired an extra source of income.

It is the intellectuals, the officials and professional people who have suffered most. The inflation hit them hardest, whereas many farmers benefited from it.

If once we can start demobilizing the army our economy can recover. The actual size of the army today is about three and a half million men. A standing army of a million is all that should be necessary in the future. This great man power when released should be used partially on public works. Although these are relief projects decent wages must be paid; the worker for his part must actually work. The state should set an example in providing model conditions of pay, shelter and medical care. We can obtain equipment from UNRRA. One-third of our UNRRA allocations is to go for relief, two-thirds for rehabilitation. We have asked for trucks, large power plants, flour mills, cement. It would be a mistake to utilize UNRRA supplies mainly for relief, for then we could never lift China out of her poverty.

Our great difficulty is lack of shipping. For instance, Formosa has coal, sugar and rice, but needs to import textiles. I have asked UNRRA to send us ships. We also need ships to move the bean crop from Manchuria. We have proposed that the Chinese Government should give half the bean crop for relief in Europe in return for help in transporting it.

The most difficult job facing us is in the war-ravaged areas. In Kwangsi, for instance, many cities are almost entirely destroyed. In Hunan, Changsha is eighty percent destroyed. In Hupeh in the Laohoko area the see-saw warfare wiped out whole towns and villages. Shelter is a tremendous problem in these places. I have proposed that we cope with this problem by such measures as giving credits for the purchase of material for those who can make bricks and tile and also to lumbermen; put up public shelters for the very poor and allocate loans for property rebuilding for those who still have any property.

We also have a tremendous personnel problem and our first need is for medical doctors. We have typhus in Nanking, malaria in Kiangsu and Formosa and cholera still in Kwangsi. Secondly we need river conservancy personnel.

As regards foreign capital investment in China and the general line of our economic development there is considerable difference of opinion. There is an argument as between the relative merits of state and private enterprise. However, we are all agreed that we don't want any Morgans in China. All the railroads should be state-owned. Steel production will have to be mainly a government enterprise because of the capital required. Private enterprise is not to be excluded. Oil will be completely government-owned, also hydroelectric power. The general idea is that the basic or controlling sectors of the economy will be government-owned or controlled.

Now the rural population is threatened by depression. What is to be done? We should, I think, take a lesson from the New Deal. In China a New Deal would be economical instead of wasteful. In the United States work had to be invented and many of the projects of the WPA were useless; but in China there is a tremendous need for public works—roads, railways, canals, dike repairs.

During the war the peasants took down their old spinning wheels and looms which had not been used for years. Small-scale industry was revitalized. For instance, seventy alcohol factories for fuel were established in Szechwan alone and forty of them are still operating.

There would be absolutely no difficulty in finding desirable and necessary public works on which the peasants could use their free time. I myself advocate the building of more roads and railways, the improvement of rivers and embankments. These would be costly but not inflationary public works because the yield from them in increased national income would be very great. The biggest job we have on hand now is the repairing of the dikes on the Yellow River and building up the embankment. Three million United States dollars have been given for this through UNRRA and we ourselves have contributed fifty million Chinese dollars.

The maintenance of large armies has in fact constituted a Chinese substitute for WPA. It is obvious how greatly the country would benefit if the millions who are now soldiers were employed on the public works so urgently needed in China.

At the time I interviewed him, Dr. Tsiang was still optimistic. "If only fools on both sides, here and in America, don't spoil everything," he said, "we shall be able to surmount our difficulties."

Two months later when I saw him again in Shanghai, Dr. T. F. Tsiang was already a much worried and less-happy man. Late in 1946 he resigned his job and rumor had it that he had been unable to get along with T. V. Soong. This, combined with La Guardia's rash decision to embargo supplies to China, made his position untenable. It was clear from his talk with me that his ideas were basically right, whatever his performance may have been. His aim was reconstruction, industrial development and aid to small-scale enterprise. This in itself must have put him at loggerheads with the bankers, big merchants and financiers of Shanghai whose fortunes are independent of general prosperity and who think in terms of trade rather than production.

Dr. Tsiang is an outstanding example of a liberal and an economist forced out of an important post by the opposition of Chinese financiers, his inability to stop corruption among his subordinates, and the Communist wrecking of all plans for reconstruction.

Many other liberals who think they could put China to rights if given office would no doubt experience the same disillusionment and would fail similarly. They lack the necessary backing of a strong and prosperous middle class. They are at the mercy of those who have political power derived either from foreign support, or a provincial army or from connections in high places in the government.

Amelioration of the desperate poverty of the Chinese peasants depends upon industrial development to provide alternative employment; the application of modern scientific techniques to the land to increase its yield and above all to ensure a larger production per man; the finding of ways to tap and organize investment credit for rural use; and a government strong enough to enforce its laws for the protection of the farmer.

Similarly as regards the coolies and factory workers, as long as the peasants are on the border line of starvation, and periodic famines send a flood of destitute men and women to the cities, wages must remain low.

Rural reconstruction and reform, together with a rise in the present miserable standard of living of the working class, are impossible without peace.

CHAPTER XIV

Can China Remain Chinese?

YEARS ago Bertrand Russell told me he thought Moscow and Peking the two most beautiful cities in the world. I lived in the former for nearly six years but I saw Peking for the first time in February 1946. I had little time to explore it, either then or two weeks later on my way back from Yenan. My time was occupied mainly with interviews, but I managed to visit the Forbidden City and see the Temple of Heaven. I received at least a faint impression of the glories of Imperial China.

Peking is as different from Shanghai as Moscow is from New York or from Washington. Its main streets are as wide and straight as the boulevards of Paris, whereas Shanghai streets are narrower than London's and more crowded. Surrounded by its ancient walls and built on a great plain not far from the desert, the ancient capital of China bears even less resemblance to ramshackle Chungking, sprawling over the cliffs above two rivers amid the lush vegetation of the Southwest. Nor does Peking show any of the scars of war so evident in Chungking. The Japanese even freshened up the paint of the blue, gold and green dragon design on the ceiling of some of the buildings in the Forbidden City.

Since V-J Day there has been a strong movement in China to re-establish the seat of government at Peking, which is so much better suited than any other Chinese city to be the capital of the nation. There are sound economic reasons for transferring the center of power to the North in proximity to China's iron and coal, since only by developing the resources of the Northern and Northeastern provinces can China solve her economic problem and become strong. But the proximity of Russia is thought to make Peking too dangerous a site for the capital. One recalls how the short distance between Leningrad and Soviet Russia's frontier caused Lenin to transfer the capital of the U. S. S. R. to Moscow.

Peking reminded me faintly of Moscow. There is the same contrast between the vivid colors of ancient palaces, temples and churches, and the dirty and decrepit wooden houses in the poorer parts of the city. Peking is, however, not disfigured by the ugly jerry-built tenement houses put up in Moscow since the revolution, the only sign of comparative modernity being the fine nineteenth-century European houses in the Legation quarter. The beautiful private homes and gardens hidden behind high walls along narrow alleys are Chinese in style, and well cared for by the "gentry" who live in them. In Moscow, except for Stalin and the other leaders who live behind the Kremlin's high red walls, the ruling class lives in new buildings with modern comforts, while most of the fine old houses have become slums. The old is gradually being torn down or obscured by the new and year by year less of the old beauty remains. In Peking the old stands out in greater splendor against the sordidness of the present.

Both cities are built around walled palaces, but the successors of the Czars live in the Kremlin, while the Forbidden City of Peking is a museum and a park. A few of its buildings are now used as residences or offices for the military, but it is open to the public. The grim towers of the Kremlin and the bulging cupolas of Moscow's churches are in a different world from Peking's graceful palaces and temples. Old Moscow's architecture is a product of the marriage between Byzantium and Tartary; Peking is pre-eminently Chinese in spite of its lama temples and Mongol relics. But there is the same Oriental love of color and in winter the same beauty of sparkling snow under blue skies.

In Peking where Kublai Khan once held his gorgeous court, one feels the influence and closeness of the lands beyond the Great Wall which march with Russia's frontiers, and out of which came the conquerors of both countries in the thirteenth century. One remembers that both Moscow and Peking were once a part of the huge Mongol Empire conquered by Ghengis Khan and his successors. Both cities have, or had, their Tartar walls. In Moscow the area inside the wall is called "Kitaiski gorod," meaning Chinese city. In Peking the Tartar city surrounded by a massive gray stone wall with gates is the main part of the town. While I lived in Moscow the whitewashed Tartar wall was pulled down to clear the way for traffic.

Yet it is in Russia rather than in China that Tartar influence left a permanent imprint. Chinese civilization was too old and widespread and its attractions too great for the barbarians from beyond the Wall, the mountains and the desert to extinguish it. Instead they were absorbed into the great stream of Chinese culture. Neither the Mongols nor the Manchus changed the character of Chinese civilization.

The Slavs were still too barbarous to resist the Mongol influence when the Golden Horde settled itself in South Russia. Moscow itself became an important city under Russian princes who owed their existence to the services they performed as tax collectors and vassals of the Tartar conquerors.

Two hundred years after they had come as conquerors the Tartars were defeated and became an oppressed minority in Russia, but their influence survived. Russia's civilization, although largely Byzantine Greek in origin, is strongly colored in modes of thought and behavior by the Tartar strain.

Perhaps it was the people of Peking who reminded me of Moscow. Their dark, nondescript, worn, padded clothing makes the same drab impression, and the drovers with their fur or leather caps would pass unnoticed in the streets of Moscow, driving the same sort of primitive carts. There are even droshkies, as in Russia, with similar miserable thin horses.

On the other hand, the coolies, rickshamen and shopkeepers of Peking are anything but Russian in manners and behavior. Unlike the unfriendly, bitter, ragged rickshamen of Shanghai who abuse you most when you pay them well, those of Peking are clean, decently dressed and courteous. They bow and thank you for payment and they talk as they pull. Some must earn their living largely out of the commission they receive from the shops they take you to. Incidentally, when I was there, there were more beautiful things still to be bought in Peking than in Shanghai and at more reasonable cost. You could still find lovely old embroideries, exquisite jewelry and ornaments.

I happened to get hold of a man who had been Count Ciano's rickshaman in days gone by. He spoke a little English and was happiest if he could take me sight-seeing. He was very proud of his city and knew about as much as an official guide. One notes the contrast between Peking, a Chinese city where the foreigner lives as a guest, and Shanghai, a foreign metropolis reflecting in exaggerated form all the bustle and hustling competitive spirit of the West.

The day I left Chungking I met a United States Army sergeant who spoke Chinese. He said to me: "There are a number of Chinese words which I learned in college, but never heard spoken until I went to Peking. The word for civilization, for instance. In Peking it is frequently used, but I never heard it in Chungking."

I wished I had met him sooner, for he knew China well and was entirely free from either political or racial prejudices—exceptional qualifications. Why this intelligent young man was only a sergeant I never discovered. His was the arduous and difficult task of searching through the Chinese countryside to discover the fate of lost American fliers in the war. His superior was a Hawaiian-Chinese United States Army captain, and their relations were as friendly as their skin and hair were different. The captain, a debonair, elegant and cheerful youth, taught me a few Chinese words and phrases on the flight to Shanghai, but he knew less about Chinese history and culture than the sergeant, and he was far more anxious to go home.

In our ride to the Chungking airport the sergeant told me of his adventures. "I have heard much about the starvation among the peasants of Szechwan but I really haven't seen signs of it. In all the villages I have been in, the people seemed very healthy. They have to give up a lot of grain to the government, but they have plenty of vegetables, which are untaxed. I think, perhaps this is the source of their physical strength. Just look." He pointed to the fertile green hillsides on both sides of the road. "They grow a fresh crop every few weeks, and maybe their abundant supply of vegetables compensates for the lack of meat and insufficient rice."

The contrast between China North and South is sharply brought home to one by air travel, which almost abolishes time but not geography. I had left Chungking in springlike weather with the trees green and the lush vegetation giving promise of plenty, but in Shanghai it was still very cold, and to the north the earth was brown and hard and sprinkled with snow.

There can be no better way to approach Peking than by air. Suddenly after hours of flying over the dull brown flatlands of North China, where the little villages are lost in the vast expanse, the great Imperial City appears beneath you, huge and square, surrounded by massive walls. Here and there, as we came near, a tall building caught the rays of the setting sun, and before reaching the airfield to the west of the city I had a glimpse of the Summer Palace and the lake around which its gardens are set out. For the first time I was seeing the

China of old pictures or designs on porcelain—delicate bridges and pagodas and birds skimming over the water.

I remembered that European Powers had sacked the Summer Palace in 1900 when they crushed the Boxer Rebellion. But the menace of barbarian invasion from the north was now closer than the decaying or retreating forces of Western imperialism. Peking, for centuries the fount of Chinese culture and seat of ancient learning, fears an older danger than that of the British and French gunboats which arrived in South China a century ago. It was easy to conjure up a vision of the savage Mongol and Manchu hordes which had swept in across the plains from the north and northeast to conquer China.

Just inside the Forbidden City the guide points out to you the hill where the last of the Ming Emperors hanged himself when the Manchu banners broke through the gates of Peking, three hundred years ago. Later, when I went to Manchuria from Tientsin in a tiny "flying jeep," we swooped low over the Great Wall, which had been useless to halt the barbarian invasions in the past, and could not now impede the incursions of the semi-Mongol Muscovites and their Chinese disciples. In the old days China could absorb her conquerors. Today the technical superiority of the West and its imitators and the insidious weapons of propaganda have deprived China of her long-lost advantage of being the most civilized and prosperous nation in the world.

Peking is one of the most-beloved cities on earth. Hu Shih, when he lived in America, had told me how he longed to return there. Lao-Shê, author of *Rickshaw Boy,* had said to me in Chungking that he dared not go back to Peking. "One just cannot work there, one is too happy." Arch Steele, who had lived in Peking before the war, was determined to end his days there, and he and his wife offered me a courtyard in their dream house when I was ready to retire from the futility of modern life.

I found George Peck, with whom I had had strenuous political arguments in Chungking, in a little Chinese house outside the Forbidden City. He had retired from the O. W. I. to write books at leisure in Peking, where he lived cheaply in Chinese style in beautiful surroundings. General Worton, Chief of Staff to General Rockey commanding the United States Marines in North China, considered coming to Peking like coming home.

The few days I spent in Peking before and after my visit to Yenan enabled me to feel its charm and appreciate its effect on all manner and conditions of men. I also understood better why the Chinese, battered and weak and poor, cling to their cultural values.

Peking is no Rome to the Chinese; it is not even one of the oldest cities of China. But because China's last three dynasties ruled from there, because for centuries it was the seat of government and the center of learning, because more of Old China survives there in monument and atmosphere than anywhere else, and because Peking is so close to Russia's power, I was most conscious here of the "ideological" conflict between the Soviet Union on the one hand, and China and the West on the other.

Li Tsung-jen, the general from faraway Kwangsi in South China, was now commander of the Generalissimo's headquarters in Peking. My interview, which took place in a beautiful old palace inside the Forbidden City, was extended for hours and included a simple lunch served in a hall of the long-dead Manchu Emperors. Li Tsung-jen had been in command of the forces which won the battle of Taierchwang in the north in 1938—about the only victory China had in the first year of the war. He and Pai Chung-hsi (the Mohammedan general who is now Minister of National Defense) had flung their troops into the defense of the Wuhan cities in 1938 and seen their own province fall defenseless to the invaders that same year. Their present responsible positions were proof of the falsity of the accusation that no one can enjoy power in China without a personal or provincial army to back him up.

I remembered Li Tsung-jen not only as a patriot but also as a philosopher and an intelligent student of history and economics. With him one could tire the sun with talking about all the problems of mankind. He had been a favorite of mine in the old days and had been called "Freda's General" by the Hankow Last Ditchers. So when we met again he talked to me frankly. First he told me in detail the sad story of Russia's depredation and duplicity in Manchuria. What shocked him most was not the crimes of the Russian soldiers but the "barbaric and uncivilized way of thinking" of the Soviet Government. He recognized China's inability to match Russia's military might, yet when I asked him whether China's situation was not hopeless, he replied:

"No, not hopeless. In the end right is always triumphant. I am sure of it. How could China have endured for so many thousands of years had we not believed in a moral law, and were not virtue, which is truth, in the long run stronger than injustice and lies?"

Was this faith the source of China's strength in adversity? Militarily weak as she is, torn by civil war and with a corrupt and inefficient administration, China's inner strength, derived from belief in a moral law, has in fact enabled her to resist longer against greater odds than any nation in the modern world. In spite of my conviction that the virtues which preserved China in the past can no longer save her today, I was almost ready to believe, for a moment, that she might survive in the future as in the past and outlive her conquerors. Could she escape the fate of those who place their trust in the technically efficient Frankenstein monster they have created? Could Sun Yat-sen's hope ever be realized of a China learning enough from the West to make her strong and prosperous, but rejecting both the Western and Russian ideologies?

For nearly a hundred years after the invasion of the Western world, China tried to save her culture by refusing to take the same path as Japan. She had bent before the aggressors instead of imitating them. For three decades the Kuomintang had sought to emancipate and modernize China, with the help first of Russia, then of America, while not relinquishing her own distinctive social values and philosophy. The end is not yet, but the fate of China is likely to be determined within the next few years.

In the past China was invaded only by barbarians without an ideology who wanted to rule her and enjoy the benefits of Chinese civilization, not to change it. They were easily absorbed. Today the "barbarians" from beyond Sinkiang, Mongolia and Manchuria have a theory, a concept of social and economic order and a "religion" which could extinguish China's independent culture. Already in Communist China the cultural effects can be seen. The pictures and woodcuts, ornaments and children's playthings produced in Yenan are more Russian in style than Chinese.

The influence of Russia over the Chinese Communists is already greater than that of the West over the rest of China. The Soviet Union is closer to China as a whole in spite of its totalitarian form of government, because Stalin rules over a people also still largely medieval in thought and in standard of life.

The differences between a Chinese and a Russian intellectual are far greater than those between Western man and a Chinese scholar. The Confucian and the Greco-Roman-Christian concepts of the "good, the true and the beautiful" are much closer akin than the Chinese and Communist ideologies. But the problems of the Chinese and the Russian peoples are similar. Their poverty, their ignorance, their crying need for freedom from starvation or penury—these make them brothers. They live almost identically miserable lives and both can easily be led to hate the prosperous, easy-living, mechanically advanced Westerners.

The fate of China will be decided according to which proves stronger: her closer affinity to the West in ideas and culture, or the pressures to solve her economic and political problems along Russian-Communist lines.

The student of ancient and medieval European history has some comprehension of the Chinese problem, because not only the economic frame but also the long forgotten values of medieval Christendom are nearer to China's today than those of our modern Western civilization.* But since Chinese civilization and history are unique in many respects, only a scholar who has devoted his life to the study of Chinese language, literature and history could bring clarity into our judgments of present-day China. Unfortunately the Sinologists usually fail to relate their knowledge of the past to the problems of today or to write popular books. As Bertram D. Wolfe pointed out in reviewing the latest edition of Kenneth Scott Latourette's monumental work, *The Chinese: Their History and Culture,* books on China have a way of flowing in two divergent channels that have no point of contact with each other. On the one hand there are the dependable and illumating works of scholars, such as Latourette, which are little read except by specialists; on the other there are the books by "reporters and special pleaders, brash and arrogant and misleading but popular in form and intended for wide distribution." Whereas the scholarly work is likely to recognize the Chinese Revolution as an attempt to transform China in terms of her own heritage, the books

---

* For instance, E. H. Tawney, the medieval historian, wrote one of the best books available on China's agrarian problem, *Land and Labor in China,* and the sociological theorist Karl Mannheim wrote on the Confucian society.

by popular authors and journalists usually ignore China's past and her right to a development of her own, treating the Chinese Revolution either as a belated attempt to "catch up with" Western civilization, or as an abortive Communist revolution.

For the most part the scholars have left a free field to the experts who presume to pass judgment and affix their little labels according to what is good or bad, true or false, progressive or reactionary in their own narrow view and in our particular Western "era of progress."

Dr. Paul M. A. Linebarger, son of the Judge Linebarger who was Dr. Sun Yat-sen's friend and biographer, is one of the few exceptions. Brought up in China and with a scholar's knowledge of its history, traditions and classical learning, he is also a modern political scientist, who served in China during the war as an intelligence officer and expert on psychological warfare. His book on *The Political Doctrines of Sun Yat-sen* is an illuminating study of the essence of the Principles which are the Bible of the Kuomintang, and of their relation to Confucianism and the basic philosophy of the Chinese people. His *Government in Republican China* gives an account both sympathetic and objective, realistic and understanding of China's recent history and her cultural and ethical values.

According to Dr. Linebarger, Sun Yat-sen's precepts and teachings were an attempt, not to displace Confucianism, but to revive, develop and adapt it to modern conditions. Sun believed that "Chinese nationalism and the regeneration of the Chinese people had to be based on the old morality of China, which was superior to any other morality that the world had known, and which was among the treasures of the Chinese people. . . . He praised the ancient Chinese superiority in the field of social science, while stressing the necessity of Western knowledge in the field of the physical and applied sciences alone."

The basic concept of Confucianism had been that the underlying problem of society is "ideology": the character of the moral ideas prevalent among the individuals composing it. According to this view, where there is no common body of ideas a society can hardly be said to exist. If, on the other hand, the great majority of people accept and believe in the same moral laws there is harmony (which in Chinese incorporates the ideograph used to denote peace). "The state existed only for the purpose of filling out the shortcomings of social harmony."

In a society—such as Confucius dreamed of—where there was no disagreement in outlook, policy would not be a governmental question; if there were no disharmony of thought and behaviour, there would be no necessity of enforcing conformance to the generally accepted criteria of conduct. From this standpoint, government itself is socially pathological, a remedy for a poorly ordered society. Men are controlled indirectly by the examples of virtue; they do good because they have learned to do good and do it unquestioningly and simply. Whatever control is exercised over man is exercised by their ideology, and if other men desire to control they must seek it through shaping the ideas of others. As its full expression, such a doctrine would not lead to mere anarchy, but it would eliminate the political altogether from the culture of man, replacing it with an educational process. Ideological control would need to be supplemented by political only if it failed to cover the total range of social behaviour, and left loopholes for conflict and dispute."*

I have quoted thus at length from Dr. Linebarger's book because it seems to me impossible to try to understand China without attempting to get at the basic ideas which still shape the thoughts and aspiration of her people.

It is, of course, obvious that the Chinese do not live up to the Confucian precepts any more than the Western world lives according to Christian teaching. Nevertheless one has to understand men's ideals in order to understand their behavior and their politics. The trouble in modern China is that the "loopholes for conflict and dispute" are now so large that the garment of social behavior has become a tattered rag. Sun Yat-sen, however, thought that a new one could be woven out of the same old raw material to fit a modernized China.

He thought of himself as a rebuilder and not a destroyer of the ancient Chinese culture or morality. Confucius had said, "Investigate into things, attain the utmost knowledge, make the thoughts sincere, rectify the heart, cultivate the person, regulate the family, govern the country rightly, pacify the world." The central point of his teachings, the doctrine of *jen*, "in the simplest terms means fellow feeling for one's kind . . . to love fellow men, in other words to have a feeling of sympathy toward mankind. Intellectually the relationship becomes

* *The Political Doctrines of Sun Yet-sen*, page 30.

common purpose, emotionally it takes the form of fellow feeling."* In those days, the Chinese considered their own society and civilization as practically identical; outside it were only barbarians. Sun Yat-sen endeavored to readjust the Confucian concepts to fit a national state among other nations. But the original concept of Chinese civilization as coterminous with world civilization renders it easier for the Chinese than for other nations to embrace the concept of world peace and unity on the basis of a universally accepted ethic.

The basic antagonism between Marxism and Sun Yat-sen's adaptation of the ancient Chinese ethics is obvious. The Marxists believe that men will be good if the economic system abolishes classes and class warfare. The Chinese believe that if men are taught to be virtuous the economic, social and political system is unimportant.

Sun Yat-sen categorically rejected the materialist interpretation of history and the concept of class warfare, saying that Marx had been not a physiologist of society but a pathologist who knew only its diseases. Sun was also more concerned with China's general poverty than with the injustices of the distributive system, as was natural since, as he said, China had no large, privileged wealthy class. Above all, Sun Yat-sen reflected the Chinese mentality which disregards theoretical absolutes and seeks for the golden mean. The empiricism and reasonableness of the Chinese approach to life and social problems are mirrored in Sun's teachings.

Sun Yat-sen was characteristically Chinese in the emphasis he put on men, rather than on rules and principles, and in his belief in an intellectual and moral elite. He thought that "if China were ruled by the right sort of men, programs would be correct according to the expediency of the moment." He had too much faith in the capacity of "ideological control" to prevent the corruption of men by power. Hence he did not foresee the degeneration of his party. Nor for that matter did Lenin, with his contrary concepts of how to create the good society, foresee the transmutation of the Bolshevists into total tyrants.

Neither the Communists nor the Kuomintang have proved the truth of their theories. The "common man" still "eats bitterness" in both societies. But it is important to recognize the basic antagonism

---

* *History of Chinese Political Thought,* by Liang Ch'i-ch'ao. Quoted by Dr. Linebarger, *op. cit.*

in ideology and hence the absurdity of thinking that the two sides in China can ever agree. The Kuomintang is much stronger than the Communists because, even though it may honor Sun Yat-sen's precepts more in the breach than in the observance, its "bible" is Chinese, whereas that of the Communists is alien.

The tragedy of the Kuomintang lies not only in its incapacity to resist the "diseases of defeat" which have corrupted it, but also in its failure to develop a vital, vigorous body of revolutionary doctrine to stand up against the Communist counterrevolution. The writings of Sun Yat-sen, like those of Confucius before him, have become a Sacred Book instead of being kept alive by the adaptation, development and modification of his doctrine to changing conditions.

Sun Yat-sen can hardly be blamed for this. He specifically stated that the greatest difficulty is to know, not to act; and that since it was often imperative to act without sufficient understanding, his plans should be revised on the basis of knowledge obtained the hard way—what he called learning through the "hardship of errors." He had the wisdom to recognize that means determine ends, saying: "No matter what you do, success lies in good method." In this respect also he held views diametrically opposite to the Communists who believe that the end justifies the means.

Chiang Kai-shek, whatever his failures or successes as a ruler, evidently sincerely believes in the teachings of Sun Yat-sen; his failures can be ascribed as much to the "National Father's" mistakes as to his own. If the Communists denounce Chiang Kai-shek's book *China's Destiny* as "fascist," they have no right at the same time to say they believe in the Three Principles of the People and are loyal to Sun Yat-sen's teachings. If, as they maintain, Chiang is a "fascist" because in his book he seeks to inspire his people with pride in their past, and because he writes about the ill effects of imperialist aggression, then not only was Sun Yat-sen a "reactionary" or "fascist" but all patriotism must be regarded as wicked and all modern nations must be similarly smeared.

Chiang's enemies may say that anyone who glorifies the past or seeks to restore ancient virtues or ethics is a reactionary. But in view of the mess we "progressive" moderns have made of the world it seems to me doubtful whether everything old is necessarily bad. Although I doubt whether China can become strong enough to survive in our world of power politics, while preserving or reviving her ancient concepts of man's place in society and of what constitutes "virtue," I do not think we have the right to assume that we have all the answers to the problems of our era. As the eminent Sinologist Latourette remarks, "China's political structure has endured longer than any other ever devised by man, and, measured by the area and the number of people governed, was one of the most successful in history . . . the Chinese culture whose disruption the present generation has witnessed, and the civilization of the West which brought about the revolution . . . are *both* notable achievements of the human genius, and it would be difficult to decide which is the more admirable."*

The paradox of the situation, it seems to me, is that whereas our problems today are mainly moral ones, we consider economics predominant; the Chinese, on the other hand, whose problems are primarily economic, insist that the revival of public and private morals is the primary need.

No one can read *China's Destiny* with an open mind and a little knowledge of Sun Yat-sen's teachings without recognizing that the Generalissimo is but expounding, and to some extent bringing up to date, the teachings of the man who is now called "The Father of the Nation."

Chiang insists, like Dr. Sun, that the traditional Chinese concepts of the relation of man to society are more valid than the West's pragmatic, or class-war, philosophy. Like Dr. Sun, he believes that China can learn physical science and techniques from us and yet cling to her traditional ethics. According to both of them China's weakness today is largely due to the degeneration of her social customs and morals, which in turn is represented as the result mainly of imperialist aggression and the corruption which resulted from it. Chiang inveighs against the tendency of individuals "to take private interests as a basis for determining good or evil" and ascribes to this the coming to power "in country and villages" of "depraved and frivolous persons," and of crafty men "acting illegally, sacrificing public safety and other people's happiness for their own selfish desires."

Chiang lists the old ethical standards of the Chinese people as follows: "Loyalty, filial piety, benevolence, love, trust, honesty, peace

---

* *The Chinese: Their History and Culture*. The Macmillan Company.

and righteousness"; and adds that "the four cardinal points for which China stands as a nation are propriety, righteousness, modesty and humility."

Since these words and their meanings could be variously interpreted, it is worth while quoting further from *China's Destiny.**

By the experience of 5000 years of rule and the vicissitudes of disorganization and decline, our people have acquired the virtue of understanding modesty, knowing humiliation, enduring disgrace and shouldering hardships. Because of understanding modesty, we are capable of accepting our lot. Because of knowing humiliation, we are capable of perseverance. Because we are capable of accepting our lot, we do not oppress or insult other races. Because we are capable of perseverance, we do not accept oppression or insults from other races. Because we are capable of enduring disgrace, the strength of our race is accumulated inwardly, and is not exposed outwardly. Because we are capable of shouldering hardship, the determination of our people is enduring and is not spasmodic.

It seems to me that the qualities of the Chinese people are here correctly stated; or at least that the claims made for them by the Generalissimo are somewhat less extravagant than the patriotic utterances of the spokesmen for other nations. It is also to be noted that the virtues of the Chinese people enumerated by Chiang Kai-shek are quite different from those on which either the West or Russia prides itself. There is, for instance, no mention of bravery in battle; instead, the emphasis is on endurance, perseverance, and restraint toward others.

Having specified the qualities which the "men of old" are held to have possessed, Chiang goes on to state that during the last century China's "national prestige and the morality of the people have deteriorated to a point which had never been reached before in 5000 years. . . . The nation and the people revealed weaknesses in political, economic, social and psychological spheres due to outside interference and internal dangers. These conditions came into being to an extent unprecedented in history, and they almost destroyed our power of recovery and rehabilitation."

It is obvious that one of China's gravest problems today is the split between those who, like Sun Yat-sen or Chiang Kai-shek, believe that China can save herself by revitalizing her ancient ethics and

* A private rendering of this passage from the original.

concepts of man's duty to society, and those with the diametrically opposite view that China should effect as radical a transformation of her ideas and morality as of her economy. The conflict is not even only two-sided. The radicals—those who want to discard the past completely—are themselves divided among those who want to follow Russia and those whose eyes are fixed on the West.

Chiang writes that China wrongly went from one extreme to the other: from blindly opposing the foreigners to submission; from arrogance to self-pity and mockery of the remnants of her own culture. He writes: "Everything foreign came to be considered right, and everything Chinese wrong." The Chinese, he insists, should have had enough self-confidence to know what is good and what is bad in both and to have kept their minds on Chinese needs and China's survival. Instead, as he rightly observes, "the fight for democracy or Communism represented nothing but the opposing ideas of England and America and of Soviet Russia." Thus the copying of the West caused Chinese culture to "fall into disunity and ruin."

The ancient virtues which he insists are still valid are not, says Chiang, destructive of society or conducive to aggressive policies or tyrannical government. The true Chinese character, he concludes, has "self-respect but not conceit; humility but not subservience."

Although we in the West may be too inclined to believe that politics can be only the clash and accommodation of opposing interests, and international relations a question of power, it is also to be doubted whether the Confucian and Christian ideal of harmony through adherence to virtuous and wise precepts is realizable. But I see no reason to call those Chinese who believe that the good society can be attained only through wisdom and virtue more "reactionary" than those who believe it can be established by force, hate, fear and liquidations.

It must nevertheless be acknowledged that Sun Yat-sen's insistence on virtue as primary and economics and social reform as secondary handicapped his successors in the performance of the difficult task history has assigned to them. The Kuomintang Party was left with a very vague idea of what to do once China achieved national independence. His Third Principle, that of "the people's livelihood," or "economic well-being," was stated in broad and at times seemingly contradictory terms.

Sun's vagueness with regard to the practical application of his theory of "distributive justice" had the advantage of enabling the Kuomintang to appeal to all elements of the population in the struggle for national liberation, but left his successors without a definite policy sanctified by his name. The independence of China has been achieved for a moment in so far as the unequal treaties are concerned, and China is, at least in name, a Great Power. The question now is "Where do we go from here?" and the "Sacred Books" do not contain the answer. So many different meanings can be read into them that both the Kuomintang and the Communists of today claim to be the executor of Sun's will, and within the ranks of the Kuomintang itself there are directly opposite views as to the course which Chinese reconstruction and reform should take.

Sun Yat-sen did, however, lay down certain basic principles for economic development and reform. His economic theories were empirical and related specifically to China's situation. The scarcity of capital and magnitude of the required industrialization necessitated the launching of huge state enterprises together with governmental restrictions on the use to be made of capital in private hands. He advocated a mixed economy with "all matters that can be and are better carried out by private enterprise" left in private hands and "encouraged and protected by liberal laws," and all "matters that cannot be taken up by private concerns and those that possess monopolistic character" taken up by the government as national undertakings.

In respect to the industrial revolution which China must carry out if she is not to be submerged as a nation, Sun Yat-sen went into considerable detail and drew up specific plans. It was with regard to the precise method of ensuring "distributive justice" that he was vague, since according to his belief virtue is the primary requisite.

A study of his writings leaves no doubt that Sun Yat-sen had hoped to unite China, shape her into a nation state and bring her back into the vanguard of civilization by the acquisition of Western scientific knowledge and mechanical techniques, while repudiating both the Western and Russian ideologies. He worked for revival of the ancient morality which had once made China great and prosperous and enabled her to outlive every other civilization. What he did not foresee was that China, instead of being re-cemented by faith in her own cultural values, would split vertically. Instead of young China combining a Chinese Confucian Renaissance with an industrial revolution, there is a continual struggle between the adherents of various imported ideologies. Not only do the Marxist Communists fight the Kuomintang, but within the Kuomintang there is conflict between those who regard the essence of Sun Yat-sen's teachings to be their attachment to the Confucian past and who are nowadays called reactionaries, and those who have adopted Western pragmatic concepts of one kind or another and are called liberals.

There is also a horizontal division in China, at least in so far as the liberals and progressives are concerned. While the mass of the people are still living in the Middle Ages, a large proportion of the educated classes belong to the modern world, pulled this way and that by the diverse currents of liberal and Marxist and Stalinist political thought. It is as if China belonged simultaneously to two worlds revolving on different axes and knowing little about each other. In the small world of the intellectuals political discussion and ways of thought and living are similar to those of the West. In the other there is the vast silent reality of Old China, familistic in organization, Confucian and Taoist in its concepts of life, unheeding of the currents of modern thought, entirely absorbed in the bitter struggle to keep alive or to win a modicum of security by fair means or foul.

Political discussion is similar to that which goes on in America. This in itself makes it largely unreal, a kind of shadowboxing unrelated to the real problems of government in China. For China's problems cannot be solved by American or European methods.

The liberals inside the government, faced with the stern realities of the Chinese economic and political situation, are poles apart from those without responsibility who still live in a dream world of nineteenth-century democratic ideals. The latter could make a great contribution to Chinese progress if given jobs and allowed to learn by experience. Too many Chinese liberals become useless or go sour through frustration. Others join the Communists in despair or disgust, or in the false hope that the Communists are sincere in their democratic professions. Others still, like some of the leaders of the Democratic League, see alliance with the Communists as a means to force their way into the government. Basically, however, the trouble is that there isn't room for everyone at the top, and it is only in the higher ranks of government service that the income is adequate.

There is a certain analogy between the position and the reactions of many of China's educated middle class and those of the Indian intelligentsia under the British. They turn against the government because the government makes no use of their talents or their knowledge. It is, unfortunately, all too true that in China old men, and useless and corrupt men, are kept in high office while many an able young man cannot get a job because he has no relative or patron in the administration. Before the war with Japan there were positions and opportunity in industry and trade and the professions, but since the economy is now stagnant on account of the civil war there are few jobs for the Chinese youth of the middle classes outside government service. And the salaries of those who have government jobs are so small on account of the inflation that they do not earn enough to live on if they are honest.

Many of the criticisms of the government made by the opposition are entirely valid. Others are completely unrealistic since they take no account either of the exigencies of the war and its legacy of destruction, disorganization and demoralization, or of the dead hand of the past which lies so heavy on the Chinese people and blocks even the sincerest efforts at reform. The Communists solve the problem of conservatism and ignorance by forcibly changing the people's way of life, ignoring prejudices and ancient concepts of right and wrong. China could be dragged out of medievalism by force and terror as Russia has been. But the price would be an end to all hope of her development into a democracy, the annihilation of her distinctive culture, and a bitterer servitude for her people than any they have yet experienced. On the other hand the world will not wait for China's gradual emergence as a modern state through a process of education, persuasion and peaceful reform. China will not be able to preserve her independence unless she hurries the process of modernization. Hence the dilemma of the liberals—a dilemma which is well understood by those inside the government but too often ignored by its critics outside. How can China become strong and united, and thus able to survive as a nation, without abandoning the democratic path? How can a process of development normally requiring centuries be accomplished in a decade or two without resorting to compulsion, dictatorship and terror? How avoid foreign conquest or Communist tyranny without resorting to tyrannical methods of "persuasion"?

Dr. Y. C. Koo, whom I have already quoted with regard to China's agrarian problem, said to me in Chungking:

What we are up against is China's cultural heritage: the attitude of our people toward life. This has brought us many misfortunes as well as enabled us to endure them. A Chinese desires many children more than anything else in life. An old man is happy, even when he is desperately poor, if he has many grandchildren around him. Yet birth control is as essential as any economic reform for China.

Our philosophy, our teaching, our traditional attitude, is to endure rather than to strive actively to change our conditions. We are, of course, changing and have been changing for a long time. But only passively. We accept and endure but we do not actively try to control, for our own benefit, the new forces which affect our lives and change our environment. Dynamic changes are actually now proceeding but not fast enough.

I asked him how he thought the presence of the Americans in the most backward parts of China, the sight of American mechanical devices and so forth, affected the Chinese people. "How do you think the coolies dragging their heavy loads feel about the Americans rushing by in their trucks? Do they envy them and hate them? Do they even visualize the possibility of ever living the easy lives of Americans?"

His reply was that the Americans in China were having a great effect, providing a powerful stimulus toward change and progress, but I wondered if he, or anyone else, could guess at what would be the final result. Would the Chinese hate the opulent Westerners as in the past, or try to follow us?

I am not a Sinologist, nor have I spent long enough time in China to become impregnated with the Chinese view of life, traditions and atmosphere. But if only because I used to study history I have a dim conception of what a miracle of readjustment most Americans and Europeans expect of the Chinese people. "Changing the whole course of our civilization in a few years is more than the people can bear" was the way it was expressed to me by Chiang Mo-lin, Secretary of the Executive Yuan and former president of Peking University. I had met him at a dinner party the evening before given by P. H. Chang, now consul general in New York. I had not known who he was but had been so impressed by his knowledge, intelligence and calm philosophical outlook that I asked to meet him again.

A thin elderly man looking worn and ill, he holds one of the highest positions in the government, though you would never have guessed it from his manner or from the simple way he lived. It was early morning and he received me at his home, which was unguarded and indistinguishable from the other little houses on the street. He said:

It is as if Americans were required overnight to change their style of cooking and their sanitation, and live the Chinese way. The changes we have to make in the course of our civilization, the adaptations and the breaks with the past, are more than our people can bear in a short period of time. We are expected to become a democracy overnight and adopt Western individualist concepts of life and government. The bases and the cement of Chinese civilization, the virtues we have cultivated, are not suited to the life we must now force ourselves to lead. Loyalty which keeps people together; filial piety which keeps the family united; frugality which means that one consumes as little as possible in order to support more people; diligence which enables one to produce a little more in order to be able to keep more people alive—these are the four virtues we have understood, and which have been passed on by word of mouth from time immemorial. They are ingrained in the habits of our people.

In America everyone understands machinery, and machinery is the basis of civilized life. In China the four virtues are understood by everyone, for they were the basis of our civilization and the source of the strength and endurance of our people. Today what was once our greatest asset has become a liability. The practice of these virtues does not make us efficient in production. It is natural for us to try to employ as many people as possible in a business, to spread the work and the income. whereas you on the contrary seek continually to decrease the amount of labor, lowering the cost of production. What you regard as inefficiency and nepotism or corruption is to our people a natural way of doing one's duty to one's family by maintaining as many relatives as possible. It is considered a virtue, not a crime.

Men like Chiang Mo-lin live in two worlds and understand the values of both. Talking to them one appreciates the immense difficulties of the Chinese Government. Many foreign critics of China think only that China is backward and that a "good" government could find remedies for the poverty and "inefficiency." They ignore or minimize the tremendous obstacles to change and reform according to our pattern among a people which has endured for thousands of years with quite different values from ours. Not that the Chiang Mo-lins believe that China can or should remain set in her old ways. That would mean death to her as a nation; enslavement by the efficient West or the ruthless Russians. But they know that the Government of China is powerless to change her people's way of life and habits of thought "overnight."

The liberals outside the government are certain they could put China to rights if they had the power; those in the administration know the immensity of the tasks confronting the country and the obstacles to progress which even a dictatorship could not quickly overcome. Chiang Mo-lin is a scholar and a man of integrity in an important position, something like a vice-prime minister. But he knew that in spite of his considerable powers neither he nor anyone else could remake China against the will of her voteless millions. The Communists and those of like mind would remold China by force as old Russia was remolded by the Bolsheviks. But neither Chiang Kai-shek nor those around him are dictatorial-minded in this sense.

China's real defect in our modern world, in which "patriotism" and subordination of the individual conscience to the state have been carried so far everywhere, and to the nth degree in Nazi or Communist States, is her soft, old-world, in some respects "medieval," morality. The Chinese can be cruel and corruption is rife among them, but they have a profound sense of the dignity of the individual and his right to personal freedom. Freedom may often mean only the right to starve, but it is at least better to starve in freedom than to work in a concentration camp. In China's technologically backward economy, nature, or fate, sometimes government, appear as the cause of human misery rather than a class or a system.

No foreigner in China can fail to be struck by the *social* democracy evident in human relations. People of widely different social levels, rich or poor, official, merchant, scholar, peasant or worker, talk to each other without constraint as one human being to another. There is little subservience. Even the coolies and the poorest of peasants do not feel or act like slaves. They may beg but they do not cringe, and poverty does not cause them to lose their self-respect. Morally at least, they are free men.

One afternoon in Chungking, after spending an afternoon with a Chinese friend of Durdin's at his home, I commented on the fact that it would be hard to imagine people in America spending hours in an icy cold room, sitting on hard chairs, drinking only tea and discussing the problems of mankind. "Yes," Durdin said simply, "there is a profound ethical basis to Chinese civilization."

I used to be a Marxist, but I no longer believe that all human ills, injustices and wrongs can be remedied by material advancement. The Chinese are the most cheerful people in the world, and are happy in circumstances which we should consider intolerably wretched, because of their attitude toward life and their appreciation of the basic human needs which a "high standard of living" does not necessarily, or even normally, satisfy in a mechanical universe.

All this is not to argue that the Chinese people should be left in poverty, misgoverned, close to starvation, frequently dying of hunger. It is only an answer to the type of thinking which concludes that China should copy us in every way or be given no choice but to imitate either the West or the U.S.S.R. The Chinese have values worth preserving. It is silly to label everything old as reactionary and therefore bad, to want to extinguish completely the values, principles and beliefs which have enabled the Chinese to outlive all other civilizations, and to be happy with a modicum of material comforts, gadgets and conveniences.

The peasant certainly needs better tools, chemical fertilizers, land reform, more to eat, better clothes and a higher standard of life. But it seems to me not only arrogant but absurd to say that the Chinese villagers are "emotionally starved" because they do not have movies, newspapers or radios.

In this mixed-up era of ours with its changing landmarks there is an extraordinary confusion of values, meanings and labels. It is customary among so-called progressives to put the labels "reactionary, fascist, corrupt" on all anti-Communist elements, and "liberal, progressive, democratic" on those who are sympathetic toward the Soviet Union and its disciples abroad. As Winston Churchill said in Parliament, a reactionary has come to mean anyone who reacts against an armed Communist.

Just as bad money drives out good, so the bastard terminology of the "Left" has debased our whole verbal coinage. The word liberal no longer means an opponent of tyranny and lover of freedom but is instead often used to denote a Russophile or a person friendly to Communists. There is a similar ambiguity as regards the word progressive. Too many people fail to sense that, since the political world also is round, there are times when the conservatives are the liberals and to progress means to move toward tyranny.

In China, whose values and whose economic and political problems are so different from ours, the glib use of Western labels is peculiarly inappropriate. It renders impossible anything but a superficial analysis of the political situation. It is, for instance, erroneous and misleading to label as wicked and corrupt reactionaries all the Chinese who believe with Sun Yat-sen that China should preserve her ancient morality while adapting herself to the modern world. Nor is it true that such "reactionaries" are always also corrupt, and the "liberals" usually honest. A Chinese may be both corrupt and liberal, or conservative and poor without a stain on his character. Another may be an efficient administrator and dishonest, or inefficient and honest. One Chinese official may believe in a Western democratic and capitalist development for China and be entirely self-seeking; another may cling to China's traditional ethics and yet be a patriot.

Confusion has been worse confounded by the identification of a Chinese progressive with a Russophile. One finds even such writers as Lin Yutang, who no longer have any sympathy with the Communists and ought to know better, describing Sun Fo (son of Sun Yat-sen) as a "great liberal social thinker and a great admirer of Russia." As if it were possible both to be a liberal and an admirer of totalitarian tyranny! Moreover in the economic and political policies he advocates for China Sun Fo is anything but a liberal. He has argued for a Russian-orientated policy, and he wanted China to embark on an autarchic economic development with strict state control of the national economy. Had his plans been accepted, both Chinese free enterprise and foreign capital would have been placed under such handicaps that China would perforce have followed a Russian line of development. Certainly no commercial treaty could ever have been signed by China and the United States had Sun Fo's views prevailed.

On the other hand, there is the case of Chen Li-fu and his brother, usually signaled out in books on China as the arch-reactionaries who have grouped the worst elements of the Kuomintang in the "C.C. clique." Actually this clique, best known through Leftist gossip, has about as much reality as the "Cliveden Set" in England before the war which was largely a figment of Communist imagination. Chen Li-fu is accused of being a reactionary mainly because he has waged an unrelenting war on Communism. The economic policies he advocates are liberal in the original meaning of the word. He opposed Sun

Fo and was largely instrumental in getting the government to abandon the state capitalist plans for reconstruction which might have condemned China to industrialize without benefit of foreign aid, a policy which would mean enslaving the people, as in Soviet Russia, in order to squeeze out of them the necessary capital for the development of state enterprise.

Chen Li-fu incidentally is one of the most incorrupt officials in China. He has neither lands nor houses nor cash in the bank, and his worst enemies admit that he is honest. His real crime in the eyes of Western "liberals" is his uncompromising opposition to Communism. He is one of the best exponents of Sun Yat-sen's Principles and claims to have drawn 23,000 young men away from Communism. I don't know how he can make any exact calculation of this sort, but undoubtedly his lectures and writings have been a potent force in China. In his view the two weak points of the Communists are their lack of knowledge of Chinese culture and history, and their doctrine of ends justifying means. To him their doctrines are completely destructive of morality, and he is convinced that once this is demonstrated the Chinese will not accept them.

In 1938, when I first met Chen Li-fu, he was Minister of Education and already the bête noire of the Leftists. I had expected to meet a monster since I had heard so often that he was a "hidebound reactionary" and the scourge of all liberals. I found a slim, delicate-featured man with the face of an ascetic and the eyes of a dreamer, dressed in a long Chinese robe of spotless white linen which enhanced the spirituality of his finely molded features. Friends and enemies alike had to recognize an outstanding personality in this intelligent representative of the Confucian tradition. Even in those days I appreciated that it was a little too glib to label him simply as a reactionary. He just does not fit into any of our Western categories.

In conversation with him in Chungking in 1946 I found Chen Li-fu far more concerned with agrarian poverty and rural stagnation than many of the Western-orientated Chinese who are designated as liberals in America. His views of what was wrong and of what ought to be done echoed those of the nineteenth-century American Populists who blamed the gap between farm income and farm debts on the monopolists of finance and transport, or those of later midwestern American opponents of "Eastern financiers" and their political representatives. Only in the case of China the bankers are "Western." He said:

> China's banking structure is mainly to blame for our rural backwardness. It grew out of the ideas and practices of banking developed by foreigners in the foreign concessions who were naturally interested in trade, not in China's agricultural or industrial development. Even today Chinese banks concentrate on commerce and pay almost exclusive attention to the cities.

Enlarging on this theme he said that the foreigners were not to be blamed for this state of affairs, but it was the main cause of China's present critical economic situation. Large amounts of capital were lying idle in the cities, or used in speculation instead of in productive enterprise, and the inflation could never be checked so long as production did not increase all over the country.

He continued:

> Some means to reform the banking system must be found. Capital must be made to flow to the villages to be lent out at low interest rates through co-operative societies of all kinds. The banks must be made to serve agriculture first, industry second and commerce last, instead of the other way round.

It seemed to me that Chen Li-fu's ideas were very close to Sun Yat-sen's and that if he is a reactionary, so also was Sun Yat-sen. The falsity of such a label lies in using a Western yardstick to judge the Chinese.

Chen Li-fu is a conservative in the sense that he believes in, and wants to preserve, the qualities and philosophical and ethical values of China's old civilization. This does not mean that he wants China to remain backward, "feudal," poor and misgoverned. On the contrary, he is an engineer who shares Sun Yat-sen's vision of a China rejuvenated and strengthened by Western physical science and techniques; and it was he who while Minister of Education insisted on more students studying technical subjects and fewer literature and philosophy. He is a conservative in the sense that he does not believe that the West has anything new and better to offer in the social sciences. He rejects completely Marxist materialism and the latter-day Western morality which has come to be expressed almost entirely in economic terms. As he said to me in Chungking: "China should open her doors to welcome Western civilization, but she should not forget the good points of her own."

When asked by a *Time* correspondent what he considered the nearest counterpart in the West of his interpretation of *San Min Chu I,* Chen Li-fu replied: "The evolutionary program of the British Labor Party." Such a man can hardly with justice be called a reactionary.

Chen Li-fu in his talks with me in 1946 was far more outspoken about Russia than most government officials and had no faith in the pathetic efforts being made to avert Russian aggression by soft words. Perhaps this is the main reason why he is always awarded the role of chief villain in the Kuomintang government by Communist-sympathizing journalists. Few of the latter ever sought him out to talk to him and ascertain his real views, although he was easily accessible in his unpretentious office near the Press Hostel. I consider him one of the most intelligent and best-informed men in China and not unprogressive except in the sense that "progress" has come to signify a partiality for Communist dictatorship. This also was the opinion of my old friend the Canadian ambassador, General Odlum, who always said "Nonsense" when anyone referred to Chen Li-fu as a reactionary or a "fascist."

CHAPTER XV

China: Focus of Conflict

"WHAT'S the use? Russia is too big, too crafty, too cruel for us to fight. She will conquer in the end. Why not give up now and be friendly?"

These are not the words of some popular columnist today pleading that we should "get along with Russia" at all costs. It is a quotation from a dispatch written by Edwin Conger, the United States Minister to China in 1903, when Russia was already threatening to acquire dominion over China.

In the same period Secretary of State John Hay wrote: "I take it for granted that Russia knows as we do that we will not fight over Manchuria."

Half a century later, on February 11, 1945, the President of the United States promised Russia at Yalta that the "claims of the Soviet Union" to a pre-eminent position in Manchuria should "be unquestionably fulfilled after Japan has been defeated."

Theodore Roosevelt had said that although the Open-Door Policy was an excellent thing, it must "completely disappear as soon as a powerful nation determines to disregard it and is willing to run the risk of war."

Franklin D. Roosevelt did not consider the integrity of China and the Open Door even worth not fighting for. At a time when Russia was in no position to challenge America the President of the United States voluntarily offered Stalin control over Manchuria's main ports and all her railways, and promised to force the Chinese Government to agree.

Had President Roosevelt studied the record of the past, or if he had not willfully insisted on placing his trust in Stalin's good intentions, he must have recognized the enduring truth of what the *London Times* wrote in 1895:

It is obvious that with Russian fleets in the harbor of Port Arthur and a railway connecting that place with the Siberian trunk line, Manchuria would practically become a Russian province, the Chinese capital itself would be in Russia's grip, and every power in any degree interested in Chinese affairs would have to effect a fundamental revision of the arrangements by which its position and commercial interests are at present secured.

For half a century Russia's ambition to acquire hegemony over the Far East was frustrated by Japan. Today, thanks to the annihilation of Japan's power by the United States and the concessions made at Yalta, Russia is back where she was before Japan defeated her in 1905.

China, terribly weakened by the long unequal struggle with Japan and torn asunder by the civil war which Russia encourages, cannot defend herself. If the United States does not give full and effective support to the Chinese Government, there is no barrier to Russia's advance. If Russia through the instrumentality of the Chinese Communists should acquire *de facto* control of Manchuria and most of North China, the Kremlin will have succeeded in winning what the Czars failed to acquire fifty years ago—a position in which Russia can "defend" China against the West, but no one can defend China against her.

Japan was both raised up and cast down by the West. It is always possible that she will be revived again as a counterweight to Russia, but it is unlikely that she will soon play an independent role. The period from the first Sino-Japanese War in 1894 to the end of the second one in 1945 thus appears as only a break in the continuity of the three-cornered conflict among Russia, China and the West.

In the seventeenth century, when Russia had first tried to force her way down the Amur River to the Pacific, the Manchu dynasty which then ruled China was young and vigorous enough to repulse her. Forced to admit defeat the Czars accepted a frontier to the north of the Watershed for a century and a half. By 1854 the weakness of the Chinese Government at Peking and the Crimean War combined to incite Russia to make inroads on Chinese territory. The Czar demanded that China allow her right of way down the Amur to protect her Pacific coast line from Anglo-French attack. China, at that time involved in the Taiping Rebellion, was unable to resist when

Russia took control of the river and of all the territory to the north of it. As an English historian has neatly expressed it, the "only" gain Russia had to show for a three-year war against Turkey, England and France was the seizure of a couple of hundred thousand square miles of *Chinese* territory.* China, of course, had had no connection with the conflict out of which the Crimean War began. As so often in subsequent years she was made to pay the price in other people's quarrels.

The territories of which Russia had taken possession were sparsely inhabited and not of vital importance to the Celestial Empire. China was far more fearful of the vigorous aggression of Britain and France in the South than of Russia, and Japan was not yet a Great Power. Anticipating the policy of the Soviets, the Czar in 1858 came forward as China's protector. As her reward for acting as mediator between the Manchu Emperors and the Western Powers, which had already twice defeated China, Russia obtained formal possession from the Chinese Emperor not only of the territories north of the Amur but also of the seacoast as far as Korea and inland to the Ussuri River. A few years later Russia claimed and took Sakhalin from Japan in return for Russia's renunciation of all claims to the Kurile Islands.

By this time the process of extortion and counterextortion at China's expense was well under way. From the First Opium War in 1838 until 1922, first England and France, then Russia, then Germany and Japan almost tore China to pieces. Territory was seized from her. Colonial areas called concessions were established on Chinese soil at Shanghai and in other so-called Treaty Ports. China had to agree to foreigners in China being exempted from Chinese law and from Chinese taxation (extraterritoriality). Foreign gunboats had the freedom of her rivers and her coasts. Foreign soldiers guarded their nationals even in the capital city of Peking. Foreigners controlled her customs in order to collect the interest due on money borrowed from abroad to pay the "indemnities" imposed on her for being militarily too weak to resist aggression. Her government was forbidden to protect her industries or increase its revenues by being held to a maximum tariff of five percent on imports. The ports occupied by the Powers as "leased territory," together with the land close to the

* G. F. Hudson in *The Far East in World Politics*.

railroads which were constructed in the second half of the century, became foreign territory from which China could be attacked if she resisted any demands made on her, and from which the Powers could make war upon one another on Chinese soil.

Thus China was tied hand and foot by the Powers to prevent her from either thrusting them out or building herself up into a strong state. Each concession wrested from her by one Power was at once demanded by the others. The United States, although refraining from armed aggression, insisted under the "most favored nation" clause of her treaties with China that all privileges obtained by others should also be enjoyed by Americans.

By the end of the nineteenth century Russia was threatening to acquire a dominant position in China, not as an "aggressor" but as a friend anxious to "protect" China against Britain and Japan, but naturally requiring "strategic facilities" for this purpose. So when England's ward, Japan, defeated China in 1895, Russia, backed by Germany and France, prevented the victorious Japanese from taking Southern Manchuria and Port Arthur. She virtuously proclaimed that no nation was to be allowed to increase its territorial possessions at China's expense.

In those days it would have been difficult to know to which Power to award the palm of hypocrisy.

In 1894 a formal Russo-Chinese Treaty of alliance gave Russia the right to use all Chinese ports in time of war. She was also promised a naval base in Southern Manchuria, and by 1898 was demanding the "lease" of Port Arthur—all of course for China's "protection." To the uneasy British it seemed that Russia would soon be in a position from which she could "quietly watch the dissolution of the Chinese Empire."

Meanwhile Germany had taken possession of the Port of Tsingtao in Shantung; and France had obtained a "leasehold" on the Kwantung Coast between Indo-China and Hong Kong and a railway concession to connect Tonkin and Yunnan. France was also claiming most of South China as her "sphere."

England, at that time at the height of her industrial and maritime supremacy, and in possession of Hong Kong, was naturally opposed to annexation of Chinese territory by other Powers and to exclusive "spheres" for Russia, France, Germany or anyone else.* Free trade is always the cause of the strong, and it was England, not America, who first enunciated the principle of the Open Door. England then, like America today, stood to gain most if China were not partitioned. But the British knew they could not themselves halt Russia now that the completion of the Trans-Siberian Railway had enabled Russia to escape from the domination of British sea power. Russia then as now was the only Great Power able to exert military pressure directly on China. Like the United States in the present era, England herself could not, or would not, fight to preserve the Open Door so long as there seemed any other way to safeguard her interests.

If partition was to be the order of the day the British Government was going to make sure that England got the lion's share. At all costs she was going to prevent any other Power turning the whole of China into a colony. So in April 1898 after Russia had obtained Port Arthur, Britain joined in the new scramble for territories and "spheres of influence." She demanded and obtained from China the "lease" of Weihaiwei in Shantung and claimed as her "sphere" the whole Yangtze Valley.

At the close of the nineteenth century, the battle for concessions in China had thus taken the form of conflicts for "spheres of influence" within which a foreign Power sought exclusive right to capital investment, mainly in the form of railways. The demands of Russia, France and England, in particular, became so all-embracing that the conflicts among the Powers could no longer be resolved at China's expense. There would soon be so little of the Celestial Empire left to divide up that a major war in Europe was an immediate danger.

When Russia's ally, France, came into direct conflict with England over railway construction rights in Central China, the situation was saved for the moment by America's active entry into Far Eastern politics with the doctrine of the Open Door. The United States became the protagonist of the policy which served both her own and

---

* Andre Nolde, in his *La Chine de Chiang Kai Chek*, Paris, 1946, opens his book with the thesis that the Open Door was a hypocritical British and American invention for preserving a status quo favorable to the U. S. and the British Empire. He says of the Open-Door principle: "Principe inspiré en apparence d'un libéralisme économique de bon aloi, en réalité avantageux surtout pour les positions commerciales et bancaires déja acquises par la Grande-Bretagne et les Etats-Unis."

England's interests best, but which England was not in a good moral position to espouse.

Fifty years earlier, and nearly a hundred years before General George Marshall arrived in Chungking on his ill-fated mission, his namesake, Humphrey Marshall, had written from China to the State Department:

> It is my opinion that the highest interests of the United States are involved in sustaining China . . . rather than see China become the theatre of wide spread anarchy, and ultimately the prey of European ambition.

Opposition to either the partition of China or her domination by any one Power had thus been recognized as the best policy for America long before she joined hands with England to try to stop Russia. This aim did not preclude deals at China's expense if and when it seemed that American interests could be preserved by sacrificing China's. Nor did it prevent the United States from claiming for American citizens all the privileges or special rights given to others under the unequal treaties which China was forced to sign. The United States kept its hands clean. Americans did not themselves send generals with armies to force concessions from China. But as early as 1844 America's first commercial treaty with China ensured her not only "most favored nation" treatment in respect to customs dues, but also included the provision: "If additional advantages or privileges of whatever description be conceded by China to any other nation, the United States [will] be entitled thereupon to complete equal and impartial participation in the same."

A later treaty, that of 1858, obtained for American citizens in even wider terms the right to share in any and all privileges, economic or political, which China might be forced to concede to any other nation.

The "Open-Door" Policy as enunciated by John Hay in 1899 was the logical outcome of America's desire to defend her commercial interests in China without fighting either the Chinese or the aggressors in China. It seemed a cheap way to defend both principle and self-interest.

The interests of America were not sufficiently involved in Far Eastern trade to warrant either an imperialist policy or real aid to China. On the other hand, if only other nations could be persuaded to act according to the principles enunciated by the United States, America's trade and investment in China would be safeguarded. If they would not, then the United States would be compelled to find another way of preserving her interests and the balance of power. In any case American principles were not to be allowed to stand in the way of American nationals enjoying what other less virtuous nations obtained by force.

The United States, accordingly, under Theodore Roosevelt, went along with Britain in helping Japan and encouraging her to fight Russia. An American loan helped finance Japan in the Russo-Japanese War, and the United States acted as mediator in the peace signed at Portsmouth in 1905. This peace denied Japan the full fruits of her victory, but Russia, in spite of her defeats, was less exhausted than Japan and might have continued the war to her advantage had not the United States persuaded the Czar to make peace.

Prior to the Russo-Japanese War, the victim over whose body it was fought had attempted to take a hand in the determination of her fate. In 1900 the Chinese, goaded beyond endurance, tried to shake off their chains by massacring the hated white men on her soil. The British, French, Germans, Russians, Japanese *and* Americans laid aside their rivalries for a moment to crush the Boxer Rebellion in blood and fire. Having sacked Peking and taught China her lesson, they could safely renew the conflict among themselves.

Japan's defeat of Russia in 1905 saved the United States from the necessity of swallowing its principles in order to secure its interests. Japan at first was too weakened by her dearly bought victory to acquire exclusive domination over Manchuria and hegemony over China. But when, during the First World War, Japan thought she had the opportunity to reduce China to vassalage while the European Powers were busy trying to exterminate one another, the United States abandoned lofty principle for compromise. In 1917 when Japan presented China with the Twenty-one Demands which would have converted the whole Republic into a vassal state, Secretary Lansing, while continuing to oppose "in principle" special rights and privileges for any power in China, signed a document recognizing Japan's "special interests in China, particularly in the part to which her possessions are contiguous."

In 1919 at the Versailles Peace Conference President Wilson, in pursuance of his "great design," a League of Nations, went even farther. He agreed, over China's protests, to let Japan keep control of the Chinese province of Shantung* in order to get her signature to the Covenant of the League of Nations, just as, a generation later, President Franklin D. Roosevelt was to betray both China and Poland at Yalta for a similarly worthless Russian promise of support for a United Nations organization.

In 1922, at the Washington Conference, the United States could afford to adhere to principle again, since she no longer had any "great designs," since Russia and Germany were out of the picture for the time being, and since Japan could be kept in order without risk of war. Japan was forced to give up Shantung, to clear out of Russian Siberia and to sign the Nine-Power Treaty, guaranteeing the territorial integrity of China and her national independence.

This treaty was intended to ensure a hands-off policy by all the Great Powers. But it did not free China from the shackles on her sovereignty imposed during the previous century. The "Open-Door" Policy remained what it had been since its inception, a device to prevent any one Power gaining an advantage over the others by seizure of territory or acquisition of exclusive rights. In John Hay's words it was intended to "protect all rights guaranteed to friendly Powers" by preserving "China's territorial and administrative entity."

The unequal treaties remained in force, and Japan retained her "special rights and privileges" in Manchuria. No concessions were made in 1922 to China's aspirations to real independence. She was expected to "set her house in order" but it was still cluttered up with foreigners who got in her way and rendered her task impossible.

The Washington Conference was accordingly a bitter disappointment to the Chinese. They had hoped that the Western Powers would not only cease extorting new concessions but would allow China to develop into an independent modern state. Instead, as Wang Ching-wei said at the time, China was freed "from the Japanese policy of independent violent encroachment" only to leave her a victim "to the co-operative slow encroachment of all the Great Powers."

Sun Yat-sen had originally been confident enough of Western aid in China's reconstruction to submit plans for the development of

* This had already been agreed to by Britain and France in secret treaties signed during the war.

China's economic resources to the mutual benefit of the West and China. He had written that it was his hope that "the present spheres of influence can be abolished, international and commercial war done away with, internecine capitalist competition got rid of, and, last but not least, the class struggle between labor and capital avoided."

He did not turn to Communist Russia for help in the emancipation of China until compelled to recognize that only force could enable the Chinese people to win their freedom.

The 1923 to 1927 period of Kuomintang-Communist-Russian collaboration came during the brief period when the Soviet Government still hoped to win world power through the support of the working class and the oppressed "colonial peoples," rather than by building up the greatest military machine in the world. Lenin had denounced all the special rights and privileges of Czarist Russia in China, which Stalin was to claim a quarter of a century later. Russia appeared to Sun Yat-sen as the only country willing and able to help China in her struggle for liberation.

After Sun's death the Kuomintang-Communist alliance successfully swept all before it from 1925 to 1927. It seemed then that Soviet Russia might acquire what the Czars had fought in vain to achieve, a virtual hegemony over China, or China's absorption into Russia's empire as an ally and protectorate. This very real threat to the Open Door and all it stood for in the way of imperialist privilege and commercial interests led the United States to join hands with Britain in supporting the moderate forces of Chinese nationalism led by Chiang Kai-shek.

Had not the Comintern, locked in the struggle between Stalin and Trotsky, played its hand so badly, China might have remained Russia's friend instead of becoming America's.

The mixture of Right and Left policies adopted by the Comintern ruined Russia's chances. Had the line of sincere collaboration with what Marxists call the "bourgeois revolution" been followed, Sun Yat-sen's aim of a non-Communist China allied to Russia, and freed from Western Imperialist exploitation, might have been achieved. But Stalin, in his efforts both to destroy the Trotskyist opposition in Russia and to steal its fire, lost the chance of creating either a friendly non-Communist China or a Communist-dominated China. He forbade the Chinese Communists to organize the peasants, workers and soldiers into Soviets ready to seize power over the New China to be established after the "Imperialists" and the war lords had been defeated, this being the Trotskyist strategy. He insisted instead that the Chinese Communists subordinate themselves to Chiang Kai-shek's orders and do nothing to prepare for the eventuality of a break. But, at the same time, he declared that Chiang Kai-shek and the Kuomintang would later on be annihilated by the Communists in a social revolution, thus making it certain that a break must come.

Naturally Chiang Kai-shek and the Right Wing of the Kuomintang decided to be liquidators instead of waiting to be liquidated. Thus the Comintern under Stalin's guidance both destroyed the possibility, if it ever existed, of turning China's national revolution into a Communist revolution, and threw away the chance of lasting co-operation between the Kuomintang and the Communists.

The civil war which began in 1927, and has been openly renewed since V-J Day, was the price China paid for the repulse of Russia. It acted as a continual brake on the new government established at Nanking in 1927. It split the forces which might have rejuvenated China and enabled her to grow strong enough to resist her external enemies. It helped Japan as today it helps Russia.

China under the Kuomintang became sufficiently united and nationally conscious to resist Japan and deny her victory. But both the split with the Communists and the very short period vouchsafed to the government to reconstruct China and create a modern army, before Japan attacked in full force in 1937, destroyed the early hopes of the Kuomintang Revolution. China today, as at the end of the nineteenth century, is too weak to stand up to Russian pressure. She is again what she was before the rise to power of the Kuomintang—the victim of power politics and the focus of world conflict.

In affliction there is comfort in the misery of others. The Japanese can today console themselves with the thought that the Chinese, who got Japan into her present situation by refusing to be conquered quietly, have not even won the right to be left alone to reconstruct their country. Russia has taken over from Japan the "divine mission" of keeping China disunited and preventing her reconstruction and development into a strong modern state. And China's Western friends now echo the criticisms of the Kuomintang Government formerly given by Japan as an excuse for her aggression.

In the year following his country's defeat a Japanese with an ironic sense of humor could comment on the fact that Japan under General MacArthur was somewhat better off than China. Japan was at least being protected from the Communist menace from within and without, while China was being urged by the United States to take Russia's agents into her government, and the Chinese Communists were completing the material destruction which Japan had begun. By 1947 more economic assistance was being given by the United States to occupied Japan than to China. China, like Poland, was finding that it was better to have fought America than to have been her ally.

Nevertheless, in spite of all the weaknesses of China; in spite of the strains and stresses which must have broken a people with less patience and fortitude; in spite of the fact that victory meant merely the exchange of one aggressor for another; in spite of the failures of the Kuomintang Government and its inability to fulfill the tasks it had set itself in the twenties—in spite of all this, China under Chiang Kai-shek has attained too high a degree of national consciousness and self-respect for the wishes of her people to be ignored. She has not reverted entirely to her nineteenth-century position of being only a pawn in international power politics.

The struggle today is not one for greater or lesser spoils in China. It is no longer a conflict among the Powers for territory, concessions or special rights and privileges, but one to decide who shall determine the direction of China's development and her orientation in world politics. The century-old struggle over the body of China has been transformed into one for control of her mind and heart. Today there is an ideological war in which Chinese fight Chinese, instead of foreigners fighting Chinese or one another.

Until the defeat of Japan there was a three-cornered contest as among Communism, represented by Russia, Western or Anglo-American political and economic ideas, and Japan's force-backed propaganda for a greater East Asia ruled by herself. By reverting to the obsolete pattern of nineteenth-century direct colonial conquest Japan threw away her opportunity to unite and lead the Orient against both the declining imperialism of the West and the rising Soviet imperialism. Today there remains only the conflict between the West and Russia.

The Japanese never had any real chance of success. Not only their brutal and stupid methods but also the reactionary nature of the elements and principles they appealed to, nullified their military strength. They could win battles and occupy territories but they could not win sufficient adherents to secure their conquests.

For a few years the threat of Japanese conquest united China and held in abeyance the basic conflict between the Moscow-orientated Communists and the Western-orientated National Government. As soon as Japan's defeat at America's hands became a certainty the conflict was resumed. Today it holds the center of the stage. Two opposite principles of unification, two opposing philosophies, ways of life and paths out of medieval backwardness, the Communistic and the democratic, tear China apart. She cannot progress until the conflict is resolved. She stands at the crossroads and cannot take the path to modernization or reform either to the Right or the Left, either into Russia's orbit or America's, until one side or other is victorious and dominant.

During my stay in China and for a year afterward China was held suspended and impotent. She could do nothing to solve her problems because America compelled her to try to resolve by negotiation and compromise an irreconcilable conflict. We continued to insist that the ills she suffered from were of internal origin, in spite of all the evidence that the poison which was wasting her away was administered by an outside agency. True that China was herself diseased. But left alone she could have recovered. The Communist abscess would disappear if she were allowed to regain health and strength through reconstruction and peaceful reform. But Russia's aim was to weaken her further by aggravating the disease.

Viewed historically, and without reference to the diverse motives of those who determined it, American policy showed little difference in the attitude adopted toward Russia in 1945-46 and toward Japan in the thirties. The difference consisted only in the greater degree of benevolence displayed toward Russian aggression.

In the years preceding the Tripartite Pact of 1940 among Germany, Italy and Japan, America had expressed disapproval of Japan's bullying of China and had refused to recognize the puppet or semiautonomous states she set up in Manchuria and North China. Nothing, however, was done to stop Japan while it could have been done without risk of war.

The United States, unlike England, sought to save face by giving lip service to principles, but actually she too was prepared to compromise with the aggressors at China's expense. Her official protests and Ambassador Grew's representations in Tokyo were all concerned with only the preservation of America's interests in China, and America continued to supply Japan with the sinews of war until six months before Pearl Harbor.

By regarding the fate of China as of comparatively minor importance to that of Europe, and by disregarding the real menace from Japan in its preoccupation with the more distant and uncertain menace of Germany, the United States brought on the Pacific War it had sought for forty years to avoid by seeking a basis for compromise with the Japanese aggressors. Instead of saving China and curbing Japan when it could have been done without war, America and Britain let Japan build up the strength to attack them. Even after Pearl Harbor the same line of high talk and low practice was followed. At Cairo a promise was given to China that all territories stolen from her should be returned to her; at Yalta the promise was secretly annulled.

In 1946 and 1947, America similarly sought to avoid a showdown in the Far East by her support of Chinese Communist claims. Thinking she might safeguard her interests by conciliating the Chinese Communists she weakened China and strengthened Russia for the future war which only uncompromising support of the Chinese Government could avert.

"First lofty principles, then disillusionment, then compromise"*—this was as true of America's Far Eastern policy in 1946 when General Marshall attempted to bring about a compromise with Russia's agents, the Chinese Communist Party, as it had been in the years when Ambassador Grew in Tokyo and Secretary Hull in Washington hoped to preserve American interests in China by appeasing Japan while professing disapproval of all her acts of aggression.

Implementing principle requires sacrifice, and sacrifices are acceptable to a people only when real or imagined vital national interests are involved. The downfall from principle to compromise to abandonment of principle in America's foreign policy has been due to her lack

---

* *The Big Three*, by David Dallin, Yale University Press.

of interest in world affairs. The basic truth which explains the contradictions in American policy is, simply, that so long as the majority of Americans were uninterested in the fate of China, no American Government could afford to stand on principle. Thus, again and again, confronted with the grim realities of power politics, the United States has sought a compromise.

This was easily understandable, even justifiable, in the past when the United States was vowed to isolation, and before she had become involved, following Pearl Harbor, in the hardest and bloodiest war in her history. It is not so easy to understand why at the height of her military power in 1945 the United States voluntarily renounced what had been the aim of her Far Eastern policy for fifty years—a united and independent China.

For the sake of the doubtful and unnecessary entry of Russia into the war against Japan, and for Stalin's blessing on his "great design" of a United Nations organization, President Roosevelt at Yalta made the whole war against Japan meaningless. Japan would never have attacked at Pearl Harbor if we had been prepared to let her hold Manchuria and North China, which in effect meant domination over the whole of China. Yet at the very time when the blood of so many Americans shed in the Pacific had ensured the certain defeat of Japan, the United States sought to bring Russia into the war at a price enabling her, instead of Japan, to dominate the Far East. Not only has history few examples to show of such a mean betrayal of an ally as the Yalta deal giving Russia Port Arthur and control over the railways of Manchuria, but it is hard to call to mind an equally unintelligent and purposeless sacrifice of the fruits of victory by a strong Power. As Wellington Koo said to the Cleveland Council on World Affairs in January 1947, the concessions made to Russia at Yalta without consultation with China were "a curious and practically unique instance of one ally asking a price of another at the expense of a third for co-operation in what was morally and politically a common cause."

The treatment of China by President Roosevelt was paralleled only by the treatment of Poland. In Europe as in Asia the the ally which first resisted Axis aggression was sacrificed at Yalta to the ambitions of Hitler's successor as the scourge of democracy.

The Chinese ambassador to the United States was also correct when he stated in the same speech that the Yalta deals had placed responsibility on the United States "for stability and security" in the Far East. Having opened the door to Russian aggression, we obligated ourselves to protect China.

It is obvious now that it should have been the objective of American policy to keep Russia out of the Far Eastern War, instead of bribing her to come in. Russia would not then today, as in 1895–1904, hold the initiative in the Far East. Thanks to the weakening and deterioration of the Kuomintang Government and to the existence of a strong Chinese Communist Party and army as well as to the elimination of Japan, the Russians have a far better chance than under the Czars to acquire domination over China.

As paper compensation for the sacrifice of China to Stalin's ambitions, the United States maintained her Big Four rank—a meaningless gesture unless America can nullify the Yalta deal by giving China sufficient support to resist Russia. Pretensions to greatness are dangerous without the means to support them, and by agreeing to Russia's demands in Manchuria the United States deprived China of control over the one region developed into an industrial base, of her one hope to become strong, independent and "a bulwark of world peace."

America's Far Eastern policy until Yalta was based on a combination of self-interest and principle. Self-interest required equal opportunity for American trade; morality required opposition to the dismemberment of China or its becoming the colony of any one Power.

Today the commercial motive should be vastly reinforced by the security motive, but this is not yet obvious to the whole American people. Having been led by propaganda during the Second World War to believe that there were only two "wicked" and aggressive nations, Germany and Japan, it was natural that Americans should have believed that having killed the dragons they could safely go home.

Older nations, like England, have learned something from history. They know that different roles are played by different actors from epoch to epoch, and that yesterday's ally may be tomorrow's enemy. Americans, after their long period of isolationism, forgot the lessons their forefathers learned too well. A people whose ancestors forswore participation in "the interminable quarrels of Europe" fought in two world wars believing that a crusade against the wicked could rid the world of sin. The fact that Japan was our ally in World War I, and our enemy in World War II, did not teach the necessary lesson which centuries of experience have demonstrated to other nations. The United States agreed to let Russia have the Kuriles with as little thought for the future as it had when Japan took over the Marshall and Caroline Islands after World War I. Not only did the United States refrain during the war from using its tremendous power, and the dependence of its allies on its resources and production, to ensure its own future security, but also in the Far East America agreed to sacrifice the ally who had been fighting Japan for eight years, but who was weak, to the ally who was neutral and was strong.

In the Far East, as in Europe, Russian policy has been anything but enigmatic. It is indeed far easier to understand than America's vacillating, ambiguous and contradictory actions and reactions.

Stalin confronts the countries within his reach with a simple choice: Join us or be destroyed. The pattern for Greece is precisely the same as for China, or for that matter for America. Naturally Stalin's chances of immediate success are greatest in the countries which are worst governed, have suffered most from the war, and are close to Russia's borders. Greece and China have been softened up for conquest by misery and despair, injustice and misgovernment. But even in the case of America, strong, prosperous and free, Stalin can hope eventually to succeed, provided his depredations elsewhere can force us to ruin ourselves in the effort to bolster up weak nations, rather than meet the Soviet challenge at the source.

The course of events in the Far East since the Sino-Soviet War began in 1937 demonstrates with particular clarity Stalin's masterly opportunism. Of course, no nation in its foreign policy, not even the United States, ever acts entirely on principle. Few, however, have ever matched the Soviet Government's in cynical "realism," readiness to change sides and disregard for its pledged word.

From 1937 until Japan's defeat, the Soviet Government gave or withheld support to China, bargained with Japan and made deals with her at China's expense, called on the Chinese Communists to fight Japan or to fight the Chinese Government, kept or broke its treaties with Japan, according to what suited the short-range aim of Russian security and the long-range objective of dominion over

China. Stalin was thus able, without fighting Japan, to win far more than the United States which sacrificed so many lives in the bloody battles on the islands and atolls of the Pacific.

America's diplomacy was as weak as her armed forces were strong. Stalin, playing from weakness, showed himself a master of power politics.

Although World War II started in China, and the United States was brought into it by Japan, America's eyes continued to be fixed on Europe. Most Americans have only a hazy idea of what went on in the Far East during the war, and even less interest in what has happened since Japan's defeat. The fate of Europe, whence came the fathers or ancestors of most Americans, has naturally seemed of paramount importance in spite of the lesson of Pearl Harbor. At postwar international or Big Three conferences the Far East was usually omitted from the agenda. Moreover the official policy of whitewashing Russia withheld from the American public knowledge of Russia's actions in Asia long after the real face of the Soviet Union had been revealed in Europe.

In 1943 and 1944 the Press Censor forbade any realistic appraisal of the chances for and against Russia's entry into war against Japan. The negotiations, pacts and deals between Moscow and Tokyo were ignored or misrepresented so that no offense might be given to Stalin by adverse comment. When, for instance, on March 30, 1944, Russia and Japan signed a five-year nonaggression pact, the *Army and Navy Journal* was virtually alone in recognizing its implications and the benefits it conferred on Japan.

Obviously the agreement was materially as well as politically helpful to Japan's war effort. Not only did Russia recognize Manchukuo and repeat her promise not to attack Japan, but the former one-year leases of fisheries in Russian waters was replaced by a firm five-year agreement. The fish supplies thus assured to Japan were calculated as equivalent to at least the output of a hundred thousand farms. This gain far outweighed the annulment of Japan's oil and coal concessions in Russian Sakhalin, since Japan at the time possessed plenty of coal in Manchuria and oil in the Dutch East Indies. Nevertheless, almost every editorial writer and commentator in the United States succeeded by some abstruse process of reasoning in representing the pact as evidence of the identity of Russian and American purposes.

Immediately after this agreement Chinese Intelligence Reports showed that Japan had withdrawn several of her famous Kwantung Army divisions from Manchuria to Central China. So the Soviet Union enabled the Japanese to put more power into the drive they launched that spring along the Hankow-Canton Railway than they had displayed for several years. At the same time they launched a spring offensive on India. But the Chinese were alone in asking whether Japan would have dared to weaken its Manchurian defenses without an understanding with Russia which went even farther than their "nonaggression" or neutrality pacts. The American press had nothing to say concerning this evidence of something in the nature of Russo-Japanese collusion.

In 1946 in Peiping, where I interviewed two of the top-ranking Japanese generals in Chinese hands, I received some interesting answers to the questions I put concerning Russo-Japanese relations.

At my request, General Sun Lien-chung, commander of the Eleventh War Area, had arranged for me to meet General Nemoto and Major General Watanabe, both of whom were Kwantung Army officers who had served throughout the Sino-Japanese War in North China and Manchuria.

We met in a dark-walled, gloomy room inside the compound where thousands of Japanese soldiers awaited repatriation after their surrender. Japanese sentries guarded the entrance to the "prison" and there was no sign of any Chinese guards. Except for my interpreter, a woman major in the Foreign Affairs Department of the Eleventh Chinese War Zone, I was entirely surrounded by Japanese, military or civilian. As we faced one another across the red baize-covered table and sipped tea in a room furnished with stiff Western-Japanese-style chairs, I might have thought I was back in the Japan I had known twenty years before, asking questions about the cotton industry in the reception room of some large factory.

General Watanabe was slim, with a high forehead, beautiful hands and pale aristocratic features. He never smiled, and looked and behaved altogether like a legendary Samurai. Nemoto was thickset, broad-shouldered and ruddy of countenance, the hearty and jovial type of Japanese who is represented in the movies as grinning and saying "so sorry" as he decapitates his victims. Both were immaculately groomed in well-tailored uniforms. They no longer wore the swords which used to be an inseparable part of Japanese military attire but they held themselves as erect and as proudly as in the days of their glory and absolute power. The really arrogant type of Japanese was, however, represented by one of their civilian aides, a handsome young man in a well-tailored Western suit, whose contempt for Japan's conquerors, or for everyone but himself, had set his mouth in what seemed a perpetual sneer.

By a strange coincidence the Japanese interpreter, Mr. Fujita, a smiling, anxious-to-please and rather plump civilian, had once been a fellow student of mine at the London School of Economics. My interpreter, Major Shuping Kuai, had studied at Oxford University and we had all three belonged to the University Labor Federation in those distant postwar, or prewar, days. In spite of the many changes in international alignments and the death everywhere of the liberal hopes we had all once cherished, we met as old friends rather than as representatives of the victorious and vanquished nations. The interview became something in the nature of an historical post-mortem and soon even the tight-lipped Japanese generals began to unbend.

They did not relax their vigilance in respect to any remarks they may have been inclined to make concerning Soviet Russia. As Major Shuping Kuai remarked afterward, the Japanese were obviously anxious to say nothing which the Russians might consider inimical. As far as possible they tried to obscure the connection between Japan's war and Germany's. But they could not be expected to understand that the Soviet Government would not like them to reveal how good Russo-Japanese relations had been in spite of the Russo-German War.

In answer to my questions they stated that, following the Sino-Russian Treaty of 1944, Japan had considered Russia friendly enough for ten Kwantung Army divisions to be released from defending the Manchurian frontier to go south to attack the Chinese Nationalist forces.

General Nemoto also referred to the relief with which they had heard of the earlier Russo-Japanese Pact, that of April 1941. He had been in command of a division in Manchuria facing Russia's troops only 400 meters away. There were frequent border incidents and everyone was uneasy. After the pact was signed it was felt that nothing would happen between Japan and Russia, and he himself had been transferred to North China.

I asked him how the pact affected the Chinese Communists. He replied that according to Japanese Intelligence reports some were very put out and disappointed, while others maintained that it was only a provisional, temporary agreement. He thought that there had been two schools in the Chinese Communist Party, one resenting and one justifying Soviet Russia's friendly relations with Japan. He did not think that the pact had had any influence on the Communists in their attitude toward the Japanese. But he really did not know because the Japanese commanders were not much concerned.

"We never," he said, "attached much importance to the Chinese Communists as a military force. They were a nuisance, of course. They interfered with our communications now and again. But our main objective was always the National forces. Never at any time were orders issued to consider the Chinese Communist forces as a major military objective. There were small skirmishes with them but these were of little importance. It was not until after we surrendered in August 1945 that the Communists came to exert military and political influence in North China."

General Watanabe broke in to give me some figures of Japanese casualties in fighting the Communists *after* V-J Day. With considerable indignation he said that in Shansi alone the Japanese had lost 515 killed, 519 wounded and 133 missing. The total for North China was about five times that figure. The Japanese had been obligated by the terms of the surrender to guard communication lines and give themselves up only to the National Government forces. They were often attacked by the Communist forces. In southern Shantung 4,000 Japanese had been surrounded by 100,000 Communist troops but had nevertheless fought their way through to Tsinan to surrender to the National Government authorities.

Bringing the conversation back to Russo-Japanese relations during the war, I asked: "Can you explain to me why Japan did not attack Russia? Did you refrain from going to Germany's help because you were confident that the pacts with Russia would be honored; that Russia would not attack Japan in any circumstances?"

General Nemoto gave an evasive reply saying that he did not know, that he had been in China all the time, not in Tokyo, but he thought Japanese Intelligence had been very poor. They had never known what the Allies intended. Then he said: "I thought after we got into war with the United States that Japan must lose or compromise. I hoped for a compromise peace but thought that if we could not get this we should surely fight to the death. The way in which the war ended was a great shock to me. I could never have imagined such an end as our surrender before our armies were destroyed."

"But," I said, "what I have never been able to understand is why, if you were so certain that you could not win in a war against America, you failed to go to Germany's aid. Surely your only hope lay in Germany's not being defeated. Why then did you not go to war against Russia before American aid to Russia could turn the tide, save the Soviet Union and make Germany's defeat a certainty?"

Again he evaded an answer. Instead of replying to my question he started to explain why Japan had attacked America in 1941. "The oil situation was acute. Japan had either to surrender to economic pressure or play her last card in order to get oil from the South Seas. There was no alternative but to bend our knees or declare war on America and Britain. It was a desperate move."

Watanabe said: "Before Pearl Harbor we thought Japan must lose the war, but that the nation could be built anew on the ashes." And raising his head with dignity he added: "I still think so. Everything is finished. We have ceased to be a military nation. There will be a new Japanese nation in a new shape. I am optimistic concerning future Sino-Japanese relations. Japan used to dictate her will by means of her military power. That power is gone. Japan is now inferior even to China in military power. We have got to begin anew on the basis of real friendship with China. Now that we cannot dictate there is an opportunity for real friendship and co-operation."

"Yes," I said, "the Chinese are not revengeful. Japan can be happy that the Chinese are reasonable. Maybe in the future, if you change your attitude, the outcome of this war will prove to have been beneficial to both nations."

My conversation with the Japanese generals in Peiping had been interesting, but I had not learned what I wanted to know. As a historian I am still puzzled by Japan's failure to help Germany, since Germany's defeat entailed her own doom. Were the Japanese too fainthearted, or too stupid, or too farsighted? Did they rely until past the eleventh hour on Russia intervening to save them as a counterweight against a China bound to the United States? Or did they carefully and cleverly calculate that if they avoided war with Russia they would suffer only the mild punishment of an American occupation and would be protected from massacre and rape, and from the Communist menace at home as well as abroad?

Whether or not those who led Japan to defeat now regret that they let Germany down, or are happy that they refrained from fighting Russia and sharing Germany's fate, the prisoners of Nuremberg must have realized long before they were hanged that their greatest mistake was the honoring of their commitments to Japan.

Had not Germany at once declared war on the United States following Pearl Harbor, there would have remained an isolationist and an anti-British opposition to American participation in the war against Germany. Certainly it would have proved far harder for the United States administration and the British to direct America's main war effort against Hitler. Public opinion would almost certainly have forced a "defeat Japan first" instead of "defeat Hitler first" strategy. This would have prevented Russia's emergence as the principal victor of World War II, since it would have entailed directing the flood of Lend-Lease to China instead of to Russia.

In 1942 Russian and British interests converged to swing the scales against Germany instead of Japan. Churchill came to America in January 1942 to avert the danger of the "arsenal of democracy" diverting its huge output to the Pacific away from the war in Europe. Stalin and his henchmen, in their more subtle fashion, concentrated on minimizing Japan's guilt and the danger she represented.

Ambassador Litvinoff, shortly after his arrival in the United States, told the press that Hitler had "inspired" Japan's attack on us, leaving entirely out of account her war on China and all the other acts which entitled Japan to be regarded as an aggressor in her own right. The Soviet Union's former ambassador to the United States, Alexander Troyanovsky, went farther. In a booklet he published in Moscow called *Why the United States Fights against Hitlerite Germany,* he said that the Japanese had been "tricked" into war with the United States and England.

At the same time Russia assured Japan that she need have no fear of the Soviet Union. On January 23rd, 1942, Japan's Foreign Minister, Shigenori Togo, told the Diet that when Japan attacked America she received assurance from Russia that the Soviet Government would observe the 1941 Neutrality Pact to the letter.

The combined influence of the Communists, the Russophiles and the Anglophiles was amply sufficient to counteract the emotions of the American people. The people, as distinct from the administration and the press, wanted to fight the Japanese, who had attacked them, more than they wanted to fight the Germans against whom the United States had, in fact, been waging an undeclared war for more than a year before Pearl Harbor.

Even the *New York Times* called Japan the "slave and jackal of Hitler"—an absurd statement since if it had been true Japan would certainly have helped Germany by attacking Russia.

There is little use in speculation over might-have-beens. But it is worth remembering that had a "Japan first" strategy been adopted, the postwar situation would have been far more favorable to America and to the cause of democracy. Not only would China have been given a chance to emerge from the war as a Power strong enough to maintain peace in the Far East, thereby releasing America from the necessity of maintaining armed forces in the Western Pacific, but Russia would have been so worn down as to be unable to succeed Germany as the dictator of Europe and the menace to world peace. Both the totalitarian powers of Europe, instead of only one of them, might have been destroyed.

It will, of course, be said that Russia would have made a separate peace with Germany had we not given her the lion's share of Lend-Lease, and had not President Roosevelt at Teheran and Yalta promised to give her all and more than Germany had fought to win. Even so, would not this have been better than the postwar situation which confronts us? The Nazis would have been defeated, or would have surrendered, even if we had not given way to Russia's imperialist demands. Perhaps more Americans would have died in World War II, but their sons would not have a third world war in prospect.

Penny-wise and pound-foolish is an old English proverb which fitly describes President Roosevelt's secret Yalta deals with the dictator of all the Russias. The American lives saved in one generation will seem few if another world war comes because we allowed Soviet Russia to step into the shoes of both Germany and Japan. Since Russia never made more than a token contribution to the defeat of Japan, not even the pennies were saved.

It may be argued that Yalta did no more than set the stamp of American approval on what Russia would in any case have done.

With or without the blessing of the United States, the Red Army would have swept into Manchuria as soon as Japan was bombed to defeat. The sacrifice of China was in fact made much earlier when we decided to defeat Hitler first and poured out Lend-lease to Russia while telling China she must continue to endure unaided. In so doing, all hope of a future balance of power in the Far East was destroyed short of American armed support of China. Nevertheless it is difficult to understand why President Roosevelt strove to bring Russia into the Far Eastern War instead of trying to keep her out.

There were in fact two wars, not one. Japan and Germany were allies but not partners. In the Second World War, as in the first, Japan showed herself indifferent to both the ideologies and the interests of her allies. To the Japanese militarists the conflicts among the white peoples were just so many opportunities to build up their own Asiatic empire. In her eleventh-hour negotiations in Washington in November 1941, Japan showed that she would be as ready to join our side as she had been a quarter of a century earlier if we would accept her claim to dominate China. During the First World War she refused the one service she rendered her allies, the convoying of British and French ships through the Mediterranean, until assured by secret treaty that she would be given the special rights and territories she claimed in China. In the Second World War she showed more concern in maintaining good relations with Russia than with preventing Germany's defeat.

The record of relations between the Germans and the Japanese after they signed the Anti-Comintern Pact in 1936 shows clearly that both were pursuing their own national policies with little or no regard for the convenience or interests of the other. In German eyes that first alliance constituted an assurance against Russia's involvement in Germany's conflict with Britain or France, or a preparation for joint war on Russia. But for Japan it constituted something similar to the Anglo-Japanese alliance of 1904: an assurance that Germany would hold the ring for her while she devoured China as England had done in 1904-1905 when Japan fought Russia to decide who would dominate China.

Encouraged by the evident desire of the Roosevelt administration to find a basis for reconciliation with Japan, Tokyo endeavored to reconstruct her relations with the West regardless of her alliance with

Germany. Only when it became clear that America was no more prepared to recognize than to hinder Japanese conquests in China, did Japan sign the September 1940 Tripartite Alliance with Germany and Italy.

Russia equally with Japan reaped the benefit of America's half-and-half Far Eastern policy. Since Japan was too bogged down in China to be counted by Germany as an effective ally against Russia, Hitler in August 1939 made his about-turn in foreign policy. The Stalin-Hitler Pact announced to the world that Germany had decided to turn against the West instead of against Russia. The dominant group of Japanese militarists were ready to follow suit since they had never wanted to fight Russia and were even less inclined to challenge the Soviets after Japan's defeat in the border conflict at Nomonhan in the early summer of 1939. Indeed, as it subsequently turned out, Hitler was to find it far harder in the future to pry Japan loose from Russia's embrace than it had been to get Moscow and Tokyo to kiss and make friends following the Stalin-Hitler Pact.

The new and more binding alliance with Germany which Japan concluded in September 1940 was not directed against Russia. It bound the signatories to go to war against any Power not then involved in the European or China War which should become involved in the future, but Russia was specifically exempted from its provisions. It was directed solely against America. As we now know from German secret documents, made public by the State Department in 1946, the Tripartite Alliance was intended to exclude Russia from the war and mark out for her "the role of a sort of neutral silent partner in the war against the Anglo-Americans."

It was therefore only natural that Japan should shortly afterward (April 1941) conclude her first Neutrality Treaty with Russia.

Japan's Tripartite Alliance with Germany and Italy and her treaty with Russia marked her recognition that she could not obtain dominion over China with America's consent and must therefore better her chance of gaining her ends through alliances with the enemies of Britain, France and America.

Japan miscalculated in the case of America though not with regard to the attitude of the Soviet Government. The Tripartite Alliance of September 1940, which Germany and Japan had hoped would keep America out of their respective wars, galvanized the United States into beginning to stop the supply of oil and scrap iron which had hitherto fed Japan's war machine.

Nevertheless, since Japan could not, in any event, fulfill her "divine destiny" if America continued refusing to recognize her conquests, she all along stood to gain most by America's involvement in Europe's War and Russian neutrality in the Pacific War. Germany did in fact divert the thunder from Japan for several years, and Japan gave Germany little help in return. Japan's miscalculation was in thinking that America would not have the power or will to go on fighting her after Germany's defeat. Hence the hopes for a compromise peace which had been entertained by the Japanese generals I interviewed in Peiping. The atom bomb destroyed that chance if it ever existed.

In the Russo-German War which began in June 1941, Japan tried to play the role of mediator as unsuccessfully as Germany had formerly done between Japan and China. The Germans were as intransigent and foolish as the Japanese had been. Henceforth Japan and Germany each went her own way. By her failure to reciprocate for Germany's declaration of war against the United States by going to war against Russia, Japan doomed herself to eventual defeat. She could not survive Germany's collapse. But, by maintaining good relations with Russia, the rulers of Japan must have hoped to hedge on the outcome of the war. In any case Japan won great immediate advantages and, perhaps, some permanent ones. She freed most of her army for operations against China, the United States and the British Empire; she won nearly two years in which to consolidate her empire against the coming American attack; and she enjoyed the by no means inconsiderable advantage of the Chinese Communist split with Chungking and the direction of Communist military operations mainly against the Chinese National Government.

Lastly, but of greatest importance after her defeat, Japan avoided incurring the bitter hostility of Communist sympathizers and Russophiles in America and Britain and thus came out of the war with lighter losses than Germany.

There may never have been a secret understanding between Russia and Japan in addition to their pacts and treaties, but they certainly had a strong mutual interest. Both equally desired that Lend-Lease and America's war effort be directed against Germany.

Those who, year after year, had expected Russia to enter the war against Japan were as unrealistic as they were ignorant of Stalin's real interests and policies. He had gone to war with Germany only because Russia was attacked. Why should he fight Japan unless attacked? Not only did the Soviet Union need to avoid a war on two fronts, but, once Germany's defeat was assured, the longer Japan could resist, and the heavier losses she could inflict on the United States and Britain, the more Russia would benefit. Moreover, from Stalin's point of view, the longer China suffered the better. The balance of forces in the postwar world would be just so much more in the Soviet Union's favor the weaker China became, and the greater the opportunity offered to the Chinese Communists to dismember her.

It was accordingly only "realistic" on Stalin's part to sign yet another treaty with Japan on March 30, 1944. It had become important to Stalin to keep Japan in the fight and encourage her to launch her last great offensive in China by assuring her that it would be safe to withdraw the Kwantung Army from the Russian border. Any further victories which Japan could now win in China would serve to prepare the way for the Communist postwar offensive.

Stalin, however, made one important miscalculation. The rapid advance of America's naval forces in the Pacific, the efficacy of her air force and, above all, the atom bomb brought the war against Japan to too sudden a conclusion. Russia barely had time to scramble into it before peace was signed. She managed to grab Manchuria, but she was excluded from any share in the occupation of Japan. The game she was able to play in Europe could not be played in the Far East.

Japan certainly had good reason from past experience to hope for the compromise peace which the Japanese generals told me they had desired. Had not America and Britain for years insisted only on the preservation of their interests in the Far East? Had not the United States as late as the spring of 1941 agreed to recognize Manchukuo and mediate a Sino-Japanese peace if the Japanese Army would withdraw from China? And did not a large section of the American press speak of Chiang Kai-shek's government in much the same abusive terms as Japan had used?

However wrongly Japan may have diagnosed American policy, her leaders may have been wiser than they knew when they decided that discretion was the better part of valor in relations with the Soviet

Union. By not going to war against Russia they failed to act like Samurai, but they avoided incurring the virulent enmity of the Communists and their sympathizers in America and England. There was never the same loud cry for vengeance against the Japanese people as against the German people. The Death March of Bataan and other atrocities and ill treatment of Americans at Japan's hands led to no dire reprisals on the Japanese people after our victory as on the Germans.

There was no Morgenthau Plan for Japan, nor did she lose any Japanese territories, nor did she suffer a Russian occupation and the looting which goes with it. All Japanese war prisoners except those in Russian hands were sent home, whereas both Britain and France still held German prisoners as "slave laborers" two years after V-E Day.

Japan was allowed to retain a government, while Germany was shorn of her territories, divided up, allowed no government of her own and in general dealt with much like an African colony in the bad old days when "the natives" had no rights and there was no justice but the will of the conquerors.

No doubt the wisdom, statesmanship and soldierlike qualities of MacArthur were largely responsible for the civilized, even chivalrous treatment of Japan. But he would have been powerless had the Russians occupied half of Japan and had their friends in America insisted on the crucifixion of the Japanese people. There is no doubt at all that Japan profited greatly in the hour of her defeat by not having incurred the lasting hatred of Communists and Russophile "liberals" everywhere in the world. Articles such as the widely circulated ones of John Hersey describing the terrible sufferings of the Japanese people when we dropped the atom bomb were not matched by any similar sympathetic accounts of the sufferings of the German people under the blockbuster raids which killed or maimed uncounted numbers of German civilians.

Stalin's miscalculation of the length of time it would take America to defeat Japan after Germany's collapse caught him far short of his goal on V-J Day. In Europe he was able to establish a dominant position. In the Far East America still holds the whip hand. The United States has of course been wary of using it. Instead of giving full support to the Chinese National Government which stood by us through every disappointment, insult and injury, we spent our efforts in 1946 in trying to hoist the Communists into a position in which they could render China's Government impotent. Nevertheless, largely because the Communists and Russia tried to take all, instead of being satisfied with a large half of the loaf, China is still on our side of the Iron Curtain. She may not remain so. The Chinese Communists, backed by Russia, may still destroy Chiang Kai-shek and his government. It must, indeed, seem hard to understand in the Kremlin why Chiang should cling to the Western democracies who seem not to wish to save him and his government from the Communists, whereas Stalin could and would probably be only too happy to help him if he would join with Russia against America.

The whole jigsaw puzzle of Far Eastern relationships fits into place if one observes the shape of Russia's policy. Stalin gave China aid and ordered the Chinese Communists to stop the civil war and form a united front with the National Government from 1937 to 1939, because he was then afraid of Japan.

Following the Hitler-Stalin Pact, since there was not yet a Russo-Japanese Pact, the united front was still maintained in China but was severely strained. Following the first Russo-Japanese Pact, that of April 1941, what amounted to an undeclared civil war began in China. Following Hitler's attack on Russia in June 1941, since the Japanese refrained from attacking the Soviet Union, the Chinese Communists still remained virtually at war with the National Government of China. The Soviet Government itself, however, refrained from open expression of hostility toward China until 1944 when America's counteroffensive in the Pacific began to gather strength.

By 1944 when America's victory was certain and Stalin needed no longer fear Japan, he started calling her an aggressor for the first time and prepared to break his treaties with the Japanese. Likewise it was now safe for the Soviet press to start openly denouncing America's ally, the government of Chiang Kai-shek. The stage was already set for the postwar Russo-American conflict in China.

CHAPTER XVI

Conclusion: America's Stake in China

STOPPING overnight at Iwo Jima, at Eniwetok in the Marshall Islands, and on tiny Johnson Island, I arrived in Hawaii by Marine plane four days after leaving Tsingtao in North China. The vast Pacific Ocean no longer seemed an impenetrable barrier to attack on America after this rapid flight.

The tiny garrisons of Army or Navy personnel on the little islands won at such terrific cost in the war with Japan were now no longer more than hostages to fortune. In Honolulu I saw William L. White's *They Were Expendable* which tells the tragic story of the American sailors and soldiers in the Philippines who had to bear the brunt of Japan's sudden attack a few years ago. The picture was not just a reminder of our unpreparedness in the past. If and when Russia and her allies in China chose to attack us, the marines I had left in North China would be as expendable as Bill White's heroes. But when I got home, the American people were still pretending in the case of Russia, as formerly in the case of Japan, that there was no danger.

Whether or not Hitler was right when he said that the bigger the lie the easier it is to make people believe it, there is no doubt that the untruths people want to hear are those most frequently believed. Looking on the bright side of things is sometimes an advantage, but it is dangerous when it degenerates into fatuous self-delusion. No Communist Fifth Column could ever do so much to soften up the American people and weaken their defenses as the politicians, newspapermen and radio commentators who glossed over the ugly realities of the international situation and lulled America into a false sense of security. By playing up to the universal human weakness of thinking that something cannot be true because we do not wish it to be true, they had caused the United States to sheathe its sword before the battle was half won.

No people are perhaps so prone to wishful thinking as the Americans. The comparatively happy circumstances of their lives, their wealth and industrial achievements, their short and successful history as a nation, and the softening of their critical faculties by the optimistic advertising to which they are continually subjected, combine to weaken their resistance to "Pollyannaism."

Since every prospect would be pleasing if the Soviet Union were democratic and "peace-loving" and its rulers sought only for "security," the editors, the columnists and the commentators who propagated escapist myths and told us we could "get along with Russia" received a ready hearing in the United States. Just as stories with happy endings are best sellers, and sad tales ending in tragedy are transformed in Hollywood studios into fairy tales in which virtue is always triumphant and rewarded, so in international affairs the optimists who turn a blind eye on unpleasant facts have been preferred, while the Cassandras have prophesied in vain.

Eventually, of course, truth prevails. This is the virtue of democracy and a press free except for its need to please its readers. But the cost of wishful thinking is high in loss of opportunity, time and lives.

In the eighteenth century Samuel Johnson wrote, "I know not whether more is to be feared from streets filled with soldiers accustomed to plunder, or from garrets filled with scribblers accustomed to lie." In our enlightened modern age, more scribblers live in penthouses than in garrets. For years the columns of almost all the best-paying magazines were open to the propagandists, the optimists and the wishful thinkers. What they wrote, however false, unrealistic or silly, was what people wanted to hear. Circulation was what mattered, not truth, or the search for it. Any writer who warned against the Soviet Union had a hard time getting heard, not only during the war, but for more than a year after V-E Day. To question Russia's right to call herself a democracy was regarded in wartime as tantamount to being a Nazi sympathizer; and still today many honest writers are frightened when the Communist-sympathizing press labels them reactionaries, Red baiters or fascists.

It is possible to argue that all the whitewashing of Russia, like the pretense of unity among the Big Three, was necessary during the war in order to delude the enemy. But lying is always a two-edged weapon. To deceive the enemy it was also necessary to deceive the American people. A habit of thought was engendered in the United States which enabled the Soviet Union to get away with murder, both literally and figuratively, in Eastern Europe, the Balkans and Manchuria. When the smoke of battle had cleared away, it was found that all that victory had brought was a change in color, from black to red, in the totalitarian power which dominates most of Europe.

Until 1947 pretenses were kept up. Good money was thrown after bad in the first year of Truman's Presidency in the effort to obscure the basic Russo-American conflict by further sacrifices of small nations and democratic principles.

When at long last the facts of international life were presented to the public, the fiction was still maintained in some quarters that, if Roosevelt had lived, Communist Russia and the United States would have remained friends. Many would not admit that such "friendship" as ever existed was due solely to Russia's wartime dependence on American aid, and the willingness of the United States Government to make enormous concessions to Stalin at the expense of small or weak allies. The destruction of all liberty in Eastern Europe and a large part of Central Europe by Russia and her satellites, far from being attributed to the errors of President Roosevelt, was regarded as an unpredictable calamity, or due to Roosevelt's death and Stalin's consequent "distrust" of America and Britain.

In spite of all the sophistry, propaganda and wishful thinking distilled upon the air and in the press, by 1946 very few people still believed, in so far as Europe was concerned, that the Soviet Union was nonaggressive, and that its disciples, the Communist Parties, are apostles of peace and collaboration.

Unfortunately, as regards the Far East, the illusions about Communism persisted. In Asia we continued to appease Russia, in the person of the Chinese Communists, long after we had begun saying "thus far and no farther" in Europe. Just as earlier in combating the Axis, China's struggle against Japan was disregarded long after we had awakened to the Nazi menace, so in respect to the threat of Red fascism, China is still left to bear the brunt while we preoccupy ourselves with Europe.

Rarely does history afford a nation the choice to learn from its past mistakes. But America is now confronted with a situation so similar to that preceding World War II that one still hopes that the lesson of the past will be impressed on the Western world in time to avoid a third world war.

We could have stopped Germany and Japan without war if we had acted soon enough and been prepared to risk war while the enemies of democracy were still too weak to resist us. We could stop Russia now without risk of war, whereas soon the totalitarians will have subjected enough people and built up sufficient strength to believe they can destroy us. Once Stalin is able to meet us on equal terms, who doubts that he will attack us?

The enemies of democracy at home and abroad naturally seek to weaken our hands by confusing our minds. We are told that no aid should be given to the enemies of Communism unless they are pure and undefiled. Naturally, if our allies must all be democratic while Russia grasps the hand of any state or faction which is ready to support her totalitarian tyranny, America will be isolated.

Our choice in China as in Greece is not one between democrats and dictators. It is a choice between those who could be persuaded and assisted to transform their countries into democracies and those who are irrevocably committed to the support of Communist tyranny.

Late as it is, the United States could still embark on an intelligent, farsighted and realistic China policy. Such a policy would need to take account of the following facts:

China first of all needs relief from the intolerable burden of maintaining a world strategic line between two power systems. The United States, if she wishes to prevent China's being sucked under by Soviet Russia, must help foot the bill and cease expecting the Chinese alone to hold the line for the democratic world.

Secondly, in the realm of economics, we must recognize that United States' aid to China, although large in comparison with all prewar financing, is still minute in comparison with the size of her population and the immense task of reconstruction and reform. United States' aid must be directed in such fashion as to effect real improvement in limited areas or sections of China's economy because, however much we pour into China, we cannot relieve her poverty at once everywhere. But the Chinese people are industrious and able to live on little. China's productive forces could be revived by a much smaller per capita expenditure than is required in Europe. Two or three billion U. S. dollars would probably suffice, only part of which needs to be in the form of intergovernmental loans, the rest being obtainable from export balances secured by Chinese exports to Japan's former Asiatic markets.

As a military poorhouse, on the other hand, China's dead weight is so tremendous that even ten or fifteen billion dollars might not save the situation for the democracies.

American aid to China cannot be mere relief. It must be accompanied by a positive Chinese effort to decontrol her economy, remove impediments to normal trade, and eliminate racketeering, hoarding, speculation, black-marketing, maladministration and the fiscal irresponsibility which has resulted in runaway inflation.

China needs an Old Deal, not a new one. She is not yet fit for a controlled economy which even in advanced countries affords vast opportunities for graft. China must do her part, but only American political and economic support can enable the Chinese Government to allow free enterprise to quicken China's economic development.

In the political sphere it must be recognized that the Chinese being the heirs of the oldest civilization in the world are peculiarly sensitive to questions of prestige. This is true not only of officials but of the middle class and more intelligent workers, who can feel the international atmosphere even if uninformed as to details. Some Chinese feel they are being exploited by Americans. Many more feel they have been abandoned.

The uninformed or prejudiced criticism of China, so freely voiced in the American press for years past, has acted like an irritant on an open wound. The Chinese themselves are well aware of their faults and realize, perhaps better than their foreign detractors, what is wrong with their government. But public reprimands by American representatives may do more harm than good, since they intensify the government's desire to "save face," and render it less inclined to institute the drastic reforms which would constitute an admission of past errors.

The public pillorying of China encourages the Xenophobes and reactionaries, strengthens the Communists and weakens the liberal forces. As one of the latter said to me: "I may know that I have an ugly ill-tempered wife, but I very much resent it when a stranger tells me so in public."

The Chinese need help and constructive practical advice, not moral lectures. We cannot help them, or ourselves, unless we recognize that the root cause of their demoralization is the seeming hopelessness of their situation in face of the Communist destruction coming on top of the eight-year war against Japan, and the denial of American aid until they come to terms with those who profit from China's distress.

A clear statement of United States support for China would supply the political morale and sense of security without which all reform in China is impossible.

We should recognize that aid to China cannot be effective unless we take account of Chinese susceptibilities and Communist propaganda. We should take measures to insure that any financial assistance given to China by the United States be used to further the well being of the people and China's reconstruction; but we shall get nowhere if we seem to be treating China as a colony by demanding that Americans administer the funds we supply or control the economy of the country. There are honest and competent Chinese. We could insist, privately, on such men being put in positions of responsibility. We should also insist on proper auditing of expenditures. We could use our influence to bring about reforms. But we should never forget that Chiang Kai-shek is between two fires: that both the reactionaries who do not want to see China modernized under Western influence and the Communists who strive to bring her into Russia's orbit seize on every opportunity to accuse the National Government of delivering China to American "imperialists."

Strategic backing, economic and other reforms must all take time to show results. But a grand American gesture assuring the Chinese of their right to sovereignty and independence, with an American reaffirmation of interest in China's fate and assurance of even small-scale military and economic aid, might still check Soviet Russia, rally the liberal forces whom we have hitherto discouraged and save the day in China.

The United States cannot afford to disregard China and say "a plague on both your houses" to Nationalists and Communists. The Russian colossus is double-headed and faces both East and West; and the last war taught us that America is more likely to be attacked from Asia than from Europe.

The Chinese nation is the largest and oldest in the world, and if it goes Communist, there is little doubt that all Asia will eventually follow her. China is estimated to have a population of at least 450,000,000. India, freed from British rule and also deprived of British protection, has nearly as many people. Add Indo-China, Burma, Malaya and the Dutch East Indies and you have more than a billion people—about half the population of the world.

The Soviet Government already controls at least a quarter of a billion people in Europe and Asia. If a billion Asiatics are harnessed to the war machine of expanding Communism, the forces of democracy will be as outnumbered as the British when they faced Nazi-dominated Europe alone.

If, on the other hand, China succeeds with our help in becoming a democracy the scales will be weighted in favor of a free world. Yet, since V-J Day, with self-defeating obstinacy we have insisted that China admit the Communists to a share in her government, and have done nothing to prevent Russian encroachment in the North.

Only American political, economic and military aid can enable China to pull herself out of the slough of despond into which eight years of war against Japan, followed by an equally destructive civil war, have plunged her. Only American encouragement and advice can give the battered, weak and demoralized Chinese Government the energy and hope to reform itself, and the strength to prevent the Communists dragging China step by step into Russia's orbit.

All the time I was in China, and for a year afterward, America, like a blind giant, continued to destroy with one hand what she was striving to build up with the other. Understanding that the emergence of a strong and independent China is the one hope for lasting peace in the Far East and for American security, we continued to vacillate as to how to help such a China to come into being.

Since one group at home advocated transferring our support to the Chinese Communists in the belief that they could be "detatched" from Moscow, and another group advocated continuing support of the legitimate government of China, the United States backed both and thus perpetuated civil war.

The foreign policy of a democratic country depends on public opinion. The isolationist sentiments of the American people and the desire of her soldiers to go home were skillfully exploited by the Communists and their sympathizers to weaken United States policy. Since we either could not, or would not, give China the necessary military support to resist Russia, we fell back on a policy of conciliating Russia's agents in China, the Communist Party.

The forgotten truism that foreign policy is determined by domestic politics was never more clearly demonstrated than by the attitude of the United States toward China. President Truman had to try to satisfy both the conservatives and the followers of Henry Wallace. Hence the ambiguity of his foreign policy. The friends and influence which the Democratic administration hoped to win at home by sitting on the fence in China prevented its pursuing an effective and realistic policy and strengthened the enemies of democracy abroad.

The international situation is too grim for party politics or the satisfaction of being proved right to be allowed to stand in the way of America's vital interests. Nor can the United States safely continue to play the role of Little Red Riding Hood in a big bad world.

Until now Stalin could calculate that, every time Russia bared her fangs and gobbled up some weak nation, Americans would turn their heads away until Russia once again assumed the disguise of a peace-loving, democratic, friendly power. Even the hard words which the United States spokesmen began to utter in 1947 did not have to be taken too seriously. The Truman speech of March 12, 1947, stating that it must be the policy of the United States to support free peoples "resisting attempted subjugation by armed minorities or by outside pressures" was followed by Marshall's Harvard speech denying that United States policy was directed "against any country or doctrine."

American policy during the first half of 1947 was reminiscent of Stephen Leacock's story about the wife who, after deciding to leave her husband, insisted at the last moment on taking him along when she eloped in her lover's automobile. Having decided to break with Russia and aid the countries struggling to avoid coming under Communist domination, the United States hastened to assure Stalin that, after all, we had no intention of combating Communism, or any "ideology."

It is still possible to hope that the hesitant, vacillating and contradictory American policy, which has succeeded the war and postwar period of appeasement, will develop into a logical, world-wide, bold and statesmanlike use of American power and influence.

Perhaps the lesson learned in Europe through what the Chinese call the hardship of error will be applied in the Far East before China breaks or is partitioned.

When I left China it was already obvious that American policy had reached an impasse. General Marshall's return and his recall of our troops from China early in 1947 left a free field for the spread of Soviet-Communist power. Some Americans now see no other course than our concentration on a satellite Japan as the last line of defense of the democratic world in the Western Pacific. This would mean the adoption of a completely defeatist attitude—the final abandonment of the hopes for which so many young Americans gave their lives in the Pacific, in Burma and in China. For just as Japan is a natural fortress and springboard for war, so China is a potential citadel of peace. A peaceful democratic and strong China linked with America by bonds of friendship is our only insurance against another war in the Pacific.

It is not yet too late for us to adopt a policy which might bring such a China into being. We must cease making impossible demands on China. We must be realistic and unafraid. We must cease listening to the siren voices which assure us that the Chinese Communists are not real Communists. We must adopt a clear and uncompromising line in our Far Eastern policy without fear of Soviet Russia's reaction or the outraged protest of Communist sympathizers at home. We must be prepared if necessary to intervene in China to give her the strength to become a democracy regardless of the abuse of those who designate America as imperialistic. We must be prepared to challenge Russia in the interests of peace and freedom while she is stilll too weak to dare risk war with us.

In Europe we have seen the Iron Curtain crash down between us and millions of lost allies in Yugoslavia, Poland, Finland, Latvia, Lithuania, Estonia, Hungary, Rumania and Bulgaria. We must not repeat the same mistake in China—that of abandoning to the totalitarians the nations which with our help could become democracies.

In that speech to Congress on March 12, 1947, President Truman asked for $400,000,000 to assist Greece and Turkey. Yet while prepared to pour aid into Greece to enable a far from "perfect" government to combat the Communist menace we continued to insist that China should take the Communists into her government. As was said in Congress, "We can't go on embracing Communists in China and fighting them in Greece."

The Greek Government, in President Truman's words, "has been operating in an atmosphere of chaos and extremism. It has made mistakes. The extension of aid by this country does not mean that the United States condones everything that the Greek Government has done or will do."

The Chinese Government is certainly no worse than the Government of Greece. It also is operating in an atmosphere of chaos and extremism. It fought longer with less aid than any country which resisted the Axis. It can even claim to have made better use of its scanty allocation of about a dollar a head than the Greek Government which received more than fifty dollars per person and was yet incapable of preventing starvation.

Why do we consider, with indifference, the subjugation of China's enormous population by Moscow's agents aided by ruin and starvation, or positively encourage it, while we are awake to the necessity of saving Greece? There is no other explanation of the inconsistency of American policy East and West than the success of Communist sympathizers in selling us the idea that the Chinese Communists are "not real Communists."

You cannot, however, fool all the people all the time. The truth must eventually prevail in a free country. Our awakening to the realities of the world situation will not long be confined to Europe. If the patient Chinese can continue to be patient a little longer, Chiang Kai-shek's faith in America surely will be justified.

My life has spanned two worlds. I have experienced the grim reality of Stalin's Russia where the people are never free either from hunger or the shadow of terror, and hope only that tomorrow will not be even worse than today. *I know* that our Western democratic world, despite all its shortcomings, is infinitely preferable to Communist tyranny. We need to change with the changing times, but progress is not progress if it leads us back to tyranny.

I hope that self-delusion, or a sense of guilt, or the infiuence of so-called progressives who believe in the face of all the evidence that Soviet Russia has established a "new and better" form of democracy than ours, will not prevent the United States from using its power to establish an American world order in conjunction with its allies.

I do not believe that the world can be saved in our atomic age through agreement among the nations. Even if there were no Soviet

Union thirsting for world power, it would not be possible by universal agreement to reconcile the ambitions, hatreds, jealousies and the inequalities in resources of the nations. Co-operation and lasting peace are possible only under the aegis of a strong Power.

What is needed today is a new kind of world hegemony. Not the old exploitation of "colonial peoples" by white men boasting of their superior civilization. Not the imperialism of the Soviet Union with its hypocritical slogans and terror, its apparatus of brute force, its looting, concentration camps and chain gangs. But a Pax Americana as the only alternative to a Communist totalitarian world or the destruction of civilized life through an atomic war.

I am aware that Americans abroad, whether they come as allies or conquerors, have not displayed their best qualities. They may be unfitted for the exercise of world power. But what is the alternative? Badly as Americans may have behaved in Europe and Asia, they are not feared and hated like the Russians who strip bare the lands they occupy. The brutal treatment of Germany and the starvation for which the Morgenthau Plan and the Yalta and Potsdam Agreements are responsible, are already regretted by most Americans and by the British. By now it is obvious that the Communists hoped that if they could induce us to behave as cruelly as the Nazis, the conquered would be driven by despair to become Soviet Russia's allies.

It remains true that we cannot stand on principle to repel the Communist onslaught unless we cease to be guided by the Communist doctrine of ends justifying means and to disregard justice in dealing with weak allies and defeated enemies.

How many nations today would ask nothing better than to become American satellites? The Russian press may shout that the United States wants to dominate the whole world. If only this were true! Unfortunately for the world, there seems little chance of America using her few years of "atom monopoly" to order the world a little nearer to the heart's desire of all mankind. Americans want neither the glory nor the responsibility of using their power for good ends or bad ones. Whatever they call themselves, nine out of ten Americans are isolationists at heart. The American dream still beckons. They do not yet grasp that by entering two world wars they have so altered the balance of forces on this globe that it is no longer theirs to decide for or against full participation in world affairs.

When President Roosevelt insisted on unconditional surrender, he committed the American people to all the burdens and responsibility of empire. We could not destroy Germany and Japan as nations without also assuming responsibility, not only for the fate of the peoples of the defeated nations whom we disarmed, but also for the defense of all Europe and the Far East against the Russian colossus.

Some desire empire. Americans are having imperial power and responsibility thrust upon them. Willingly or unwillingly, they have got to accept the responsibilities of world power or submit to the dictation of others. They must rule or be ruled.

The next year or two will decide whether we are to wait for Russia to become strong enough to attack us from the west or from the east, or whether we shall use our power while there is yet time to prevent a third world war which we might lose.

We could still make of the United Nations a real force for peace instead of a debating hall for the apportionment of the spoils of victory. If we would place our stupendous power behind a United Nations composed only of such nations as are, or desire to become, democracies and are prepared to submit disputes to the arbitrament of an international tribunal, the walls of the totalitarian world would crumble.

This then is the lesson which is borne in on me by my flight around the world and my third visit to China:

If we appease the Russian aggressor as we once appeased the Japanese aggressor we shall go down to ruin. If we abandon China we lose all Asia. The Chinese Communists are better than the Russians, but they are on the other side—the side which inevitably finds itself pulled into the orbit of Stalin's totalitarian tyranny. It is too late for us to the redeem the Russian Revolution and set Communist Russia back on the path of liberal socialism. But it is not yet too late for us to deflect China's democratic national revolution back onto the course outlined by that noble democrat, Dr. Sun Yat-sen.

We have a last chance in China. We may go on having a last chance for quite a long time, but it will be a chance on which the odds rise day by day against us. Our own inertia and confusion at home, the strident offensive of Soviet power backed by mighty fifth columns everywhere in the world, the increasing demoralization of the abandoned and too sorely tried Chinese—all these put time on the hostile side. Our last chance to reform the Chinese Government, re-equip the Nationalist armies, support loyalist China against foreign-aided rebels seeking to bring the Chinese under Soviet hegemony, is at its best right now. History has many turnings and surprises. I will not pretend to say that this day or that marks the decisive turning point. But there seems to me no doubt that China's destiny and our own will be decided in the near future.

If we abandon China now, either because we put Europe first or because of our misunderstanding of the Far Eastern situation, the war will have been fought in vain. We shall condemn ourselves and our children to life in an America geared for war. There will be no other choice. External events—not domestic politics—will dictate our economic policies, our yearly military and naval budgets, our strategic diplomacy. But if we save China, and anchor her firmly in the world of free nations, we will secure an unbalance of power in our favor. We can then outwait Communist Russia. We can compete with the Kremlin by challenging the Soviets to a competition of known benefits, not an auction of raw military power.

The chance of peace is now, if only we will look at things as they are, and not as we should like them to be. The choice before us is one of taking a very small risk of war now to obviate the certainty of war in the future; or waiting until the rulers of Russia shall have extinguished liberty over so great a part of the earth that they will have far better hopes of defeating us than Hitler ever had.

Good things could come out of the peace which it is still within our power to establish in Asia as in Europe: prosperity, strong but moderate armament, a chance for federalism, the hope of a settled world. But we will not keep this chance long—not with the same odds. We can win now with courage, generosity, intelligence and understanding. We may be able to win at much greater cost later on. But the day may come when invasion, civil war, hypocrisy and terror will extinguish all our freedoms and we will join forsaken China in the endless night of Communist "liberation."

INDEX

INDEX

Abyssinia, 239
Academy of Sciences, 192
Acheson, Dean, 247, 248
Action Française, 187
Air Transport Command, 15, 17, 31, 84
Alaska, 22
Alien Property Custodian, 55
Alla, 89, 90
Altai, 261
American-Chinese Agricultural Mission, 313
American Committee for Non-Participation in Japanese Aggression, 16, 98
American National Foreign Trade Council, 106
Amur River, 354-355
Anglo-Japanese Alliance, 376
Anshan, 229, 231, 238
Anti-American demonstrations, 301
Anti-Comintern Alliance, 189, 376
Arabia, 17
Army and Navy Bulletin, 251, 369
Army Medical Service, 41
"Asiatic system" of rent payments, 311
Associated Press, 220, 222, 223, 279
Assyria, 18
Ataturk, Kemal, 172
ATC, *see* Air Transport Command
Atkinson, Brooks, 201
Atom bomb, 23
Australia, 91
Austria, 259
Aying Yung, 184
Azores, 17

Balkans, 384
Baltimore Sun, 220, 223, 228
Barbey, Vice-Admiral Daniel E., 67
Bataan, 380
Battle for Asia, Snow, 200
Battle of Taier-chwang, 332
Beard, Charles A., 307
Belden, Jack, 212
Bethlehem, Jerusalem, 17
"Big Three," 68, 383
Big Three, The, Dallin, 365
Bodine, Cornelius, 260
Bohlen, Maj. ———, 36
Bolshevik Party, 159, 183
Border Governments, 128, 158
Border region, 151, 158, 167, 297
Borodin, 182
Bowerman, Miss ———, 90-91
Boxer Rebellion, 181, 331, 359
Bretton Woods, 323
British-American Tobacco Co., 224
British Empire, 18, 22, 23, 27
Broadway Mansions, 100, 113
Brooks, Sgt. ———, 144
Browder, Earl, 197
Brown, Constantine, 62
Brussels Conference, 53
Bucharin, 183
Buck, Dr. J. Lossing, 47, 314, 315, 316-318, 320
Bulgaria, 172, 200, 259, 390
Burma, 17, 31, 32, 36, 113, 202, 209, 260, 265-266, 388, 390
Burma Road, 209-210
Butterfield and Swire, 103
Byrnes, James, 239-240
Byzantium, Turkey, 157, 328

Cairo, Egypt, 365
Calcutta, India, 17, 31
California University, 313
Canton, 33, 177, 180, 183, 210, 287, 290

Capone, Al, 307
Caraway, Gen. Paul, 270-272
Carlson, Col. Evans, 202, 212
Caroline Islands, 368
Carter, E. C., 193, 216
Casablanca, Morocco, 16, 17
Cathay Hotel (Shanghai), 85
C. C. clique, 349
Central Bank of China, 49, 57
Central Executive Committee, 42, 197, 243, 247, 306
Chahar, Iran, 77, 150
Challenge of Red China, The, Stein, 152
Chamberlain, Neville, 53, 196
Chamber of Commerce (Shanghai), 178
Chang, Dr. Carson, 57, 307
Chang, P. H., 345
Chang Chia-ngau, 307
Chang Chun, 107, 124, 125-126, 243, 292
Changchun, 75, 221, 222-224, 234, 244
Chang Hsin-fu, 224, 238
Chang Hsueh-liang, 121-122, 189, 295
Chang Kuo-san, 154
Chang Lan, 307
Changsha, 40, 202
Chang Shen-fu, 162
Chang Tso-lin, 179
Chang Wen-ching, 121-122
Chao, Gen. ———, 233
Chao, Mrs. ———, 153
Charles I, 141
Chefoo, 245, 263
Chen, Eugene, 187
Chen, Jack, 187
Chen, Mary, 40, 121
Chen Cheng, Gen. ———, 262, 291
Chen Chih-mai, 60, 255, 286
Cheng Chen-yu, 321-322
Chengtehfu, 77
Chengtu, 316
Chen Li-fu, 124, 257, 349-352
Chen Ming-shu, Gen. ———, 41-43
Chennault, Gen. Claire, 207, 209, 213; and Stilwell, 211
Chen Tu-hsiu, 182-183
Chen Yi, 136
Chialing River, 33
Chiang Kai-shek, Generalissimo, 24, 40, 41, 42-43, *et passim;* and Chinese Communists, 70-72, 77-78, 80-81, 117, 124, 134, 135, 136, 195, 249-251, 261-262, 361-362; and Kuomintang, 177-183, 243, 282-284, 287-309; and Lend-Lease, 207; and Mao Tse-tung, 215; and Marshall, 75, 246, 257; and Stilwell, 209-214; and Sun Yat-sen, 338-341; and Wedemeyer, 269, 271-272, 278, 280; and the United States, 248, 255-256
Chiang Kai-shek, Mme., 39, 46, 130-132, 144, 211, 280, 290, 299, 302
Chiang Lung-chi, 141
Chiang Mo-lin, 345-347
Chicago Daily News, 65, 114, 220
Chicago Sun, 223
Chicago University, 312
Chien Chun-su, 158-159, 160, 162, 164-165
Chihfeng, 76-77
China, A. Kaiming Chiu, 312
China-American Chamber of Commerce and Industry, 106
China-American Council of Commerce and Industry, 208
China at War, Utley, 131, 194, 280
China Campaign Committee, 98
China Industry Company, 49
China's Destiny, Chiang Kai-shek, 308, 309*n.*, 338, 339
China Textile Industries, Inc., 55
China Weekly Review, 195
Chinchow, 220, 222, 232, 233, 234
Chinese Air Force, 233
Chinese Central News Agency, 128, 154, 261, 262, 284, 298*n.*
Chinese Combat Command, 271
Chinese Customs Service, 103

Chinese Embassy (Washington, D. C.), 60
Chinese Intelligence reports, 370
Chinese Ministry of Foreign Affairs, 262
Chinese National Aviation Corporation, 84, 100
Chinese Secret Service, 266
Chinese: Their History and Culture, The, Latourette, 324, 339*n.*
Chinese Training Center, 271
Chinese Universal Trading Co., 106
Ching Kiang, 297
Chingwangtao, 67
Chiu, Dr. A. Kaiming, 312
Chiulungpo Airport, 32
Chou En-lai, Gen., 77, 78-79, 80, 81-82, 116-123, 125, 206, *et passim*
Christian Century, 201
Christian Science Monitor, 129
Chu, Chi-chien, 121, 295-296, 320
Chu, Dr. H. T., 190
Chungking, 17, 28, 30, 31, 33, 37, 40, *et passim;* correspondents in, 34-36, 63, 113-115, 129-133, 226, 239; industries, 49-51, 56; student demonstrations, 65-66, 167-168, 240
Churchill, Winston, 73, 105*n.*, 196, 307, 348, 374
Chu Teh, 76, 160-161, 165-167, 205, 218
Ciano, Count ———, 329
Cleveland Council on World Affairs, 366
"Cliveden Set," 349
CNAC, *see* Chinese National Aviation Corp.
CNRRA, 108
Collins, John W., 216
Comintern, 25, 26-27, 79, 169, 173, 178, 180, 182, 183-184, *et passim*
Comintern Executive Committee, 188, 189
Commercial Press, 125
Commercial Treaty, 248
Communist, bureaucracy, 18; dictatorship, 18, 19; ideology, 18, 123, 255, 334; Army, 121, 145, 154, 160
Communist Academy, 179, 192. *See also* Academy of Sciences
Communist International, 171, 173
Communist International, 193
Communist News Service, 167
Communist Party (British), 186
Communist Party (Chinese), 62, 78, 79, 117, 119, 122, 123, *et passim*
Communist Party (French), 187
Communist Party (German), 79, 169, 187
Communist Party (Russian), 159, 160, 161, 162, 183, 193, 282, 304
Communist Party (U. S.), 168
Communist Party Headquarters, 115, 116, 117, 139
"Complex Problem of China," Linebarger, 147
Comrade L, 26
Confucianism, 134, 325, 335-338, 341, 343
Conger, Edwin, 353
Correspondents, *see* Chungking, Manchuria, Mukden
Coué, Dr. Emile, 61, 275
Crimea, 174
Crimean War, 354-355
Cromwell, Oliver, 136
Crow, Carl, 315
Cushing, Richard, 222, 225
Czechoslovakia, 105

Daily Worker, 72, 167
Dairen, 63, 64, 65, 67, 89, *et passim*
Dallin, David, 365*n.*
Davies, Joe, 124, 179, 307
Davies, John, 212
Davis, Spencer, 220, 223
Dead Sea, 17
Demobilization, 17, 20-21, 259
Democratic League, 43, 50, 56-58, 77, 124-125, 126, 129, *et passim*

Dimitrov, 187-188, 192, 193
Domesday Book, 311
Doolittle, Gen. James, 114
Dragon Throne, 121
Drake, Sir Francis, 18
Dream We Lost, The, Utley, 312
"Dr. Haber," 26-27
Duma, 181
Durdin, Tillman, 65, 113-114, 116-117, 129, 153, 154, 162, *et passim*
Dutch East Indies, 97, 369, 388

Ebner, Charlotte, 114, 220
Economic Facts, 316
Edward I, 135
Egypt, 17
Eighth Route Army, 144, 190, 194, 231-232, 244, 245
Eldridge, Fred, 212
Eleventh Chinese War Zone, 370
Emancipation Daily, 155, 167
England, *see* Great Britain
Eniwetok, 382
Estonia, 390
Executive Yuan, 36, 50, 54, 55, 63, 118, 243, 258, 322, 345
Export-Import Bank, 95

Far Eastern Survey, 204
Far East in World Politics, The, Hudson, 355
Farmers Bank, 318, 323
Feng Yu-hsiang, 182, 243
Field, Marshall, 307
Filan, Frank, 220
Finland, 172, 390
First Opium War, 355
Five-Year Plans, 183
Forbidden City, 327, 328, 331, 332
Ford, Henry, 307
Formosa, 136, 324
Fourteenth Air Force, 209
France, 102, 141, 174, 178, 184, 187, 192, 197, 208, 255, *et passim*
Franco, Gen. Francisco, 172, 187, 279
French Concession, 101
Fujita, 371
Fukien, 41
Fushan, 231
Fushun collieries, 224
Fu Ssu-nien 53, 125, 137, 299

Gauss, Clarence E., 95, 98, 214, 267
George, Henry, 321
Germany, 18, 19, 21, 22, 32, 66, 86, 91, 93, 94, 104, 172, *et passim*
Gestapo, 225
G-5, 99, 274
Ghengis Khan, 328
Gloria ———, 90
"God Save the King," 135
Goethe, 157
Golden Horde, 329
Gould, Randall, 26, 110-111, 226-227
Government in Republican China, Linebarger, 335
"Grandmother of the Guerrillas," 153
Great Britain, 16, 18, 19, 20, 32, 68, *et passim;* and the United States, 22-23; and China, 178, 356-359; and Japan, 27-28. *See also* Hong Kong, Shanghai, England
Great Wall of China, 233, 278, 328, 329, 331
Greece, 105, 260-261, 368, 390-391
Greek Government, 391
Grew, Joseph, 204, 365
Grosse, Lev, 86, 87

Haber, "Ypsilon," 26
Hahn, Emily, 53, 205, 206
Haichow, 163
Handy, Tom, 273
Hankow, 31, 33, 34, 35, 41, 113, 125, 132, 134, 150, *et passim*
Hankow-Canton Railway, 370
"Hankow Last Ditchers," 34, 113
Hanyang, 181
Harbin, 88, 223, 224, 230, 238, 248, 297

Harriman, Averill, 241
Harvard Law School, 60
Hawaii, H. I., 17
Hay, John, 353, 358, 360
Henry VII, 135
Hersey, John, 380
Hilton, James, 139
Hiroshima, Japan, 23
History of Chinese Political Thought, Liang Ch'i-ch'ao, 337
Hitler, Adolf, 32, 94, 105, 136, 169, 172, 186, 187, 196, *et passim*
Hodge, Gen. John R., 261
Hogan, Col. Pendleton, 274
Holland, 192
Hollywood, 144
Holy Land, 17
Honan, 37, 182, 185, 324
Hongkew, 93, 94
Hong Kong, 65, 104, 108, 205, 356
Honkeiko, 231
Honolulu, H. I., 382
Hopei, 297, 298
"Hostel Number 2," 277
Ho Ying-chin, 291
Hu, T. A., 49-50
Huang, Gen. J. L., 39, 137
Hudson, G. F., 355*n.*
Hull, Cordell, 307, 365
Hulutao, 67, 235
Hump, the, 31, 207, 210
Hungary, 172, 200, 259, 390
Hupeh, 29, 36, 182, 324
Hurley, Gen. Patrick, 29-30, 70-72, 75, 97, 135, 213, 214, 215, 235, 279
Hu Shih, Dr., 310, 331
Hutchison, Claude B., 313

India, 31, 38, 97, 113, 388
Indo-China, 388
Inflation, 44-48, 54-56, 107-108, 144-145, 323, 351
Inner Mongolia, 29
Institute of Pacific Relations, 192-193, 204, 205, 216, 316
International Monetary Fund, 322
International News Service, 114, 220, 223
International Peace Hospital, 148-149
International Settlement, 101
"Intourist" Hotel, 220, 223. *See also* Yamato Hotel
I. P. R., *see* Institute of Pacific Relations
Iron Curtain, 244, 257, 381, 390
Isaacs, Harold, 176*n.*, 179*n.*
Isolationism, 19
Italy, 22, 239, 377
Iwo-Jima, 382

Jacoby, Annalee, 181
Jacquerie, 178
Japan, 15, 21, 22-24, 25, 28, *et passim;* and China, 27, 30, 33, 62-63, 94-97, 181, 196-197, 201, 257, 283-284, 309, 363-364; and the United States, 98*n.*, 359-360, 366. *See also* Russia, Sino-Japanese War, Russo-Japanese War
Japan's Feet of Clay, Utley, 41, 53, 116, 148
Jehol, 29, 76-77
Joffe, A., 176
Johnson, Samuel, 383
Johnson Island, 382
Judd, Walter, 21, 200-201, 209

Kaiser, Henry, 307
Kalgan, 249, 262, 297-298, 305
Kang Hsin-chi, 294
Kansu, 322
Karachi, 17
Karlov, Gen. ———, 223
Kellis, Col. ———, 232-233
Kiang Kang-hu, 294
Kiangsi, 25, 163, 185, 297, 322, 324
"Kitaiski gorod," 328
Konoye, Prince ———, 284
Koo, Wellington, 366
Koo, Dr. Y. C., 313, 322-323, 333, 345

Korea, 29, 174, 225, 258, 260, 261, 278, 355
Kovtoun-Stankevitch, Andre, 231, 239
Kowloon, 65
Kremlin, 172-173, 192, 218, 245, 328, 354, 381, 394
Kublai Khan, 328
Kullgren, John, 102
Kung, H. H., 43, 46, 51-53, 57, 59, 292, 306
Kunming, 17, 20, 31, 36, 56, 111, 154, 207
Kuo Mo-Jo, 125, 307
Kuomintang, 24-25, 41-42, 43, 48-49, 51, 57, 59, 66, 104, *et passim;* and Chinese Communists, 68-69, 77-79, 80-82, 118-120, 122-129, 189, 193-195, 217-218, 242; with Communists, 177-178, 283-284, 288-289, 298-299; and land, 321-322; and Russia, 178-184, 361-362
Kurile Islands, 22, 241, 355
Kwangsi, 322, 324, 332
Kwantung, 322, 356, 368
Kwantung Army, 206, 370, 371
Kweichow, 37, 91
Kweilin, 207, 265, 271
Kweiyang, 265

Labor Party (British), 186, 352
La China de Chiang Kai Chek, Nolde, 357
La Guardia, Fiorello, 325
Lancashire, England, 310
Land, 38, 188-189, 310-326; and population, 311-315; division, 162-163, 185
Land Administration, 319, 321
Land and Labor in China, Tawney, 334*n.*
Land Utilization in China, Buck, 315
Lansing, Robert, 359
Laohoko, 324
Lao-shê, 153-154, 331
Latourette, Kenneth Scott, 334, 339
Lattimore, Owen, 193, 291
Latvia, 390
Leacock, Stephen, 389
League of Nations, 187, 359-360
Legislative Yuan, 53, 55
Lend-Lease, 19, 32, 41, 104-105, 126, 195, 207, 213, 221, *et passim*
Lenin, Nikolay, 64, 76, 127, 159, 160, 164, 166, 173, 174, *et passim*
Leningrad, 327
Liang Ch'i-ch'ao, 337*n.*
Liaotung Peninsula, 230
Lieberman, ———, 220
Life, 150
Li Li-san, 183, 184, 186, 218
Lim, Dr. Robert, 38-41, 148
Linchow-Tushan line, 265
Lindsey, Michael, 80
Linebarger, Judge ———, 335
Linebarger, Dr. Paul, 147-148, 294, 335-336
Ling Ching, 145, 150-151, 152
Linton, Col. ———, 35, 274
Lin Tsu-han, 315
Lin Yutang, 198, 203, 307
Lippmann, Walter, 72-73, 307
Lithuania, 390
Li Tsung-jen, 209, 237-239, 332-333
Litvinoff, Ambassador Maksim, 374
Liu, Mrs. Herman, 307
Logan, Col. ———, 272
Lo Lung-chi, Dr., 56, 129, 307
Lominadze, Besso, 183
London, 20
London Daily Express, 223
London News Chronicle, 33
London School of Economics, 27, 371
London Times, 353-354
Long March, 185
Loo Chi-teh, Dr., 39, 40
Lost Horizon, Hilton, 139
Louis XIV, 42
Lung, Tiger, 57-58, 291
Lu Tso-fu, 307

MacAfee, Capt. ———, 272
Macao, 65
MacArthur, Gen. Douglas, 363, 380
McClure, Gen. Robert, 279
McCormick, Anne O'Hara, 94
McGaffin, ———, 220
McLaughlin, Rev. Wilfred, 163
MacNair, Prof. ———, 312
Magna Carta, 307
Malaya, 32, 388
Malinovsky, Rodion, 222, 223, 236
Manchester Guardian, 27
Manchu dynasty, 135, 307, 354
Manchukuo, 76, 80, 196, 248, 379, 396
Manchuria, 21, 23, 29, 32, 63, 64, 67, *et passim;* and the United States, 221, 235, 237, 246, 278; Chinese Communists in, 76-77, 234, 245-247, 260-264; correspondents in, 130, 220-231, 238; Red Army in, 28, 34, 62, 67-68, 85, 163-164, 201, 219-241, 242, 244-259, 376
Mannheim, Karl, 334*n.*
Mao Tse-tung, 78-79, 80, 137, 145, 147, 157, 159, 161, *et passim*
Marshall, Gen. George C., 24, 47, 63, *et passim;* 123, 126; and Chinese Communists, 74-77, 169, 217-218, 244-249, 253-255; as Secretary of State, 259-260; failure in China, 251-255
Marshall, Humphrey, 358
Marshall Islands, 368, 382
Martin, Pepper, 220
Marx, Karl, 298, 311, 337
Marxist Communists, 343, 348
Ma Yin-ch'u, Prof., 48-49
Menzies, 232-233
Merwin, Rev. Wallace C., 201
Miao Chia-min, 56
Middleton, Brig. Gen. ———, 95
Mikhailovitch, 205, 282
Miner, Charles E., 111
Mission to Moscow, Davies, 307
Molotov, Viachislav Mikhailovich, 61, 68*n.*, 172, 254, 259
Mongol Empire, 328
Mongolia, 333
Moorad, George, 241
Moosa, Spencer, 35, 129
Morgenthau Plan, 392
Moscow, 24, 25, 26, 30, 43, 68, 70, 74, 79-80, 81, 85, 123, *et passim*
Mo Teh-hui, 125
Mountbatten, Lord Louis, 210, 273
Mowrer, Edgar Ansel, 217
Mukden, 75, 89, 165, 226-227, 232, 238, 242, 244, 245, 261; correspondents in, 220-221; destruction by Russians, 221-224, 226-232
Municipal Building (Shanghai), 302
Mussolini, Benito, 136, 159, 196
Mutual Broadcasting Company, 220
MVD (secret police of Russia), 64. *See also* NKVD

Nanking, 47, 85, 140, 182, 195, 215, 248, 249, 258, 289, 294, 324, 362
Nanking College of Agriculture and Forestry, 318
Nanking Government, 24, 182
Nanking Road, 25
Nanking University, 316
National Agricultural Research Bureau, 317
National Assembly, 58, 122, 126, 143, 250, 254
National Government, 28, 29, 34, 42, 45, 47, 48, 49, 56, 64, 65, *et passim*
Nationalist Armies, 33, 40, 63, 67, 76, 80, 119, 143, 146, 167, *et passim*
National Revolutionary Party, 24
National Salvation Association, 124, 125
National Socialism, 174
Nelson, Donald, 49, 208*n.*
Nemoto, Gen. ———, 370-373
N. E. P., *see* New Economic Policy
Neumann, Heinz, 183

New Bridge, 40
New Deal, 325
New Democracy, The, Mao Tse-tung, 197, 199
New Economic Policy, 159
New First Army, 260
New Fourth Army, 150
New Life Movement, 39, 131, 280
New Yorker, 205
New York Herald Tribune, 72, 77, 263, 303
New York Post, 217, 220, 223
New York Shanghai Tiffin Club, 286
New York Times, 65, 94, 113, 162, 220, 223, 242, 248, *et passim*
Nile Valley, 16
Nine-Power Treaty, 53, 360
1941 Neutrality Pact, 374
Nineteenth Route Army, 41, 96
Ninth Route Army, 245
NKVD, 89, 230
Nolde, Andre, 357*n.*
Nomonhan, 377
North Africa, 17
North China Daily News, 110-111
Northwestern University, 154
Noulens, 25-26
Novosty Dnya, 86

Oberlin College, 52
Odlum, Gen. Victor, 28, 79, 267, 270, 352
Okamura, General, 197
Olmsted, Gen. George, 99-100
Open Door Policy, 22, 353, 357-359, 360, 361
Operations Division of the U. S. War Dept., 268
Opper, Fritz, 220, 221, 226, 228
Oriental Economist, The, 30
Osaka, 228
O.S.S. (U. S.), 40, 232
Outer Mongolia, 64, 261
Overseas Press Club, 239
O. W. I., *see* U. S. I. S.
Oxford University, 371

Pacific Affairs, 204
Pacific Ocean Cabinet, *see* Institute of World Economy and Politics
Packard, Reynolds, 220, 226
Pai Chung-hsi, Gen., 262, 332
Palace Hotel (Shanghai), 25
Palestine, 97
Pan-American Airways, 100
Paris Conferences, 251
Pattern for World Revolution, Haber, 26
Pauley, Edwin S., 225
P.C.C., *see* Political Consultative Council
Pearl Harbor, 16, 22, 98*n.*, 100, 204, 301, 365, 366, 369, 373, 374, 375
Peck, George, 331
Peiping, 76, 78, 113, 115, 121*n.*, 139, 215, 220, 224, 237, *et passim;* U. S. Marines in, 276-277
Peiping Government, 283, 287
Peiping-Hankow-Canton Railroad, 206, 262
Peiping University, 345
Peking, 121*n.*, 169, 182, 295. *See also* Peiping
Peking University, 125
People on Our Side, Snow, 205
People's Political Council, 55, 306, 320
Pepper, Claude, 307
Peron, Gen. ———, 81, 172, 216
Persia, 17, 18, 29
Peter, King, 205
Philadelphia Record, 72
Poland, 72-73, 105, 170, 171, 172, 200, 207, 218, 255, 360, 363, 366, 390
Political Consultative Council, 50, 58*n.*, 111, 113, 115, 120-121, *et passim*
Political Doctrines of Sun Yat-sen, The, Linebarger, 335, 336*n.*
Political Science clique, 124, 243

Port Arthur, 63, 64, 65, 67, 224, 229, 263, 354, 356-357, 366
Portsmouth, England, 359
Potsdam, Germany, 282, 392
Potter, Phil, 220, 228
Pravda, 97
Present Strategy and Tactics of the Chinese Communists, 190, 191
Presidium of the Politbureau, 197
Press Censor, 369
Press Hostel, 34, 35, 36, 40, 85, 113, 114, 115, 129, 150
Problems of Leninism, Stalin, 19*n.*
Public Salvation Grain Levy, 145
Puy, Maj. ———, 40-41

Quebec, Canada, 213
Quebec Conference, 105*n.*

Race Course (Shanghai), 302
Rand, Christopher, 263, 303
Rangoon, Burma, 210
Reader's Digest, 111
Realpolitik, 73
Red Army, 18, 25, 63, 76, 77, 111, 119, 140, 143, 152, 154, *et passim*
Red Cross, 16, 91, 276
Red Cross (British), 90, 91
Red Cross Club, 36
Red Cross Medical Commission, 38-39
Red Star Over China, Snow, 185
Reinbold, Rev. ———, 202
Ribbentrop, von, Joachim, 172
Richelieu, Cardinal, 135
Rickshaw Boy, Lao-shê, 153, 331
Rigg, Maj. Robert B., 216
Rivière, Claude, 111-112
Robertson, Walter, 78
Rockey, Gen. ———, 277, 331
Rome, Italy, 18, 157
Rook, Gen. Lowell W., 109*n.*
Roosevelt, Eleanor, 307
Roosevelt, Franklin D., 23, 66, 69, 73, 164-165, 166, 188, *et passim*
Roosevelt, Theodore, 23, 353, 359
Roots, Dr. Logan, 31, 232
Rumania, 170, 172, 200, 259, 390
Rural Reconstructive Society, 124
Russell, Bertrand, 327
Russia, 16-19, 27, 32, 38, 44, *et passim;* and China, 21-24, 27-28, 32, 34, 61-68, 71-74, 79-83, 85-89, 309, 312, 333-334, 354-356, 373-381; and Japan, 23, 196, 201, 361-362, 379; and Kuomintang, 176-181; and the United States, 23-24, 239-241, 251, 353, 367-368, 383-386, 389-394
Russian Foreign Office, 68
Russian ideologies, 333, 342
Russian Revolution, 191
Russo-Chinese Treaty, 356
Russo-German War, 371
Russo-Japanese Pact, 196-197, 204, 206-207, 208, 290, 371, 381
Russo-Japanese War, 164, 359, 370
Russophile, 348, 349, 375, 380

Sakhalin, 29, 355, 369
Salisbury, Lawrence, 205
Salween, 202, 209
San Min Chu I, 42, 104, 127, 137, 199, 200, 287, 352
Scott, Col. Don, 37, 274
Semi-Mongol Muscovites, 331
Seventh Congress (Comintern), 187, 193
Shanghai, 17, 24-25, 27, 29, 32, 36, 41, 47, 50, 52, *et passim;* Americans and British in, 99-101, 110-111, 275-276; Japanese in, 91-96; Russians in, 87-88; government, 101-112
Shanghai Country Hospital, 85
Shanghai Evening Post, 26, 85, 110-111, 116, 205, 226, 227
Shansi, 52, 194, 322, 372
Shantung, 360, 372
Shantung War, 261
Shao Li-tze, 63, 124, 179, 243, 307
Shensi, 322

Shensi-Kansu-Ningsia Border Region, 141, 146-147, 151, 153, 167, 185
Shigenori Togo, 374
Shihchiachuan, 297
Shuping Kuai, Maj., 371
Siam, 81, 189
Siberia, 22, 24, 89, 227, 228, 236, 258
Sinkiang, 29, 333
Sino-Japanese War, 32, 34, 45, 103, 194-195, 197, 202-204, 241, 261, 284, 289, 354
Sino-Soviet Treaty, 32, 34, 62, 63-64, 65-68, 77, 163-165, *et passim*
Sino-Soviet War, 368
Sixth Army (China), 270
Smedley, Agnes, 39, 150, 201, 212
Snow, Edgar, 35, 142, 171, 185, 195-196, 200-201, 205, 315
Social Democratic Party, 57, 124
Socialism, 174
Sokolsky, George, 62
Soldiers, American, 16-17, 21, 33, 36, 41, 151, 152, 274-275; Chinese, 37-41, 270-272. *See also* Demobilization, Red Army
Soong, T. V., 43, 46, 49, 50-57, 59, 66, 121, 136, 236, 243, 292, 325
Soong-Molotov Treaty, 30
S. O. S., 271
Soviet Foreign Office, 173
Soviet Government, 66, 68, 69, 70, 74, 81, 86, *et passim*
Spain, 279
Stalin, Joseph, 18-19, 23, 24, 25, 29, 30, 32, 61, 64-66, *et passim;* and Chiang Kai-shek, 179-180, 288, 361-362; and Hitler, 186-187, 207
Stalingrad, Russia, 204
Stalin-Hitler Pact, 195, 204, 208, 290, 377, 381
Starr, Cornelius V., 85, 100
Stars and Stripes, 35, 89, 225, 227, 229, 275, 276
Steele, Arch, 77, 113-114, 129, 241, 331
Stein, Gunther, 152, 201
Steinbeck, John, 307
Stewart, Col. ———, 233
Stilwell, Gen. Joseph, 29, 75, 126, 151, 252, 265, *et passim;* and Chiang Kai-shek, 209-214, 291; and Chinese soldiers, 212, 265; and Lend-Lease, 207-208; recall, 208-209, 213-214
Stimson, Henry L., 204
Stratemeyer, Gen. G. E., 272-273, 274
Strong, Anna Louise, 150
Stuart, Findlay, 103
Stuart, Leighton, 249
Süchow, 163
Suez, 102
Summer Palace (Peking), 330, 331
Sun Fo, 49, 51, 59, 63, 66, 79, 124, *et passim*
Sung Chu-hsieng, 224
Sun Lien-chung, Gen., 370
Sun Yat-sen, 66, 81, 127, 133, 135, 137, 166, 176, *et passim;* and Communists, 176; and Russia, 360-361; teachings, 335-343
Sun Yat-sen, Mme., 26, 124, 131, 258, 274-275
Sun Yat-sen Institute, 317
Supreme Defense Council, 322
Szechwan, 32, 46, 50, 51, 56, 59, 113, 125, 318, 322, 330, 325
Szepingkai, 262

Taierchwang, 202
Tai Li, 40, 266
Taiping Rebellion, 181, 354
Ta Kung Pao, 303
Tang En-po, Gen., 37, 94-95
Tartars, 174, 328-329
Tartary architecture, 328
Tawney, E. H., 334*n.*
Taylor, George, 211
Teheran, Persia, 375
Temple of Heaven, 327
They Were Expendable, White, 382
Third Party, 124

Three Principles of the People, 122, 137, 166, 177, 193, 194, 287, 338, 350. *See also San Min Chu I*
Thunder Out of China, White and Jacoby, 181, 192, 216
Tientsin, 88, 112, 174, 222, 232, 234, 277
Tientsin-Shanhaikwan Railroad, 245
Time, 115, 298*n.*, 352
Tito, Marshal, 109, 168, 171, 205, 305
Tokyo, 114, 228, 365, 369, 376
Tolum, 77
Tonkin, 356
Torossian, Vincent, 88
Tragedy of the Chinese Revolution, Isaacs, 176, 179
Trans-Siberian Railway, 357
Treaty Ports, 355
Trieste, Italy, 205
Tripartite Alliance, 364, 377-378
Tripoli, 16
Trotsky, Leon, 178, 183, 361
Troyanovsky, Alexander, 374
Truman, Pres. Harry, 30, 74, 75, 220, 240, 248, 251, 384, 389, 390-391
Tsiang, Dr. T. F., 323, 325-326
Tsingtao, 276, 356, 382
Tu Li-ming, 130
Tungting Lake, 202
Turkey, 390
Twenty-one Demands, 359
Twin Stars over China, Carlson, 202

Ukraine, 105, 109, 261
United Nations, 278, 360, 366, 393
United Nations World, 307
United Press, 220, 223, 261
United States, 15, 19, 20, 21, 27, 61, 66, 67, 68, 100, 126, *et passim*
U. S. Army, 20, 86, 151, 267, 276, 277, 281, 382
U. S. Army Air Force, 91, 207, 215, 272
U. S. Army Hdqtrs., 99, 207, 270, 274
U. S. Army Liaison, *see* O.S.S.
U. S. Army Post (Yenan), 159
U. S. Far Eastern policy, 21-24, 28-30, 73-75, 251-257, 357-360, 365-368, 390-391. *See also* Open Door Policy
U. S. Information Service, 72, 275, 331
U.S.I.S., *see* U. S. Information Service
U. S. Marine Corps, 20, 202, 215, 245, 251, 276, 277, 331
U. S. Military Intelligence, 102
U. S. Navy, 20, 86, 215, 234, 239, 245, 267, 276, 382
U.S.S.R., *see* Russia
"Unity of the Workers of the World," 174
University Labor Federation, 371
UNRRA, 19, 31, 101, 105, 108-110, 232, 260, 282, 324-325
Ussuri River, 355

Vaughn, Miles, 258
V-E Day, 380, 383
Versailles Peace Conference, 359
Vigil of a Nation, The, Lin Yutang, 203
Vincent, John Carter, 252, 256-257
"Vinegar Joe," *see* Stilwell, Gen. Joseph
V-J Day, 21, 28, 30, 46, 47, 113, 197, 202, 209, 215, 257, *et passim*
Vladivostok, Russia, 225, 229, 230
Vocational Education Association, 124

Walker, Gordon, 129
Walker, John, 115
Wallace, Henry, 124, 172, 258, 307, 389
Wang, Dr. ———, 40
Wang Ching-wei, 182, 257, 290, 360
Wang Ming, 193-194
Wang Shih-chieh, 126, 129, 136, 243, 307
Wang Shih-wei, 153
Wang Yao-wu, Gen., 40, 261
Wang Yen-pei, 157
Wang Yun-wu, 125, 307
"War Communism" in Russia, 38

Washington, D. C., 31, 151, 213, 246, 263, 264, 360
Watanabe, Maj. Gen. ———, 370-373
Wedemeyer, Gen. Albert C., 29, 67, 75, 137, 138, 201, *et passim;* and Chinese army, 269-274; and Communists, 235, 269, 279-281; replaces Stilwell, 214, 265-267
Weihaiwei, 357
Weimar Republic, 169
Weller, George, 65, 114, 116, 129, 142, 168, 232, 244-245
Welles, Sumner, 176
West China Development Co., 51
Western Powers, 24, 32, 64, 65, 93, 96, 103, 134, 166, 176, *et passim*
West Point Military Academy, 272
Whampoa, 291
White, Theodore, 35, 181, 201, 202
White, William L., 382
White Russia, 105, 109, 261
White Russians, 87-88, 229
Whittlesea Hall, 149
Why the United States Fights against Hitlerite Germany, Troyanovsky, 374
William the Conqueror, 311
Willkie, Wendell, 196, 306
Wilson, Capt. ———, 36
Wilson, Sgt. Dick, 89, 229, 230-232
Wilson, Woodrow, 359-360
Wolfe, Bertram D., 334
Wong Wen-hao, 235-237, 307, 312
World War I, 64, 368, 376
World War II, 16, 177, 198, 259, 367, 368, 369, 374, 375, 376, 384
Worton, Gen. ———, 277, 331
WPA, 325
Wrath in Burma, Eldridge, 212
Wu, Miss ———, 90
Wu, K. C., 130, 142, 240
Wu, S. Y., 51, 79
Wuchang, 181
Wuhan cities, 32, 33, 39, 180, 181-182, 202, 332. *See also* Hankow
Wuhan Government, 46
Wu Men-yu, 152
Wu Te-chen, Gen., 69-70

Xenophobes, 386

Yale Review, 147
Yale University Press, 365
Yalta, 23, 64, 72-73, 164-165, 226, 235, 239, 241, 242, 278, *et passim*
Yalu River, 229
Yamato Hotel, 220, 226
Yangtze River, 33, 111, 209, 278
Yangtze Valley, 215, 317, 357
Yeaton, Col. Ivan, 149, 151
Yeaton, Mrs. Ivan, 151
Yellow River, 325
Yen, the educator, 307
Yenan, 78, 81, 139-141, 152-158, 160, 161, 162-164, *et passim;* army post, 149-151, 205, 297; children in, 143-144; trade, 144-146
Yenan Emancipation News, 162
Yenan Guest House, 144
Yenan News Agency, 168
Yenan Observer Group, 140
Yenan University, 141, 142-143
Yenching University, 52
Yen Hsi-shan, 146
Yen River, 152
Yingkow, 63, 67, 235
Yin Kou, 231
Young, Robert, 307
Youth Party, 77, 124
Yuan Shih-Kai, 121
Yugoslavia, 105, 109, 170, 172, 200, 205, 390
Yung Hsiung-Kuan, 161, 167
Yunnan, 20, 31, 56, 58, 291, 356
Yu Ta-wei, 122, 296, 307

Zionism, 172

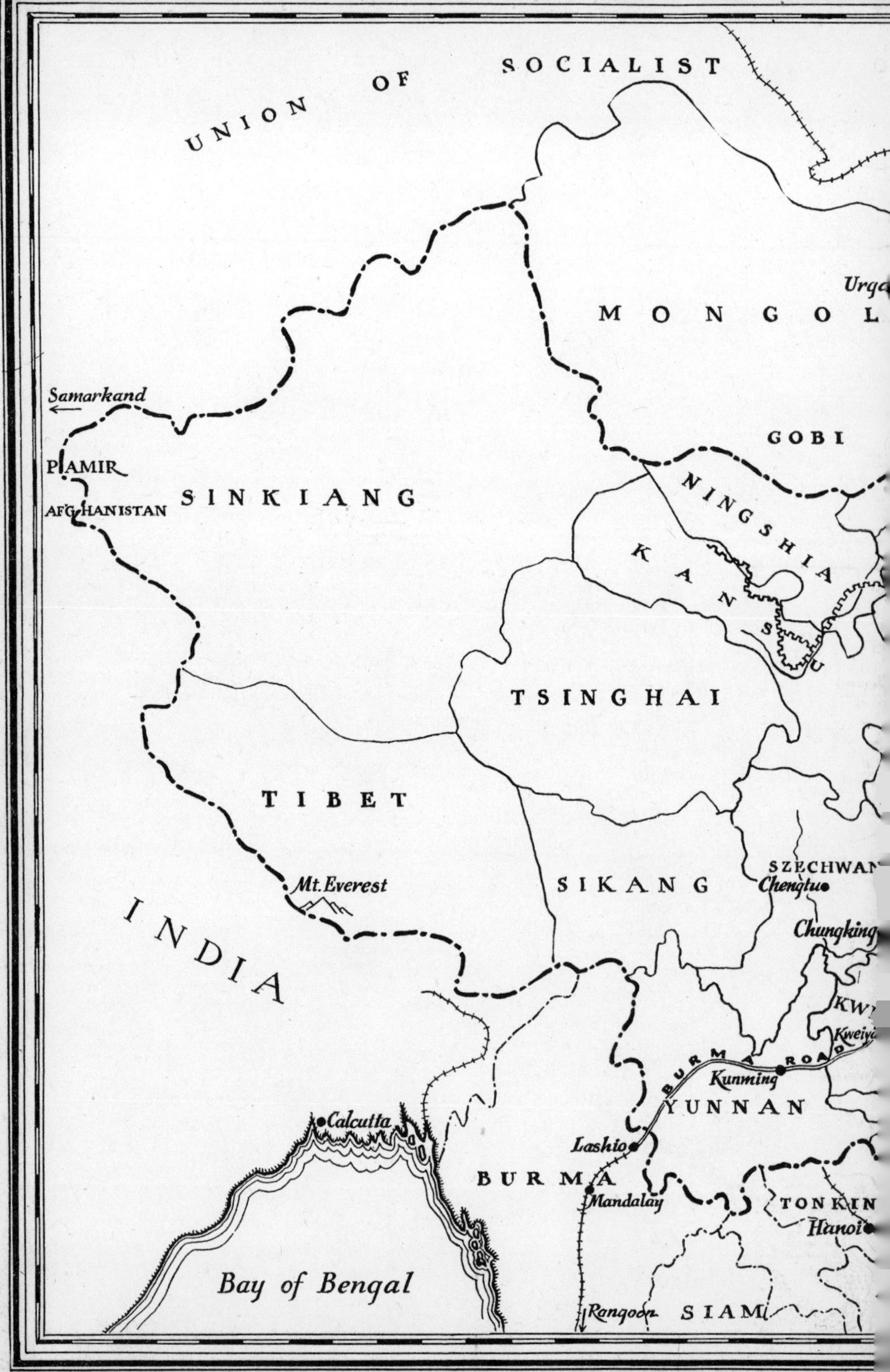
UNION OF SOCIALIST
MONGOL
Urga
GOBI
Samarkand
PAMIR
AFGHANISTAN
SINKIANG
NINGSHIA
KANSU
TSINGHAI
TIBET
SIKANG
SZECHWAN
Chengtu
Chungking
Mt. Everest
INDIA
KWE
Kweiya
BURMA ROAD
Kunming
YUNNAN
Calcutta
Lashio
BURMA
Mandalay
TONKIN
Hanoi
Bay of Bengal
Rangoon
SIAM